CAE
Practice Tests
with key

Charles Osborne

THOMSON

TM

Australia • Canada • Mexico • Singapore • Spain • United Kingdom • United States

Thomson Exam Essentials: CAE Practice Tests
Charles Osborne

Publisher: *Christopher Wenger*
Director of Product Development: *Anita Raducanu*
Director of Marketing: *Amy Mabley*
Editorial Manager: *David Baker*
Developmental Editor: *Tasia Vassilatou/Process ELT*
Production Editor: *Sarah Cogliano*
International Marketing Manager: *Eric Bredenberg*
Sr. Print Buyer: *Mary Beth Hennebury*

Project Manager: *Howard Middle/HM ELT Services*
Production Management: *Process ELT*
(www.process-elt.com)
Copy Editor: *Process ELT*
Compositor: *Process ELT*
Illustrator: *Nick Dimitriadis*
Cover/Text Designer: *Studio Image & Photographic Art*
(www.studio-image.com)
Printer: *G. Canale & C.S.p.a*

For more information contact Thomson Learning, High Holborn House, 50/51 Bedford Row, London WC1R 4LR United Kingdom or Thomson Heinle, 25 Thomson Place, Boston, Massachusetts 02210 USA. You can visit our web site at http://www.heinle.com.

ISBN: 1-4130-0985-9 (with key)

Text Credits
Page 8: From "Peach of an Idea", by Richard Wray. Copyright © THE GUARDIAN 2004. **Page 34:** From "Mind your languages", by Matthew Brace. Copyright © GEOGRAPHICAL 1999. **Page 60:** Adapted from "Explorers Still Seek El Dorado in the Mountains of Peru", by Juan Forero. Copyright © 2004 by the New York Times Co. Reprinted with permission. Text has been modified to facilitate reading comprehension. **Page 62:** From "On yer bike", by Tim Dowling, THE GUARDIAN. Copyright © Tim Dowling 2003. **Page 104:** From "Countdown to extinction for world's great apes", by Tim Radford. Copyright © THE GUARDIAN 2003. **Page 126:** From "Hybrid Homes", by William Underhill and Malcolm Beith. From Newsweek, September 20 © 2004 Newsweek, Inc. All rights reserved. Reprinted by permission. **Page 150:** From "Bred to soar", by Jeffrey P.Cohn. Copyright © ORGANIZATION OF AMERICAN STATES 2004. **Page 170:** "Close encounters of the wild kind", by Christian Amodeo. Copyright © GEOGRAPHICAL 2004. **Page 172:** From "Back to basics", by Ashley Seager. Copyright © THE GUARDIAN 2004.

Photo Credits
The publishers would like to thank the following for permission to use copyright images:
Page 192 top © AP Photo/Marco Ugarte, bottom © AP Photo/Kathy Willens; page 193 bottom © Brand X Pictures/PictureQuest; page 194 lower middle left © Brand X Pictures/PictureQuest; page 195 bottom right © Corbis; page 196 bottom © Bob Evans (pp 50%)/Painet; page 198 top © Bill Bachmann/Painet, bottom right © AP Photo/Chris O'Meara; page 200 top © Comstock Images/PictureQuest, middle right © AP Photo/Richard Drew, bottom © AP Photo/Marcio Jose Sanchez; page 201 top © AP Photo/Doug Mills, middle left © Jack Iddon/Painet, middle right © Mark Downey/Painet, bottom left © AP Photo/ Mariana Eliano, bottom right © AP Photo/Kevin Frayer; page 203 bottom centre © Words & pictures LLC/Painet; page 204 © Andre Jenny/Painet; page 205 top © Corbis/PictureQuest, bottom © Steve Skjold/Painet; page 207 top © Brand X Pictures/Picture Quest, middle right © IT Stock Free/PictureQuest, bottom © Blend Images/PictureQuest; page 208 bottom centre © Goodshoot/PictureQuest; page 209 top left © RubberBall/PictureQuest, top right © Corbis/PictureQuest, middle right © AP Photo/Michel Euler; page 210 bottom left © Bill Bachmann/Painet, bottom right © AP Photo/David Brauchli; page 211 top © Comstock Images/PictureQuest; page 212 bottom right © Corbis/PictureQuest; page 213 top © AP Photo/Peter Morgan, middle left © AP Photo/Dmitry Lovetsky, middle right © AP Photo/Lennox, bottom © AP Photo/Damian Dovarganes; page 214 bottom © AP Photo/Gaurav Tiwari.
© Index Open: Page 192 middle left; page 193 top, middle right; page 194 upper middle, bottom right; page 195 middle; page 196 top; page 199 top; page 202 top, bottom left; page 203 middle right, bottom left, bottom right; page 207 middle left; page 208 top, bottom left, bottom right; page 209 bottom right; 211 bottom left, bottom right; page 212 middle left.
© Photos.com: Page 192 middle right; page 193 middle left, middle right; page 194 top, lower middle centre, lower middle right, bottom left, bottom centre, page 195 top, bottom left; page 198 bottom left; page 199 middle, bottom; page 200 middle left; page 202 middle, bottom centre, bottom right; page 203 top, middle left; page 204 top; page 209 middle left, bottom left; page 210 top; 212 top left, top right, middle right, bottom left; page 214 top.

Contents

Thomson Exam Essentials is a new series of materials for students preparing for the major EFL/ESL examinations, such as First Certificate in English (FCE), Certificate in Advanced English (CAE), Certificate of Proficiency in English (CPE), International English Language Testing System (IELTS), Test of English as a Foreign Language (TOEFL®), Test of English for International Communication (TOEIC®), and others. The series is characterised by the close attention each component pays to developing a detailed knowledge of the skills and strategies needed for success in each paper or part of the exams.

CAE Practice Tests helps learners become aware of CAE exam requirements, offers details about the format and language in the exam and helps learners develop exam skills necessary for success. The book also provides extensive practice in all parts of the exam, using the actual test format.

Taking the CAE Exam

The CAE is at Level 4 of the series of Cambridge ESOL Examinations: Level 1 is the Key English Test, Level 2 the Preliminary English Test, Level 3 the First Certificate in English, and Level 5 the Certificate of Proficiency in English. CAE is also at Level 4 of the ALTE framework (ALTE, the Association of Language Testers in Europe, promotes transactional recognition of levels of language proficiency and certification). It is also classified as being at C1 level of the Common European Framework. The CAE is widely recognised in commerce and industry, and by universities and similar educational institutions, as proof that the holder of this qualification can do office work or take a course of study in English.

The exam, which is usually held twice a year, consists of five Papers:

Paper 1, Reading (1 hour 15 minutes): There are four parts. Tasks include multiple matching, multiple choice comprehension questions and gapped texts. The focus is on understanding gist, main points, detail and structure, as well as deducing meaning.

Paper 2, Writing (2 hours): There are two parts, each requiring candidates to produce one or more pieces of writing – a newspaper or magazine article, contribution to a leaflet or brochure, notice, announcement, personal note or message, formal letter, informal letter, report, proposal, review, instructions, directions, competition entry, information sheet, memo – written for a given purpose and target reader.

Paper 3, English in Use (1 hour 30 minutes): There are six parts. Tasks include multiple choice cloze, open cloze, error correction, word formation, register transfer and gapped text, focusing on lexis, structure, spelling and punctuation, register, and cohesion and coherence.

Paper 4, Listening (45 minutes approximately): There are four parts with recorded texts. Tasks include sentence completion or note taking, multiple choice comprehension questions and multiple matching. The focus is on understanding specific information, detail, gist, interpreting context and recognising attitude and opinion.

Paper 5, Speaking (15 minutes approximately): There are four parts, generally involving two candidates and two examiners, focusing on candidates' ability to use transactional, interactional and social language.

Preparing for the CAE Exam

In preparing for the five Papers, the following points should be taken into account:

Reading: Candidates need to be familiar with a range of reading material, such as newspapers, magazines, journals, non-literary books, leaflets, brochures etc. It is important for them to realise that different reading strategies can be used for different parts of the Reading Paper. For example, scanning to find specific information is the best strategy to adopt for Parts 1 and 4, and candidates should not feel they have to read every word in the text(s). On the other hand, in Part 2 candidates need to skim the main text for gist before they consider the various linguistic devices which mark the logical and cohesive development of the text (words and phrases indicating time, cause and effect, contrasting arguments, pronouns, repetition, use of verb tenses etc.).

Writing: In Part 1 candidates need to be able to process the information provided in the rubric as well as in input texts and use this information appropriately to write a text for a target reader. Candidates must practise covering all the points provided in the input. In Part 2 candidates have to choose one of four tasks, and as for Part 1, their writing must have a positive effect on the target reader. Candidates need to be aware of the style, layout and register that each task demands, and their texts must be well organised and coherent and display good control of language. Candidates who do not have relevant business or work experience are advised not to choose question 5.

English in Use: Candidates need to develop grammatical awareness and become familiar with grammatical patterns and collocations. They also need a good knowledge of vocabulary and are advised to learn whole phrases rather than single words in isolation. In Part 1 candidates are required to complete each gap in a text with the correct word or phrase. This part tests phrases, collocations, phrasal verbs, idioms and linkers. To complete Part 2, candidates need to understand the structure of the language. Answers must be syntactically and semantically correct. In Part 3 candidates can expect to deal with one of two possible task types. In the first type, they will be required to identify extra words in a text which are incorrect. In the second type, they will be required to identify spelling or punctuation errors in a text. In both cases, there will be sixteen lines to be corrected. No more than five of these lines will have no errors in them. In Part 4 candidates are required to complete two texts with one appropriate word in each gap. Each word is formed from a prompt word, and candidates need to be aware of the principles of word formation – affixation, internal changes to a word, formation of compound words. In Part 5 candidates need to show that they are aware of features of style and appropriateness by transferring information given in one text into another. The texts will be in different registers, and answers must be grammatically accurate as well as stylistically appropriate. In Part 6 candidates are required to complete a gapped text with an appropriate phrase or short sentence in each gap. The task tests awareness of discourse features, particularly cohesion and coherence.

Listening: Practice with pre-listening tasks (focusing on developing an expectation of what might be said) is essential here, as is thorough familiarity with a wide variety of spoken English, in terms of discourse types, accents, speeds of delivery and degree of background noise. Listening for different purposes should also be exercised: to understand gist, identify context or attitude or find specific information.

Speaking: Candidates need practice in using spoken English effectively, which includes the mastery of conversational skills (such as turn taking and the appropriate way to participate in a discussion), providing full but natural answers to questions, requesting clarification and speaking clearly and audibly at all times. Candidates should practise listening carefully to instructions and remembering what they are asked to do. It is important to react to visual prompts rather than simply describing them, using speculative or hypothetical language whenever possible. They also need to be able to use the right kind of language for exchanging information or opinions, giving reasons, speculating, hypothesising, agreeing, disagreeing, politely justifying and negotiating.

Further information can be obtained from the Cambridge ESOL website: www.cambridgeESOL.org.

CAE Practice Tests: contents

CAE Practice Tests in the **Thomson Exam Essentials** series prepares candidates for the CAE examination by providing **8 full practice tests**, which accurately reflect the latest exam specifications.

There are **3 guided tests** at the beginning, which feature **essential tips** to practise exam strategy. These tips offer guidance and general strategies for approaching each task. Other tips offer advice relevant to specific questions in the guided tests. These 3 guided tests will help students prepare for each paper, while the following **5 tests (without guidance)** will offer students thorough practice at a realistic exam level.

The CDs or cassettes accompanying the book include the audio materials for all the Listening Papers. These accurately reflect the exam in both style and content. Moreover, the audio materials for Tests 1 and 2 have been recorded with the repetitions and full pauses, exactly as in the exam itself.

A **writing bank** includes sample answers for the kinds of tasks that occur in Paper 2 (Writing), writing tips in the form of notes and **useful phrases** for the particular task types. Varied **visual materials** for Paper 5 (Speaking) have also been included, while a **language bank** supplies useful phrases and expressions for use in the Speaking Paper.

There is also a **glossary** for each test, explaining vocabulary that is likely to be unfamiliar to students.

Clear and straightforward design simplifies use of the book. **Exam overview** tables ensure that key information is readily accessible, while a specially designed menu makes it easy to navigate through the different parts and papers of each practice test.

CAE Practice Tests: principles

In writing this book, three guiding principles have been observed:

Firstly, that it should be useful for teachers, students sitting the CAE exam for the first time and students re-sitting the exam, whether they are working alone or in a class. Students approaching CAE for the first time would be best advised to work through the book linearly, developing their skills and confidence; those re-sitting the exam can consult the Exam overview tables to concentrate on particular areas for targeted revision. The **"without key"** edition can be used by students working in a class, while the **"with key"** edition includes a detailed **Answer key**, ensuring that students working alone can benefit from support while attempting these tests.

The second principle is that the questions should accurately reflect the range of questions found in the CAE exam. Thus students obtain guidance concerning the general content and the best way of approaching the tasks from the questions themselves. Seeing the questions in this light – as instructions to the candidate from the examiner rather than intimidating challenges – also helps students feel less daunted by the whole experience of sitting a major exam like this.

The third principle is that the texts used in the practice tests should be varied, representative of those used in the exam, and interesting. Everyone finds it easier to learn if the subject matter is relevant to his or her lifestyle and interests. In choosing, editing and creating the texts here, we have done our utmost to ensure that the experience of working with this book is as stimulating and rewarding as possible.

Charles Osborne, January 2006

Essential tips

▶ In this part of the exam, you are required to read a text to find specific information, which may include an opinion or the expression of an attitude.

▶ Read the instructions, the title and the questions.

▶ Skim through the text quickly to get a general idea of what it is about. Don't worry if there are words or phrases you don't understand.

▶ Read each question again and make sure you understand what it is asking. Underline the key words in the question (the words that show you what you should look for in the text).

▶ Scan the text for ideas or words that relate to the question. Read the relevant part of the text carefully.

▶ The questions will not cover every aspect or part of the text.

Question 3: A 'gap in our understanding', means there is something we do not know. The word 'evolution' means the way living beings have developed. Which part of the text mentions that we do not know how living beings have developed?

Question 9: Find a phrase that means 'substances that are found in living organisms'. The same idea will probably be expressed in more formal language.

Question 10: Think carefully about the key words in the question. Do you know the meaning of 'fluctuation' and 'emissions'? Even if you don't, you know from the question that the emissions come from a star, so look for a part of the text that mentions something coming from a star.

Answer questions **1–15** by referring to the magazine article on page **7** which discusses life in the universe.

Indicate your answers **on the separate answer sheet**.

For questions **1–15**, answer by choosing from the sections of the article (**A–F**). Some of the choices may be required more than once.

Note: When more than one choice is required, these may be given **in any order**.

In which section of the article are the following mentioned?

a recently developed method of detecting planetary systems	**1** ....
a reason for believing that life has evolved on other planets	**2** ....
a crucial gap in our understanding of evolution	**3** ....
the significance of a planet's temperature	**4** .... **5** ....
a hope that a planetary system like ours may have been discovered	**6** ....
protection against dangerous radiation	**7** ....
objections to the way money is spent	**8** ....
substances that are found in living organisms	**9** ....
fluctuations in emissions from a star	**10** ....
speculation about the history of a planet	**11** ....
future space missions	**12** ....
speculation that life may not be common in our solar system	**13** ....
a reason for restricting ourselves to our own solar system in the search for life	**14** ....
possible extra-terrestrial mining activity	**15** ....

Life in the Universe

A There are billions of galaxies in the universe and countless billions of stars, so to many people it seems unlikely that our own planet is unique in having the physical conditions that permitted sentient beings to evolve. It is, therefore, interesting to speculate about the criteria a planet would have to meet in order to sustain life. Clearly, one of the most important must be a stable star providing a steady source of energy – a sun – to fuel the processes of life. A planet would need an almost circular orbit at a uniform distance from this sun: an elliptical orbit would bring the planet very close to the sun and then take it very far away. This, in turn, would mean that the planet would be both too hot and too cold for life during the course of a single revolution around the sun. Then, the planet itself would need to have the constituent elements of life, including carbon, phosphorus, sulphur, nitrogen, hydrogen and oxygen. It would also need a good supply of liquid water, which appears to be essential in the chemistry of biological systems. Furthermore, it would need to have a large enough mass so that its gravitational force could hold onto an atmosphere.

B From observing the planets closest to us, it seems that our own solar system provides only a small window of opportunity for life to have a chance. Venus, our closest neighbour, is almost identical to the Earth in terms of size, but is too hot for life as we know it, simply because it is closer to the sun. Moreover, unlike the Earth, it lacks a magnetic field, which is crucial in shielding life from cosmic rays. Our other neighbour, Mars, is more promising. It shows signs of erosion caused in the past by some kind of fluid, possibly water. It even has a thin atmosphere. Consequently, it has been the focus of many space missions, and several exploratory craft have landed on its surface and conducted tests to detect signs of life. But so far, findings have proved inconclusive.

C Until recently, we have confined ourselves to our own solar system in the search for life, partly because we have not had evidence for the existence of other solar systems. Furthermore, our telescopes have not been powerful enough to detect planets. But not long ago, a technique was developed that could ascertain reliably whether stars have planets orbiting them. Basically, this technique relies upon our ability to detect with some degree of precision how much light a star is giving off. If this changes for a brief period, it is probably because a large object – a planet – is passing in front of it. At first, the technique could only establish the existence of a very large planet with an elliptical orbit that brought it into close proximity to the star. This was one of the limitations of the technique: life could not exist on such large planets. Furthermore, the orbit of the planet would preclude the possibility of other, smaller planets orbiting the same star. Therefore, that particular planetary system could be effectively ruled out in terms of the search for life.

D However, astronomers using an Anglo-Australian telescope in New South Wales now believe they have pinpointed a planetary system which resembles our own. For the first time, they have identified a large planet, twice the size of Jupiter, orbiting a star like the sun, at much the same distance from its parent star as Jupiter is from the sun. And this is the vital point about their discovery: there is at least a theoretical possibility that smaller planets could be orbiting inside the orbit of this planet. The discovery also raises the distinct possibility that many other stars will turn out to have planetary systems. The next step is to train telescopes on some of the stars nearest to us. We are getting closer to solving the question of how common solar systems like ours are.

E Moreover, within the next few years, a new generation of space telescopes will be built, and they will be powerful enough to spot not just planets of Jupiter's dimensions but ones with a mass similar to ours, with orbits lasting approximately a year. But even if we do eventually find planets that have physical conditions similar to Earth's, what are the chances that life has actually evolved on them? Any attempt to answer the question comes up against a fundamental difficulty. We simply do not know how life originated here on Earth, so when we try to decide how probable it is that life will be found on other planets, we can only make educated guesses.

F There are often voices raised in opposition to the vast sums invested in space research, but Dr Marisa Matherson of the Kramer Space Institute feels the investment is worthwhile. 'For a start, it would add greatly to our knowledge of the universe,' she says. 'As our telescopes are further refined, we will locate more and more planetary systems similar to our own. Whether or not they sustain life, we will at least be better able to see our own world in relation to the rest of the universe.' Matherson also hopes that by the third decade of this century, spaceships will be sent into outer space with the sole purpose of studying likely planets. There is even a possibility that valuable mineral resources could be discovered on these planets and exploited commercially, which would further justify funding exploratory missions.

PAPER 1	Reading	▶	Part 1
PAPER 2	Writing		Part 2
PAPER 3	English in Use		Part 3
PAPER 4	Listening		Part 4
PAPER 5	Speaking		

For questions **16–22**, choose which of the paragraphs **A–H** on page **9** fit into the numbered gaps in the following newspaper article. There is one extra paragraph which does not fit into any of the gaps.

Indicate your answers **on the separate answer sheet**.

Peach of an Idea

Regent's Park in central London was recently the site of a festival of music and fruit, marking the fifth birthday of Innocent, the drinks company set up by three college friends who wanted to bring a bit of nature to the table. It all began five years ago, when Adam Balon, Richard Reed and Jon Wright were contemplating starting their own business. They took £500 worth of fruit to a music festival in west London, made a huge batch of smoothies – fruit drinks blended with milk and yoghurt – and asked their customers for a verdict.

16

Looking back, they now admit that they were amazingly naive about starting a business, thinking it would just take off once they had the recipes and packaging figured out. In fact, the three budding businessmen had nine months living on credit cards and overdrafts before they sold their first smoothie.

17

The appeal of Innocent's products lies in their pure, unadulterated ingredients, plus a dash of quirky advertising. As one campaign put it, their drinks are not made *from* fruit, they *are* fruit.

18

Most are made from concentrated juice with water – and perhaps sweeteners, colours and preservatives – added. 'We didn't even know about that when we started,' Adam explains. 'It was when we started talking to people and they said, "OK, we'll use orange concentrate," and we said, "What's concentrate?" and they explained it and we said, "No, we want orange juice"'.

19

'Everyone knows what they're supposed to do,' says Richard. 'But we just don't, especially when you live in a city and it's pints of lager and a kebab at the end of the night. We just thought, "Wouldn't it be great to make it easy for people to get hold of this natural fresh goodness?" Then at least you've got one healthy habit in a world of bad ones.'

20

In essence, explains Jon, Innocent plans to simply freeze some of its smoothies, possibly with a bit of egg thrown in to make it all stick together. To help testers make up their minds about which combinations work, the yes and no bins will be dusted off and put out again.

21

'You've just got to put that in the category of "never say never",' says Richard. 'But the three of us go away once every three months to talk about what we want out of the business and we are all in the same place. So as long as we are excited and challenged and proud of the business, we are going to want to be a part of it.'

22

'We have got annoyed with each other,' admits Adam. 'But the areas we have had fallings-out over are things where we each think we have reasons to be right. So it's been about really important stuff like the colour of the floor, the colour of the entrance, or what to paint the pillar.' 'We really did nearly jump on each other about that,' adds Jon. 'Was it going to be blue or green?'

A 'Naivety,' adds Richard, who is always ready with a soundbite, 'can be a great asset in business because you challenge the status quo.' Although Innocent's drinks are fiendishly healthy, the company has always been very careful not to preach.

B Despite the temptation to do so, they have so far refused all offers. This might not last, of course, but while it does, it will have positive consequences for the fruit drinks market.

C At the Regent's Park event the team tried out one of their new ideas – extending their range of products into desserts. 'We always try and develop something that we actually want, and for us there is this problem of Sunday evenings when you sit down with a DVD and a big tub of ice cream and it's nice to munch through it, but my God, is it bad for you,' Richard adds.

D Innocent's refusal to compromise on this point presented them with some problems when they first started talking to potential suppliers, Adam says. This was when they discovered the truth about the majority of so-called 'natural fruit drinks'.

E 'We originally wrote this massive long questionnaire,' says Richard. 'But then we thought, if you're at this festival and it's sunny, the last thing you want is to fill out a survey. So we decided to keep it simple and ask literally, "Should we stop working and make these things?" We had a bin that said yes and a bin that said no, and at the end of the weekend the yes bin was full of empty bottles. We all went in to work the next day and quit.'

F They also seem to have managed to stay friends. They still take communal holidays, and the fact that each member of the team brings a different and complementary set of skills to Innocent seems to have helped them avoid any big bust-ups over strategy.

G Innocent now employs 46 people and Fruit Towers – as they call their base – has slowly expanded along the line of industrial units. The company has managed to establish a dominant position in the face of fierce competition. This year Innocent became Britain's leading brand of smoothie, selling about 40% of the 50 million downed annually by British drinkers.

H Having created a successful business from this base, is there a temptation to sell up and go and live on a desert island? With consumers becoming increasingly concerned about what they put in their stomachs, premium brands such as Innocent are worth a lot of money to a potential buyer.

Essential tips

▶ This part of the exam tests your understanding of how a text is organised and, in particular, how paragraphs relate to each other. For example, a paragraph might give details about an idea mentioned or discussed in a previous paragraph, or it may present another side of an argument discussed in a previous paragraph.

▶ Read through the main text quickly to get a general idea of what it is about. Don't worry if there are words or phrases you don't understand. Find the main idea in each paragraph.

▶ Look for links between the main text and the gapped paragraphs. The gapped paragraph may have links either to the paragraph before it or to the paragraph after it, or even to both.

▶ Look for theme and language links. For example:
  • references to people, places and times.
  • words or phrases that refer back or forward to another word, phrase or idea in the text. For example, if the first line of a paragraph says something like 'This becomes clear when we look at ...', 'This' refers back to something expressed in the previous paragraph.
  • linking devices such as 'firstly', 'secondly', 'furthermore', 'on the other hand', 'however'. These will help you to find connections between paragraphs.

▶ When you have found a paragraph that may fill a gap, read the paragraph that comes before it and the one that comes after it to see that they fit together.

▶ Re-read the completed text and make sure it makes sense.

Question 16: The last sentence in the previous paragraph describes how Balon, Reed and Wright 'asked their customers for a verdict'. Which gapped paragraph describes how customers gave their opinion?

Question 18: The paragraph following the gap starts by describing how 'Most are made'. Most what? What could be made from 'concentrated juice with water'? Look for a paragraph that mentions something which could be made in this way.

Question 21: In the paragraph following the gap, one of the owners of Innocent implies that something seems unlikely because he and his colleagues are still a good team. Which gapped paragraph poses a question which this paragraph answers?

PAPER 1 Reading

PAPER 2 Writing

PAPER 3 English in Use

PAPER 4 Listening

PAPER 5 Speaking

Part 1
Part 2
Part 3
Part 4

Read the following magazine article and answer questions **23–29** on page **11**. On your answer sheet, indicate the letter **A, B, C** or **D** against the number of each question. Give only one answer to each question.

Indicate your answers **on the separate answer sheet**.

The Beauties of the Stone Age

Jane Howard views some works of ancient art

I have just come home after viewing some astonishing works of art that were recently discovered in Church Hole cave in Nottinghamshire. They are not drawings, as one would expect, but etchings, and they depict a huge range of wild animals. The artists who created them lived around 13,000 years ago, and the images are remarkable on a variety of counts. First of all, their sheer number is staggering: there are ninety all told. Moreover, fifty-eight of them are on the ceiling. This is extremely rare in cave art, according to a leading expert, Dr Wilbur Samson of Central Midlands University. 'Wall pictures are the norm,' he says. 'But more importantly, the Church Hole etchings are an incredible artistic achievement. They can hold their own in comparison with the best found in continental Europe.' I am not a student of the subject, so I have to take his word for it. However, you do not have to be an expert to appreciate their beauty.

In fact, it is the wider significance of the etchings that is likely to attract most attention in academic circles, since they radically alter our view of life in Britain during this epoch. It had previously been thought that ice-age hunters in this country were isolated from people in more central areas of Europe, but the Church Hole images prove that ancient Britons were part of a culture that had spread right across the continent. And they were at least as sophisticated culturally as their counterparts on the mainland.

News of such exciting discoveries spreads rapidly, and thanks to the Internet and mobile phones, a great many people probably knew about this discovery within hours of the initial expedition returning. As a result, some etchings may already have been damaged, albeit inadvertently, by eager visitors. In a regrettably late response, the site has been cordoned off with a high, rather intimidating fence, and warning notices have been posted.

An initial survey of the site last year failed to reveal the presence of the etchings. The reason lies in the expectations of the researchers. They had been looking for the usual type of cave drawing or painting, which shows up best under direct light. Consequently, they used powerful torches, shining them straight onto the rock face. However, the Church Hole images are modifications of the rock itself, and show up best when seen from a certain angle in the natural light of early morning. Having been fortunate to see them at this hour, I can only say that I was deeply – and unexpectedly – moved. While most cave art often seems to have been created in a shadowy past very remote from us, these somehow convey the impression that they were made yesterday.

Dr Samson feels that the lighting factor provides important information about the likely function of these works of art. 'I think the artists knew very well that the etchings would hardly be visible except early in the morning. We can therefore deduce that the chamber was used for rituals involving animal worship, and that they were conducted just after dawn, as a preliminary to the day's hunting.'

However, such ideas are controversial in the world of archaeology and human origins. Dr Olivia Caruthers of the Reardon Institute remains unconvinced that the function of the etchings at Church Hole can be determined with any certainty. 'When we know so little about the social life of early humans, it would be foolish to insist on any rigid interpretation. We should, in my view, begin by tentatively assuming that their creators were motivated in part by aesthetic considerations – while of course being prepared to modify this verdict at a later date, if and when new evidence emerges.'

To which I can only add that I felt deeply privileged to have been able to view Church Hole. It is a site of tremendous importance culturally and is part of the heritage, not only of this country, but the world as a whole.

▶ This part of the exam tests your detailed understanding of a text, including the views and attitudes expressed.

▶ Read through the text quickly to get a general idea of what it is about. Don't worry if there are words or phrases you don't understand.

▶ The questions follow the order of the text. Read each question or question stem carefully and underline the key words.

▶ Look in the text for the answer to the question. One of the options will express the same idea, but don't expect that it will do so in the words of the text.

▶ The final question may ask about the intention or opinion of the writer. You may need to consider the text as a whole to answer this question, not just the last section.

Question 23: An option can only be correct if all the information contained in it is accurate. Look at option A: are the images in Church Hole 'unique examples of ceiling art'? The text says they are 'extremely rare in cave art' – is this the same? Look at option B: are the images in Church Hole 'particularly beautiful'? And are they 'paintings'?

Question 25: Look at option A. What does the writer say about the discovery of the images being made public? Look at option B. If something is 'vulnerable to damage', what might happen to it? Look at option C. The text says 'many people probably knew about the discovery within hours of the initial expedition returning'. Is this the same as saying many people visited the cave within hours? Look at option D. Have the images definitely been damaged? When may the damage have taken place: before or after the measures were taken?

Question 27: Sometimes you will find words from the options in the text. Be careful: the meaning in

the text is not necessarily the same as that in the answer options. Here, option D says the hunters 'worshipped animals in the cave', but the text says the cave was used for 'rituals involving animal worship', which is not the same thing.

23 According to the text, the images in Church Hole cave are
   A   unique examples of ceiling art.
   B   particularly beautiful cave paintings.
   C   superior in quality to other cave art in Britain.
   D   aesthetically exceptional.

24 What is the cultural significance of these images?
   A   They indicate that people from central Europe had settled in Britain.
   B   They prove that ancient Britons hunted over large areas.
   C   They reveal the existence of a single ice-age culture in Europe.
   D   They suggest that people in Europe were more sophisticated than Britons.

25 According to the text,
   A   the discovery of the images should not have been made public.
   B   the images in the cave are vulnerable to damage.
   C   many people visited the cave within hours of its discovery.
   D   the measures taken to protect the images have proved ineffective.

26 Why were the images not discovered during the initial survey?
   A   They were not viewed from the right angle.
   B   People were not expecting to find any images.
   C   Artificial light was used to explore the cave.
   D   The torches used were too powerful.

27 What conclusions does Dr Samson draw from the lighting factor?
   A   Rituals are common in animal worship.
   B   The artists never intended to make the images visible.
   C   The images were intended to be visible at a certain time of day.
   D   Ice-age hunters worshipped animals in the cave.

28 According to Dr Caruthers,
   A   we cannot make inferences from cave art.
   B   the images in Church Hole do not serve any particular function.
   C   experts know nothing about life 13,000 years ago.
   D   the function of such images is open to question.

29 It seems that the writer
   A   can now envisage the life of ice-age hunters more vividly.
   B   was profoundly impressed by the images in the cave.
   C   has now realised the true significance of cave art.
   D   thinks the images should receive more publicity.

PAPER 1 Reading ▸
- PAPER 2 Writing
- PAPER 3 English in Use
- PAPER 4 Listening
- PAPER 5 Speaking

Part 1
Part 2
Part 3
Part 4

Answer questions **30–44** by referring to the newspaper article on pages **13–14**, in which the writer reviews performances given in his own home.

Indicate your answers **on the separate answer sheet**.

For questions **30–44**, answer by choosing from the reviews of the performances in sections **A–D** of the article. Some of the choices may be required more than once.

In which review are the following stated?

Performers worked seasonally at one time.	**30** ....
The venue did not allow for a performance of a particular art form.	**31** ....
The performance reminded the writer of an unusual performance he had once enjoyed.	**32** ....
The performers were free to devise their own programme.	**33** ....
The performers had been recommended to the writer.	**34** ....
The behaviour of the performers was contrary to the writer's expectations.	**35** ....
The performance challenged the conventions of an art form.	**36** ....
Performances of this sort used to be very popular.	**37** ....
The performance prompted someone to reconsider a prejudice about an art form.	**38** ....
The performance had unexpectedly sophisticated requirements.	**39** ....
An element of the performance was distressingly realistic.	**40** ....
One of the artists performed despite a handicap.	**41** ....
The performance comprised a number of extracts from various works.	**42** ....
The performers derived pleasure from audience participation.	**43** ....
One participant revealed an unexpected talent.	**44** ....

Essential tips

▸ Part 4 is similar to Part 1, though the text here is longer. As in Part 1, you are required to scan a text for specific information.

▸ Read the instructions, the title and the questions.

▸ Skim through the text quickly to get a general idea of what it is about. Don't worry if there are words or phrases you don't understand, especially since this text is long.

▸ Read each question again and make sure you understand what it is asking. Underline the key words in the question (the words that show you what you should look for in the text).

▸ Scan the text for ideas or words that relate to the question. Read the relevant part of the text carefully.

▸ Remember that the part of the text that gives the answer for each question will almost certainly not use the same words; instead, it will express the idea in a different way.

Question 32: The word 'reminded' is used in the statement. Think of other words or phrases that convey this idea and scan the text for them. Then check that the part of the text you find also expresses the idea of an experience that was both unusual and enjoyable.

Question 36: If the statement is expressed in formal or difficult language, you need to examine it carefully. What is meant by 'the conventions' of an art form? This must refer to the conventional or usual way of doing something. Find a performance that was unusual in relation to a conventional or ordinary performance of that art form (opera, puppet show, jazz or theatre).

Question 38: A 'prejudice' is a negative opinion someone has about a person or thing. Find a section of a review that describes how someone reconsidered an opinion or changed their mind about the art form.

That's Entertainment!

Felix Masterson decided to engage artists to put on performances
in his own home for his family's private enjoyment. Here is his report.

A Opera Recital

For the first of our 'home performances' we decided
on opera, a form of art that especially moves me. The
other art form that I adore – ballet – could hardly be
performed in the confined space of a normal house, no
matter how much ingenuity was employed! My wife
and I were particularly looking forward to the
performance by Footstool Opera, a touring company
that specialises in mounting productions in confined
spaces, often coming up with a programme to order as
suits the occasion. When I was planning the event, I
imagined the opera company would bring with them a
high-quality sound system of some sort to provide
musical accompaniment, but the manager informed
me that all they required was 'a piano in good working
order'. I hastily arranged for our ancient upright to be
tuned, and to my relief, pianist Antonia Holmes
pronounced it entirely satisfactory when she tested
the instrument before the performance. We had made
it clear that no particular requirements would be
imposed upon the performers, so they gave us a
medley of familiar pieces from popular operas, and
my daughter – who had previously been of the view
that opera was unspeakably idiotic – was entranced. If
I were to be brutally honest, I would have to say that
the performers, apart from one tenor, were not in the
top class. But I don't imagine many people would
notice this, and it certainly didn't detract from our
enjoyment of the evening.

B Puppet Show

Having grown up with that curiously British
phenomenon of puppet theatre, the Punch and Judy
show, I was determined to find one of the traditional
practitioners of the art and secure his services. Alas,
times have changed. There was once a time when no
seaside resort in the country was complete without a
Punch and Judy show on the pier, but today puppet
theatre of this sort can hardly compete with video
games at holiday resorts. Besides, who can afford to
work only during the summer months? Consequently,
there are, according to the theatrical agencies I
contacted, none of the old-fashioned puppeteers left.
However, I did manage to find a puppet theatre
company called Little Man Theatre that included
traditional Punch and Judy shows in its repertoire, so I
went ahead and booked them. They arrived with a
surprising number of boxes and cases. Naively, I had
expected a miniature theatre to require a minimal
amount of equipment. In this case, the size of the
venue did indeed present a problem, though the nature
of the difficulty was the reverse of what I had feared.
We actually had some trouble making out the words of
the crocodile character, largely – I suspect – because
William Daniels, one of the two puppeteers, was
suffering from a terrible cold, complete with high fever
and a voice virtually reduced to a croak. Like a true
pro, though, he struggled through the performance
bravely. And once the first act was under way, I began
to appreciate why so many props were needed. This
wasn't Punch and Judy as I remembered it but a
twenty-first century version of the story, requiring a
staggering number of scene changes. A breathtaking
performance, and though I felt sad at the demise of the
old-time favourites, our children enjoyed it immensely.

C Jazz Concert

I had initially set myself the task of finding performers
of whom I knew absolutely nothing, simply by sitting
down with the Yellow Pages, when a colleague of my
wife's started raving about a particular jazz ensemble.
It seemed churlish to do otherwise than engage them
and The Hot Jazz Quintet turned out to be a group of
highly professional musicians who appeared to make a
point of being scrupulously polite and tidy. It was as
though the stereotype image of the egocentric
musician were being overturned in front of my very
eyes: a surprising experience for anyone old enough to
have seen The Who smash their instruments live
onstage several decades ago.

Despite being in such close proximity to the musicians, it had not occurred to me that we would be required to adopt a more active role until the saxophone player handed my son a set of bongo drums and invited him to join in. As luck would have it, Mike is a percussionist with his school orchestra, and he was able to acquit himself creditably, to the delight of the professionals performing for us. Not being a connoisseur of this type of music myself, I had frankly not been prepared to enjoy this evening as much as the other members of my family. This perhaps makes it more of a tribute to the Quintet that I found myself getting quite carried away by the intricate rhythms and spectacular solos.

D Murder Mystery Theatre

We invited Murder Incorporated, a theatre company that specialises in murder mysteries, to perform *Death Calls* for us, and to those of you who have not been initiated in the workings of 'murder mystery theatre', a word of explanation is needed. This is no ordinary production. In fact, one could claim that it doesn't really come under the category of theatre at all, and it is not normally presented on a stage, either. The basic idea is that a murder is 'committed' just out of sight of the audience. After the 'body' is found, the task of the audience is to work out who the murderer is by following up on certain clues.

A few moments after the actors had arrived, when we were still under the impression that preparations were being made for the performance, a piercing scream caused us all to rush out into the hall. There we stumbled – literally – over a body oozing fake blood that was so convincing it almost caused my wife to faint. Yes, it had started. As we followed the actors around the house for scenes in various locations, we tried to work out who the murderer could be. It was a fascinating experience, and I have to report that my wife proved to be a brilliant sleuth, solving the mystery in record time. *Death Calls* was a masterpiece of condensed theatre that had me fondly recalling a production of *2001, A Space Odyssey* at the Edinburgh Fringe Festival, which featured a cast of two, an audience of two and an old car as the venue. Highly recommended.

Essential tips

▶ In Paper 2 you must answer two questions. The question in Part 1 is compulsory. In Part 2 there are four questions, and you have to answer one of them.

▶ You may be asked to write an announcement, a competition entry, a contribution to a leaflet or brochure, directions, a formal letter, an informal letter, an information sheet, instructions, a memo, a newspaper or magazine article, a notice, a personal note or message, a proposal, a review or a report. All of these will be written for a particular purpose and target reader.

▶ Part 1 tests your ability to understand information from a variety of sources and produce a piece of writing that re-presents all the necessary information in an appropriate style.

▶ Read the instructions carefully and underline the key words that tell you what you are being asked to do. Usually, you are asked to produce one piece of writing in Part 1, but you may be asked to produce two pieces of writing. In this case, check how many words each should be.

▶ The input information for Part 1 consists of about 400 words and can be from a number of different texts: notes, letters, reports, advertisements, diagrams etc. Read the input information carefully. If the material is in the form of a chart or diagram, make sure you understand what information it conveys.

▶ Think about the appropriate register for your writing: formal, semi-formal, neutral or informal. If you are writing a report or proposal, consider whether to use headings and bullet points or numbered lists.

▶ Don't try to write out your answer in a rough draft before you produce a final draft; you will not have enough time. Instead, plan carefully what you will say in each section/paragraph of your writing.

▶ Divide your writing into three sections: introduction, main body and conclusion. Think about what you will say in each part. Plan approximately how many words should be in each section of your writing.

▶ Write your article, letter, report etc. Use your own words as far as possible; don't copy the information from the input texts.

▶ When you have finished, check your spelling and punctuation. Make sure the examiner can read your writing.

▶ See the **Writing bank** on page 216 for examples of different types of writing.

1 You are a member of a youth club in the small town of Northgate. The local government planning department has announced that it intends to build houses on a piece of open land called Northgate Common. Your youth club is opposed to the plan. The committee of the youth club have asked people living and working in the area near Northgate Common to fill in a questionnaire, and have used the information to make the poster below.

You have offered to write an article for the local newspaper describing the situation. You have also been asked by the committee to write a brief letter to your local Member of Parliament, Ann Winters, explaining why you are opposed to the plan. Read the poster below and the notice on page **17**, to which you have added your comments. Then, **using the information carefully**, write the **article** and the **letter** outlined on page **17**.

Save Northgate Common!

The local Planning Department wants
to build houses on Northgate Common and
use the rest of the land to make private gardens.

Is this what *you* want?

Replies to a recent questionnaire suggest it isn't!

Build a community
centre there: **31%**

Leave it as it is: **47%**

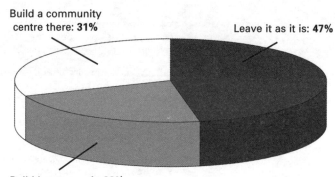

Build houses on it: **22%**

Come to a public meeting!
Saturday 17ᵗʰ March in the Town Hall!

NORTHGATE COMMON

Consultation? When?

After consultation with local residents, the Northgate and District Planning Department hereby announces that planning permission has been granted for a housing project on the area of unused land known as Northgate Common. Work on the project is scheduled to begin in September of this year.

Only 3 months away: should have been told earlier!

Not unused: parkland for sports, children playing, walks etc.

The project foresees the construction of 12 semi-detached private residences, two storeys high, whose architectural design will be in keeping with the character of other structures in the vicinity.

Cheap housing for local people?

The buildings themselves will occupy 62% of the common, and permission has also been granted for the purchasers of the land, Stonton Highbread, to acquire the remaining 38% for the purpose of developing private gardens for the use of the residents in the new development.

Why not public gardens?

Now write:

- an **article** for the local newspaper (approximately 150 words).
- a **letter** to Ann Winters (approximately 100 words). You do not need to include postal addresses.

You should use your own words as far as possible.

Essential tips

▶ Here, you are asked to write an article and a letter. Think carefully about the register and tone that are appropriate for each. What publication is the article for? Who is going to read your article? Who is the letter to?

▶ In your article you must describe the 'situation'. What information should you give? Is it necessary to mention who 'you' are in this article?

▶ Instead of trying to use all the information in both pieces of writing, decide which information is needed in each. For example, in the letter you need to explain 'why you are opposed to the plan'. This suggests you do not need to describe the plan, only to explain what you dislike about it. Where can you find information to use here?

▶ The handwritten comments next to the notice provide you with information, but you will have to use an appropriate sentence structure. For example, the first comment is 'Consultation? When?' How could you express the idea conveyed by these words in a sentence?

Essential tips

▶ In Part 2 you must choose one task. However, you should be familiar with all the possible types of text you might need to write.

▶ Read each question carefully. Before you choose a question, ask yourself if you know enough vocabulary on the subject and can employ it in the required register and text type.

▶ In Part 2 questions you have more freedom to use your imagination and come up with information that is not in the input material.

Question 2

▶ Although the word is not mentioned in the question, you are being asked to write an article expressing your opinions.

▶ Think about the style that would be appropriate: formal, semi-formal or informal?

▶ The question makes it clear that you should concentrate on two aspects of travel: (a) why it is important and (b) how you would benefit. This suggests that the two main sections of your article should be about these aspects.

▶ Plan carefully what to say in each part of your answer to avoid repeating yourself, and to ensure you include as many relevant points as possible.

▶ You also need an introduction and a conclusion. What could you say here?

▶ Remember that you should use your imagination – when you explain what you would like to do on a journey, for instance.

▶ Make sure you have enough time to check your answer.

Choose one of the following writing tasks. Your answer should follow exactly the instructions given. Write approximately 250 words.

2 You see the following announcement in a travel magazine and decide to enter the competition:

FREE TRAVEL IN EUROPE!

Are you under the age of 25?
Are you interested in travelling around Europe?

Write to us explaining why travelling is good for young people, and indicate how you yourself would expect to benefit from a trip around Europe.

The writer of the best entry will win a free EuropeRail monthly travel pass.

Send your entry to:
EuropeRail, P.O. Box 242, London

Write your **competition entry**.

3 You have seen the following announcement in an international magazine:

Modern technology:
saving our time or wasting our money?

Does modern technology really make our lives easier, or are the machines and devices we buy a waste of money? We want to know what you think.

Write an article, giving at least two examples of useful machines or devices and two examples of machines or devices that we could easily do without.

Write your **article**.

4 Read the following extract from a letter that you received from an international youth organisation:

> We are conducting a survey on the importance of regional culture to young people around the world. Please write us a report for this survey, describing how young people in your region feel about the history and culture of that region, and how you think this may change in the future.

Write your **report**.

5 You have been asked to write an information leaflet for employees who are new to your company. You should give a brief outline of:
- the structure of the company
- its aims and principles
- its main activities
- its plans for the future

You should also mention any other points that you think are important.

Write the **text for the leaflet**.

Essential tips

Question 4

▶ In order to answer this question, you must be familiar with the format of a report. You need to write clear paragraphs and use headings. You may also want to use other features such as bullet points or numbered lists.

▶ Remember that a report must have a clear introduction and conclusion as well. In your introduction, state what the report is about and who it is for. In your conclusion, summarise the information contained in your report. See the Writing bank on page 216.

▶ You need to include information about the culture and history of your region. At the same time, your task is to produce a good piece of writing, so as long as the points you make sound reasonable, they do not all have to be factually correct. For instance, if you want to say that young people in your region are interested in the history of this part of the country, you could invent a survey that shows 65% of young people say they are 'very interested' in history. It doesn't matter if this survey was never actually carried out.

▶ The question asks you to give your opinion about how the situation may change in the future. Therefore, you can use the first person to say what you think (e.g. 'I think', 'I believe'), but keep the formal style that is appropriate for a report.

PAPER 1 Reading

PAPER 2 Writing

PAPER 3 English in Use ▶ | Part 1

PAPER 4 Listening | Part 2

| Part 3

PAPER 5 Speaking | Part 4

| Part 5

| Part 6

For questions **1–15**, read the text below and then decide which answer best fits each space. Put the letter you choose for each question in the correct box on your answer sheet. The exercise begins with an example (**0**).

Example:

0	B	0

Essential tips

▶ Read through the whole text to get a general idea of what it is about.

▶ The correct option must have the correct meaning. It can also be part of a phrase, collocation, idiom, phrasal verb or expression.

▶ The correct option must fit in the sentence structurally. All the four options will be the right part of speech (noun, adjective, verb, adverb etc.), but only one will be correct in the context of the sentence. For instance, the correct option may be the only word that is followed by a preposition which comes after the gap. So check the words on either side of the gap carefully to see what collocates with them.

Question 2: One of the options does not collocate with 'time'. Of the other three options, only one has the correct meaning of 'best'.

Question 4: Only one of the options forms a fixed expression with 'what is' which has the required meaning here: 'in addition' or 'moreover'.

Question 7: Only one option collocates with 'convinced'.

Question 11: The correct option must mean something like 'get used to'. Be careful, though: one option has this meaning when it is in the form of a past participle and is preceded by 'be' or 'get'.

Nature's Clocks

Our biological clocks govern almost every (**0**) ...... of our lives. Our sensitivity to stimuli (**1**) ...... over the course of the day, and our ability to perform certain functions is subject to fluctuations. Consequently, there is a(n) (**2**) ...... time for tasks such as making decisions: around the middle of the day. Anything that (**3**) ...... physical co-ordination, on the other hand, is best attempted in the early evening. What is (**4**) ...... , there is a dramatic drop in performance if these activities are (**5**) ...... out at other times. The risk of accident in a factory, for example, is 20% higher during the night (**6**) ....

Primitive humans lived their lives in tune with the daily cycle of light and dark. Today we are (**7**) ...... convinced that we can impose schedules on our lives at (**8**) .... Sooner or later, however, we pay a (**9**) ...... for ignoring our natural rhythms. A good example is jet lag, caused when we confuse our body's biological clocks by (**10**) ...... several time zones. People suffering from jet lag can take several days to (**11**) ...... to new time zones, and have a reduced ability to make decisions, which is a worrying thought, as serious (**12**) ...... of judgement can be made. And this may be just the (**13**) ...... of the iceberg. An increasing (**14**) ...... of people suffer from seasonal affective disorder (SAD), a form of depression that can be (**15**) ...... by living in artificial conditions. SAD can be serious, and sufferers may even need to take antidepressant drugs.

0	**A** event	**B** aspect	**C** field	**D** division
1	**A** modifies	**B** ranges	**C** varies	**D** wavers
2	**A** peak	**B** summit	**C** maximum	**D** optimum
3	**A** requests	**B** demands	**C** dictates	**D** stipulates
4	**A** more	**B** else	**C** different	**D** up
5	**A** made	**B** done	**C** carried	**D** performed
6	**A** labour	**B** work	**C** duty	**D** shift
7	**A** powerfully	**B** firmly	**C** steadily	**D** highly
8	**A** whim	**B** determination	**C** will	**D** desire
9	**A** price	**B** fine	**C** fee	**D** cost
10	**A** landing	**B** penetrating	**C** crossing	**D** travelling
11	**A** accustom	**B** adjust	**C** change	**D** alter
12	**A** errors	**B** mistakes	**C** inaccuracies	**D** fallacies
13	**A** peak	**B** pinnacle	**C** top	**D** tip
14	**A** amount	**B** quantity	**C** number	**D** proportion
15	**A** triggered	**B** developed	**C** created	**D** launched

PAPER 1 Reading

PAPER 2 Writing

PAPER 3 English in Use ▸ Part 1

PAPER 4 Listening **Part 2**

PAPER 5 Speaking Part 3
 Part 4
 Part 5
 Part 6

Essential tips

▸ Read through the whole text to get a general idea of what it is about.

▸ Decide what word or words in the sentence are grammatically related to the gapped word; this will help you decide what part of speech is needed (auxiliary verb, pronoun, article, preposition etc.).

▸ Read the whole sentence to see if the word you need is part of a longer or parallel structure such as 'not only ... but also ...'.

▸ It may be that two or even three words could fit in the gap, so do not assume the word you are thinking of is wrong if you can also think of one or two alternatives.

Question 16: Read the whole sentence carefully. You will notice that each half talks about a certain type of tourist. The second group is referred to as 'others', so what word could be used together with 'tourists' to refer to the first group?

Question 18: The gapped word is part of a phrase: 'follow ... somebody's footsteps'. If you can't immediately think of the gapped word, try to find a word that sounds right: you may well have heard the phrase before.

Question 24: Think of the meaning of the sentence and the text as a whole. If oil dispersed effectively, would there be a problem?

Question 27: It should be clear that you need a preposition here. The previous sentence mentions cruise ships, and now the possibility of a collision involving an iceberg is raised. Which preposition is used with 'collision' in this context?

Question 29: The word you need may be part of a simple expression. You may be able to find the correct word by reading the sentence aloud.

For questions **16–30**, complete the following article by writing each missing word in the correct box on your answer sheet. **Use only one word for each space.** The exercise begins with an example (**0**).

Example:

0	*there*	0 __ __

Danger Facing Antarctica

Antarctica is becoming a popular tourist destination and in the last decade (**0**) .... has been a dramatic increase in visitors to the area. (**16**) .... tourists simply want to see the last unspoiled continent, (**17**) .... others have more active pursuits such as adventure sports in mind. And of course, there are also those adventurous souls who want to follow (**18**) .... the footsteps of the great polar explorers. (**19**) .... , environmentalists are concerned that the booming tourist industry may (**20**) .... endangering the Antarctic environment and sowing (**21**) .... seeds of its own destruction.

One of the problems facing the area is pollution resulting from tourism. Careless visitors throw rubbish into the sea, not realising (**22**) .... harmful this can be to wildlife. (**23**) .... danger is oil spills. In the freezing waters, oil does (**24**) .... disperse effectively. Consequently, oil from even a small spill (**25**) .... remain a hazard to wildlife for many years. And this is a very real danger: some of the cruise ships visiting Antarctica have not been reinforced to (**26**) .... into account the dangers. A collision (**27**) .... an iceberg could cause a disaster of major proportions. This is (**28**) .... no means a far-fetched notion. From (**29**) .... to time icebergs do appear in these waters, and global warming means that massive chunks of ice are breaking (**30**) .... the continental ice sheet more and more frequently. If a ship collided with one of these, it could spell disaster for tourism.

In most lines of the following text, there is **either** a spelling **or** a punctuation error. For each numbered line **31–46**, write the correctly spelt word or show the correct punctuation in the box on your answer sheet. Some lines are correct. Indicate these lines with a (✔) in the box. The exercise begins with three examples (**0**), (**00**) and (**000**).

Example:

0	*fundamental*	__ 0 __
00	*cruise'*	__ 00 __
000	✓	__000__

Essential tips

▶ Read through the whole text to get a general idea of what it is about.

▶ You are only looking for two types of mistakes here, spelling and punctuation, so don't waste time wondering about other possible mistakes. Punctuation mistakes can include the use of commas, quotation marks, apostrophes, question marks, full stops and capital letters.

▶ No more than five lines of the text will be correct, so it is unlikely that two consecutive lines will be correct. When you find a line that is correct, look especially carefully at the line before and after it for mistakes.

▶ Look in particular for the sort of spelling that causes problems in English: the use of 'ie' or 'ei', for instance, or the use of double consonants.

▶ Punctuation mistakes are often easier to see when you consider a whole sentence, not just one line. For example, if the sentence includes direct speech, check that there are quotation marks at the beginning and the end of the direct speech, which may be on different lines.

Cruising

0	There has been a fundamentall change in attitudes towards cruise
00	holidays. At one time the phrase 'Mediterranean cruise conjured
000	up images of rich elderly people sitting in deckchairs. And it
31	certainly was the case that a fourtnight on a luxury cruise ship
32	cost a great deal more than the average person could aford.
33	But today cruising is one of the most popular holiday options
34	for people in the Uk, and last year the number of people choosing
35	this way of spending their liesure time topped the one million
36	mark for the first time ever. The most important change, though
37	is in the type of person who goes cruising. Holiday company's
38	are trying hard to attract younger customers, and these days
39	the larger cruise ships have a huge range of entertainment facilities
40	on-board. There are nightclubs, theatres and restaurants, of course,
41	but you can also find rock-climbing walls and even ice rings on the
42	bigger vessels. Activities ashore have also been modifyed, so when
43	the ship docks at some exotic port, the passengers can indulge
44	there taste for adventure sports like dog-sledding and abseiling.
45	Cruise ships provide childcare servises, too, enabling parents to
46	enjoy a relaxing holiday and a brake from the duties of parenthood.

Question 36: A word or group of words may be separated from the main sentence between commas to show that the information conveyed is additional to the main sentence. Here, there is a comma before 'though'. Is it correct? If it is, do you need a comma after it as well?

Question 37: It may be correct to use an apostrophe and 's' with the word 'company' if the meaning fits with the sentence. Does it in this case?

Question 39: Long words may look correct even if a letter is missing. Is there an example of such a word in this line?

Question 46: There is a spelling mistake in this line involving a homophone: a word which sounds the same as another word but has a different meaning and spelling.

PAPER 1   Reading

PAPER 2   Writing

PAPER 3   English in Use   ▶   Part 1
Part 2
Part 3
Part 4
Part 5
Part 6

PAPER 4   Listening

PAPER 5   Speaking

Essential tips

▶ Read through each text to get a general idea of what it is about.

▶ For each gap decide first what sort of word you need: noun, verb, adjective or adverb. Then decide what form of the word you need. If it is a noun, do you need the singular or plural form? If it is a verb, what form of the verb? Does the word need to have a positive or negative meaning?

▶ The spelling of the root may change when different forms are derived from it, so be careful (e.g. explain – explanation).

▶ In some cases, you will need to make more than one change. For example, you may need to add both a prefix and a suffix (e.g. ordinary – extraordinary – extraordinarily), or two suffixes (e.g. increase – increasing – increasingly).

Question 47: The word after the gap is a noun, so you need an adjective here. The context will tell you whether the adjective must be positive or negative.

Question 48: The meaning of the phrase with the gap is that 'he is … for an original idea'. You need an adjective here. Be careful with the spelling.

Question 54: There is an article before the gap, so the gapped word must be a noun. The context tells you that the new credit card is to be used instead of the old one. What noun derived from 'place' means 'a thing that is used instead of something else'?

Question 55: The word 'should' before the gap shows that you need a verb. The context tells you that the meaning of this verb is 'to be certain'.

For questions **47–61**, read the two texts below. Use the words in the boxes to the right of the texts to form one word that fits in the same numbered space in the text. Write the new word in the correct box on your answer sheet. The exercise begins with an example (**0**).

Example:

0	*considerable*	0

FILM REVIEW

Driving Left

Bob Wilson's new film is ample proof, if any were needed, that he deserved the (**0**) .... praise he received for his first full-length feature. In *Driving Left* (**47**) .... novelist Brett Dasher decides to boost his failing career. (**48**) .... for an original idea, he resolves to commit a crime and then write a book about it. Of course, it has to be an (**49**) .... clever crime if he is ever going to sell this story. So Dasher makes up his mind to (**50**) .... the President of the United States. The plot itself is (**51**) .... , with too many implausible twists and turns. But Wilson directs with his usual (**52**) .... , and this reviewer, at least, was very impressed. The film is (**53**) .... the best of this summer's releases.

(**0**)	**CONSIDER**
(**47**)	SUCCESS
(**48**)	DESPAIR
(**49**)	EXCEPTION
(**50**)	PERSON
(**51**)	BELIEVE
(**52**)	BRILLIANT
(**53**)	EASY

INFORMATION LEAFLET

We are pleased to send you your new VISTA credit card as a (**54**) .... for your old one. You should (**55**) .... that you sign your new card straight away. Please also note that you are responsible for the (**56**) .... of your old card. This is to prevent it falling into the hands of any (**57**) .... person who might attempt to use it. We advise you to check immediately the details on your new card, including the (**58**) .... date. There is one (**59**) .... difference between your new VISTA credit card and your previous cards. Credit card fraud is on the increase; (**60**) .... , we have introduced a new security measure: a Personal Identity Number. Please (**61**) .... this number, which you will be required to produce when purchasing goods or services.

(**54**)	PLACE
(**55**)	SURE
(**56**)	DESTROY
(**57**)	AUTHORISE
(**58**)	EXPIRE
(**59**)	ESSENCE
(**60**)	CONSEQUENCE
(**61**)	MEMORY

PAPER 1 Reading

PAPER 2 Writing

PAPER 3 English in Use ▶
    Part 1
    Part 2
    Part 3
    Part 4
    Part 5
    Part 6

PAPER 4 Listening

PAPER 5 Speaking

Essential tips

▶ Read through each text to get a general idea of what it is about. Your task is to find words or phrases that complete the gaps in the second text so that the meaning of the first text is conveyed.

▶ The first text will be formal and the second informal, or the other way around.

▶ For each gap decide what information is required and underline the part of the first text that gives this information. You will need a more formal or less formal way of expressing this idea.

▶ The words you use – no more than two for each gap – must be grammatically correct in context.

Question 62: The words in the informal text are 'put up visitors'. You need a verb that can express this idea more formally.

Question 65: The cloakroom attendant was rude. Which noun expresses what he/she did not show? There are two possible answers.

Question 68: We are told there was only fish or meat, but there should have been vegetarian dishes as well. Look carefully at the sentence: you need a noun and also a word to connect it to the words 'fish or meat'.

Question 72: An adjective is needed here. It must convey the information that this person didn't do anything about the complaint. What (negative) adjective describes someone who does not assist or help when there is a problem?

For questions **62–74**, read the memo from a company executive to her secretary. Use the information in the memo to complete the numbered gaps in the formal letter. The words you need **do not occur** in the memo. **Use no more than two words for each gap**. The exercise begins with an example (**0**).

Example:

0	*complain about*	0

MEMO

To: Anne Hathaway
From: Edna Marples

Anne, please write to the manager of the Coronation Hotel about the end-of-year party and tell him we were not happy. Explain we are old customers: we use the hotel to put up visitors and our last few parties there were fine. But this year we had some complaints:

- We asked them to keep spaces free in the car park for the directors – they didn't.
- The cloakroom attendant was rude.
- There weren't enough chairs at the top table for dinner.
- We couldn't turn up the sound system for the speeches.
- They only gave us a choice of fish or meat (they said they'd definitely have some vegetarian dishes, too), the drinks were lukewarm, and the tables hadn't been done up to look nice.

We told the hotel's Events Co-ordinator about the problems, but she didn't do anything. So if they want our custom, they should make it up to us – maybe 10% less on the price of the summer picnic?

FORMAL LETTER

I am writing to (**0**) .... your arrangements for our company's end-of-year party. We use your hotel to (**62**) .... visitors, and we have been satisfied with your service in (**63**) .... However, there were several problems at our party this year. Firstly, there were no spaces (**64**) .... in the car park for our directors, although we had requested them. Secondly, the cloakroom attendant didn't treat guests with the proper (**65**) .... Thirdly, there was a (**66**) .... chairs at the top table. Moreover, it was impossible to adjust the (**67**) .... on the sound system, so people couldn't hear the speeches. As for the meal, there was no (**68**) .... fish or meat, whereas we had been (**69**) .... some vegetarian dishes. The drinks had not been properly (**70**) .... , and the tables had not been (**71**) .... When we approached the Events Co-ordinator, she was most (**72**) ....

We would appreciate a gesture from you as (**73**) .... One possibility might be a 10% (**74**) .... our summer picnic.

PAPER 1 Reading

PAPER 2 Writing

PAPER 3 English in Use ▶ Part 1
Part 2
Part 3
Part 4
Part 5
Part 6

PAPER 4 Listening

PAPER 5 Speaking

Essential tips

▶ Read through the text to get a general idea of what it is about.

▶ This part of the exam tests your understanding of the structure of a text: how phrases and clauses fit together.

▶ The options may be similar: they may all be clauses beginning with 'to', for example, or clauses beginning with a conjunction. However, only one option will fit each gap.

▶ Three of the options don't fit any of the gaps.

▶ Look carefully at words in the options that refer to or link with a preceding clause or sentence in the main text.

Question 76: The words before the gap, 'the one', refer to a person, so a clause beginning with 'who' would fit here. Two of the options begin with 'who', but only one is followed by a singular verb.

Question 77: The main idea in this sentence is that students should think about what to do during their gap year, so the correct option for this gap will relate to that idea.

Question 79: The sentence would be complete even without the words in the gap. Therefore, the correct option must provide extra information about the way universities work. Look for the option that conveys this information and that has the appropriate structure.

Question 80: The sentence is about what students – 'they' – can do in their gap year, so look for an option that continues this idea, with a verb in the correct form.

For questions **75–80**, read the following text and then choose from the list **A–J** given below the best phrase to fill each of the spaces. Write one letter (**A–J**) in the correct box on your answer sheet. Each correct phrase may only be used once. **Some of the suggested answers do not fit at all**. The exercise begins with an example (**0**).

Example:

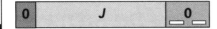

| 0 | J | 0 |

Filling the Gap

Rather than going straight from school to university, more and more school leavers are taking a year out **(0)** .... The benefits of a gap year are obvious. Young people with some experience of life outside an educational institution, even if just for a year, will probably be better able to concentrate on their university studies **(75)** .... Clearly, if a company is faced with several candidates for a position, all similarly qualified, it makes sense to opt for the one **(76)** ....

However, students should consider carefully what they want to do during this year, **(77)** .... Spending a year perfecting one's surfing technique on the beaches of California, for instance, may be appealing but the skills gained in this way are hardly likely to impress Human Resources managers.

Employers particularly like young people who have worked during their gap year, whether in paid employment or on a voluntary basis, **(78)** .... Many business people feel that universities, **(79)** ...... , aren't very efficient at teaching the 'people skills' necessary for a position in management. For this reason, voluntary service overseas with charities and aid organisations is becoming a popular choice for gap year students. They can develop the competitive edge they want **(80)** ....

A while providing a sound academic education

B and at the same time do some genuinely useful work

C but few employers are happy with the management skills taught at university

D since this will have helped them develop teamwork and communication skills

E but prefer not to think seriously about a career at that time

F who has gained extra skills during a gap year

G and they will also improve their chances of employment after graduating

H who have finished school and passed all their exams

I and how to employ their time to the best advantage

J so they can travel, learn some skills, or simply get further experience of life

Essential tips

▸ Read the instructions and find out the subject of the recording.

▸ Read the questions carefully and think about the sort of information you might need to complete the gaps.

▸ Each gap is completed by one, two or three words, or a number.

▸ Decide what grammatical form the gapped word or words should have.

▸ You will hear the words you need on the recording, but not in the same sentences as the questions. You need to listen for the ideas expressed on the recording.

▸ You will hear the recording twice, so you will have a chance to fill in any gaps you miss the first time.

Question 1: What sort of word could come after 'in': a time, a place, or an expression with the preposition 'in'? Listen for any of these.

Question 4: The recording is about a medicine, and this sentence mentions an acid that can affect something or somebody quite badly. Who or what could this be?

Question 6: The sentence is about something that happened or lasted for nearly seventy years, so you should listen for information about this period. Also consider what could fit with the phrase 'into the way aspirin works'.

Question 8: The gapped word must describe something like a plant, which can be grown without artificial chemicals, so listen for a word with this meaning.

You will hear a writer talking about a book she has written on the subject of aspirin. For questions **1–8**, complete the sentences.

You will hear the recording twice.

The story of aspirin

Doctors in [**1**] treated their patients with a medicine derived from the bark of the willow.

Edward Stone believed that [**2**] was similar to quinine.

The active ingredient of aspirin was isolated in [**3**]

Unfortunately, salicylic acid can affect the [**4**] quite badly.

The first commercially available aspirins were made by Bayer, a [**5**]

However, there was little [**6**] into the way aspirin works for nearly seventy years.

Some scientists think that people over [**7**] should take aspirin to prevent certain diseases.

It appears that [**8**] grown without artificial chemicals also contain the active ingredients of aspirin.

Essential tips

▶ Read the instructions and find out the subject of the recording.

▶ Read the questions carefully and think about the sort of information you might need to complete the gaps.

▶ Part 2 is like Part 1, except that you only hear the recording once. Therefore, it is particularly important to remember that the questions are in order.

▶ You will hear the words you need on the recording, but not in the same sentences as the questions. You need to listen for the ideas expressed on the recording.

Question 12: What word can go with '... of miles'? Listen carefully for the form of the word.

Question 13: The word 'unfortunately' shows that something bad can be spread by the dust.

Question 14: We are told that something in or on the sea can be destroyed. Remember, you might not hear the word 'destroy', but you will hear a word or phrase with this meaning.

Question 16: The speaker will probably say that something results from the increase in desert dust storms, or that the dust storms cause something. However, he may use different words to express this.

You will hear a talk on the subject of desert dust storms. For questions **9–16**, complete the sentences.

Listen very carefully as you will hear the recording ONCE only.

Desert Storms

There has been an increase in the [____ 9 ____] of dust storms recently.

Normally, even [____ 10 ____] winds don't disturb the crust on top of the desert sand.

[____ 11 ____] and overgrazing have also contributed to the problem.

The dust can travel [____ 12 ____] of miles before it falls to the ground.

Unfortunately, the dust can spread [____ 13 ____] to distant places.

If the dust falls on the sea, it can destroy [____ 14 ____]

The dust that lands on the ice in Greenland is causing it to [____ 15 ____]

One consequence of the increase in desert dust storms is [____ 16 ____]

PAPER 1 Reading

PAPER 2 Writing

PAPER 3 English in Use

PAPER 4 Listening ▸
  Part 1
  Part 2
  Part 3
  Part 4

PAPER 5 Speaking

Essential tips

This part of the exam is usually a multiple-choice task, but it could also be a sentence-completion task. If it is a sentence-completion task, look back at the tips for Parts 1 and 2. If it is a multiple-choice task, read the following tips:

▸ Read the instructions and find out the subject of the recording.

▸ Read the questions or question stems carefully and underline the key words.

▸ The questions follow the order of the recording, but the final question may be about the recording as a whole.

Question 17: Option A suggests most people, especially the critics, liked the ballet; option B implies some people liked it and some didn't; option C implies most people didn't like it; and option D implies that people who love animals liked the ballet. Which of these ideas does the recording convey?

Question 20: Think about different ways to express that something 'is of greatest interest to audiences'. You should also be prepared for the information to be given in a different order. For example, the speaker may describe something that happened and then say afterwards that it interested audiences.

Question 21: The question tells you that Stan will talk about something that went wrong when he saw the ballet. Which option best describes what happened?

You will hear part of an interview with Stan Levin, a dance critic, about a modern ballet production involving animals. For questions 17–22, choose the correct answer **A**, **B**, **C** or **D**.

You will hear the recording twice.

17 We gather that the ballet being discussed here
  A has received general critical acclaim.
  B has caused considerable controversy.
  C has not been well received on the whole.
  D has become popular with animals-lovers.

18 It appears that the function of the dogs in the ballet is to
  A reflect what happens to the human characters.
  B act as a contrast to the human characters.
  C show how primitive beings behave in a civilised society.
  D symbolise homeless people.

19 How does Stan feel about the increasing use of technology in dance?
  A He thinks this trend has gone too far.
  B He prefers more traditional approaches to dance.
  C He does not approve of it in principle.
  D He believes it is creating a new art form.

20 What aspect of the ballet is of greatest interest to audiences?
  A the way the dogs behave during dance sequences
  B the way the dogs perform their tricks
  C the sight of the dogs in a pack
  D the way the dogs copy the actions of one character

21 What caused the lapse in mood during the performance Stan saw?
  A the inability of the dogs to concentrate
  B the audience's unwillingness to accept the dogs
  C the behaviour of a member of the audience
  D the inability of dogs and humans to work as a team

22 What aspect of the performance made the most powerful impression on Stan?
  A the implicit potential for violence
  B the aggression shown by the dogs
  C the bond between the dogs and the tramp
  D the primitive appearance of the dogs

PAPER 1 Reading

PAPER 2 Writing

PAPER 3 English in Use

PAPER 4 Listening ▶ | Part 1
Part 2
Part 3
Part 4

PAPER 5 Speaking

Essential tips

▶ Read the instructions and find out who will be talking and what they will be talking about.

▶ You have two tasks to think about at the same time, each relating to one type of statement made by the speakers. So the first time you hear each speaker be prepared for a piece of information that corresponds to an option in the first task; the second time listen for a piece of information that corresponds to an option in the second task.

▶ The answer options do not repeat what the speakers say; they express the ideas in different words. Read each option carefully, and be prepared to hear the information expressed in a different form.

▶ Each task has three options you do not need.

Questions 23–27:
Option A: If something has a 'social function', what does it have? How might you express the idea that learning English has a social function?

Option H: If this option is correct for one of the speakers, it must mean that the person had 'an injury'. What words could be used to express that you were injured?

Questions 28–32:
Option G: What ways are there to express that something is a commitment? If you commit yourself to do something, what do you do or say to yourself or to other people?

Option H: How else could a speaker talk about 'genetic make-up'? Can you think of any expressions, perhaps more informal ones, that convey the idea that some characteristics are genetically controlled?

You will hear five short extracts in which different people talk about fitness and health.

You will hear the recording twice. While you listen you must complete both tasks.

Task One

For questions **23–27**, match the extracts with what each speaker says about his or her reasons for attending a gym regularly, listed **A–H**.

A The gym has a social function for me.

B I want to be fit for a specific event.

C My company pays for me to attend a gym.

D I must keep fit because of my medical condition.

E Being fit gives me a sense of achievement.

F Attending a gym is an absolute necessity for me.

G I come here with the members of my cycling club.

H I started exercising regularly after an injury.

Speaker 1	23
Speaker 2	24
Speaker 3	25
Speaker 4	26
Speaker 5	27

Task Two

For questions **28–32**, match the extracts with the opinion each speaker expresses about fitness and health generally, listed **A–H**.

A My lifestyle is unhealthy in the long run.

B Keeping fit is a habit.

C I find it hard to commit myself to exercising.

D City life doesn't encourage walking as exercise.

E Exercise machines are extremely boring.

F You can't separate health and lifestyle.

G It's easier to get fit if you think of it as a commitment.

H I'm sure your genetic make-up has a lot to do with fitness.

Speaker 1	28
Speaker 2	29
Speaker 3	30
Speaker 4	31
Speaker 5	32

Essential tips

Part 1

▶ In this part of the exam, you must show that you can use English appropriately to interact with another person in a social context. You will be expected to answer questions about yourself, but you should also listen to what your partner says and be prepared to ask him/her questions.

▶ It is easy to say too much or too little when you are nervous, so try not to do either of these.

▶ When the examiner or your partner asks a question, don't interrupt them. Listen politely until they have finished.

▶ Make sure you answer the question you have been asked and don't go off at a tangent to talk about something different.

▶ Don't try to prepare for this part of the exam by learning a speech off by heart – it will sound unnatural.

▶ Here you are asked to talk about where you live. Make sure you express some opinions, even if you do not feel very strongly about the subject.

Part 2

▶ In this part of the exam, you have to talk on a subject for one minute. This may not sound much, but it is quite a long time when you have to talk without interruption in an exam situation. Make sure you practise talking for this length of time.

▶ Listen carefully to the examiner's instructions. He/She could ask you to compare things, contrast them, identify them or speculate about them.

▶ Here you are asked to do two things: to compare and contrast the photographs, and to speculate why someone is doing something or what advantages something might have. Make sure you answer both parts of the question.

▶ Don't interrupt while the other candidate is talking; listen carefully. The examiner will ask you a question related to what the other candidate has been talking about. You should answer this question briefly (in about twenty seconds).

Part 1 (3 minutes)

The examiner will ask you a few questions about yourself and then ask you to talk to your partner. For example, the examiner may ask you:

- Where do you both live?
- What do you like and dislike about this area?
- If you moved to another area, where would you like to live?

Part 2 (4 minutes)

You will each be asked to talk for a minute without interruption. You will each be given a set of photographs in turn to talk about. After your partner has finished speaking, you will be asked a brief question connected with your partner's photographs.

Costumes (compare, contrast and speculate)

Turn to pictures 1–4 on page **192**, which show people in costumes.

Candidate A, compare and contrast these pictures and imagine what could have prompted these people to dress in this way.

Candidate B, which of these costumes would you feel most comfortable in, and why?

Working environments (compare, contrast and speculate)

Turn to pictures 1–4 on page **193**, which show different working environments.

Candidate B, compare and contrast these workplaces, saying what advantages and disadvantages you could imagine for them.

Candidate A, which of these environments would you prefer to work in, and why?

Part 1
Part 2
Part 3
Part 4

Part 3 (4 minutes)

Modern times (discuss, evaluate and select)

Turn to the pictures on page **194**, which show aspects of modern life.

Talk to each other about which two of these pictures you would choose to illustrate that modern life has both advantages and disadvantages.

Part 4 (4 minutes)

The examiner will encourage you to develop the topic of your discussion in Part 3 by asking questions such as:

• Which aspects of life in the past, which no longer exist, do you think were positive? Could they be revived? Why (not)?

• Should developments in technology be restricted in any way? Why (not)?

• What sort of difficulties do young people face today, but that previous generations did not have to confront, or not to the same extent?

• Why do older people sometimes become nostalgic about the past?

Essential tips

Part 3

▶ In this part of the exam you and the other candidate have to work together to perform a task such as finding a solution to a problem.

▶ Listen carefully to the examiner's instructions.

▶ You have three minutes for the task, so it is important that you really discuss the issue. You must ask your partner about his/her views and not only give your own.

▶ There is no right or wrong answer. The only important thing is to come to a conclusion. However, don't try too hard to persuade your partner; it is perfectly acceptable if you each come to different conclusions.

▶ Here you have to choose two photos that illustrate the advantages and disadvantages of modern life. You could begin by discussing the positive and negative aspects of each item. Then you can move on to a discussion of which two photos would be the best examples.

Part 4

▶ In this part of the exam you will be asked to talk about the subject discussed in Part 3. Usually, the discussion will be more abstract and general.

▶ You should demonstrate your conversational skills by listening carefully to your partner and then commenting on what they have said, perhaps agreeing or disagreeing, or adding a new idea.

▶ Make sure you don't just give one-word responses to your partner's questions. Practise the conversational devices used in discussions, including expressions like 'In my opinion', 'It seems to me', 'I don't entirely agree'.

▶ Here you are asked to discuss attitudes to the past. You should not talk for too long, even if the subject is of great interest to you. Neither should you try too hard to think of something new and fascinating to say. It is perfectly acceptable to express familiar opinions, as long as you express them well.

PAPER 1   Reading   ▶   Part 1
PAPER 2   Writing   Part 2
PAPER 3   English in Use   Part 3
PAPER 4   Listening   Part 4
PAPER 5   Speaking

Essential tips

▶ You can approach this part of the exam in two slightly different ways. However, you should begin by reading the instructions and the title of the text. Then you can either skim the text first before you read the questions, or read the questions first before you skim the text. Experiment and see which way works better for you.

▶ Remember: you don't need to read the whole text in detail, and it would waste valuable time if you did.

▶ Read each question carefully again, and then scan the text for the answer. The text will probably not use the same words to express an idea as the question, so think about the meaning of what you read.

Question 3: Think of other terms or expressions for the key words here: 'important', 'group' and 'consumers'. In the context of advertising, marketing and sales – the subject of this text – what does 'consume' mean? For example, if you consume a product, what do you do? Now look for these ideas in the text.

Question 7: The word 'regulation' can have different meanings, but this text is about a form of advertising and how it is governed by law. Therefore, in this context 'regulation' will probably mean 'law' or 'rule'. A 'paradox' brought about, or caused, by a law suggests that as a result of the law, something which is normally illegal is legal, or vice versa.

Answer questions **1–14** by referring to the magazine article about product placement on page **33**.

Indicate your answers **on the separate answer sheet**.

For questions **1–14**, answer by choosing from the sections of the article (**A–D**). Some of the choices may be required more than once.

In which section of the article are the following mentioned?

a tendency to blur the distinction between fact and fiction   **1** ....

the difficulty of obtaining information   **2** ....

an important group of consumers   **3** ....

a technological development   **4** ....

data compiled from monitoring TV programmes   **5** ....

concerns that restrictive laws would come into effect   **6** ....

an apparent paradox brought about by regulation   **7** ....

a more critical attitude that develops with time   **8** ....

a tendency to reject patronising advertisements   **9** ....

the cost of advertising   **10** ....

advertising that would have the opposite effect to the one intended   **11** ....

the inability to draw conclusions from numbers alone   **12** ....

the adverse consequences of placement on a certain age group   **13** ....

the need for accurate data   **14** ....

The Growth of Product Placement

A Product placement, the positioning of consumer goods in films and television programmes as a form of advertising, is growing in popularity. Though figures are notoriously hard to come by, it seems clear that many major companies are paying high fees to see their products feature in blockbusters or even TV soaps. Moreover, the function of product placement within an integrated marketing policy is also changing. In the eyes of many industry insiders, placement used to be merely a supplement to a standard ad campaign, but now it is being increasingly adopted as a stand-alone tactic. The introduction of video recorders that can automatically skip commercials and only record the programmes lent further impetus to a form of marketing that can camouflage itself and thus evade this form of consumer-imposed censorship. But perhaps the most powerful incentive to use product placement was the fear that legislation would be introduced to regulate conventional forms of advertising more strictly. This fear has, to a certain extent, proved justified: in many countries advertising regulations are enforced rigorously. Not only do they stipulate that certain products cannot be advertised on certain media, but they also concern themselves with what a TV commercial may or may not imply. It is not permitted to suggest that any alcoholic product bestows benefits on the consumer, for instance.

B Now that placement is thriving, complaints from consumer groups and others are also multiplying. Among the objections most commonly cited is that product placement appears to the gullible as factual information ('this character uses this product') and therefore bypasses their critical faculties. They don't realise fully that a marketing ploy has been adopted, so they are more likely to be a victim of the deceit. This argument draws ammunition from the tendency among some viewers of soap operas to believe, at least with one part of their minds, that events and characters on the screen are real. Another objection relates to the ease with which product placement evades the regulations related to advertising. Thus commercials for alcohol are banned entirely in the UK, but a scene in a film showing the hero drinking a certain brand of whisky will not – and indeed, in our present climate cannot – be subject to censorship. And yet, it may be more effective than the type of commercial that is banned. Moreover, placement may expose children to unsuitable products, with parents unaware of what is happening and powerless to prevent it. And there is little doubt that exposure to certain modes of behaviour can encourage copy-cat posturing among the young or the immature.

C What other factors have contributed to the cascade of product placement images that fill our screens? One is the tendency, frequently identified, of consumers in any given market to become more discerning in their response to advertising as they are exposed to more of it over a period of time. Indeed, it is increasingly difficult to distinguish, on the level of the images employed, between placement moments and more sophisticated 'slice of life' ads. The ads show beautiful people using a certain product, as do certain sequences in films and TV programmes. If the scene from the film had a voice-over, it could very well pass as an ad – at least, a sophisticated one. A further reason for the growing incidence of placement is that consumers are tired of being talked down to. Rather than have a disembodied voice urging them to spend their money in a certain way, they prefer to observe how role models spend their money and then draw their own conclusions. And if this is true of consumers in general, it is particularly applicable to the young, those much sought-after purchasers in the 16 to 24 age group, who are intensely aware of fashion and image but equally strenuous in their rejection of authority. It has even been claimed that standard advertising for certain products aimed at niche youth markets would damage sales rather than improve them, since the target consumers tend to turn their backs on products perceived as mainstream.

D Until recently, placement has not been accorded the same status as more traditional forms of advertising, and little attempt has been made to track the incidence of placement or to measure its effectiveness. But now tracking has begun; major TV networks will be scanned for placement, and it will be possible to calculate how many seconds a certain product has been visible on prime-time television. This is not to say that the effectiveness of placement can be deduced from such a simple statistic alone. However, if it is ever going to be possible to calculate the precise effects of this, or indeed any, marketing device, such figures will be necessary. The information provided will also include a breakdown of positioning – in this context, the foreground/background differential: is the product merely on view or actually being used?

In the broader context, what with globalisation proceeding apace, it seems safe to say that product placement will be playing an even more important role, particularly for lifestyle and youth-orientated products, and especially in view of the difficulty any regulatory organisations would have in policing this marketing device.

PAPER 1 Reading ▶

PAPER 2 Writing

PAPER 3 English in Use

PAPER 4 Listening

PAPER 5 Speaking

Part 1
Part 2
Part 3
Part 4

For questions **15–20**, choose which of the paragraphs **A–G** on page **35** fit into the numbered gaps in the following magazine article. There is one extra paragraph which does not fit into any of the gaps.

Indicate your answers **on the separate answer sheet**.

Mind your languages

Thousands of the world's languages are dying, taking to the grave not just words but records of civilisations and cultures that we may never come to fully know or understand. It is a loss of which few people are aware, yet it will affect us all. Linguists have calculated that of the 6,000 languages currently spoken worldwide most will disappear over the next hundred years. As many as 1,000 languages have died in the past 400 years. Conversely, the handful of major international languages are forging ahead.

15

But the vast majority of the world never had need of phrases in Heiltsuk (a Native Indian language from the Canadian Pacific coast of British Columbia which is now dead). Nor will most people be interested in learning any of the 800 languages spoken on the island of New Guinea or the 2,400 spoken by Native American Indians (many of which are threatened), but their deaths are robbing us of the knowledge needed to write many chapters of history.

16

Documenting a threatened language can be difficult and dangerous, requiring consummate diplomacy with tribes, some of which may be meeting outsiders for the first time and may well be wary about why these strangers need so much information about their language. 'Some peoples are extremely proud of their language while others are sceptical of the "white man", believing he now wants to rob them of their language as well,' says Kortlandt.

17

'There are about 200 Tibeto-Burman languages, only about ten of which have been properly described,' says Kortlandt. 'We now have fourteen PhD students describing different, unknown languages.' The problem is it can take years to document a language. 'We are

generally happy when we have a corpus of texts which we can read and understand with the help of a reliable grammar and dictionary provided by a competent linguist, preferably including texts of some particular interest,' says Kortlandt.

18

To non-linguists it must seem an odd issue to get worked up about. Why waste so much time saving languages spoken by so few and not concentrate on the languages of the future that most of us speak? Why look back instead of forward? 'Would you ask a biologist looking for disappearing species the same question?' Kortlandt asks. 'Or an astronomer looking for distant galaxies? Why should languages, the mouthpiece of threatened cultures, be less interesting than unknown species or galaxies? Language is the defining characteristic of the human species. These people say things to each other which are very different from the things we say, and think very different thoughts, which are often incomprehensible to us.'

19

Take, for example, the vast potential for modern medicine that lies within tropical rainforests. For centuries forest tribes have known about the healing properties of certain plants, but it is only recently that the outside world has discovered that the rainforests and coral reefs hold potential cures for some of the world's major diseases. All this knowledge could be lost if the tribes and their languages die out without being documented.

20

Kortlandt is blunt about why some languages have suffered. 'If we look back to the history of the Empire,' he says, 'for social, economic and political reasons, a majority never has an interest in preserving the culture of a minority.'

A Frederik Kortlandt, Professor of Comparative Linguistics at Leiden University in Holland, has a mission to document as many of the remaining endangered languages as he can. He leads a band of language experts trekking to some of the most inaccessible parts of the earth to save such threatened languages.

B This is one of the factors worrying Paul Qereti, a linguist in Fiji in the South Pacific. There are hundreds of known remedies in Fiji's forests. The guava leaf relieves diarrhoea, the udi tree eases sore throats, and hibiscus leaf tea is used by expectant mothers. There are possibly scores more yet to be discovered. We will only be able to find them and benefit from their properties through one or more of the 300 languages and dialects spoken on the Fijian islands. If the languages die, so too will the medicinal knowledge of naturally occurring tonics, rubs and potions. Science could be left wondering what we might have found. English is now spoken by almost everyone in Fiji and Qereti is teaching Fijians how to speak their own disappearing native languages and dialects.

C In September this year, like-minds met in Kathmandu for a conference on how to save some Himalayan languages spoken by just a handful of people. A great number of languages in the greater Himalayan region are endangered or have already reached the point of no return.

D As Kortlandt stresses, 'If you want to understand the human species, you have to take the full range of human thought into consideration. Language is the binding force of culture, and the disappearance of a language means the disappearance of culture. It is not only the words that disappear, but also knowledge about many things.'

E Kortlandt knows a language is disappearing when the younger generation does not use it any more. When a language is spoken by fewer than forty people, he calculates that it will die out. Every now and then language researchers get lucky. Kamassian, a southern Samoyed language spoken in the Upper Yenisey region of Russia, was supposed to have died out, until two old women who still spoke it turned up at a conference in Tallinn, Estonia in the early 1970s.

F According to the *Atlas of Languages*, Chinese is now spoken by 1,000 million people and English by 350 million. Spanish, spoken by 250 million people, is fast overtaking French as the first foreign language choice of British schoolchildren.

G Kortlandt is one of several linguists who have sounded the alarm that humankind is on the brink of losing over fifty percent of its languages within the next generation or two. 'This loss may be unavoidable in most cases,' says one authority, 'but at the very least, we can record as much as we can of these endangered languages before they die out altogether. Such an undertaking would naturally require support from international organisations, not to mention funding.'

Essential tips

▸ Remember: in this part of the exam you need to understand the structure and organisation of a text: how its paragraphs work together.

▸ First look at the instructions and the title of the text. Then skim the gapped text for the general meaning and notice how it develops ideas, opinions or events.

▸ You may need to consider more than one gap at a time in order to work out which paragraph goes where. Do not rely simply on recognising repeated names, dates etc.

Question 15: In the paragraph after the gap, the word 'But' shows that a contrast is being described. It is likely that the contrast is between the extinct or threatened languages referred to and the 'major international languages' mentioned in the paragraph before the gap.

Question 16: In the paragraph following the gap, the name of a person – Kortlandt – is mentioned, but there is no indication who this person is. It is likely that the gapped paragraph gives some details about him.

Question 19: The paragraph after the gap describes the kind of knowledge that could be lost if certain languages become extinct. Which gapped paragraph introduces this theme?

PAPER 1 Reading ▶ Part 1
PAPER 2 Writing   Part 2
PAPER 3 English in Use   Part 3
PAPER 4 Listening   Part 4
PAPER 5 Speaking

Read the following magazine article and answer questions **21–26** on page **37**. On your answer sheet, indicate the letter **A**, **B**, **C** or **D** against the number of each question. Give only one answer to each question.

Indicate your answers **on the separate answer sheet**.

The Cinderella Story

The basic story is very old indeed and familiar to most of us. The heroine, Cinderella, is treated cruelly by her stepmother and mocked by her two ugly stepsisters. And even though her father loves her, she can't tell him how unhappy she is because her stepmother has bewitched him. One day Cinderella's stepmother and stepsisters are invited to a ball at the royal palace. Cinderella is told she cannot go and is understandably very unhappy. However, her fairy godmother comes to the rescue and, waving her magic wand, produces some beautiful clothes for Cinderella as well as a carriage to convey her to the ball. There, she dances with the handsome prince, who falls in love with her, not only because she is beautiful but also because she is good and gracious. Cinderella has been warned that the magic will wear off at midnight, so when the clock strikes twelve, she hurries away, leaving behind her a glass slipper. Next day, the prince, smitten by her charms, comes looking for the girl whose foot fits the glass slipper. He finds Cinderella and they marry amid general rejoicing.

Just a sweet, pretty tale? Not in the view of Ellen MacIntosh, who has written extensively about fairy tales. 'This story features the stock, two-dimensional characters of most fairy tales, and little character development is attempted,' she says. Indeed, although her comment does make one wonder why simplicity of this sort should be out of place in a story for children. Be that as it may, Ellen's main problem is with what the story implies. 'Instead of standing up to her cruel stepmother and absurd stepsisters, Cinderella just waits for a fairy godmother to appear and solve her problems. But wouldn't you want a daughter of yours to show more spirit?'

The story is enduring, whatever its shortcomings, and it doesn't take much in the way of analytical skills to see its influence on a number of recent Hollywood productions, all aimed at girls aged five to fifteen. In these versions for the silver screen, the Cinderella character no longer has to clean the house and has no siblings to make her life a misery, though she persists in not showing much backbone. The character of the rich and handsome stranger, however, is retained, and in some cases really is a prince. The role of the fairy godmother is often played by coincidence or sheer luck; we live in an enlightened age when even very young children might reject the notion of fairies. The wicked stepmother may be transformed into a villain of some sort. In the majority of film versions, the heroine has a profession and is even permitted to continue working after marrying her prince – this is the twenty-first century, after all.

Doesn't the success of these films indicate that the story has relevance to children even today? 'Yes,' admits Ellen, who sees its message as being rooted in a fundamental childhood desire for love and attention. 'Most children experience a sense of inner loneliness as they are growing up and empathise with the protagonist who faces some sort of test or challenge. This can be seen in the original story of Cinderella, where the fairy godmother tells the heroine that she must learn to be gracious and confident if she is to go to the ball. She has to grow spiritually, and by maturing, she becomes attractive to the prince, thus ensuring that the ending of the story will be happy. 'In the later versions, this element is missing,' says Ellen, 'and the theme of the story is simply that a girl's role in life is to be more beautiful than other little girls so that she can carry off the prize: the handsome prince. Is this really what we want girls to grow up believing?'

▶ Remember: in this part of the exam you need to understand the details of a text, as well as the writer's opinion, attitude and purpose.

▶ You can approach this part in two slightly different ways. However, you should begin by reading the instructions and the title of the text. Then you can either skim the text first before you read the questions, or read the questions first before you skim the text.

▶ There will be five, six or seven questions or question stems. Read each question carefully and, without looking at the options, scan the text for the answer or for a suitable and accurate way to complete the question stem.

▶ Think about the meaning of what you read, and only then see if you can match the relevant section of the text with one of the options.

▶ The correct option is unlikely to use the same words as the text to express an idea.

Question 21: You are being asked about the writer's view, not Ellen MacIntosh's. Look for a section of the text where the writer describes Ellen's ideas and then gives her opinion of these ideas.

Question 23: This question is about films based on the Cinderella story. Look in the text for the word 'film' or any other word which means the same thing, for example, 'movie'. When you find the relevant section of the text, read it carefully. Then see which option corresponds precisely to what the text says.

Question 26: Even though you may be nervous and in a hurry, you must think carefully about the meaning of the questions. Which word in the question stem shows you are being asked to find a *difference* between the original story and the modern version?

21 What does the writer imply about fairy tales?
  A Fully developed characters would improve them.
  B The stories are very basic.
  C It is unrealistic to expect character development.
  D It is a mistake to consider them sweet and pretty.

22 What is Ellen's main objection to the Cinderella story?
  A The heroine is treated cruelly.
  B The heroine is not assertive enough.
  C The ugly stepsisters are figures of ridicule.
  D The stepmother is a stereotypical character.

23 In film versions of the Cinderella story
  A the prince is invariably replaced by a rich stranger.
  B two characters from the original story are omitted.
  C luck plays a greater role than in the original story.
  D the Cinderella character no longer has to work.

24 Modern variants on the story generally
  A portray Cinderella as a successful professional.
  B imply that Cinderella will become a real princess.
  C reflect children's beliefs.
  D make concessions to modern women's lives.

25 In Ellen's view, what makes the Cinderella story so appealing?
  A Children can identify with the heroine.
  B Little girls enjoy being challenged.
  C It has an element of magic.
  D Cinderella is more beautiful than other girls.

26 Unlike the original tale, modern versions of the Cinderella story
  A suggest that girls do not need strength of character.
  B do not require the heroine to develop.
  C underestimate the power of love.
  D are aimed solely at young children.

PAPER 1	Reading	▶	Part 1
PAPER 2	Writing		Part 2
PAPER 3	English in Use		Part 3
PAPER 4	Listening		**Part 4**
PAPER 5	Speaking		

Essential tips

▶ The text for Part 4 is longer than that for Part 1, but the basic idea is the same.

▶ Don't waste time reading the text in detail. You only need to match specific information in the text with the questions.

▶ The text is on two pages, so be careful. In the exam, you will be able to fold out the second page so that you can access any part of the text at a glance.

Question 32: Some questions use language which you will need to think about carefully. Here, for example, the question is about the need to do other jobs to make money, but this simple idea is expressed formally. The reverse may also occur: the question may express an idea in simple language but the text will use more formal language.

Question 35: A 'leisure pursuit' is a hobby; an 'alternative' leisure pursuit is one different to the hobby already mentioned. You know from the title that this text is about people who have made their hobbies into their careers, so find a section of the text where someone talks about taking up another hobby.

Question 39: Here, a key word is 'unexpected'. All the people in this text were able to turn their hobby into their career, so they all probably had a talent or, at least, a certain ability. But which person had an unexpected talent?

Answer questions **27–41** by referring to the newspaper article on pages **39–40**, in which people talk about turning their hobbies into careers.

Indicate your answers **on the separate answer sheet.**

For questions **27–41**, answer by choosing from the sections of the article **A–F**. Some of the choices may be required more than once.

In which section of the article are the following mentioned?

the pleasure of teaching young people	27 ....
valuable experience gained from voluntary work	28 ....
an enhanced appreciation of other people's work	29 ....
neglecting a job	30 ....
thoughts about the future	31 ....
the financial necessity for engaging in other ventures as well	32 ....
encouragement from a family member	33 ....
advice from a specialist	34 ....
finding an alternative leisure pursuit	35 ....
the value of assessing one's abilities objectively	36 ....
identifying potential customers	37 ....
an impulsive decision	38 ....
un unexpected talent for a particular job	39 ....
a feeling of apprehension before making a major change	40 ....
academic qualifications which were never used	41 ....

Turning a **Hobby** into a **Career**

It may seem idealistic or risky to exchange one's regular job for the uncertainty of earning your living from a hobby – but more and more people are attempting to do just that.

A I had piano lessons when I was young, and I did have some talent. But it soon became obvious I'd never be good enough for a career on the concert stage. In a way, I was lucky. If I hadn't realised early on that I'd never make it as a performer, I probably would have carried on dreaming that my big break would come. As it is, I became a music teacher instead, and in my free time I started to dabble in the technical side of music production. Then an aunt died, leaving me some cash, and I suddenly realised I could finally set up my own recording studio! Of course, there is a downside to turning a hobby into a career. I love my job so much that I used to work seven days a week, but after a while I realised I was getting burnt out – you need to switch off occasionally. My job has definitely added depth to the way I listen to music; now I can really understand why someone's using a certain technique or piece of equipment.

B I studied medicine, but when I finished medical school I had a sort of crisis. I suddenly knew I couldn't go on with it! I'd have been an awful doctor. But I was keen on amateur dramatics and I enjoyed putting on plays at the local youth centre, especially coaching budding actors. So I started wondering if I could make a living from teaching drama. A friend suggested I should set up as a freelance teacher and offer acting lessons for children. It was tricky and at first, I couldn't work out how to find customers who would pay for their children to attend the kind of courses I wanted to run. Then someone at an organisation called Business Link, which helps people set up their own businesses, suggested advertising on the Internet! I was contacted by a surprising number of interested people, and five years down the line I'm doing all right. The classes themselves aren't terribly lucrative, but I supplement my income by giving talks to amateur dramatics societies, writing articles for magazines and organising trips to see shows in London. It's not a bad life.

C When I left college I started working in a bank, but my heart was never really in it. The problem was partly the environment: I don't like working in an office. I'm more of an outdoor person – and I'd always been crazy about surfing. Well, one summer while I was in Cornwall on holiday, I got chatting to the owner of a surf shop. He said he wanted to sell up and I jumped at the chance to buy the business from him! Looking back, I can see how lucky I was. It's incredibly difficult to set up a shop like that from scratch. Besides, being such an avid surfer myself, I assumed a lot of other people must share that interest – which isn't the case! Obvious when you think about it, but it took me a while to realise what a naive attitude that was. Now that I've learnt the ropes, I'm thinking either of expanding – more shops, managers and so on – or diversifying, perhaps producing my own surf boards! I actually think the second option is more likely because it's a subject which interests me a lot.

D I'd always been a serious amateur photographer, and when I left school I wanted a job that would allow me a lot of free time for my hobby. So I got a job as a waiter, working evenings only. Around that time I also offered to help my uncle out in his studio. He was a professional photographer, and I'd go along at the weekends and act as general unpaid dogsbody. I got an insight into the business, which made me wonder whether I too could earn a living from photography. So I saved, set myself up as a professional photographer and tried to survive solely on my earnings from selling pictures. However, after a while I realised it simply wasn't going to happen. So I swallowed my pride and got some work as a sales representative for one of the big camera manufacturers, which takes me round the country to trade fairs and so on, demonstrating the latest equipment. I'm doing quite well in that line of work, although I've noticed one odd thing: now that my hobby is my work, more or less, I've had to find another way to switch off. In fact, I've taken up fishing.

E My first job was with an insurance company, but I was hardly a model employee. I loathed my job, and instead of selling insurance, I used to wander around the city's numerous art galleries. I have no creative talent of my own, but I can recognise it in the work of others. I soon picked up quite a lot of knowledge about contemporary art. Then one day I got talking to the manager of an art gallery. She mentioned a new gallery that was going to be opened and suggested I apply for the job of manager. At first, I was doubtful, but I realised I had nothing to lose, so I applied and was asked to go for an interview. I think the fact that I was so obviously crazy about art impressed the owners. To my surprise, I've turned out to be quite a good saleswoman. Of course, most people come into the gallery just to look around, but when someone shows an interest in one of the works on show, I don't immediately start to persuade them to buy it. I just chat about the work and what makes it interesting to me. People feel reassured when they sense your enthusiasm.

F I wanted to study graphic design when I left school, but I didn't have good enough grades to go on to art school. Instead, I got a job in a garage, and for the next ten years I worked as a car mechanic. But while I was working, I did some evening courses in industrial design and got lots of books on the subject. I was interested in the practical side of construction, too: I even built a car of my own from spare parts. Then I got the idea of building a bike – a four-wheel delivery bike – and the next thing I knew, my wife was urging me to set up my own company! I had to take a very deep breath before I finally took the plunge. I'd done my best to prepare for it, taking a course in business management in my spare time, and I knew I'd be working longer hours for less money, at least at first. The big difficulty was the uncertainty of not knowing how much would be coming in each month. And things were pretty tough for the first few years, although I never regretted it. Looking back, I can see that I underestimated the amount of paperwork I'd have to do. I somehow thought I could just concentrate on the nice stuff – designing!

Essential tips

▸ In Paper 2 you must answer two questions, so it is essential to use your time effectively. This does not mean you should start writing at once and write as much as you can! You must take the time to prepare before you begin writing.

▸ Make sure you understand the instructions. Read the question several times, underlining the key words that describe your task.

▸ Think about the register of your writing: should it be formal or informal? What layout is appropriate?

▸ You need to understand the input – the information you are given – and use it to produce a piece of writing.

  • In Part 1 you are given a lot of input. It is worth spending time to read and study the information, checking that you understand it. Make sure you use all the information necessary to answer the question fully. Underline the key points you must mention.

  • Pay particular attention to input material in the form of charts or diagrams. The information they contain is as important as that in any other input material, but greater effort may be needed to understand it.

▸ The input for the Part 2 questions is much shorter. You must use the information given, but you will also need to provide some information yourself – use your imagination intelligently. You will need to spend time preparing your answer, as for Part 1.

▸ Don't write a rough draft – there isn't time for that. Make a plan instead.

  • Your writing should normally have three sections: an introduction, the main body and a conclusion. Note down approximately how many words should be in each section.

  • Note down a few words or phrases to remind yourself what you must say in each section.

  • Take a few minutes to look at your plan and make sure the information flows well. If it doesn't, you can still change your mind and put something in the conclusion instead of the main body, for instance.

▸ See the **Writing bank** on page 216 for examples of different types of writing.

PAPER 1 Reading

PAPER 2 Writing ▶ | Part 1 | Part 2 |

PAPER 3 English in Use

PAPER 4 Listening

PAPER 5 Speaking

1 You are the student representative on the executive committee of Oldtree College, where you are studying. Recently, an article from a former student was published in the local newspaper, criticising the way the college has changed. The principal of the college has asked you to write to the newspaper, responding to the article. In your letter she would also like you to publicise a college reunion which is being organised.

Read the extract from the former student's article below, on which the principal has made some notes, together with the principal's memo on page **43**. Then, **using the information carefully**, write the **letter** outlined on page **43**.

Oldtree Gone Downhill

A former student expresses disappointment

by *Hilda Cooper*

Twenty years after graduating from Oldtree College I thought I'd have a look at the old place again. Oh, how sad! The <u>lovely sports pavilion</u> has gone – don't students enjoy cricket and football these days? In its place is an ugly new <u>accommodation block</u>. There was litter everywhere and the students looked distinctly unfriendly with their sloppy clothes and surly faces. In an atmosphere like this, how can <u>academic standards</u> be maintained? What can explain this sad state of affairs?

New sports centre shared with City College

Accommodation needed: 70% more students over last 15 years

Higher proportion of students get top grades than 20 years ago!

MEMO

To: The Student Representative of the Executive Committee
From: The Principal
Re: The College Reunion (weekend 25–26th May)

Following the discussion at last week's meeting of the Executive Committee, we have received approval to organise a college reunion to which the graduates of the last ten years will be invited. The reunion will be mainly a social event with a concert and disco. However, we also need to make both old students and the general public aware how Oldtree College has changed in the last twenty years:

- There are almost 7,000 students now.
- Over 20% of students are from overseas (a big increase).
- We offer a much wider range of courses (especially vocational).
- More graduates leave with the highest possible grade.
- The college is more involved with the community (e.g. evening classes for retired people).

Could you write to the local newspaper explaining this and mention the college reunion as well?

Now write a **letter** to the editor of the local newspaper as requested by the principal (approximately 250 words). You should use your own words as far as possible. You do not need to include postal addresses.

Essential tips

▸ You are asked to write a letter to a local newspaper, so what register is appropriate? Should you use headings? What about abbreviations or contractions?

▸ Underline the important information, which includes the handwritten comments next to the article. Then decide where to include this information when you plan your letter.

▸ Your letter is in reply to an article, so what would you put in the introduction to your letter? How would you explain who you are and why you are writing?

▸ You are told that this letter is primarily to respond to the article, so the points you make should be in the main body of your letter. You also have to make additional points about the college reunion. Which part of your letter could contain this information?

▸ It may be effective to end your letter with a simple and powerful statement. Could you say anything personal (in your character here as 'student representative')? Perhaps you could give your own personal, positive view of the college.

PAPER 1 Reading

PAPER 2 Writing ▶ Part 1 / Part 2

PAPER 3 English in Use

PAPER 4 Listening

PAPER 5 Speaking

Choose one of the following writing tasks. Your answer should follow exactly the instructions given. Write approximately 250 words.

2 You would like to start a radio station at the college where you are a student. You have decided to send a proposal to the principal, asking for permission and practical assistance. Your proposal should include the following:
- why you think the radio station would be beneficial
- what sort of programmes you would begin with
- what sort of support, practical and financial, you would need

Write your **proposal**.

3 You have seen the following advertisement in an international magazine for young people:

Competition

All over the world, more and more people are migrating from the countryside to cities. What are the attractions of city life? What about the disadvantages? What will life in our cities be like in the future?

**Write and tell us your views.
We will publish the best entry.**

Write your **competition entry**.

Essential tips

▶ In Part 2 you must answer one question, so think carefully about the task that you feel most comfortable with. Are you confident you know which register to use and if a particular format or layout is necessary? Do you have a good range of vocabulary relevant to this task? Can you express clear views on the subject (if the question requires you to do so)?

▶ If you are required to give opinions, don't try to think up or express complex or original ideas. Your main task is to show you can use written English in the way the question demands, and you shouldn't worry if the views you express are familiar.

▶ You may have to think up additional information for Part 2 questions, so before you decide which question to answer, make sure you can come up with other information or details.

Question 2

▶ What style would be appropriate for this proposal? Bear in mind that the proposal is written by a college student to the principal of the college.

▶ Consider your three sections: introduction, main body and conclusion. The introduction could state simply what you want, and the conclusion could repeat this request, perhaps with some extra force or promise of success. The words 'Introduction' and 'Conclusion' could also be headings. What will the main body contain? What will the heading(s) be?

▶ Be careful when you use bullet points. You are giving a list, and the contents of the list should all be correct in grammatical terms. For example, you should not say:

A radio station would be:
- a good way to tell students about social events.
- inform local people about college events.

However, you could say:

A radio station would be a good way to inform:
- students about social events.
- local people about college events.

▶ Don't worry about precise figures, for example, how much money would be needed to start the radio station. You are not expected to know this.

4 A British television channel is interested in making a documentary called *Transports of Delight*, which will feature public transport all over the world. You have been asked to write a report for the channel, addressing the following questions:
- What means of public transport in your region are the most popular?
- What is being done to improve these facilities and encourage the use of public transport?
- What more could be done?

Write your **report**.

5 A colleague of yours, Andrew Armstrong, has applied for a job in the sales department of a multinational company, and you have been asked to write a character reference for him. You should indicate how long and in what capacity you have worked with him, what business skills and experience he has, and how his personal qualities would make him a good candidate for the job.

Write your **character reference**.

Essential tips

Question 5
▸ As with every Question 5 in Part 2, it is best to attempt this only if you are familiar with English in working situations.

▸ In order to answer this question, you must be familiar with the format of a character reference, which usually begins with the heading 'To Whom It May Concern', and then a sub-heading which is the person's name.

▸ You need to provide the information requested in the question. Decide which information will go in the various paragraphs.

▸ What qualities would an employer look for in a job candidate? Can you think of some specific qualities that would make a person good at the job mentioned here?

▸ Finish your character reference by saying you would be glad to provide any further information that may be required.

Essential tips

▸ Read the title and the whole text quickly for general meaning.

▸ Remember: the gapped word may be part of an idiom, expression or phrasal verb. It may collocate with another word, or be part of a fixed phrase.

▸ If you do not know which option to choose, read out the sentence with each of the options in turn. Choose the option that sounds best in context.

▸ Check the clauses and phrases on each side of the gap to see whether the presence of a word here dictates the choice of word for the gap.

Question 3: The correct word must be applicable to 'canals'. If you have an option that is used in a clear, concrete sense to mean a different sort of structure to a canal, it will probably not be correct here. Is there a word that can be used in a general sense?

Question 6: Two options have the correct meaning, but only one of them is followed by 'with'.

Question 7: Sometimes it helps to picture a scene. How would a horse walk along the side of a canal pulling a boat? Quickly or slowly? With effort or easily? In a straight line or wandering from side to side? One of the options suggests the appropriate way of walking.

Question 14: The word 'up' after the gap suggests that the correct option is part of a phrasal verb. The meaning is clear here – the boats can be renovated to make them attractive.

For questions **1–15**, read the text below and then decide which answer best fits each space. Put the letter you choose for each question in the correct box on your answer sheet. The exercise begins with an example (**0**).

Example:

0	B	0

Modern barging

There has been a (**0**) ...... change in the way the canals of Britain are used. The (**1**) ...... network of canals that covers much of the country (**2**) ...... back to the industrial revolution, when goods were transported along these (**3**) .... The canals themselves, the (**4**) ...... waterways of the country, were dug by teams of men. This was no (**5**) ...... feat in the days before mechanised diggers. It was also necessary to construct a system of locks, which raise and lower boats so they can (**6**) ...... with the varying height of the canals themselves. Barges – simple boats without engines – were used to carry the freight, and horses would (**7**) ...... along the side of the canal pulling these vessels. Many of the people working on the boats would themselves live on the water, in a long boat with cramped living (**8**) ...... : a narrowboat.

As the railways and roads (**9**) ...... popularity as ways of transporting freight, the canals fell into (**10**) ...... ; many of them became (**11**) ...... with weeds and rubbish. But over the last few decades Britain appears to have rediscovered these (**12**) ...... of engineering. A growing number of people each year (**13**) ...... the delights of canal holidays. Narrowboats can be (**14**) ...... up to be very comfortable, and these days they are (**15**) ...... by an engine and not pulled by a horse.

0	**A** prime	**B** fundamental	**C** downright	**D** deep-rooted
1	**A** extensive	**B** far-flung	**C** ample	**D** widespread
2	**A** comes	**B** looks	**C** throws	**D** dates
3	**A** roads	**B** paths	**C** routes	**D** ways
4	**A** inbuilt	**B** inland	**C** internal	**D** interior
5	**A** modest	**B** mean	**C** minor	**D** tiny
6	**A** balance	**B** compensate	**C** cope	**D** handle
7	**A** trudge	**B** canter	**C** stroll	**D** meander
8	**A** rooms	**B** apartments	**C** spaces	**D** quarters
9	**A** increased	**B** obtained	**C** gained	**D** assumed
10	**A** disuse	**B** obsolescence	**C** redundancy	**D** negligence
11	**A** impeded	**B** choked	**C** hindered	**D** congested
12	**A** records	**B** testimonies	**C** constructions	**D** monuments
13	**A** investigate	**B** revel	**C** sample	**D** approve
14	**A** done	**B** worked	**C** customised	**D** converted
15	**A** equipped	**B** supplied	**C** drawn	**D** powered

Essential tips

▶ Read through the whole text to get a general idea of what it is about.

▶ Remember: the gapped words will probably not be complex or specialised words. Most of them will be structural items like articles, pronouns or prepositions. A few may form part of common expressions etc.

▶ Look at the whole sentence, or even bigger sections of the text, to see if the word you need is part of a longer or parallel structure. For example, you might need the word 'other' in the expression 'on the other hand', which will be clear if you find 'on one hand' in the previous sentence.

Question 20: The structure 'as ... as' is often used with adjectives to compare two things which are the same. Can you think of an expression with 'as ... as' that has the more abstract meaning of 'to the extent that'?

Question 22: This gap is in a long sentence, so read the whole sentence carefully. There is a verb after the gap: 'appear'. What is its subject? Can it be 'the tribe', which occurs earlier in the sentence?

Question 24: The word 'than' later in the sentence indicates that the gapped word must be part of a comparative structure. The context tells us that these people are not good at counting. What adjective could be used with 'no' to express the idea that they are as good at counting as a baby is at speaking?

Question 28: Read the whole sentence. The first part of the sentence must mean something like 'it seems that the Piraha ...'.

For questions **16–30**, complete the following article by writing each missing word in the correct box on your answer sheet. **Use only one word for each space.** The exercise begins with an example (**0**).

Example:

0	*order*	0

Finding the Right Word

A recent study has suggested an answer to a question that has occupied philosophers for centuries: Do people need words in (**0**) .... to think? A tribe living in the Amazon basin could provide the answer. The Piraha tribe (**16**) .... be small – there are only about 200 members all told – (**17**) .... they exhibit a fascinating cultural peculiarity. These people have no words for numbers, (**18**) .... from 'one', 'two' and 'many'. What is more, (**19**) .... words for 'one' and 'two' are very similar. As (**20**) .... as anyone can tell, this tribe has never had (**21**) .... sort of vocabulary for numbers, but (**22**) .... appear to survive quite well without it.

It was soon realised that these people might supply an insight (**23**) .... the way our minds work. Studies have shown that adult members of the tribe are no (**24**) .... at counting than a baby is at speaking. (**25**) .... they were shown a row of objects and asked (**26**) .... duplicate the number they saw, they could not get beyond two or three before starting to make mistakes. This applies even to adults who appear reasonably intelligent in (**27**) .... other way.

So it looks (**28**) .... though the Piraha are not very good at counting simply because they (**29**) .... not have a vocabulary for numbers. This would suggest that human beings in general cannot think if they have no words to do (**30**) ....

Essential tips

▸ Read through the whole text to get a general idea of what it is about.

▸ Some of the spelling mistakes may involve words that sound the same (or nearly the same) but are spelled differently, such as 'way' and 'weigh'. To find mistakes like these, you need to read the text carefully, thinking about every word.

▸ Spelling mistakes can be difficult to find for another reason: in English, words are often not pronounced as one would expect. For example, the words 'rough', 'though' and 'through' sound quite different!

Question 31: The apostrophe in English can be used to show possession, but it can be an abstract sort of possession or association, as in the phrase 'the country's past'. Can you find an example like that here?

Question 35: If you read a text quickly, you might confuse words that look similar. In this line there is an example of a mistake that native speakers often make!

Question 37: When we speak, we often do not pronounce certain letters. In this line there is an example of a mistake that involves leaving out such a letter.

Question 43: When you are looking for punctuation errors, read the whole sentence, even if it goes over two or three lines. What pair of punctuation marks should be used in this line and the line before?

In most lines of the following text, there is **either** a spelling **or** a punctuation error. For each numbered line **31–46**, write the correctly spelt word or show the correct punctuation in the box on your answer sheet. Some lines are correct. Indicate these lines with a (✔) in the box. The exercise begins with three examples (**0**), (**00**) and (**000**).

Example:

0	✔	__ 0 __
00	*birth,*	__ 00 __
000	*extremely*	__ 000 __

Eels

0   Eels, those snake-like fish that live in rivers all around England

00   and swim out to the Atlantic to give birth have recently become

000   extremly popular in expensive restaurants throughout the country.

31   This is particularly surprising in view of the eels reputation as a

32   cheap and rather unapetising food, popular in the East End of

33   London. Their it is still possible to find market stalls selling eels

34   that have been preserved in jelly. However, smoked eel is today

35   regarded as quiet a delicacy, and restaurants in a number of other

36   european countries are also seeing a surge in demand. It is perhaps

37   ironic that the reputation of a diffrent fish has declined over a

38   similar period. Fresh samon is now so cheap that people no longer

39   regard it as a desirible food in the way they did a few years ago.

40   Does this indicate that the actual taste of the fish is not as important

41   as it's price and image? Anton Bewley, chef at the exclusive Bewley's

42   Restaurant in London, thinks foods go in and out of fashion. 'People

43   love to feel they have discovered the next big trend, he says. At the

44   moment, eels are considered fashionably interesting and new, but

45   it is hard to predict wether this popularity will continue for many

46   years; in the long-term, people may rediscover their dislike of the eel.

PAPER 1 Reading

PAPER 2 Writing

PAPER 3 English in Use ▶

PAPER 4 Listening

PAPER 5 Speaking

Part 1
Part 2
Part 3
Part 4
Part 5
Part 6

Essential tips

▸ Read through each text to get a general idea of what it is about.

▸ Remember: you may need to make more than one change to the root word. For example, you may need to add both a prefix and a suffix to the root word (e.g. courage – encourage – encouragement), or two suffixes (e.g. mad – madden – maddening).

▸ Check the whole sentence to be sure you have used the correct form of the gapped word. Sometimes, however, even that is not enough. The gapped word must make sense in the text as a whole.

Question 48: The meaning of the root verb doesn't seem to have much to do with the words around the gap here, but there is a noun from this verb which means 'department' or 'part of a large organisation'.

Question 52: If you look at the verb in this clause, you will see that an adverb based on the noun given would make sense.

Question 55: The word after this gap is a noun, so perhaps an adjective is required. Think about the whole sentence and decide whether the adjective needs to be positive or negative.

Question 61: The verb 'be' is often followed by an adjective. What adjective can be formed from 'refund' that expresses the idea that the money can be refunded?

For questions **47–61**, read the two texts below. Use the words in the boxes to the right of the texts to form one word that fits in the same numbered space in the text. Write the new word in the correct box on your answer sheet. The exercise begins with an example (**0**).

Example:

0	*educational*	0

JOB ADVERTISEMENT

Sales Manager

Wilson Pickert has been a publisher of quality (**0**) .... books for the last 35 years. The (**47**) .... increase of sales in Central Europe in the last few years has led to the creation of a new (**48**) .... , which aims to consolidate our position in this market and expand it even further. We are therefore seeking an (**49**) .... and competent Sales Manager to head this unit. The (**50**) .... candidate is expected to bring (**51**) .... and commitment to the task facing him/her. He/She will have experience in the publishing industry and be able to pursue our aims in this market (**52**) .... We are able to offer a (**53**) .... salary and excellent fringe benefits. Please contact the Human Resources Manager, Wilson Pickert, 14 Library Place, London W13IF for more details.

(**0**)	**EDUCATE**
(**47**)	PRECEDENT
(**48**)	DIVIDE
(**49**)	ENERGY
(**50**)	SUCCEED
(**51**)	CREATE
(**52**)	AGGRESSION
(**53**)	COMPETE

EXTRACT FROM ONLINE SHOPPING CATALOGUE

Ordering Clothes from *SuperQuick*

Simply place the items you want in your virtual shopping basket and proceed to the checkout. Make sure that you click on the payment (**54**) .... you prefer. In the (**55**) .... event that you have any difficulty, phone our helpful hotline for assistance. Our experienced (**56**) .... are trained to deal with any problems quickly and (**57**) ....

As soon as you have placed your order, we will send you e-mail (**58**) .... of your purchases. If, for any reason, goods are returned to us, we will ensure that you receive (**59**) .... of the fact. If you are (**60**) .... with any of the items you have purchased, simply return them to us. But please note that while the cost of the goods is (**61**) .... , postal expenses are not.

(**54**)	OPT
(**55**)	LIKELY
(**56**)	OPERATE
(**57**)	EFFICIENCY
(**58**)	CONFIRM
(**59**)	NOTIFY
(**60**)	SATISFY
(**61**)	REFUND

For questions **62–74**, read the notes from a meeting. Use the information in the notes to complete the numbered gaps in the formal letter. The words you need **do not occur** in the notes. **Use no more than two words for each gap**. The exercise begins with an example (**0**).

Example:

0	*residents*	0 __ __

Essential tips

▶ Read through each text for the general meaning.

▶ Remember: you need to complete the second text with one or two words (not more) in each gap. The second text must convey the same meaning as the first, but in a different register.

▶ Concentrate on the meaning of the phrase or clause containing the gap. For example, if the first text says 'Only 5% of the local population agree with the plan' and your gapped sentence is ' … who live in the area like the plan', don't waste time trying to think of a phrase that means 5%. Instead, think of a phrase that conveys the idea of 'only 5%', i.e. 'very few'.

Question 62: One way to convey the idea of '96% of people' would be to say 'almost everyone'. Can you think of a more formal expression, including 'the' and a noun which collocates with 'vast'? Do you need a preposition with this word in this context?

Question 67: The informal word is 'cut', which is often used in newspapers and speech. Which more formal word could be used in the same way?

Question 69: 15% more patients went to the unit last year than the year before. In the formal letter, a passive verb is needed which is followed by the preposition 'to'. Which word means 'allow somebody to enter'?

Question 74: The gap needs to be completed by a word meaning 'think again'. Many verbs in English meaning 'do something again' begin with 're'. There is a verb 'rethink', but a more formal word would be better.

NOTES

Meeting attended by people living in Otterbury

Topic of discussion: Proposed Closure of Accident Unit at Otterbury Hospital
✓Government wants to close unit
✓96% of people against the idea! (local newspaper sent out questionnaires)
✓Doctors and nurses also against idea

Reasons why almost everyone is against closing unit:
✓Big cut in medical services
✓More and more patients use unit (15% more patients went to unit last year than year before)
✓If unit closed, patients would have to go to Samgate Hospital, 34 miles away (can take 45 mins to get there by ambulance because road so bad!)
✓Almost 60 people at Otterbury Hospital would lose their jobs

Ask government to think again about public enquiry (refused to allow one last month)

FORMAL LETTER

I am writing on behalf of the (**0**) .... of Otterbury regarding the proposed closure of the Accident Unit at Otterbury Hospital. This plan is unpopular with the vast (**62**) .... people in the area. In a (**63**) .... carried out by the *Otterbury Gazette*, 96% of respondents indicated that they were (**64**) .... to the plan. Moreover, the (**65**) .... at the hospital are also against the closure.

There are a number of reasons for the virtually (**66**) .... opposition to the plan. Firstly, a (**67**) .... hospital services is unjustified, especially in view of the fact that the (**68**) .... people using the unit is growing. Hospital records show that 15% more people were (**69**) .... to the unit for treatment last year than the year before. Secondly, the only (**70**) .... for accident and emergency cases, if the unit is closed, would be Samgate Hospital, which is 34 miles away. Due to the poor (**71**) .... the roads, it can take an ambulance 45 minutes to get there. Finally, implementing this plan would mean that almost 60 hospital employees would be (**72**) ....

We are aware that the government refused (**73**) .... for a public enquiry into the matter last month, but we would ask you to (**74**) .... this decision.

Essential tips

▸ Read through the text to get a general idea of what it is about.

▸ Remember: even if the options begin in similar ways, they may differ in other important ways. This can help you decide which one is correct. For example, the phrases 'to live in this country' and 'to living here' both begin with 'to', but each will be preceded by a different type of clause:
  - *Many people would like* to live in this country.
  - *Some people can't get used* to living in this country.

▸ Look carefully at the words before and after a gap. What do they suggest about the gapped clause or phrase?

Question 76: The relative pronoun 'which' can refer to an object just mentioned or to the idea expressed earlier in the sentence.

Question 77: The sentence continues after the gap with the main verb, and the subject of the main verb is 'standing on a platform'. So what could the words in this gap refer to?

Question 78: A sentence can express an idea already mentioned, but in different words. Here, 'something peculiarly British' is followed by the word 'something'. Look for an option that explains 'something peculiarly British'.

Question 80: The structure of the sentence indicates that the correct option must refer to a person, so which relative pronoun will it begin with? The sentence after the gap expands on the idea by talking about 'the loner'. Could this refer to the gapped clause?

For questions **75–80**, read the following text and then choose from the list **A–J** given below the best phrase to fill each of the spaces. Write one letter (**A–J**) in the correct box on your answer sheet. Each correct phrase may only be used once. **Some of the suggested answers do not fit at all**. The exercise begins with an example (**0**).

Example:

0	J	0

Trainspotting

There are few things **(0)** ...... than the popular British hobby of trainspotting. Not that it's a complicated hobby – in fact, quite the reverse, but its very simplicity is one of the puzzling things about it. Trainspotters are people **(75)** ...... writing down in little notebooks the serial numbers of the railway locomotives they see (or 'spot') there. In the old days all large steam locomotives had names, such as The Flying Scotsman, **(76)** .... Today there are not so many names, and diesel or electric locomotives are characterless compared to steam engines. But the trainspotters are still on the station platforms.

There is a competitive element to the hobby, of course, in that each trainspotter wants to have spotted more locomotives than other enthusiasts. But standing on a platform, waiting to glimpse a particular locomotive, **(77)** ...... , seems a strange way to engage in a competition. Is there something peculiarly British about this hobby, something **(78)** ...... ? It's certainly true that you don't find trainspotters elsewhere in the world. Perhaps the explanation lies in the character of the British people. Britain is a land **(79)** .... In many countries someone **(80)** ...... might be considered strange, but in Britain the loner is respected. Doubtless, many British people think trainspotters are a little odd – but this only makes them eccentric, which is a compliment in the eyes of the British.

A which means it will never become really popular

B who would rather pursue a hobby in solitude

C which may never actually appear

D who spend hours standing on station platforms

E whose inhabitants like to think of themselves as individuals

F who know the different types of locomotive by heart

G which perhaps made things a little more interesting

H who derive enormous personal satisfaction from it

I that people from other countries can't appreciate

J that puzzle foreigners more

Essential tips

▶ As with all listening tasks, make the best use of the time you are given before you hear the recording. Read the instructions carefully, look at the title and the questions, and imagine what the recording might say.

▶ Remember: you will hear the words you need but not in the same context as the question. Note, however, that you can answer a question with a synonym, or paraphrase an idea, as long as the synonym or paraphrase completes the question appropriately.

▶ Bear in mind the question after the one you are trying to answer, so if you miss the information you need, you can move on to the next question.

Question 1: The word or words you need must describe the person's occupation or role. This sort of information might be given at the beginning of the talk, so make sure you are listening carefully from the very start of the recording!

Question 3: From the context you can guess that the speaker will mention a profession. You might try to imagine which professions a farmer and his wife might aspire to for their son.

Question 5: The speaker will say that he studied something, but remember that another way to say that you did something is to imagine what would have happened if you had not done it.

Question 8: There are many phrases with 'in' which might fit here, such as 'in luxury', but that is unlikely. Probably the word you need will be the name of a place. The text may use a different structure, so you might not hear the preposition 'in'.

You will hear part of a talk by a writer who has written a biography. For questions **1–8**, complete the sentences.

You will hear the recording twice.

An interesting character

The speaker has written a book about ▭ **1**

called Robert Tewbridge.

Tewbridge's father was a ▭ **2** in Scotland.

Tewbridge's parents wanted him to become ▭ **3**

Tewbridge earned his living by writing ▭ **4**

for various publications.

The speaker learnt a great deal about Tewbridge's character

from studying his ▭ **5**

It appears that Tewbridge and his ▭ **6**

were close friends.

Tewbridge spent many years studying ▭ **7**

He lived in ▭ **8** for the last thirty years of his life.

PAPER 1 Reading

PAPER 2 Writing

PAPER 3 English in Use

PAPER 4 Listening ▶ Part 1 / **Part 2** / Part 3 / Part 4

PAPER 5 Speaking

Essential tips

▸ Parts 1 and 2 of the Listening Paper are similar, but for Part 2 you only hear the recording once. If you miss the information you need to answer a question, don't panic; just listen carefully for the information for the next question.

▸ Be careful when you have to listen for numbers. Word stress can be very important, for instance, in distinguishing between 'sixteen' (the stress is on the second syllable) and 'sixty' (the stress is on both syllables equally).

▸ Remember: you will hear the words you need but not in the same context as the question. Note, however, that you can answer a question with a synonym, or paraphrase an idea, as long as the synonym or paraphrase completes the question appropriately.

Question 9: A number is probably necessary here. Can you guess what sort of number?

Question 11: If you have read the title and the questions, you can probably guess that these DVDs work for some time after they have been opened and then stop working because they react with something. What could that be?

Question 14: How could an object be 'used' in a magazine? You may need to include an adjective as well as a noun in your answer if the adjective gives important information.

Question 16: The verb 'end up' implies that the DVDs become something bad in the end. In what way could an object that is no longer useful 'end up' as something negative or difficult to deal with?

You will hear a talk on the subject of disposable DVDs. For questions **9–16**, complete the notes.

Listen very carefully as you will hear the recording ONCE only.

The Disposable DVD

Disposable DVD can only be viewed
for [_____ **9**__] hours.

It is kept in [_____ **10**__] until use.

When packaging opened, substance on DVD reacts with
[_____ **11**__]

Technology available to make DVD last up to [_____ **12**__]

One possible use: people buy disposable DVD
instead of [_____ **13**__] ordinary DVD.

Another possible use: [_____ **14**__] in magazines.

Strong objections to disposable DVDs from [_____ **15**__]

Problem: disposable DVDs end up as [_____ **16**__]

PAPER 1 Reading

PAPER 2 Writing

PAPER 3 English in Use

PAPER 4 Listening ▶   Part 1

PAPER 5 Speaking   Part 2
                         Part 3
                         Part 4

Essential tips

▸ Prepare for what you will hear on the recording: read the instructions and think about the subject. Consider who the speakers will be.

▸ Remember: you will not hear the exact words of the question in the recording, so concentrate on the ideas expressed.

▸ The questions follow the order of the recording, but the final question may be about the recording as a whole.

Question 18: The question refers to Betsy's feelings about expensive shops. If you hear one of the words in the options, check that Betsy is using it to talk about expensive clothes shops.

Question 19: To prepare for this question, think how you would explain the feelings in the options. In the recording you will hear one of these feelings expressed in different words.

Question 21: How might Betsy express 'most rewarding' in other words? Now think about the meaning of the options. What does 'overcome their inhibitions' in option A mean, for example?

You will hear part of an interview with Betsy Boom, owner of a chain of fashion shops. For questions **17–22**, choose the correct answer **A, B, C** or **D**.

You will hear the recording twice.

---

17 What aspect of shopping does Betsy enjoy most?
   A experimenting with different styles
   B finding a bargain
   C comparing items in different shops
   D being given advice

18 What does she dislike about expensive clothes shops?
   A There isn't a wide selection of goods.
   B The assistants are unfriendly.
   C Customers are ignored.
   D Customers are expected to spend a lot of money.

19 When people first went into one of Betsy's shops, they often felt
   A flattered.
   B amused.
   C awkward.
   D dizzy.

20 The members of staff in Betsy's shop
   A were offended at the demands Betsy made.
   B found it hard to adjust to the new surroundings.
   C disliked dealing with shy and difficult customers.
   D came to enjoy the atmosphere after a while.

21 What is the most rewarding aspect of the business for Betsy?
   A seeing customers overcome their inhibitions
   B proving to others that her idea was a good one
   C watching the staff relax in their new roles
   D being able to provide fashionable clothes at low prices

22 What does Betsy feel is the danger she faces now?
   A becoming complacent
   B growing arrogant
   C being afraid to try something new
   D suffering financially if fashions change

PAPER 1 Reading

PAPER 2 Writing

PAPER 3 English in Use

PAPER 4 Listening ▶ | Part 1
                     | Part 2
                     | Part 3
                     | **Part 4**

PAPER 5 Speaking

Essential tips

▶ In this part of the exam there are two possible task types. There is an example of the first in Test 1, page 29. Here we have an example of the second type.

▶ Read the instructions and find out who will be talking and what they will be talking about.

▶ Read the questions or question stems carefully and underline the key words. There are two questions for each speaker.

Question 23: The question stem mentions what 'most employees' think. You may hear one of the ideas in the options, but make sure that it refers to what the majority of staff think.

Question 27: What does the recording say in connection with the company's environmental policies (option A)? Can we deduce anything about its policies in the past? Option B mentions electricity, but does the recording compare the company's electricity consumption with that of other companies? Does the recording mention the company's future (option C)?

Question 31: Think about the connections between ideas. Option B, for example, suggests that the problem mentioned by the speaker is 'caused' by rising costs. For this option to be correct it isn't enough for the speaker to talk about a problem that involves rising costs or something being expensive – the speaker must also say that these rising costs create the problem.

You will hear five short extracts in which different people talk about environmental initiatives in the workplace. Each extact has two questions. For questions **23–32**, choose the best answer **A**, **B** or **C**.

You will hear the recording twice.

---

23 The first speaker thinks the attitude of most employees to good environmental practice is
  A that individual efforts would not be effective.
  B that government guidelines are required.
  C that this is the responsibility of the company.

24 She believes few office workers
  A realise how much they could do to conserve energy.
  B consider conservation a priority.
  C feel environmental issues really affect their lives.

25 What does the second speaker see as the prime motivation for companies to adopt a sound environmental policy?
  A tax concessions
  B pressure from consumers
  C a desire to move with the times

26 What attitude does he notice among young job seekers?
  A They would like a work environment that reflects their own values.
  B They feel most companies do not do enough for the environment.
  C They don't buy products from companies without sound policies.

27 What does the third speaker imply about the company she mentions?
  A It did not always have sound environmental policies.
  B It uses less electricity than other companies.
  C It has a bright future as a business.

28 What other example does she mention to illustrate a point?
  A the fact that the company's staff no longer use cars
  B the fact that the company provides its staff with a particular kind of car
  C the fact that the company no longer employs sales reps

29 The fourth speaker feels that a good image with regard to the environment
  A suggests the company is efficient in other ways.
  B attracts positive publicity.
  C appeals to investors.

30 He suggests that
  A regulations regarding the environment are bound to be ineffective.
  B employees have to make greater efforts at work.
  C companies need to explain environmental initiatives to their employees.

31 The fifth speaker mentions a problem
  A related to perception.
  B caused by rising costs.
  C is simply an attempt to boost its image.

32 She feels that the tree planting scheme run by a car manufacturer
  A should involve compensation.
  B should be linked to a calculation of environmental damage.
  C is simply an attempt to boost its image.

Essential tips

Part 1

▶ Remember: in this part of the exam you must show you can use English appropriately to interact with another person in a social context.

▶ If you are asked about a subject you don't know much about (or aren't interested in), you should still be able to express some views. Here, the subject is sports and it may be that they don't interest you. In that case, don't just say you aren't interested in them, expand on the idea and say why you aren't interested. Alternatively, you could say you yourself aren't interested but other members of your family are.

▶ Don't forget to give the other candidate a chance to speak.

Part 2

▶ Remember: in this part of the exam you have to talk on a subject for one minute, so practise speaking for this time.

▶ Listen carefully to the examiner's instructions. Is he/she asking you to compare pictures, speculate about them, identify with them?

▶ The examiner will also ask you a question related to what the other candidate has been talking about. You should answer this question in about twenty seconds.

▶ If there are two parts to the task (for example, making a comparison and then speculating on people's feelings), spend roughly half a minute on each part of the task.

Part 1 (3 minutes)

The examiner will ask you a few questions about yourself and then ask you to talk to your partner. For example, the examiner may ask you:

- What kind of outdoor activities do you enjoy?
- Which sports are popular in your region?
- Which sports do you enjoy watching and playing, and which do you find boring?

Part 2 (4 minutes)

You will each be asked to talk for a minute without interruption. You will each be given a set of photographs in turn to talk about. After your partner has finished speaking, you will be asked a brief question connected with your partner's photographs.

Anticipation (compare, contrast and speculate)

Turn to pictures 1–4 on page **195**, which show people anticipating something.

Candidate A, compare and contrast these pictures and imagine what these people could be anticipating that makes them look this way.

Candidate B, what sort of things do you anticipate with pleasure?

Being Alone (compare, contrast and speculate)

Turn to pictures 1–2 on page **196**, which show people alone.

Candidate B, compare and contrast these situations, saying how you think the person might be feeling in each.

Candidate A, when do you enjoy being alone, and when does it disturb you?

Part 3 (4 minutes)

Motivation (discuss, evaluate and select)

Turn to the illustrations on page **197**, which show how motivation is part of modern life.

Talk to each other about the importance of motivation in each of these situations and then decide in which one a powerful sense of motivation can have a positive and in which a negative effect.

Part 4 (4 minutes)

The examiner will encourage you to develop the topic of your discussion in Part 3 by asking questions such as:

- When do you think it is important for people to be motivated? Are there any times when being motivated is undesirable?

- It is often said that motivation is important in education. Do you agree? Why (not)?

- What factors motivate people to achieve something? Are these factors external or internal?

- How can people motivate themselves?

Essential tips

Part 3

▶ Remember: in this part of the exam you have to work with the other candidate to perform a task, so listen carefully to the examiner's instructions and make sure you understand exactly what you have to do.

▶ The task may be in two parts. Here, for instance, you should discuss motivation in each of the situations and then decide in which situation motivation can have a positive, and in which a negative, effect. Spend roughly two minutes on each part of the task.

▶ Don't come to a conclusion too quickly. You must talk for the period required: four minutes.

▶ Taking part in a discussion often involves agreeing or disagreeing with the other person. It is perfectly acceptable to do so in the exam as well, providing you don't confine yourself to saying you agree or disagree. You must express your reasons for doing so.

▶ Make sure you use appropriate conversational expressions for discussions, such as 'Wouldn't you say ... ?' and 'Do you agree that ... ?'

Part 4

▶ Remember: in this part of the exam you will be asked to talk further about the subject in Part 3. Usually, the discussion will be more abstract and general.

▶ Don't interrupt your partner while he/she is talking, even if you feel strongly about the subject. Listen carefully and then comment on his/her ideas.

▶ As long as you stick to the general subject, it is fine to introduce new ideas.

▶ Here, you are asked to discuss motivation. You could illustrate your points by mentioning your own experiences or those of other people, but don't get involved in telling a long story that may not be relevant.

Essential tips

Question 2: Look at the key words 'belief' and 'make a contribution'. Make sure you understand what they mean. The correct answer will probably be expressed in different words.

Question 7: If you are not familiar with a word or expression in the question, don't automatically assume you can't answer the question! Even if you don't know how 'made out' is used here, you can still look for a section of the text which says that environmental problems are not very bad.

Question 11: How can optimism be 'misplaced'? This must mean some people were optimistic, but it turned out that there was not enough reason for their optimism. Look for a section which expresses this idea.

Answer questions **1–15** by referring to the magazine article about environmental issues on page **59**.

Indicate your answers **on the separate answer sheet**.

For questions **1–15**, answer by choosing from the sections of the article (**A–D**). Some of the choices may be required more than once.

Note: When more than one answer is required, these may be given **in any order**.

In which section of the article are the following mentioned?

the belief that some solutions are deliberately not being developed	**1**	
a belief that the individual can make a contribution	**2**	**3** ....
concern that the scale of a problem may prevent action	**4**	
conservation of natural habitats	**5**	
faith in technological progress	**6**	
a belief that environmental problems are not as bad as they are made out to be	**7**	
the need for international co-operation	**8**	
inconsistent attitudes towards conservation	**9**	
the fallibility of experts	**10**	
a realisation that optimism was misplaced	**11**	
maintaining civilised standards of behaviour	**12**	
the power of vested interests	**13**	
legislation concerning certain substances	**14**	
the view that personal liberty ought to be respected	**15**	

How much does the environment matter?

Four people give us their views on environmental issues.

A Teresa Stanley, 47, housewife

I've always been keen on environmental matters, but in the seventies, when I was growing up, the subject wasn't discussed as much as it is today. Perhaps the problem was just as bad then, but fewer people understood the implications of what was going on or realised something ought to be done about it. I remember being pleased when laws restricting the use of certain pesticides came in. They appeared to signal the start of a vast movement to improve the environment, an acknowledgement that all human beings had a right to clean air and water. With hindsight, I think we were naive. There is much greater public awareness of environmental issues these days, but I still don't think enough is being done about the problem. And since it's a global issue, individual countries can't tackle it by themselves. Reducing damage to the environment really must be an international effort. In a paradoxical way, the more we discover about the extent of the problem, the less we do about it. This is because problems like global warming are so huge that ordinary individuals don't feel they could possibly make any difference. I think that's the real danger facing us today – that we'll succumb to a feeling of helplessness instead of making a concerted effort to make our planet a safer and cleaner place for future generations.

B Stan Bingley, 20, student

I must say I'm pessimistic about the extent to which we can make a real difference to the conservation of our environment. Take the problem of air pollution, for instance. So much of the waste is produced by big industry, which has tremendous financial clout and a lobby that can put pressure on governments to pass laws in its favour. I've read somewhere that it would be a relatively easy matter to mass-produce cars that run on non-polluting fuels like hydrogen or natural gas, but the oil companies are so strong they block any real progress in that direction. And in the meantime, factories and power stations add to the problem by continuing to spew out tons of poisonous gases into the atmosphere.

I know many people are under the impression that they are helping in their own little way: recycling glass, plastic and paper in the household and so on. But then you often see the same people driving huge cars that guzzle petrol. They also think nothing of flying around the world for a holiday, polluting the atmosphere with the exhaust emissions from commercial planes. They don't seem to realise that you can recycle waste paper for years to save trees being cut down, but your good deeds can be cancelled out by a single plane flight!

C Meg Darcy, 32, senior executive

I think people get worked up unnecessarily about these things, to be perfectly honest. Naturally, I'm all in favour of preserving the environment, but you have to take a balanced view of the situation. You can't simply pass laws to discourage people driving large vehicles and force them to change to tiny fuel-economical cars. People have to be allowed to make choices of their own – responsible choices, of course – on such matters. And I suspect the scientists who keep preaching doom and gloom are probably exaggerating. The other day I saw a documentary about trains, and it seems that at the dawn of the railway age, scientists confidently stated that human beings could not possibly survive a journey on one of the new steam engines: they would not be able to breathe if they travelled at such unnatural speeds! They were wrong about that, so why should we assume they are right about global warming and the rest of the doomsday scenarios? As for the so-called energy crisis, I cannot take that very seriously, either. In the next few decades scientists are bound to find viable alternative sources of energy to fossil fuels. After all, we are already using inventions like solar panels to generate 'clean' electricity. One has to be optimistic about these things.

D Syd Bayle, 56, dentist

Environmental issues are important, but I don't agree with people who become aggressive about the subject. No matter how right your ideas are, there's no justification for becoming rude or violent. You have to take the long view and persuade people by reasoned argument and by setting a good example. Besides, attitudes have changed over the years. Not so long ago people thought you were eccentric if you recycled your household waste, but these days it's common practice. I also feel that if everyone were responsible and organised about relatively little things like that, it would make a huge difference in the end. That's how we have to approach the problem: by being very conscientious and painstaking.

Of course, we also need accurate information about the real situation, and this is where voluntary groups can make a valuable contribution – by monitoring the amount of pollution all over the country. A lot of people feel they can't really trust government figures to be accurate, so it's important to be able to double-check information against an independent source. I think this applies in particular to places like moors, forests and heathland – isolated regions where wildlife is under threat. People often forget about the rare birds and other species that suffer because of the way we humans are affecting the environment, which is a great pity.

PAPER 1 Reading	▶	Part 1
PAPER 2 Writing		Part 2
PAPER 3 English in Use		Part 3
PAPER 4 Listening		Part 4
PAPER 5 Speaking		

For questions **16–21**, choose which of the paragraphs **A–G** on page **61** fit into the numbered gaps in the following newspaper article. There is one extra paragraph which does not fit into any of the gaps.

Indicate your answers **on the separate answer sheet**.

Seeking El Dorado in the Mountains of Peru

It was just a sparkle on the horizon, where the sun hit what appeared to be a flat plain on an otherwise steep mountain in the Peruvian Andes. But Peter Frost, a British-born explorer and mountain guide, surmised that the perch would have made a perfect ceremonial platform for Inca rulers. So Frost and the adventure hikers he was leading slogged through heavy jungle growth and uncovered remnants of the Inca civilisation that flourished here. They found looted tombs, a circular building foundation and the stonework of an aqueduct.

16

Recent carbon dating at Caral, north of Lima, has shown that an advanced civilisation existed here nearly 5,000 years ago. The Lord of Sipian tomb, considered one of the richest pre-Columbian sites ever found, was discovered in 1987, firing the ambitions of those hoping to make similar spectacular finds.

17

It is the mountains of the Vilcabamba range that perhaps hold the most tantalising, spectacular ruins. Vilcabamba was the centre of a great empire that 500 years ago stretched from modern-day Colombia to Chile. The Spaniards wiped out the last Inca holdouts in 1572 and then promptly abandoned much of the region. That left it to men like Mr Bingham, who in one remarkable year discovered Machu Picchu and several other important settlements.

18

The finds are significant because while modern Peru is synonymous with the Inca, archaeologists actually know very little about their civilisation. 'About ninety percent has not been investigated,' said a Peruvian archaeologist. 'There are maybe 1,000 books on Machu Picchu, but only five or six are really scientific.'

19

To many, like Frost and Reinhard, the powerful hold of discovering ruins swallowed by jungle is as strong today as it was early last century. 'It's the Indiana Jones fantasy,' said Scott Gorsuch, whose sharp eye led to the discovery of Qoriwayrachina with Frost. 'It's really not more complicated than that – the search for El Dorado, this idea that there are lost cities out there waiting to be found.'

20

Frost is not an archaeologist, but through his work as a tour guide, photographer and author of the popular travel book, *Exploring Cuzco*, he has dedicated much of the last thirty years to learning everything he can about the ancient highlanders. 'Some people like the thrill of finding something and moving on to something else,' he said. 'But you want to do something useful with it.'

21

Frost is now trying to raise money for future expeditions to Qoriwayrachina, but he is already dreaming of other finds. 'I know of two sites that are sort of undiscovered, that I'd like to discover,' he said, explaining with a wry smile that he cannot reveal their locations. 'It's not a big thing, but I feel it's wise not to broadcast intentions.'

A But he did not find them all, leaving much of Vilcabamba open to modern-day explorers. 'I've run across foundations of buildings, foundations of roads, water channels, probably dozens of them,' Frost said.

B In two lengthy expeditions to Qoriwayrachina in 2001 and 2002, a team led by Frost found a sort of blue-collar settlement spread across more than sixteen square miles. They found the ruins of 200 structures and storehouses, an intricately engineered aqueduct, colourful pottery and tombs. The people who once lived there toiled in mines or cultivated diverse crops at various altitudes. The explorers believe that Qoriwayrachina may have been used to supply a more important Inca centre, Choquequirau, but much remains unknown.

C But exploring is not all about adventure. Serious explorers carefully read the old Spanish chronicles, pore over topographical maps and charts and interview local residents, who often lead them to sites. The work also requires raising money to finance expeditions. 'Anyone can blunder around in a jungle,' writes Hugh Thompson in his recent book about exploring for Inca ruins, *The White Rock*. And indeed, the annals of Peruvian exploration are littered with failures.

D 'Peru has one of the oldest continuous civilisations in the history of the planet,' Frost explained. 'That amounts to an awful lot of culture buried under the ground or under vegetation.'

E Johan Reinhard, who holds the title of explorer in residence at *National Geographic*, is a proponent of vigorous exploration combined with serious scientific research. He says it is important to find and catalogue sites in Peru before they are looted or destroyed. 'If you don't do it now, some of these things will be gone, and they'll be gone forever,' he said.

F The previous year, 1989, saw a number of expeditions to the region in search of the mythical lost city, but the end result was similarly disappointing. Undeterred, the courageous explorer refuses to abandon his attempts to raise money for one last try.

G The discovery in 1999 of Qoriwayrachina was instantly hailed as a major find. It evoked the romantic image of the swashbuckling explorer unearthing a Lost City, an image embodied by Hiram Bingham, the American who in 1911 made the greatest Inca discovery of them all, Machu Picchu. In the twenty-first century it would seem that the remote, rugged mountains around Cuzco would have given up all of their secrets. But this region of southern Peru is still full of ruins.

Essential tips

Question 17: The last sentence of the previous paragraph mentions 'spectacular finds'. In which gapped paragraph is this theme continued?

Question 18: Look at the previous paragraph and underline the names mentioned. Are any of them mentioned in a gapped paragraph? The last sentence talks about the discoveries of Bingham. Which gapped paragraph has pronouns that could refer to them?

Question 19: Remember that when a person's name is first mentioned, the writer will often give some basic information about that person. So if a name is mentioned in the main text without any such information, look for it in one of the gapped paragraphs.

PAPER 1 Reading	Part 1
PAPER 2 Writing	Part 2
	Part 3
PAPER 3 English in Use	Part 4
PAPER 4 Listening	
PAPER 5 Speaking	

Read the following magazine article and answer questions **22–27** on page **63**. On your answer sheet, indicate the letter **A, B, C** or **D** against the number of each question. Give only one answer to each question.

Indicate your answers **on the separate answer sheet**.

On Your Bike On Your Bike On Your Bike

Every generation has its emblematic boy's toy. Once upon a time there was the golf cart: a little toy car specifically designed for middle-aged men too rich to care about looking ridiculous. Later came the beach buggy, a briefly fashionable, wildly impractical, single-terrain vehicle. One might include the motorcycle or the snowmobile on this list, were they not, in certain contexts, quite useful, but there is no doubt which pointless recreational vehicle has captured the imagination of the landed, middle-aged celebrity: it's the quad bike.

What is it about this squat, ungainly, easy-to-flip machine that celebrities love so much? As recreational vehicles go, the quad bike is hardly sophisticated. They are to the countryside what the jet-ski is to Lake Windermere. 'There's nothing cool about a quad,' says Simon Tiffin, editor of a well-known magazine. 'It's a strange thing to want to hare round beautiful bits of the country in a petrol-guzzling machine.'

But celebrities love quad bikes. Musicians, comedians, DJs, actors and sportsmen have all been photographed aboard quads. 'They're the latest rich person's toy,' says Tiffin. 'Spoilt children get them for Christmas.' Provided you've got a large estate to go with it, however, the quad bike can remain a secret indulgence. You can go out and tear up your own piece of countryside without anyone knowing you're doing it.

The quad bike's nonsensical name – 'quad' means four, but 'bike' is an abbreviation of 'bicycle', which means two – that comes to six – hints at its odd history. Originally the ATV, or all-terrain vehicle, as quads are sometimes known, was developed in Japan as a three-wheeled farm vehicle, an inexpensive mini-tractor that could go just about anywhere. In the seventies it was launched in America as an off-road recreational vehicle. In the 1980s the more stable four-wheeled quad was officially introduced – enthusiasts had been converting their trikes for some time – again primarily for farming, but its recreational appeal soon became apparent. At the same time a market for racing models was developing.

Paul Anderson, a former British quad racing champion, says the quad's recreational appeal lies in its potential to deliver a safe thrill. 'It's a mix between a motorbike and driving a car; when you turn a corner, you've got to lean into the corner, and then if the ground's greasy, the rear end slides out,' he says. 'Plus they're much easier to ride than a two-wheeled motorcycle.' The quad bike, in short, provides middle-aged excitement for men who think a Harley might be a bit dangerous. Anderson is keen to point out that quad bikes are, in his experience, much safer than motorcycles. 'With quad racing it's very rare that we see anybody having an accident and getting injured,' he says. 'In the right hands, personally, I think a quad bike is a very safe recreational vehicle,' he adds.

Outside of racing, quad bikes are growing in popularity and injuries have trebled in the last five years. Although retailers offer would-be purchasers basic safety instructions and recommend that riders wear gloves, helmets, goggles, boots and elbow pads, there is no licence required to drive a quad bike and few ways to encourage people to ride them wisely. Employers are required to provide training to workers who use quad bikes, but there is nothing to stop other buyers hurting themselves.

For the rest of the world, quad bikes are here to stay. They feature heavily in the programmes of holiday activity centres, they have all but replaced the tractor as the all-purpose agricultural workhorse and now police constables ride them while patrolling the Merseyside coastline. It has more or less usurped the beach buggy, the dirt bike and the snowmobile; anywhere they can go the quad bike can. They even race them on ice. You can't drive round Lake Windermere on one, or at least nobody's tried it yet. Just wait.

Essential tips

22 The writer claims that the quad bike
   A   now serves the same function as the beach buggy once did.
   B   is as useful as a snowmobile or motorcycle.
   C   is pointless as a recreational vehicle.
   D   will only be fashionable for a brief period.

23 What is Simon Tiffin's attitude to the people who ride quad bikes?
   A   He doesn't understand them.
   B   He thinks they are amusing.
   C   He is scornful of them.
   D   He believes they have too much money.

24 Originally, the quad bike
   A   was popular only in America.
   B   was a utilitarian vehicle.
   C   had four wheels.
   D   was used as a recreational vehicle.

25 What view is expressed by Paul Anderson?
   A   The only danger is when the rider is turning a corner.
   B   Anyone who can ride a quad bike can ride a motorcycle.
   C   Most accidents occur when people are racing quad bikes.
   D   A quad bike can be exciting without being dangerous.

26 Quad bike riders have to
   A   wear gloves, helmets, goggles, boots and elbow pads.
   B   follow basic safety instructions.
   C   take lessons if they use the bike as part of their job.
   D   have a motorbike licence.

27 According to the writer, why will quad bikes remain popular as working vehicles?
   A   They are used by the police.
   B   They are used a great deal on farms.
   C   They have virtually replaced horses.
   D   They can be used on ice.

PAPER 1   Reading   ▶   Part 1
PAPER 2   Writing   Part 2
PAPER 3   English in Use   Part 3
                                 Part 4
PAPER 4   Listening

PAPER 5   Speaking

Essential tips

Question 31: Even if you are unfamiliar with the word 'fusion', you can work out that this question is about something successful involving 'words and graphics'. Which other words or phrases could be used to talk about these elements of a book?

Question 35: To find the answer to this question, think about what a person could conjure up in his or her mind as a result of having a strong imagination.

Question 40: The words in the question are very simple, which may mean that the words used in the text will not be. Can you find a different word for 'ending' in one of the texts, and an expression or idiom that means 'unexpected'?

Answer questions **28–42** by referring to the book reviews on pages **65–66**.

Indicate your answers **on the separate answer sheet**.

For questions **28–42**, answer by choosing from the book reviews **A–H**. Some of the choices may be required more than once.

In which review are the following mentioned?

a subject whose fascination never fades	28 ....
particularly fine illustrations	29 ....
an accidental transgression	30 ....
a successful fusion of words and graphics	31 ....
an adult who helps a child	32 ....
travel between completely credible worlds	33 ....
a previous work by the same author	34 ....
the potential danger of having a powerful imagination	35 ....
children who are not interested in certain kinds of books	36 ....
children who lack self-confidence	37 ....
doubts about who the book is intended for	38 ....
a powerful evocation of a certain period and place	39 ....
an unexpected ending	40 ....
the ability to make adult themes accessible to children	41 ....
the tendency to patronise	42 ....

Books for Children

Reviews of the best children's books published this year

A Lost and Found by Peter Osgood
Ages 10+

Anje was abandoned by her mother as a baby and has grown up with foster parents, but now she resolves to track down the mother who deserted her. Osgood avoids all the traps inherent in a tale of family life, refusing to describe events in such a way as to justify the adults' actions. Instead, he portrays the situation as Anje herself experiences it, with stunning insight and accuracy, producing a moving and hard-hitting story. What is more, there is plenty of action to keep you turning the pages, and the breathtaking finale comes right out of the blue. Sensitive youngsters may find the subject emotionally haunting, but by this age children should be able to cope with the issues handled here. Highly recommended.

B Bird Fly Away by Helen Hunter-Smith
Ages 8–11

Children may well be natural conservationists, enchanted by floppy bunnies and cute doggies, but rather than simply exploit this yearning for anthropomorphic animals, Hunter-Smith has decided to tackle head-on the whole problem of how we treat animals in western society. The story revolves around a farm where Cal lives with his parents, who are desperately trying to get away from the countryside and move to the big city. The haunting pictures of the dilapidated farm buildings and scruffy animals are just one of the outstanding features in this first novel, but perhaps the major attraction of *Bird Fly Away* is that it refuses to compromise in its portrayal of poverty-stricken farmers and neglected animals. This enables young readers to understand fully the awkward issues facing the grown-ups in this world, though there is a tribute to the genre of fairy tales in the shape of a happy ending. A fine work with serious undertones.

C Cuddle by Seth Ashton
Ages 0–4

Everyone likes a cuddle; that's the premise of this charming, chunky book for the very young. Even toddlers who show no interest in the usual baby bathtime books will be entranced by the delightful narrative. In fact, this book could hardly be bettered as an introduction to the world of stories. As Eddy the Baby Elephant wanders sadly through the jungle in search of his parents, he encounters all sorts of adorable creatures, from Harold the Hippo to Tim the Toothy Tiger, and each of them sends him on his way with a nice cuddle. All Eddy has to learn to do is ask for a cuddle – and be prepared to return the favour and give someone else a cuddle when asked to do so. The sparse text is cleverly interwoven with the line drawings in such as way as to encourage reading without being too overtly didactic.

D Step Aside by Diana Courtland
Ages 8–11

Having grown up in an orphanage, Bob can only imagine what normal family life is like, and he indulges in these fantasies whenever his drab reality becomes too depressing. Problems begin to emerge when he discovers he is slipping in and out of his imaginary world without realising it – and then he finds he can't control which world he is living in. This powerful and original tale demonstrates with stunning clarity how strongly we can be drawn into our fantasies and what an uncomfortable (and ultimately terrifying) experience it can be. While Courtland clearly has talent as a writer, the younger members of the target market for this work may find the subject matter too unsettling. After all, she is really hinting at the psychological basis of a wide range of mental problems, not to mention abuse of alcohol and narcotics. If this marketing mismatch could be addressed, the book would deserve unreserved praise.

E Not in Time by Laura Rose
Ages 8–11

Child psychologists tell us that round about the age of six or seven most children are gripped by an interest in the phenomenon of time, though the extent to which they articulate this naturally varies. Books and films for older children (and adults) that deal with time travel indicate just how, well, timeless, that interest is. Laura Rose's third book once again features her popular protagonist, Heather Hornet, who discovers an old garden that is a portal to a world of the future. As Heather ventures backwards and forwards in time, she learns fascinating details about life in different epochs, each of which is entirely plausible and very real. The writer also dares to address the thorny but fascinating philosophical question of whether a visitor from the future who changes the past could thereby nullify his own existence. To discover what conclusion Rose comes to, you will have to buy the book!

F Colour My World by Ashton Lyle
Ages 2–5

My three-year-old niece loved this book, though I can't promise that every three-year-old will feel the same way. This is the story of Viji, the little boy who absolutely refuses to paint pictures in his nursery class. In a clever touch we see how the pictures themselves feel (neglected, since you ask) when Viji only paints them under extreme pressure. But a new teacher at nursery school brings out the artist in Viji by helping make his pictures come to life for him, showing him what they think and feel. So the moral here is that even though grown-ups want you to do something that you yourself have no desire to do, you might still enjoy it if you give it a go. A useful message for every child who is unwilling to try something new because of doubts about his or her ability.

G The Ghost at Number 54 by Fred Wilmot
Ages 8–11

This marvellous tale manages to make England in the 1950s seem like an interesting place – and as someone who was growing up there at the time, I can only say this is a huge tribute to the writer's skills! Wilmot captures brilliantly the drabness and grey uniformity, but also the quaint quality of life in that decade. Against this backdrop he tells the story of Alice and John as it slowly dawns on them that their house, number 54 Mafeking Place, is haunted. One striking quality in this work is Wilmot's ability to demonstrate what is going on in the minds of the adults in the story – without talking down to his young readers, as so many writers do. I won't reveal how the tale ends, except to remark that we were very fond of happy endings in the 1950s.

H The Enchanted Tree by Samantha Carson
Ages 11+

The tree in this story is not just enchanted in the figurative sense of the word: Haball the wizard has actually cast a spell over it, and this means that nobody must look at the old oak. Everyone in the village knows this, for such matters are common in this medieval world of witches, wizards and spells. Everyone except Arthur, that is, for Arthur is the son of a travelling musician who is passing through the village. We learn what happens to Arthur when he looks at the tree, and as in her first novel, Carson depicts brilliantly the isolation of childhood, the sensation that everyone except you knows the rules of the game. A gripping read that will be popular with boys and girls alike.

Essential tips

Question 1

▶ Make sure you know who you are writing for. Think about the format and register that would be appropriate for the task.

▶ Include all the essential points from the input in your writing. You will lose marks if you neglect to cover all of them.

▶ Organise your writing clearly into paragraphs and present your ideas in a logical order.

▶ Use a good range of structures and vocabulary.

1 You are studying at a college in Brighton, on the south coast of England. Recently the college social club organised a week-long trip to Edinburgh, and you were one of the people who went on the trip. Now the president of the club has asked you to write a report about it.

Read the extract from the president's memo below and also the extract from the publicity leaflet about the trip, together with your comments. Then, **using the information carefully**, write your **report**.

I have heard various reactions from people who went on the trip, including some criticisms as well as praise. The Social Club would like to organise similar trips in future, so I would be grateful if you could write a report for me. We want to know what problems there were as well as what aspects of the trip were successful. Perhaps you could also suggest how we could do better in future?

Sam Samson, President

See a completely different part of Britain!
Enjoy the <u>beautiful scenery</u>!
Listen to <u>musical Scottish accents</u>!

Didn't see much of it

Better if we'd had practice before?

Faster by train?

Sun: <u>Coach to London</u>, arrive at hotel
<u>Free time</u> in evening

Some wanted organised event on first evening

Save time by taking sleeper?

Mon: <u>Train</u> to Edinburgh

Great!

Tues: <u>Guided tour of city</u>

Wed: Day at MacTavish College:
• <u>lectures</u> on Scottish culture
• <u>language classes</u>

Some young students bored

Everyone loved it

Thur: Free day, Scottish <u>country dancing</u> in evening

A bit hard for most

Interesting, but too much for one day?

Fri: Edinburgh's <u>museums and art galleries</u>

Sat: Back to London, then Brighton

Now write your **report** for the president (approximately 250 words). You should use your own words as far as possible.

PAPER 1 Reading

PAPER 2 Writing ▶ Part 1 / **Part 2**

PAPER 3 English in Use

PAPER 4 Listening

PAPER 5 Speaking

Essential tips

Question 2: Your main task is to produce a good piece of written English, so it is not very important if the factual details you include are not entirely accurate.

Question 3: When writing about an experience you have had, make sure you include a balanced mixture of information about the experience. Don't only describe the facts, but also your views or feelings relating to them. You should also consider the best way to organise your ideas.

Question 4: Note that there are four points you must include in this piece of writing. Make sure you cover them adequately, and use your imagination to come up with the details.

Question 5: You should only attempt this question if you are clear about the format required – a proposal usually has headings and bullet points – and if you are familiar with the vocabulary required to talk about the Internet and business situations. Don't forget who 'you' are in this case: someone in the sales department of a company. How will this influence your writing?

Choose one of the following writing tasks. Your answer should follow exactly the instructions given. Write approximately 250 words.

2 A college in your region would like to send a leaflet to foreign students, giving them helpful information about the local leisure facilities they might find interesting. You have been asked to write the text. You should provide information about:
- sports and recreational opportunities
- cinemas and theatres
- cafés and restaurants

Write the **text for the leaflet**.

3 You have seen the following announcement in an international magazine:

> 'Education today often concentrates on theory and intellectual processes, but young people also need the satisfaction that comes from doing manual work.'
>
> Have you ever had any experience of physical work – anything from building a piece of furniture to cleaning windows – that gave you a sense of satisfaction?
>
> Write an article about your experience for us!

Write your **article**.

4 You recently witnessed a car accident. Nobody was seriously hurt, but there was a disagreement about who caused the accident and you had to make a statement to the police, which was an interesting experience. Write a letter to a friend describing:
- the events leading up to the accident
- the accident itself
- the reaction of the drivers and passers-by
- your experience with the police

Write your **letter**.

5 You work in the sales department of a large company, and you are keen for the company to start an online magazine. Write a proposal for your managing director telling him or her:
- what sort of information would be in the magazine
- who you would expect to read it
- how it would be publicised
- how it would be of benefit to the company

Write your **proposal**.

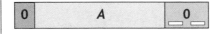
Essential tips

Question 2: The meaning of all four options could be appropriate here, but look at the structure of the sentence after the gap. Which verb can be followed by 'other people to read it'?

Question 7: Two options can be used with 'than', but only one forms a phrase with the meaning of 'except', which is the meaning required by the context.

Question 14: The correct option is clearly part of a phrasal verb, and the meaning should be apparent: 'become successful or popular'.

For questions **1–15**, read the text below and then decide which answer best fits each space. Put the letter you choose for each question in the correct box on your answer sheet. The exercise begins with an example (**0**).

Example:

0	*A*	0

The Video Loggers

One rather (**0**) ...... word that has recently entered the language is 'blog', a shortened form of 'web log'. A blog is a diary (**1**) ...... on the Internet by the person writing it – the 'blogger' – who presumably (**2**) ...... other people to read it. It is ironical that modern technology is being used to (**3**) ...... new life into such an old-fashioned form as the personal journal. And now, as the technology (**4**) ...... video cameras is making them easier to use, we have the video log, or 'vlog'. Vlogging does not require (**5**) ...... sophisticated equipment: a digital video camera, a high-speed Internet connection and a host are all that is needed. Vloggers can put anything that (**6**) ...... their fancy onto their personal website. Some vloggers have no ambitions (**7**) ...... than to show films they have (**8**) ...... while on holiday in exotic places. However, vlogs can also (**9**) ...... more ambitious purposes. For instance, amateur film-makers who want to make a (**10**) ...... for themselves might publish their work on the Internet, (**11**) ...... to receive advice or criticism. And increasingly, vlogs are being used to (**12**) ...... political and social issues that are not newsworthy enough to (**13**) ...... coverage by the mass media. It is still too early to predict whether vlogging will ever (**14**) ...... off in a major way or if it is just a passing fad, but its (**15**) ...... is only now becoming apparent.

0	**A** unlikely	**B** impossible	**C** unbelievable	**D** unique
1	**A** released	**B** sent	**C** posted	**D** mounted
2	**A** believes	**B** expects	**C** assumes	**D** supposes
3	**A** add	**B** inhale	**C** insert	**D** breathe
4	**A** about	**B** behind	**C** beneath	**D** under
5	**A** absolutely	**B** largely	**C** utterly	**D** highly
6	**A** grasps	**B** appeals	**C** takes	**D** gives
7	**A** except	**B** apart	**C** rather	**D** other
8	**A** shot	**B** photographed	**C** snapped	**D** captured
9	**A** serve	**B** employ	**C** function	**D** play
10	**A** publicity	**B** fame	**C** name	**D** promotion
11	**A** interested	**B** hopeful	**C** enthusiastic	**D** eager
12	**A** emphasise	**B** publicise	**C** distribute	**D** circulate
13	**A** earn	**B** warrant	**C** excuse	**D** cause
14	**A** fly	**B** show	**C** take	**D** make
15	**A** potential	**B** possibility	**C** ability	**D** feasibility

Essential tips

Question 16: If you look at the whole sentence, you will see that a comparison is being made using the expression 'makes more sense'. How would you expect this comparison to continue?

Question 22: The punctuation here shows that this is a question. The sentences that follow provide reasons for using this reclamation material. Which question with 'bother' is answered by giving reasons?

Question 27: The sentence explains that the clients of reclamation centres want 'items that simply can't be found these days', and then goes on to give an example: 'stone fireplaces'. Which expression using 'as' can be used to give an example?

For questions **16–30**, complete the following article by writing each missing word in the correct box on your answer sheet. **Use only one word for each space.** The exercise begins with an example (**0**).

Example:

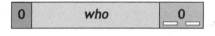

0	*who*	0

Second-hand
but better than new

Many people (**0**) .... are building their own homes or renovating existing buildings have discovered that it makes more sense to buy second-hand goods (**16**) .... to buy new doors, fireplaces or radiators. These days a large (**17**) .... of businesses offer second-hand material, though many of (**18**) .... cater exclusively for professional builders. However, there are outlets that sell to members of the public, so someone who wants to indulge (**19**) .... a spot of DIY will probably be able to find reclamation material, (**20**) .... second-hand building supplies are known, anywhere in the country.

Searching for (**21**) .... one wants can be time-consuming, so (**22**) .... bother? Is there, for example, any financial reason to make it (**23**) .... one's while? The answer, in many cases, is yes. An oak door in good condition will be considerably (**24**) .... expensive than a new one, even (**25**) .... it is only a few years old. However, the majority of clients of reclamation yards are on (**26**) .... lookout for items that simply can't be found these days, (**27**) .... as stone fireplaces several centuries old. Items like this (**28**) .... , of course, be expensive, but there are a lot of people who do not (**29**) .... paying a high price for a second-hand fireplace that is, (**30**) .... their view, better than new.

Essential tips

Question 32: Look at the expression with 'fact', which begins on line 31: is it correct to say 'in actually fact'?

Question 36: Check the way prepositions are used with verbs. Here, we have the verb 'attended' and then the preposition 'to'. It is possible to use 'to' with 'attend', but what meaning does it have? How is 'attend' used when talking about a school?

Question 46: Don't forget to check relatively simple grammatical structures, which you may overlook when you are searching for complex problems. Here, the adjective 'new' appears to be used as a noun. Is this correct?

In most lines of the following text, there is one unnecessary word. It is **either** grammatically incorrect **or** does not fit in with the sense of the text. For each numbered line **31–46**, find the unnecessary word and then write it in the box on your answer sheet. Some lines are correct. Indicate these lines with a (✓) in the box. The exercise begins with two examples (**0**) and (**00**).

Example:

0	✓	___ 0 ___
00	*from*	___ 00 ___

The oldest exam certificate

0   The oldest exam certificate ever found in Britain is a fascinating

00   object. It dates back from almost two thousand years to the era when

31   the country was under the Roman rule. This certificate, which is in

32   actually fact two bronze sheets once threaded together, survives in

33   the form of fragments, and the name of the soldier to whom it was

34   been awarded is no longer visible. However, enough of the text can

35   be read out to reveal what the unnamed soldier had done in the form

36   of academic work. Over twenty-five years he attended to a number

37   of lessons while serving in a Roman legion. These twenty-five-year

38   diplomas were very valuable, such as they were proof not only of

39   academic skills but also of citizenship. Anyone who in possession

40   of a certificate like this would be able to claim all a range of rights

41   and privileges. Consequently, these diplomas were bought and sold

42   illegally on what it would, in our age, be called the black market.

43   While the system could be abused in this way, it is although still a

44   tribute to the efficiency of the Roman Empire that efforts were made

45   to educate up common soldiers – and it also reminds us that

46   studying to pass exams is not a new by any means.

Essential tips

Question 50: Sometimes the gapped word is a compound word. The word 'tablecloth', for example, is a compound word formed from the word 'cloth', and the word 'table'.

Question 53: From the context, you can see that you need a verb with a negative meaning here. But the word before the gap is a preposition: 'for'. What form does a verb take when it comes after a preposition?

Question 55: You might take a map with you when you go out in case you get lost, so what sort of clothing would you take in case it rains?

For questions **47–61**, read the two texts below. Use the words in the boxes to the right of the texts to form one word that fits in the same numbered space in the text. Write the new word in the correct box on your answer sheet. The exercise begins with an example (**0**).

Example:

0	*response*	0

EXTRACT FROM ARTICLE

City Gardens

New York City has passed a new law in
(**0**) .... to the weather. It has been
(**47**) .... hot here this summer, and large numbers of people have fled the city. In the last exceptionally hot summer an unprecedented demand for
(**48**) .... to operate air conditioning units caused a power cut, and New York was
(**49**) .... at the mercy of the heat. But when there is a (**50**) .... , a lot of people can't escape and simply have to sit it out. New regulations stipulate that public buildings should have grassy rooftops, which slows down heat
(**51**) .... into the building. This grassy
(**52**) .... also absorbs some of the pollution in the air. The authorities are trying to enforce the new law, and the fine for (**53**) .... it is high.

(**0**)	**RESPOND**
(**47**)	BEAR
(**48**)	ELECTRIC
(**49**)	TEMPORARY
(**50**)	WAVE
(**51**)	PENETRATE
(**52**)	INSULATE
(**53**)	OBEY

EXTRACT FROM ARTICLE

Rambling

Vivian Lee explains the attraction of walking in the countryside.

Strolling around the countryside – or rambling, as it is
(**54**) .... known – is my favourite activity. All you need is a pair of stout boots and some
(**55**) .... clothing in case it rains. However, these days the very (**56**) .... of rambling, though one of its (**57**) .... for me, seems to put some people off. I sometimes think they
(**58**) .... prefer hobbies for which expensive equipment is (**59**) .... I find this odd. Surely a hobby shouldn't involve a huge effort: it should be a form of (**60**) .... And walking does just that for me: I find it
(**61**) .... relaxing.

(**54**)	COMMON
(**55**)	WATER
(**56**)	SIMPLE
(**57**)	ATTRACT
(**58**)	ACTUAL
(**59**)	DISPENSE
(**60**)	RECREATE
(**61**)	BELIEVE

For questions **62–74**, read the brochure about a weekend trip to London. Use the information in the brochure to complete the numbered gaps in the informal letter. The words you need **do not occur** in the brochure. **Use no more than two words for each gap**. The exercise begins with an example (**0**).

Example:

0	*begin*	0

Essential tips

Question 63: We are told in the first text that a 'chauffeur will be waiting'. In the second text we are told that there will be a car at the airport, 'with' someone – a chauffeur. Which simple word means something similar to 'chauffeur'?

Question 69: The first text tells us that the guide is 'bilingual'. What adjective, meaning 'able to speak a language very well', can be used in the second text?

Question 70: The word 'something' before the gap must be followed by a verb with 'to' in this context. What is available on the coach? Can we express this idea using the structure here?

BROCHURE

Our luxury city breaks commence at Charles de Gaulle Airport, Paris, where your plane departs at 16.00 on Friday afternoon. Your chauffeur will be waiting when you emerge from London's Heathrow Airport and transport you to the Hotel Splendid, located at 4 Hatton Gardens, London SW1. The hotel is within walking distance of London's main shopping area around Oxford Street and has excellent facilities, including a swimming pool and fitness centre.

On Saturday morning you will be accompanied on a sightseeing tour of London by a bilingual guide, who will provide commentary. Light refreshments will be available on the luxury air-conditioned coach. On Saturday evening you will have the opportunity to enjoy *Dogs*, the West End musical that is breaking all box office records, followed by a meal at Andrew's, where chef Andrew Logan's culinary creations cater for the most demanding tastes.

After a Sunday morning cruise along the Thames to round off a memorable weekend, you will be driven to Heathrow Airport for your return flight.

INFORMAL LETTER

According to the brochure, the weekend breaks (**0**) .... on Friday afternoon, when the plane (**62**) .... from Charles de Gaulle Airport. There'll be a car with a (**63**) .... waiting for you when you (**64**) .... of Heathrow Airport. You will be (**65**) .... to the Hotel Splendid – the (**66**) .... is 4 Hatton Gardens, London SW1. It's just a few minutes (**67**) .... to Oxford Street, and it sounds great.

You'll get to see (**68**) .... of London on Saturday, and your guide will be (**69**) .... in both French and English. You can even get something (**70**) .... on the coach. In the evening don't miss the chance to see a very (**71**) .... musical. Dinner will be at a top-class (**72**) .... , where the food will (**73**) .... even to a gourmet like you! On Sunday morning you will go on a (**74**) .... on the Thames, and then catch the plane back to Paris. Sounds good!

PAPER 1 Reading

PAPER 2 Writing

PAPER 3 English in Use ▶ | Part 1
Part 2
Part 3
Part 4
Part 5
Part 6

PAPER 4 Listening

PAPER 5 Speaking

For questions **75–80**, read the following text and then choose from the list **A–J** given below the best phrase to fill each of the spaces. Write one letter (**A–J**) in the correct box on your answer sheet. Each correct phrase may only be used once. **Some of the suggested answers do not fit at all**. The exercise begins with an example (**0**).

Example:

| 0 | J | 0 |

Boys and *Girls*

It is a question that has puzzled teachers (**0**) .... Are girls in general naturally better at certain subjects and boys better at others, or are any apparent differences due simply to cultural pressures? Some people claim that if boys tend to do better at maths and science, it is simply because they are encouraged to perform well in these subjects (**75**) .... Others believe there could be biological factors at work – that the female brain is somehow not wired to cope effectively with analytical subjects, for instance, (**76**) ....

A number of other theories also attempt to explain this difference between the sexes (**77**) .... For instance, it has been noted that girls who attend single-sex schools generally get better exam results than girls at co-educational schools. This might suggest that girls generally do not like the competitive atmosphere that exists when boys are present in a classroom. So perhaps girls on the whole are better at 'quieter' subjects such as languages because they can work alone more of the time (**78**) ....

At the same time, according to a recent survey, boys in most countries appear to be worse at reading than girls. Some schools are trying to reverse this trend (**79**) .... One way is by holding reading championships, thus making the atmosphere in reading classes more competitive. The same survey also established that the majority of men say they read mainly to get information (**80**) .... In contrast, far more women read for pleasure. Perhaps more appealing books for boys would go some way towards solving the problem!

A and not feel they are competing with others

B and girls are not

C and there is little anyone can do to change this

D and not for enjoyment

E and in their later careers

F and encourage boys to improve their skills in this area

G and this would certainly benefit society as a whole

H and they then find they enjoy the subject

I and suggest ways of changing the situation

J and sociologists for years

PAPER 1 Reading

PAPER 2 Writing

PAPER 3 English in Use

PAPER 4 Listening ▶ Part 1

Part 2
Part 3
Part 4

Essential tips

Question 1: What kinds of constructions are built these days? Do you need to include an article in your answer? Is an adjective necessary?

Question 3: From the structure of the sentence you can see that an adjective is needed here. If the wheels of a vehicle don't match so that it can't be used for practical purposes, what sort of function might the vehicle have?

Question 6: What kind of word might complete the phrase: 'The Parisii came to Britain from ...'? It could be the name of a place: a city, country etc. Remember that you will hear the word or words you want, but not in the same context as in the question.

You will hear an archaeologist talking about a recent find. For questions **1–8**, complete the sentences.

You will hear the recording twice.

An Ancient Chariot

The chariot was found at a site where [____ 1] is being built.

It was buried in a limestone chamber with a man's [____ 2] inside it.

The chariot's wheels don't match, suggesting it had a [____ 3] function.

The remains of a large number of [____ 4] were also discovered near the chariot.

The chamber was probably the tomb of the [____ 5] of a tribe.

The Parisii came to Britain from [____ 6]

Until the discovery of the chariot, it was not known that the Parisii had lived so far [____ 7]

It is hoped that the chariot can be moved to [____ 8]

Essential tips

Question 9: An adjective is needed here. What sort of adjective might you use to describe flowers?

Question 12: The word you need must be a noun, a kind of animal. Can you think of the names of some animals that might be hunted in Scotland? Listen for a word other than 'hunt', though of course with the same meaning.

Question 15: The form of the verb after this gap shows that a plural noun is needed. It must refer to plants of some kind.

You will hear a talk about the heather moors of Scotland. For questions **9–16**, complete the sentences.

Listen very carefully as you will hear the recording ONCE only.

Heather Hardship

Heather is a plant which produces many

☐ **9** flowers.

Today, heather moors cover approximately ☐ **10**

of Scotland.

The heather moors are the natural habitat of certain

☐ **11**

Many people also hunt ☐ **12** there.

The heather moors are among Scotland's

most important ☐ **13**

One reason why they have shrunk is mismanagement

by ☐ **14**

In addition, ☐ **15** have been planted

on areas formerly covered by heather.

The ☐ **16** of the heather moors

may be reversed if the land is managed better.

Essential tips

Question 17: The question is expressed in simple language. However, in the recording, you will hear the correct answer expressed in less straightforward language, perhaps using an idiom or informal expression. Even if you are not familiar with the idiom or expression, you may still be able to guess the correct answer from the context and tone of voice.

Question 21: Ellen says she thinks Tim is 'trying to dodge the responsibility for the problem'. Even if you don't know the word 'dodge', the context tells you Ellen is not pleased with what Tim has said. What could 'dodge' mean, in connection with 'responsibility'?

Question 22: Listen for an expression meaning 'make the protest effective'. It may well be that Ellen does not express this idea in a simple or direct way.

You will hear part of a radio discussion with Ellen Harrington of the Meadow Lane Residents Group, and Tim Barlow from Carton Town Planning Department. For questions **17–22**, choose the correct answer **A**, **B**, **C** or **D**.

You will hear the recording twice.

---

17 What was Ellen's first reaction when the town centre was closed to traffic?
  A She was terrified.
  B She was miserable.
  C She was delighted.
  D She was suspicious.

18 The mood of the Meadow Lane residents can best be described as
  A resigned.
  B dissatisfied.
  C furious.
  D dejected.

19 How does Tim feel about the changes in the town centre?
  A He regrets they were made so quickly.
  B He believes they were inevitable.
  C He thinks the town council should have foreseen the problem.
  D He is proud the town council went forward with them.

20 What does Tim think about the protest Ellen's group is planning?
  A He doesn't think it will accomplish anything.
  B He thinks it is not aimed at the right people.
  C He doesn't think drivers will be affected.
  D He thinks it will be dangerous.

21 How does Ellen react to Tim's comments?
  A She thinks he is being evasive.
  B She accepts his main point.
  C She thinks he doesn't understand human nature.
  D She considers his comments unrealistic.

22 What does Ellen think will make the protest effective?
  A the amount of publicity it will generate
  B the inconvenience it will cause to drivers
  C the number of demonstrators who will take part
  D the forthcoming election

Essential tips

Questions 23–27: Since you will probably not hear most of the key words in the options, you need to be prepared for words and expressions with a similar meaning. For example, instead of saying 'at school' (option A), the speaker might refer to a type of school, a certain class at school, the name of a school etc. Similarly, a speaker may use a word for a certain relative (option B), such as 'aunt', or even a description of who that person is, such as 'my sister's husband'.

Questions 28–32: Think about how someone might describe an activity to convey the idea that it is 'very dangerous' (option A), perhaps by saying what sort of accident might happen. What kind of language could be used to express this? And consider different ways of expressing the idea of 'spirit of cooperation' (option F): what would we call a 'group' in a sport?

You will hear five short extracts in which different people talk about children's free time activities.

You will hear the recording twice. While you listen you must complete both tasks.

Task One

For questions **23–27**, match the extracts with each person's explanation of how his or her child became interested in this activity, listed **A–H**.

A Our child began this activity at school.

B A relative was indirectly responsible for our child taking up this activity.

C A newspaper article sparked off interest in this activity.

D We encouraged our child to take up this activity.

E Our child began this activity as a result of a medical condition.

F A television programme inspired our child to take up this activity.

G Our child became interested in this activity while staying with friends.

H The idea for doing this activity came from reading about it.

Speaker 1	23
Speaker 2	24
Speaker 3	25
Speaker 4	26
Speaker 5	27

Task Two

For questions **28–32**, match the extracts with the opinion each speaker expresses about these activities, listed **A–H**.

A This activity is very dangerous.

B Our child's physical condition has improved.

C We were opposed to this activity at first.

D Our child takes this activity too seriously.

E We didn't understand what the activity entailed at first.

F This activity develops a spirit of cooperation.

G This activity has become quite fashionable recently.

H Our child has benefited socially.

Speaker 1	28
Speaker 2	29
Speaker 3	30
Speaker 4	31
Speaker 5	32

Essential tips

Part 1: Think about the vocabulary you need to talk about the topic. You should also consider which tenses are appropriate. For instance, you might say your father 'comes from' a certain city, using the present tense – but if you want to say when he left that city, you could use a past tense. When you describe how long you have been living in your home, you will probably need to use the present perfect continuous.

Part 2: To describe how people might feel in a certain situation, or what might have happened, you need expressions that express possibility, such as 'he might have just arrived' or 'they must be feeling tired because it looks as though ...'. However, to describe something that has happened to you, you will need to use appropriate past tenses. For instance, you might say something like: 'I remember once I was walking home and I fell over. I had been to a party, and I was feeling very tired ...'.

Part 3: An emotion or an abstract concept can be interpreted in different ways. The concept of 'pride' can be positive or negative, for example, so you should be prepared to consider different aspects of the idea given to you. Remember that the point here is not to convince the examiner or the other candidate, but to show you can express your views, argue, negotiate and reach a conclusion.

Part 4: In this part, you are asked to talk about actual events or situations and to give your opinions. After answering the question, you may go on to talk more generally about the subject, but you should always first show that you have understood the question.

Part 1 (3 minutes)

The examiner will ask you a few questions about yourself and then ask you to talk to your partner. For example, the examiner may ask you:

* Would you tell me something about the members of your family?
* Where are the members of your family from?
* Which people from your extended family do you have most contact with?

Part 2 (4 minutes)

You will each be asked to talk for a minute without interruption. You will each be given a set of photographs in turn to talk about. After your partner has finished speaking, you will be asked a brief question connected with your partner's photographs.

Departing (compare, contrast and speculate)

Turn to pictures 1–3 on page **198**, which show people departing.

Candidate A, compare and contrast these pictures and imagine how the people might be feeling in these situations.

Candidate B, can you describe a situation when you felt very excited about leaving a place?

Exhaustion (compare, contrast and speculate)

Turn to pictures 1–3 on page **199**, which show tired people.

Candidate B, compare and contrast these situations, and describe how the people might feel exhausted in different ways.

Candidate A, which kind of exhaustion do you find most difficult to get over, and why?

Part 3 (4 minutes)

Pride (discuss, evaluate and select)

Turn to the pictures on page **200**, which show examples of pride.

Talk to each other about the different sorts of pride suggested by these pictures, and then decide which two pictures you would choose to illustrate that pride has different forms.

Part 4 (4 minutes)

The examiner will encourage you to develop the topic of your discussion in Part 3 by asking questions such as:

* When was the last time you felt proud of something you had achieved?
* Do you think there are forms of pride that can be harmful?
* Would someone who never felt proud of himself or herself be unhappy?
* Are there times when you feel proud of other people? Can you give an example?

Answer questions **1–15** by referring to the magazine article about young people in the arts on page **81**.

Indicate your answers **on the separate answer sheet**.

For questions **1–15**, answer by choosing from the sections of the article (**A–E**). Some of the choices may be required more than once.

Note: When more than one choice is required, these may be given **in any order**.

Which person ...

reveals that he/she was not formally trained?	**1** ....
relishes the social aspects of success?	**2** ....
finds it gratifying to work with other artists?	**3** ....
originally wanted to work in a different field?	**4** ....
would like to reach a different audience?	**5** ....
is finding life unexpectedly hard?	**6** ....
needs to be reassured about his/her abilities?	**7** ....
has taken up a new hobby?	**8** ....
achieved success without much effort?	**9** ....
believes his/her art should not be enjoyed only by a few privileged people?	**10** ....
describes the financial consequences of success?	**11** ....
suffers physically because of his/her profession?	**12** ....
dislikes the attention of the media?	**13** .... **14** ....
had to overcome parental disapproval?	**15** ....

The Young Ones

*How does it feel to be young and successful in the world of the arts?
We asked some young people who know.*

A Sarah Hampton, 24

Naturally, I'm over the moon that my first novel, *Strange Tales,* is a bestseller, but I feel that success can be a two-edged sword. Some publishers claim if one's first novel does well, the second novel is particularly difficult because of the pressure to live up to expectations. I do hope that's not true! In some ways, my real career as a writer hasn't begun until now. I wrote *Strange Tales* the summer after I graduated from university, and the words just poured out; it didn't seem to require any struggle at all. Perhaps it's true what they say: that everybody has a novel in them. And I had no doubts I could do it. I suppose my confidence – or arrogance – can be traced back to our English teacher at school; he always said I could write for a living. But now I've got to discipline myself and work at my craft, forcing myself to write when I'd much rather do something else – anything else, some days! And I have to say, writing is more demanding and less glamorous than I had ever imagined.

B Justin Tyme, 25

Now that I've danced a few leading roles, I've been hailed by some critics as a new star. Actually, I don't think you can really talk about someone being a star in the world of dance – there are a few exceptions, of course – because classical ballet is a collaborative art, which is one aspect of it I particularly appreciate. And to be perfectly honest, I'm uncomfortable about the whole concept of being a star because the publicity can be an intrusion into your private life. As for the future, I think I would like to work in a less traditional, less conservative environment. Ballet can be such a rarified world, and you feel you are performing for a small, rich elite. I'd like to work in a company that mounts productions for children and tries to attract people who wouldn't normally dream of going to the ballet, just to give them a taste of it. I'm sure a lot of people would enjoy ballet if they ever had a chance to see it.

C Mike Thimble, 27

My paintings are now on show in a major London art gallery, and I must admit that I feel relieved at getting recognition for my work. Of course, there is a negative aspect to success as well. When people constantly tell you how wonderful your work is, the temptation is to produce more of the same, instead of moving on and exploring your medium – mine is oils – as an artist should. What's more, public attention can be exhausting, and I feel awkward about being interviewed. However, what matters most to me is not public acclaim but the praise of other artists and those critics I respect, especially because I sometimes doubt my own talent. If you go to art school, you get feedback from tutors and your peers, but I never had the opportunity, so there was never anyone looking objectively at my work. The result was I had to trust in my own abilities. This was hard, especially since I had to rebel against the wishes of my family; my father was determined I should become a lawyer like him. But he has come to terms with my decision not to pursue a legal career, and he's quite proud of my success now.

D Emma Hanratty, 28

My short film, *Hoping*, has just won an award at a major European film festival, and the dominant feeling I have is gratitude towards all the people who had faith in me. It's a long list, going back to my teacher at art school, who advised me to give up any idea of being a graphic designer and think about some other line of work. Getting the award and the recognition that goes with it was a dream come true, and I've been reaping some more tangible benefits as well. Funding for future projects is more readily forthcoming, and I've been invited to several international film festivals. I love this aspect of my work, and I find new places stimulating. I get lots of ideas for films, though of course, most of them will never see the light of day!

Life has been generous to me and I feel I owe it something in return. The best way I can repay this debt is by running classes in film-making for young people at a college of further education. In fact, I love the place and I've started taking pottery classes there just for fun.

E Geena Gel, 23

My first single has reached number one in the charts. This success has come overnight, and I'm still taken aback when people recognise me in the street, although there is a plus side – I enjoy being invited to parties. Knowing that my single is selling well is hugely satisfying, of course, but it doesn't compare with the pleasure I get from performing for a live audience. I've just completed a national concert tour and the response of my fans was overwhelming.

I'm not from a musical family. I only became interested in singing when I was sixteen, when some friends asked me to join their group as a vocalist – I took to singing like a duck to water. Naturally, I had daydreams of being a star, but some aspects of performing came as a surprise. I never would have imagined I'd get back pain from standing on stage for so long, for instance. But on balance, I'm delighted with the way things have turned out, and I'm looking forward to recording my next album in June.

PAPER 1 Reading   ▸   Part 1
    Part 2
PAPER 2 Writing   Part 3
PAPER 3 English in Use   Part 4
PAPER 4 Listening
PAPER 5 Speaking

For questions **16–21**, choose which of the paragraphs **A–G** on page **83** fit into the numbered gaps in the following newspaper article. There is one extra paragraph which does not fit into any of the gaps.

Indicate your answers **on the separate answer sheet**.

Wind of Change

The world's biggest wind farms are currently being constructed off the coast of Britain after a major policy decision by the government to invest time and money in renewable forms of energy. When the entire project is finished, it is estimated that almost eight percent of the electricity that the country needs will be generated in this way.

16

The wind farms themselves will consist of towers with fan-like blades at the top, arranged in groups of as many as 300. As these blades are turned by the wind, they generate electricity. The towers are tall enough to ensure that there will always be enough wind, even on the calmest days, to turn the rotor blades. The electricity generated from these turbines is fed by underground cable to the mainland, where it is incorporated into the national grid.

17

The reason for the delay is due to a conservative approach to new technology as well as economic considerations. Governments are notoriously reluctant to embrace new technology which has not yet proved itself, fearing that if it were to fail, the electorate would blame them. Moreover, until recently it was cheaper to generate electricity by traditional methods. However, now that fossil fuels are becoming more expensive – and the cost of mining them is also rising – the balance has shifted.

18

The way ahead is not without its problems, however. There have been a large number of complaints about wind farms on land, with critics maintaining that the tall towers and gigantic blades are an eyesore. Appearance is less likely to be a problem with offshore wind farms since they will be far enough from the coast to be virtually invisible unless the weather is exceptionally clear.

19

Environmental organisations hope that the government's commitment to wind power will encourage the use of other 'green' methods of producing electricity, though some technologies are less likely to be developed than others, at least in this country. The British Isles enjoy relatively few sunny days, so solar energy is hardly going to be a great success here.

20

It now appears likely that funds will be made available for the necessary research, especially since the British government has made it clear that it sees no future for nuclear power. Existing nuclear power stations are to be phased out gradually, though the government has been wary of providing precise dates for decommissioning.

21

In the meantime, it is encouraging to note that energy solutions which would have seemed unlikely, not to say laughable, just a few decades ago are finally starting to make an impact. It is to be hoped that this trend will continue.

A The most striking aspect of the project is the simplicity of the fundamental idea. Indeed, it seems odd that the principle, which has, after all, been applied to power windmills for thousands of years, has only very recently been used successfully to generate electricity on a large scale.

B There has been little attempt up to now to persuade the general public that wind power is the technology of the future. The government no doubt hopes that when the towers are in place and people realise they are neither a threat to the environment nor aesthetically ugly, attitudes will change.

C Some form of water power would seem a far more likely candidate for development, with tides off the coast of Britain being strong and, of course, regular. As has been the case with wind power, sizeable investment will be needed in order to produce the required technology, but the potential is certainly there.

D This is in line with the target the government set itself of producing ten percent of Britain's electricity from renewables – wind power being the most significant of these – by the year 2010. Environmental groups have hailed the government's commitment and are claiming that the future is definitely looking greener as far as energy is concerned.

E It has been pointed out by those who fear the terrible consequences of an accident that this is only a small step in the right direction. Even when the existing power stations are shut down, the huge problem of disposing of the radioactive materials from them will still have to be solved.

F Another cause for concern is voiced by wildlife organisations, fearful that migrating birds could crash into the rotating blades. Experience in other countries such as Denmark suggests this is unlikely, but the government has promised to monitor the progress of a pilot scheme at present in operation off the coast of Wales.

G Britain is not being particularly revolutionary in placing its trust in wind power. In fact, there is very little risk involved. The country is fortunate when it comes to this particular source of energy – it has a great deal of wind all year round. In a few years Britain may well become a world leader in offshore wind exploitation.

PAPER 1 Reading ▶ Part 1
                      Part 2
                      Part 3
                      Part 4
PAPER 2 Writing
PAPER 3 English in Use
PAPER 4 Listening
PAPER 5 Speaking

Read the following magazine article and answer questions **22–26** on page **85**. On your answer sheet, indicate the letter **A**, **B**, **C** or **D** against the number of each question. Give only one answer to each question.

Indicate your answers **on the separate answer sheet**.

Facing the Music

Declan Mayes, President of the Music Buyers Association, is furious at a recent announcement by the recording industry concerning people downloading MP3 music files from the Internet. Of course, there are files that can be downloaded legally for a small charge, but the uproar is not about these: it is about illegal downloads, which constitute an undoubted infringement of copyright. However, there is a great deal of controversy over whether the people who indulge in this activity should be regarded as actual criminals.

A few parallels may be instructive. If someone copies an audio music cassette for their own private use, they are, strictly speaking, breaking the law. But recording companies have usually turned a blind eye to this practice because prosecuting the few people involved would be difficult, and the financial loss to the company itself is not considered significant. At the other end of the scale, there are criminals who make illegal copies of CDs and sell them for a profit. This is far more serious, and the industry actively pursues and prosecutes pirates. Now the Music Recording Association has announced that it regards individuals downloading music from the Internet as pirates, claiming that they damage the industry in just the same way. 'The industry is completely over-reacting; it'll be a laughing stock,'

says Mayes. 'They're going to arrest some teenager downloading files in his bedroom – and sue him for thousands of dollars! This isn't going to frighten anyone into buying CDs.'

Mayes may have a point. There is a general consensus that CD pirates should be subjected to the full wrath of the law, but few would see an individual downloading music for his or her own pleasure in the same light. However, downloading music files illegally is not as innocuous as making private copies of audio cassettes. The scratchy, distorted cassette copy is a poor version of the original recording, whereas an MP3 file is of high quality and can be stored – on a CD, for example. It is this that makes the practice a powerful temptation for music fans, given the high cost of CDs.

What does Mayes think about claims that music companies could be forced out of business by people downloading music illegally? 'That's nonsense. Music companies are always whining about high costs, but that doesn't prevent them from recording hundreds of CDs by completely unknown artists, many of whom are "packaged" by marketing departments to appeal to young consumers. The companies are simply hoping that one of these new bands or singers will be a hit, and although it can be expensive to promote new artists, the cost of

manufacturing the CDs is actually very low.'

This last point would appear to be the focus of resentment against music companies: a CD is far cheaper to produce than its price in the shops would indicate, and profit margins for the music companies are huge. An adult with a reasonable income may not object to paying £15 for a CD of classical music, but a teenager buying a CD by the latest pop sensation may find that price rather steep – especially since the latest pop sensation is almost certain to be forgotten within a few months. And while the recording industry can't be held responsible for the evanescent nature of fame, given the teenage appetite for anything novel, it could lower the prices it charges – especially since technology is making CDs even cheaper to produce.

This is what Mayes hopes will happen. 'If the music industry stops exploiting the music-buying public, it can survive. Everyone would rather buy a CD, with an attractive jacket and booklet, than mess around downloading files, but the price has to be reasonable. The problem isn't going to vanish if the industry carries on trying to make a quick profit. Technology has caught up with the music companies, and trying to fight it by taking people to court will only earn money for the lawyers.' A frightening thought.

22 Mayes thinks that the recording industry's recent announcement

   A fails to take into account the difficulties of prosecuting offenders.

   B makes the industry appear ludicrous.

   C will deter consumers from buying CDs.

   D will encourage resentment of CD piracy.

23 Why does the writer feel that MP3s are unlike copies of audio cassettes?

   A Downloaded MP3 files are generally not for private use.

   B The financial losses to the music industry are greater.

   C The price of MP3s is greater than the price of audio cassettes.

   D There is a significant difference in quality.

24 Mayes implies that music companies

   A could cut costs by making cheaper CDs.

   B should not promote artists who are unknown.

   C are speculating when they promote new artists.

   D should use different manufacturing processes.

25 The writer points out that the music industry cannot be blamed for

   A the fact that fewer teenagers are buying classical music CDs.

   B the fact that fashions change quickly.

   C the poor quality of much modern music.

   D the prices that are charged for CDs in shops.

26 What does Mayes think is at the root of the dilemma facing the music industry?

   A the unprecedented speed of technological advances

   B unrealistic legal advice

   C its failure to adopt an appropriate long-term strategy

   D the rapidly changing nature of contemporary music

PAPER 1   Reading   Part 1
PAPER 2   Writing   Part 2
PAPER 3   English in Use Part 3
PAPER 4   Listening   Part 4
PAPER 5   Speaking

Answer questions **27–41** by referring to the newspaper article on pages **87–88**, in which women talk about their attitude towards cars.

Indicate your answers **on the separate answer sheet**.

For questions **27–41**, answer by choosing from the sections of the article **A–D**. Some of the choices may be required more than once.

Note: When more than one answer is required, these may be given **in any order**.

Which person …

uses her car to get to work?	**27** ....
uses her car mainly to make short journeys?	**28** .... **29** ....
has only had a driving licence for a few years?	**30** ....
has a prejudice against a particular kind of car?	**31** ....
feels safety considerations are paramount when buying a car?	**32** ....
wanted a car that would have a minimal impact on the environment?	**33** ....
didn't want to be responsible for the car at first?	**34** ....
acknowledges that she knows little about cars?	**35** ....
uses other means of transport because of rising costs?	**36** ....
drives a kind of car which is becoming increasingly popular?	**37** ....
needs a large car?	**38** ....
is an enthusiastic driver?	**39** ....
wishes she didn't need to rely on a car?	**40** ....
dissuaded someone from buying a car?	**41** ....

Women Drivers

What do women think about the cars they drive? We talked to four women about their views.

A Megan Fields

Megan Fields lives in rural Hertfordshire, just outside a small village. In recent years the bus service in the village has improved, and there is also a good link now to the nearest town. Consequently, she uses a car mainly to commute to her office almost forty miles away. Megan works normal office hours, Mondays to Fridays, and this means she has to make a round trip of very nearly eighty miles a day in the enervating rush-hour traffic. However, since the latest increases in the price of fuel, she and her husband feel they have to think more carefully about car maintenance costs.

Megan was forced to purchase a new car only a short while ago: she was recently involved in a collision with a lorry. It was an unequal contest, and Megan's car was a write-off. Fortunately, nobody was badly hurt, but Megan was shaken by the experience. She promised herself that her next car would have more robust bodywork in case anything like that ever happens again. Since their old car had been on its last legs anyway, she and her husband had been looking at the options available on the market even before the crash, and they had narrowed the choice down to three or four models. Before they made their final decision, they took a number of other factors into consideration. They wanted a car that would be fuel-efficient and that would produce as few harmful emissions as possible. Megan left the choice of car to her husband; she claims she is ignorant of the technical issues involved and has no desire to learn. She stresses that she would rather be able to manage without a car at all. However, given their circumstances, doing without a car does not appear to be a viable option.

B Vera Aziz

Vera is one of the growing number of people who have purchased an SUV – a sports utility vehicle. In her view, there is something very reassuring about the height of the vehicle, which places the driver and passengers above the majority of other road users. Though she has no statistics to back up her opinion, she is convinced that this means she would be far better off in an accident. There is another practical factor at work in her choice of vehicle: her SUV seats eight people quite comfortably, and she needs this room since she regularly ferries her two daughters and their four friends to and from ballet classes.

Vera says that a car is an absolute necessity for her. Public transport in the part of Surrey where she lives is woefully inadequate and there is no school bus, so when the weather is bad she has to drive the children to their school nearby. About once a fortnight she and her husband go up to London for the day and they need the car to get them to the local train station. Otherwise, she admits, the car stays in the garage most of the time. When asked about what influenced her choice of vehicle, she is unequivocal: safety was the crucial point, and she imagines that this is the case for the vast majority of women.

C Sue Henderson

The new charges for drivers entering inner London, coupled with exhorbitant parking fees throughout the capital, means that the situation has changed for Sue. She says she would far rather take the train to the city instead of driving in from Faversham in Kent, so these days she mostly uses the car to stock up with groceries from the local supermarket on Friday evenings. But there has been another more radical change in her driving habits over the past few months. Some good neighbours of hers, who only used their car very occasionally, were thinking of buying a new one, and Sue suggested that instead of going to the expense and trouble this would involve, they should just use hers whenever they wanted to. Sue says that some careful planning is required to make this arrangement work smoothly, but it has resulted in considerable savings for everyone concerned. She also makes the point that a scheme like this works best if people are relaxed about the car they drive and don't insist on a spotlessly clean high-performance model. Sue's present car is fairly old, large and sturdy – one of the Scandinavian models that offer their owners a sense of security. She is rather dismissive of SUVs, which she doesn't consider particularly safe. This is because she read somewhere that they can roll over quite easily. Furthermore, they are a danger to cyclists because SUV drivers tend not to notice them. Sue also has strong opinions about the jokey stereotype of the bad woman driver, which she regards as absolute nonsense. She is similarly dismissive of the idea that men are natural born drivers, claiming that statistics prove the opposite, and that men cause far more accidents than women, especially serious ones.

D Heather Adams

Four years ago Heather Adams's husband injured his leg in an accident which left him unable to drive. Heather herself then reluctantly took charge of the car, not only driving it but also making sure it was serviced regularly and generally looking after it. The Adams's children are still very young, so Heather is the only one in the family who uses the car now. In fact, she only passed her driving test three and a half years ago, so she had little practical experience with vehicles of any kind until then. Their present car is the only one she has ever driven, apart from the car at the driving school when she was learning to drive. She says she never expected to get such enormous pleasure from sitting behind the wheel, and believes that learning to drive gave her a sense of independence and confidence that she lacked when she was younger. She regards a car as an essential part of her life now – public transport in the northern city where she lives is unreliable and not convenient for her needs.

Her husband has clearly influenced her views on road safety. He believes it is important to be able to put your foot down and accelerate away from trouble. Heather agrees and clearly relishes driving a car with a powerful engine. For her, this would be a prime consideration if she were to buy another car.

1 You are the social secretary at Blackstone College, where you are also a student. Recently you organised a party for children living in the area. In your view, it was a success. However, an article published in the local newspaper was rather critical about it.

At the party parents were asked to complete a questionnaire. A fellow student has read their responses and has sent you a brief note about her findings.

Read the article, to which you have added some comments, and the note. Then, **using the information carefully**, write a **letter** to the newspaper responding to the article.

Complaints about College Children's Party

Blackstone College held its first Children's Party on Tuesday 15th, but parents say <u>the event was not a success</u>. 'They ran out of food early on – <u>there was none left by half past two</u> – and <u>there weren't enough rides for all the kids</u>,' said Helena Jackson, who brought her four-year-old son Steven. Fred Wormsley, who brought his twin eight-year-old girls, also felt that the party could have been better planned. 'We were given <u>a map of the area</u> but it didn't stop us getting lost!' Such criticisms are bound to make local residents wonder whether the college is spending <u>tax payers' money</u> wisely.

Not fair: most parents satisfied. Approx. 120 kids had good time!

OK, not enough rides – but other entertainment like clowns, jugglers etc!

OK, bad layout

Refreshments scheduled from 12 to 2!

Party paid for by students, not college!

I thought you'd be interested to find out what parents thought about our Children's Party. About 75% of those who brought kids filled in the questionnaire, so the results are a fairly good indication of the general reaction.

Sally

Survey results

General approval:	82% satisfied or very satisfied with event.
Refreshments:	62% said food and drink supplied satisfactory, though 26% said could have been organised better.
Entertainment:	Rides approved by 83%, live acts approved by 95%.
Layout of area:	Almost 60% wanted better planning to reduce crowding, especially at refreshment tent.

Now write a **letter** to the newspaper (approximately 250 words) responding to the article. You should use your own words as far as possible. You do not need to include postal addresses.

Choose one of the following writing tasks. Your answer should follow exactly the instructions given. Write approximately 250 words.

2 You decide to enter a competition for writers run by an English language club in your area. The notice you see says:

> ## 'People can never hide their deepest emotions.'
>
> Write an account of an occasion when you were strongly affected emotionally, but attempted to hide your true feelings. Describe how the situation came about and indicate whether you succeeded in concealing your emotions or not.

Write your **account**.

3 You have been asked to write a contribution for a tourist guidebook for your area, suggesting outings and day trips suitable for families. You should include information about:
- places of historical interest
- areas of natural beauty
- theme parks and amusement parks

Also include practical information about transport, opening and closing hours etc.

Write your **contribution** for the guidebook.

4 You see the following announcement in an international magazine for language teachers:

> # What makes an outstanding teacher?
>
> We want to hear your stories. Tell us about a teacher you had at school who really impressed you. Explain what it was about him or her that makes you remember this person as a great teacher.

Write your **article**.

5 There is a shortage of space at the company where you work, so the management want to try out a possible solution to the problem. The whole office area is now open-plan and members of staff no longer have a desk of their own: they simply use any desk or work station that happens to be available. You have been asked to write a report on how this arrangement is working in practice. Indicate the benefits and problems you have encountered.

Write your **report**.

For questions **1–15**, read the text below and then decide which answer best fits each space. Put the letter you choose for each question in the correct box on your answer sheet. The exercise begins with an example (**0**).

Example:

0	C	0

All in the Stars

First-time visitors to India are (**0**) ...... to be impressed by how profoundly astrology influences almost every (**1**) ...... of life on the subcontinent. In fact, the belief that the motions of remote heavenly bodies can affect events on Earth is so (**2**) ...... that several Indian universities (**3**) ...... courses in the subject. It is not, therefore, surprising that many people will (**4**) ...... an astrologer before they (**5**) ...... any important step. For example, Indian marriages are arranged with the aid of an astrologer, who will (**6**) ...... the horoscopes of the bride and groom, and also (**7**) ...... out the best date for the wedding to take place. A few years ago in Delhi, thousands of couples rushed to get married on a particularly auspicious day, with the (**8**) ...... that priests, brass bands and wedding photographers were in (**9**) ...... supply.

The role of astrology is not (**10**) ...... only to the social aspects of Indian life. Few people (**11**) ...... business without resorting to their astrologer. Major films are only (**12**) ...... on auspicious dates. Even (**13**) ...... of state are not exempt from its influence: when India (**14**) ...... her independence from Britain in 1947, the (**15**) ...... of power was carefully timed to take place after a particularly inauspicious period had passed.

0	**A** probable	**B** possible	**C** likely	**D** potential
1	**A** division	**B** facet	**C** angle	**D** sector
2	**A** widespread	**B** overwhelming	**C** intensive	**D** capacious
3	**A** offer	**B** afford	**C** supply	**D** serve
4	**A** interrogate	**B** confer	**C** interview	**D** consult
5	**A** have	**B** take	**C** go	**D** decide
6	**A** fling	**B** propel	**C** cast	**D** throw
7	**A** make	**B** work	**C** calculate	**D** determine
8	**A** effect	**B** outcome	**C** upshot	**D** result
9	**A** short	**B** deficient	**C** inadequate	**D** slight
10	**A** demarcated	**B** bound	**C** confined	**D** restrained
11	**A** engage	**B** perform	**C** carry	**D** conduct
12	**A** published	**B** released	**C** aired	**D** revealed
13	**A** affairs	**B** cases	**C** issues	**D** topics
14	**A** grabbed	**B** procured	**C** gained	**D** captured
15	**A** delivery	**B** inheritance	**C** succession	**D** transfer

For questions **16–30**, complete the following article by writing each missing word in the correct box on your answer sheet. **Use only one word for each space.** The exercise begins with an example (**0**).

Example:

0	*all*	0

Independent **Television**

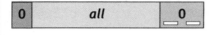

Foreigners are often surprised that there are no advertisements at (**0**) .... on the BBC television channels. The absence of commercials, as television advertisements are known, is (**16**) .... to the fact that the constitution of the BBC forbids it to accept advertising. So (**17**) .... does the BBC get the money it needs to (**18**) .... it going? In fact, the BBC is financed from revenue (**19**) .... is raised by the sale of television licences. The fee for the licences is set by the government, but (**20**) .... this, the BBC is not state run, and it is proud of (**21**) .... independence. It (**22**) .... be said that the viewers themselves pay for the BBC, since (**23**) .... who owns a television has to purchase a licence. And of course, you have to have a valid licence whether you actually watch the BBC (**24**) .... not. This arrangement dates (**25**) .... to the 1920s, when the BBC was a radio broadcaster. Some people feel the system is unfair (**26**) .... those who watch other channels but not the BBC, and there are those who fail to buy a licence, which is (**27**) .... the law. (**28**) .... an effort to combat this, the BBC has a fleet of detector vans that tour the country, checking (**29**) .... a television is being used from an address when there is (**30**) .... record of a licence having been purchased.

In most lines of the following text, there is **either** a spelling **or** a punctuation error. For each numbered line **31–46**, write the correctly spelt word or show the correct punctuation in the box on your answer sheet. Some lines are correct. Indicate these lines with a (✓) in the box. The exercise begins with three examples (**0**), (**00**) and (**000**).

Example:

0	*sympathy*	___ 0 ___
00	*retirement*	___ 00 ___
000	✓	___000___

Life begins at seventy

0	My grandmother wouldn't have much symphathy with those who
00	want to lower the age of retirement, from the present age of sixty
000	to fifty-five or even fifty. She's still working hard at the age of
31	seventy-five, and what's more, she's doing so off her own free will.
32	In fact, she's conviced that the idea of people being too old to work
33	when they reach the age of sixty-five is outdated. 'In the old days,
34	she claims, 'when the majority of people did hard physickal work
35	all their lifes, they were exhausted by the age of sixty-five. But it's
36	quite different today.' She points out, that most people do office
37	jobs and are still fit and healthy at the age of sixty-five. If we retire
38	young, we'll spend the next twenty year's watching television!
39	However, it isn't just the prospect of been bored that keeps my
40	grandmother at work. She firmly beleives that if someone is active,
41	he or she is more likely to be healthy – and she certainly intends
42	to stay in peek health for as long as possible. In her view, old age
43	doesn't really begin untill you start to lose the power to think
44	straight. And the brain, she claims is much like any other organ
45	or muscle in you're body: you have to use it and give it plenty
46	of exercise if you want it to stay in good shape.

For questions **47–61**, read the two texts below. Use the words in the boxes to the right of the texts to form one word that fits in the same numbered space in the text. Write the new word in the correct box on your answer sheet. The exercise begins with an example (**0**).

Example:

0	*delightful*	0 

EXTRACT FROM GUIDEBOOK

BERLIN

One of the most (**0**) .... things you can do when travelling is to indulge in some (**47**) .... off the beaten track. Of course, this is not to imply you should ignore the well-known landmarks, and Berlin, with its fascinating history and remarkable (**48**) .... heritage, has buildings and monuments that are well worth a visit. Who, for example, could fail to be awed by the sight of the (**49**) .... Brandenburg Gate? The major tourist (**50**) .... of the city are listed on the following pages, and you will also find (**51**) .... information on the website of the Berlin Tourist Office.

If you have time, however, head out of the city to the (**52**) .... forest of Grünewald, which provides Berliners with one of their finest recreational areas. Tread (**53**) .... when you are in the woods, though: the wild boar there may object to being disturbed!

(**0**)	**DELIGHT**
(**47**)	EXPLORE
(**48**)	ARCHITECTURE
(**49**)	IMPRESS
(**50**)	ATTRACT
(**51**)	COMPREHEND
(**52**)	PICTURE
(**53**)	CAUTION

MAGAZINE ARTICLE

COLD FEET?

It is common (**54**) .... that some people are naturally 'cold': their normal body temperature is slightly below average. But anyone who suddenly starts getting cold feet should consult a doctor, especially if other (**55**) .... such as fingers are also affected. The condition may be an (**56**) .... that there is an underlying health problem. For example, cold feet can mean your blood (**57**) .... has fallen below the level generally regarded as (**58**) .... Cold feet may also be a sign that your circulatory system is (**59**) .... If the veins in your legs have lost their (**60**) .... , there is simply not enough warm blood flowing to your feet. And of course, we cannot (**61**) .... the fact that cold feet may have psychological causes. Under stress, the body's nerves may constrict small blood vessels, which limits their ability to carry blood and results in cold feet.

(**54**)	KNOW
(**55**)	EXTREME
(**56**)	INDICATE
(**57**)	PRESS
(**58**)	ACCEPT
(**59**)	FUNCTION
(**60**)	ELASTIC
(**61**)	REGARD

TEST 4

PAPER 1 Reading

PAPER 2 Writing

PAPER 3 English in Use ▸
- Part 1
- Part 2
- Part 3
- Part 4
- **Part 5**
- Part 6

PAPER 4 Listening

PAPER 5 Speaking

For questions **62–74**, read the following extract from a rental agreement. Use the information in the agreement to complete the numbered gaps in the informal letter. The words you need **do not occur** in the agreement. **Use no more than two words for each gap**. The exercise begins with an example (**0**).

Example:

0	*moved out*	0

RENTAL AGREEMENT

Flat B, 45 Station Road

1 This agreement comes into effect on 1ˢᵗ September, after the present tenants vacate the property.

2 Tenants are allowed use of the garden, such facility also being granted to the tenants of Flat A on the floor below. Tenants are responsible for maintaining the garden in good condition.

3 The rent is £300 per calendar month. It does not include utilities such as gas and electricity, which are to be paid separately. After a rent review next January, the rent may be increased by a maximum of 2.5%. The rent is to be remitted by bank transfer.

4 Tenants are to refrain from having the central heating over 62°F.

5 Furniture must be treated with care. An inventory is attached herewith.

6 The volume of hi-fi equipment, televisions etc. is to be kept low after 8 p.m.

7 This agreement is renewed annually unless written notice is received to the contrary three months before the lease expires, i.e. three months before 31ˢᵗ August next.

INFORMAL LETTER

Dear Mandy,

We'll be moving into a new flat in September, as soon as the previous tenants have (0) .... The flat's nice and there's a garden we can (62) .... with the people (63) .... Of course, it'll be up to us (64) .... it tidy.

The rent is £300 a month although there will be gas and electricity bills (65) .... At the end of the year the rent might (66) .... although (67) .... it can do so is by 2.5%. I'll have to arrange (68) .... the rent every month straight from my bank account.

But the rules! We aren't (69) .... turn the central heating up, and we have to (70) .... the furniture that comes with the flat – the landlord has given us a (71) .... We also have to (72) .... the music after eight o'clock! If we want to move, we'll have to let the landlord know in (73) .... by the (74) .... May.

For questions **75–80**, read the following text and then choose from the list **A–J** given below the best phrase to fill each of the spaces. Write one letter (**A–J**) in the correct box on your answer sheet. Each correct phrase may only be used once. **Some of the suggested answers do not fit at all**. The exercise begins with an example (**0**).

Example:

0	J	0

Horse Sense

Hippotherapy has been used for over thirty years in some parts of Europe (**0**) .... The basic concept behind this controversial form of therapy is not hard to grasp. It is believed that people who suffer from a whole range of serious medical problems can benefit from sitting on a horse as it walks. The motion of the walking animal stimulates the rider (**75**) .... By trying to keep their balance in response to the horse's movements, patients exercise and strengthen the muscle groups (**76**) .... Hippotherapy has to be supervised by a physiotherapist (**77**) .... A professional horse handler, sometimes known as a hippologue, is also in attendance and guides the horse.

Enthusiastic practitioners claim there are several reasons why hippotherapy is so effective. The patterns of walking in humans and horses are similar (**78**) .... There are also psychological benefits, (**79**) .... Children in particular appreciate the warmth and affection that they experience through contact with this powerful but gentle animal. Connecting emotionally with the horse seems to increase their attention span, (**80**) .... Even children with attention-deficit disorders can benefit.

Of course, hippotherapy has its critics. Detractors dismiss it as an alternative treatment backed by little scientific proof that it works, and many health care agencies for disabled children and adults refuse to endorse it.

A who has received special training

B and the bond between rider and horse can play an important role in therapy

C and helps improve posture, mobility, coordination and strength

D that he or she can improve with constant attention

E and improves memory, concentration and speech

F that they would use in walking, sitting and stretching on their own

G who work together to provide the best possible therapy

H and no machine has ever been invented which can mimic the human gait

I and without being too strenuous for people who have suffered severe injury

J and is now gaining acceptance in North America

You will hear an anthropologist talking about a recent find. For questions **1–8**, complete the sentences.

You will hear the recording twice.

A Significant Find

Several fossil skulls were dug up in Ethiopia

last [_____ **1**]

There were at least [_____ **2**] adult skulls

and one that belonged to a child.

It appears that the people these skulls belong to were

our [_____ **3**] ancestors.

Anthropologists now believe that *Homo sapiens* is

[_____ **4**] from Neanderthals.

The reason why the Neanderthals [_____ **5**]

is not known.

The people whose skulls have been found probably used

[_____ **6**]

They also lived in [_____ **7**] ,

a factor which probably helped them to survive.

The early days of human evolution are still [_____ **8**]

to modern scientists.

You will hear instructions for the use of a model aircraft. For questions **9–16**, complete the notes.

Listen very carefully as you will hear the recording ONCE only.

BURNLEY FLIER

Choosing a Site

Make sure no house is closer than [_____ **9**]

Danger: keep away from [_____ **10**]

Watch out if [_____ **11**] approach.

Starting Up

Make sure there is enough [_____ **12**] (and right sort).

Get ready to [_____ **13**] to engine (only for starting).

Start engine with [_____ **14**]

First Flight

Control plane with wires and don't [_____ **15**]

At first stick to [_____ **16**]

You will hear part of a radio discussion about iris recognition systems. For questions **17–22**, choose the correct answer **A**, **B**, **C** or **D**.

You will hear the recording twice.

---

17 Jim says that the idea behind iris recognition systems (IRS)
   A   is based on state-of-the-art technology.
   B   was thought of many years ago.
   C   relies on a simple camera.
   D   requires sophisticated computer software.

18 He believes that iris recognition machines will be adopted on a large scale chiefly because
   A   they can be depended upon.
   B   they speed up the identification process.
   C   they can be connected to a wide range of secondary devices.
   D   the machines in use at present are proving very successful.

19 Iris recognition machines were used at a school
   A   to gauge the reaction of students.
   B   to stimulate interest in science lessons.
   C   to improve efficiency at a school canteen.
   D   to identify pupils entering a school.

20 Jim feels that people who object to iris recognition machines
   A   regard them as a threat to personal freedom.
   B   object to X-ray machines as well.
   C   are a very small minority.
   D   fail to appreciate how they work.

21 What does Jim say about the costs involved in registering the population?
   A   The government will not pay all the costs involved.
   B   They will depend on the scale of the project.
   C   They will be modest at the outset.
   D   They will be high initially.

22 According to Jim, what will convince governments to adopt iris recognition systems?
   A   reduced expenses
   B   public acceptance
   C   increased security
   D   ease of use

You will hear five short extracts in which different people talk about holidays that went wrong. Each extract has two questions. For questions **23–32**, choose the best answer **A**, **B** or **C**.

You will hear the recording twice.

---

23 The first speaker was most dissatisfied about
   A the flight.
   B the accommodation.
   C the trip from the airport to the hotel.

24 After the holiday the speaker discovered that the tour company
   A would not give him any money back.
   B had not printed the truth in their brochure.
   C was not used to customers' complaints.

25 The second speaker feels that problems arose because of
   A insufficient planning.
   B lack of knowledge of local conditions.
   C factors beyond the control of the organisers.

26 She will endeavour to avoid similar situations by
   A planning a more realistic itinerary.
   B choosing a different location.
   C using the services of a different company.

27 The third speaker feels that
   A he was to blame for the accident.
   B he should have rented another car.
   C he ought not to have lost his temper.

28 What was the nature of his punishment?
   A He had to pay a fine.
   B He spent two nights in prison.
   C He was reprimanded.

29 The fourth speaker
   A woke up with a headache.
   B felt very thirsty.
   C had a temperature.

30 We gather that when she was first taken to hospital
   A she could not get a first-class room.
   B she was apprehensive.
   C she realised how fortunate she was.

31 The fifth speaker was most surprised by
   A the height of the waves.
   B the behaviour of the vessel.
   C the reaction of the crew.

32 It appears that the speaker
   A travelled by hydrofoil again shortly afterwards.
   B was convinced he would never board a hydrofoil again.
   C would like the chance to travel by hydrofoil again.

Part 1 (3 minutes)

The examiner will ask you a few questions about yourself and then ask you to talk to your partner. For example, the examiner may ask you:

- What do you enjoy doing when you go away for a holiday?
- How would you describe the best holiday you have had?
- What sorts of things can spoil a holiday for you?

Part 2 (4 minutes)

You will each be asked to talk for a minute without interruption. You will each be given a set of photographs in turn to talk about. After your partner has finished speaking, you will be asked a brief question connected with your partner's photographs.

Sports (compare, contrast and speculate)

Turn to pictures 1–5 on page **201**, which show people taking part in different sports.

Candidate A, compare and contrast two or three of these situations, saying what you think the people involved enjoy about the sport.

Candidate B, which of these sports would you find most enjoyable?

Accommodation (compare, contrast and speculate)

Turn to pictures 1–5 on page **202**, which show different places where people live.

Candidate B, compare and contrast two or three of these homes, saying what you think would be the impractical aspects of living there.

Candidate A, which of these homes do you think is most practical?

Part 3 (4 minutes)

Public Transport (discuss, evaluate and select)

Turn to the pictures on page **203**, which show different forms of public transport in a certain city.

The tourist board in this city is publishing a brochure to attract visitors, and it has been decided to put three photographs on the cover, showing different forms of public transport. Which three photographs should be used in order to give the impression that this is an interesting city to visit?

Part 4 (4 minutes)

The examiner will encourage you to develop the topic of your discussion in Part 3 by asking questions such as:

- Should private cars be banned from city centres? Why (not)?
- What do you think could be done in your area to encourage people to use public transport?
- Some cities encourage people to take passengers in their cars to reduce congestion. Do you think this is a good idea, and would it work in your area? Why (not)?
- Which types of public transport do you think are the most and the least harmful to the environment?

PAPER 1 Reading ▶

PAPER 2 Writing

PAPER 3 English in Use

PAPER 4 Listening

PAPER 5 Speaking

Part 1

Part 2

Part 3

Part 4

Answer questions **1–14** by referring to the magazine article about astrology on page **103**.

Indicate your answers **on the separate answer sheet**.

For questions **1–14**, answer by choosing from the sections of the article (**A–E**). Some of the choices may be required more than once.

In which section of the article are the following mentioned?

the post once held by a writer	**1** ....
the influence of astrology on corporate decisions	**2** ....
a suggestion that people are being tricked into believing something	**3** ....
a fruitful collaboration	**4** ....
the star sign of a famous politician	**5** ....
information that an astrologer needs	**6** ....
a reason why a hypothesis is not taken seriously	**7** ....
the antiquity of astrological belief	**8** ....
recent findings that cast severe doubt on astrology	**9** ....
the timeless appeal of astrology	**10** ....
planetary positions in relation to athletic talent	**11** ....
the influence of astrology on public life	**12** ....
an attack on astrology from an unexpected source	**13** ....
the suggestion that astrology has gained adherents as a result of scientific progress	**14** ....

Not in our stars

A The roots of astrology are probably almost as old as humanity's first attempts to map the heavens. The oldest astrological records we know of come from Babylon, and astrology clearly played an important role in the life of Ancient Egypt, Greece and Rome. In fact, most cultures throughout history have believed that the stars influence our lives, and to judge by the avidity with which modern-day Britons scan the pages of newspapers for their daily horoscope, astrology is as popular today as ever it was. In fact, astrology is big business, and top astrologers with regular pages in newspapers and magazines earn huge annual incomes. Even the new technologies have been pressed into service: astrological websites are visited by millions every day, and not just by the gullible or uneducated. There are students studying science at university who admit to believing that one's star sign determines personality. Hard-headed businessmen have been known to pay for astrological predictions about the rise and fall of the stock market, and a few years ago it emerged that one large bank was using astrology to help manage its £5 billion investment portfolio. Nor is it a secret that several politicians have relied on astrologers to provide insight on matters of state – believers include former American President Ronald Reagan. Even former British Prime Minister Margaret Thatcher once told MPs: 'I was born under the sign of Libra, it follows that I am well-balanced.'

B But surely it is an irony that in our technological age so many people continue to put their faith in astrologers. After all, we are living in a period of history when science seems to have provided answers to many of the riddles and mysteries of nature. Paradoxically, however, the resultant mechanistic view of life has caused many to feel that their life has no purpose, a state of affairs also reflected by the decline in formal religious observance. Is this, perhaps, why growing numbers of people are turning to astrology with such fervour? Are they simply exhibiting a natural human longing for some meaning in their life? Do they need to feel that a higher power is controlling their destiny? Is there, after all, anything to astrology, or is the whole 'science' an elaborate hoax to bamboozle the gullible? Can an expert astrologer armed with the details of your exact time and place of birth produce an accurate reading of your character? Can he or she predict what the future holds for you, just because you were born on a certain date?

C Back in the 1950s, a French psychologist, Michel Gauquelin, published a study which seemed to lend support to the belief that the motions of distant planets can affect life on Earth. In this study, he explained that Mars is found in certain positions in the sky more often at the birth of sports champions than at the birth of other people. To be more precise, the path along which Mars appears to travel across the sky can be divided into six equal parts or sectors, with sector one starting where Mars rises and sector six ending with Mars setting. Among outstanding sportspeople, the percentage who were born in two of these sectors was not the base rate of the population at large, namely seventeen percent, but closer to twenty-two percent. Gauquelin's findings spawned considerable interest and debate, and seemed to demonstrate that the mechanism by which the stars affect our lives had a physical existence, but it was not long before he was discredited.

D Despite the debunking of the so-called Mars effect, studies supporting astrological claims continue to be published, and one of the most recent and controversial publications is a book entitled *The Scientific Proof of Astrology*. Its author is Percy Seymour, a former astronomy lecturer and member of the Royal Astronomical Society, who stresses that he does not believe in star sign horoscopes. However, he does believe that the movements of the moon and planets affect the Earth's magnetic field, which, in turn, influences the development of unborn children. Most scientists and astronomers have poured scorn on Seymour's suggestions, saying that variations in the Earth's magnetic field caused by the motions of extraterrestrial bodies are so small as to be virtually undetectable. In fact, far greater magnetic forces are created by the multitude of gadgets with which we surround ourselves these days. And yet there has been no serious suggestion that these have any significant influence on us, which should surely be the case if miniscule fluctuations in the Earth's magnetic field are capable of dictating fundamental human characteristics.

E Many eminent scientists have attacked astrology, one famous astronomer describing it as 'absurd'. Stephen Hawking, Lucasian Professor of Mathematics at Cambridge University, said that astrology became impossible as soon as early scientists found that the Earth was not the centre of the universe, an idea on which astrology was founded. But ironically, it is research done by an ex-astrologer, Geoffrey Dean, that has done the greatest damage to the credibility of astrology. Working with psychologist Ivan Kelly, Dean studied 2,000 people, all born under the supposed influence of the same star sign; indeed, most of the subjects who were investigated were born within minutes of one another, and therefore should have had many personal characteristics in common. Dean and Kelly looked at more than 100 different characteristics, including IQ levels, occupation, marital status, sociability and talent in art, all of which astrologers claim are influenced by heavenly bodies. They found no evidence of the similarities that astrologers would have predicted, and Dean was quoted as saying that astrology 'has no acceptable mechanism, its principles are invalid and it has failed hundreds of tests'.

PAPER 1 Reading ▸
- Part 1
- Part 2
- Part 3
- Part 4

PAPER 2 Writing

PAPER 3 English in Use

PAPER 4 Listening

PAPER 5 Speaking

For questions **15–20**, choose which of the paragraphs **A–G** on page **105** fit into the numbered gaps in the following magazine article. There is one extra paragraph which does not fit into any of the gaps.

Indicate your answers **on the separate answer sheet**.

Countdown to Extinction for World's Great Apes

Gorillas, chimpanzees, bonobos and orangutans – the closest living relatives of humanity – could vanish from the wild within fifty years, according to United Nations leaders who met recently in Paris. They have appealed for £15 million to save the world's great apes from extinction.

15

There is no doubt that dedicated researchers and writers have raised public awareness about the plight of the great apes, and commercially successful films like *Gorillas in the Mist* have also helped to shed light on the situation. Unfortunately, in spite of this, the decline in ape numbers has not only continued but accelerated.

16

Lowland and mountain gorillas range through nine African countries. Reliable figures on these animals are hard to come by, partly because the creatures are by nature reclusive and shy, and partly because the areas they inhabit are both remote and inhospitable. However, one estimate suggests that eighty to ninety percent of the population may have been lost in just five years, as new roads have opened up inaccessible forest to poachers, loggers and bush meat hunters. Only about 600 mountain gorillas survive in Uganda, Rwanda and the Democratic Republic of Congo.

17

The future looks equally bleak for the other African apes. Two chimpanzee species, *Pan troglodytes* and *Pan paniscus* (the bonobo or pigmy chimpanzee), are found in twenty-one African countries, but their populations are very small compared to the size of their potential range. There may be only 105,000 *Pan troglodytes*, and fewer than 20,000 bonobos left. The western chimpanzee has vanished from Benin, Gambia and Togo. Fewer than 400 remain in Senegal and 300 to 500 in Ghana. The population of chimps in Guinea-Bissau is below 200. And yet these animals are our closest relatives: chimpanzee DNA is so close to human DNA that one scientist has proposed that they should be reclassified as genus *Homo*.

18

By 2030 less than ten percent of Africa's remaining forest is likely to remain undisturbed. The picture from south-east Asia is also disturbing: by 2030 there will be almost no habitat that could be described as 'relatively undisturbed'. The total number of orangutans (*Pongo pygmaeus*) in the region is unknown, but the species is at 'extremely high risk' of extinction in Sumatra, where a population put at 6,000 three years ago has been falling by 1,000 a year. It is also endangered in Borneo.

19

'We cannot just put up fences to try and separate the apes from people,' says one official. 'Great apes play a key role in maintaining the health and diversity of tropical forests which people depend on. They disperse seeds throughout the forests, for example, and create light gaps in the forest canopy which allow seedlings to grow and replenish the forest ecosystem.'

20

It remains to be seen whether the great apes will fare any better than the dodo, or whether they will soon only survive in 2005 as sad reminders of our inhumanity. Time, which is fast running out, will tell.

A Another official has said: 'It's basic arithmetic: the multiplication of threats to the great apes, the division of their habitats, the subtraction of overall ape numbers.' To get the sums right, he added, would take the combined efforts of two UN agencies, four wildlife conventions and eighteen non-governmental organisations to raise awareness, funds and 'our conservation game to stop the great apes becoming history'.

B The UN first sounded an alarm about the rapidly dwindling numbers of great apes in 2001 and appealed for funds. But by last year, researchers on the ground had begun to reveal an even more ominous pattern of loss. They found that ape numbers in Africa had been slashed by logging, hunting and disease.

C 'The clock is standing at one minute to midnight for the great apes, animals that share more than 96% of their DNA with humans,' said Klaus Topfer, the head of the UN environment programme. 'If we lose any great ape species, we will be destroying a bridge to our own origins, and with it part of our own humanity.' He called the sum required 'the bare minimum we need, the equivalent of providing a dying man with bread and water'.

D To survive and breed, the great apes need undisturbed forest. But such earthly edens are becoming increasingly scarce. Logging, slash and burn agriculture and the ever-increasing pressure by human populations are taking their toll, and unfortunately, political instability and war have also had a devastating effect.

E UN agencies, conservation organisations, donor countries and officials from twenty-three African and south-east Asian nations have been meeting in Paris to work on survival strategies. Researchers have begun to use European satellite studies to measure forest destruction, and Unesco officials are working to improve law enforcement in African national parks.

F It is hoped that similar fund-raising activities will also prove effective in this case. Since the funds required have not been allocated by the UN as yet, it remains to be seen exactly how much will have to be supplied by private means. But it is likely to be a significant amount.

G In one population studied, researchers knew of 140 gorillas. After an outbreak of the Ebola virus, they could only find seven alive. 'The stark truth is that if we do not act decisively, our children may live in a world without wild apes,' they reported.

PAPER 1 Reading	▶	Part 1
PAPER 2 Writing		Part 2
PAPER 3 English in Use		Part 3
PAPER 4 Listening		Part 4
PAPER 5 Speaking		

Read the following newspaper article and answer questions **21–25** on page **107**. On your answer sheet, indicate the letter **A**, **B**, **C** or **D** against the number of each question. Give only one answer to each question.

Indicate your answers **on the separate answer sheet**.

The Land under the Sea

Underwater maps reveal hidden history

Ten thousand years ago, as the last ice age drew to a close, sea levels around the world were far lower than they are today. Much of the land under the North Sea and the English Channel was part of a huge region of forests and grassy plains, where herds of horses and reindeer roamed free and people lived in villages by the lakes and rivers. Then the climate gradually became warmer (a phenomenon certainly not confined to our own age!) and the water trapped in glaciers and ice caps was released. This ancient land was submerged in the resulting deluge and all that remains to tell us that it was once lush and verdant – and inhabited – is the occasional stone tool, harpoon or mammoth tusk brought up from the sea bed by fishing boats.

Now the development of advanced sonar technology, known as bathymetry, is making it possible to study this flooded landscape in extraordinary detail. A special echo sounder is fixed to the bottom of a survey vessel, and it makes wide sweeps across the sea bed. While previous devices have only been able to produce two-dimensional images, bathymetry makes use of computers, satellite positioning devices and special software to create accurate and remarkably detailed maps. For the first time an ancient river bed leaps out of the three-dimensional image, complete with rocky ledges rising up from the bottom of the valley. The sites of pre-historic settlements can now be pinpointed, and it is also possible to see in stunning detail the sunken shipwrecks that litter this part of the sea bed.

According to archaeologist Dr Linda Andrews, this technological development is of huge significance. 'We now have the ability to map the sea bed of the Channel and the North Sea as accurately as we can map dry land,' she says. She is, however, scathing about the scale of government funding for such projects. 'We have better images of Mars and Venus

than of two-thirds of our own planet! In view of the fact that Britain is a maritime nation, and the sea has had such a massive influence on us, it's an absolute scandal that we know so little about the area just off our shores!'

Once bathymetric techniques have identified sites where people might have built their homes and villages, such as sheltered bays, cliffs with caves and the shores of freshwater lakes, divers could be sent down to investigate further. Robot submarines could also be used, and researchers hope they will find stone tools and wood from houses (which survives far longer in water than on dry land) as proof of human activity. The idea of Britain as a natural island kingdom will be challenged by these findings: Britain has been inhabited for about 500,000 years, and for much of this time it has been linked on and off to continental Europe. It remains to be seen how far this new awareness is taken on board among our 'island' people.

In fact, the use of bathymetry scanners will not be limited to the study of lost landscapes and ancient settlements. It will also be vital in finding shipwrecks. Records show that there are about 44,000 shipwrecks off the shores of Britain, but there is good reason to believe that the real figure is much higher. In addition, commercial applications are a real possibility. Aggregates for the construction industry are becoming increasingly expensive, and bathymetry scanners could be used to identify suitable sites for quarrying this material. However, mapping the sea bed will also identify places where rare plants and shellfish have their homes. Government legislation may prevent digging at such sites, either to extract material for a profit or to make the water deeper: there are plans to dredge parts of the English Channel to provide deeper waterways for massive container ships.

21 We are told that the area now under the sea
    A was not previously thought to have been populated.
    B was created by the last Ice Age.
    C has yielded some archaeological artefacts.
    D was flooded, drowning the inhabitants.

22 What is the most important aspect of the new scanning technique?
    A It can pinpoint the location of shipwrecks under the sea.
    B It only requires the use of an echo sounder.
    C It can measure the depth of the sea bed with accuracy.
    D It reveals important details of underwater topography.

23 How does Dr Andrews feel about the lack of accurate maps of the waters around Britain?
    A outraged
    B resigned
    C astonished
    D amused

24 The writer suggests that a better understanding of the settlements on the sea bed may
    A inspire more young people to take up archaeology.
    B modify the attitudes of the British to their country's history.
    C provide confirmation about the dangers of global warming.
    D alter the perception other countries have about Britain.

25 Quarrying is mentioned to show that
    A there will be little difficulty obtaining funds for research.
    B underwater research should be completed as soon as possible.
    C damage to the sea bed has not been recorded accurately so far.
    D the project may have practical benefits for industry.

Answer questions **26–39** by referring to the magazine article on pages **109–110**, in which people talk about their experiences at job interviews.

Indicate your answers **on the separate answer sheet.**

For questions **26–39**, answer by choosing from the sections of the article **A–F**. Some of the choices may be required more than once.

Note: When more than one answer is required, these may be given **in any order**.

In which section of the article are the following mentioned?

establishing how the interview will be conducted	**26** ....
the importance of keeping to the point	**27** ....
revealing what motivates you	**28** .... **29** ....
awareness of body language	**30** ....
sources of information about your prospective employer	**31** ....
dressing appropriately	**32** ....
taking responsibility for past errors	**33** ....
appearing to have rehearsed responses	**34** ....
preparing inquiries to put to a prospective employer	**35** ....
foreseeing the consequences of feeling apprehensive	**36** ....
an abrupt ending to an interview	**37** ....
indicating that you view the interview as a transaction	**38** ....
a relaxed atmosphere in the workplace	**39** ....

Tell us Something about Yourself

Being interviewed for a job can be a stressful experience. We asked six people what they learnt from being in that situation.

A My first interview for a job taught me a great deal. I was applying for the position of junior account executive in an advertising company, which involves dealing with clients on a face-to-face basis. It follows that you have to be good at interpersonal skills, and unfortunately, that's not the impression I gave. Like a lot of people, I tend to babble when I'm nervous. The interviewer began by asking me to say something about myself, and I started talking about my hobbies. But I got carried away and went off at a tangent, which made a bad impression. The other lesson I learnt was that if you are asked what your weaknesses are, you really shouldn't be evasive. You could mention a weakness that can also be a strength. For example, being pedantic is not always a bad thing in certain circumstances, and you should explain how you cope with that weakness, but you have to say something.

B In my present job I have to interview applicants, and I can offer a few general tips. Firstly, a candidate should not learn a speech off by heart; you will come across as insincere, as if you have practised everything in front of a mirror. Secondly, it is crucial to understand what the interviewer wants you to talk about. For instance, an interviewer might ask about a situation where your supervisor or manager had a problem with your work. Now, what the interviewer is really after is to see how you react to criticism, and the best thing is to say that you tried to learn from this. Finally, don't try to conceal your real character. When I was interviewed for a job many years ago, the interviewer asked me at the end of our talk if I had any questions. I was very keen to get the job, so I asked what opportunities there were for promotion if I were hired. I wondered if perhaps I had been too direct, but I later discovered that employers like you to seem eager, and I think they were impressed by my enthusiasm and ambition.

C One good way to prepare for an interview is to find out as much as you can about the company you have applied to from its website and promotional material. When you are asked if you have any questions, you can show that you have done this preparatory work, which will impress the interviewer. I also think a lot of candidates are too defensive in interviews. It's not enough just to avoid giving the 'wrong' answers; you should also actively try to make a good impression. Make it clear that the interview is a two-way process: after all, you want to be sure the company is the right place for you. It's acceptable to take the opportunity, when one is offered, to interview the interviewer! One way to do this is to ask him or her some penetrating questions such as why he or she has stayed with the company for so long. Some people might think such a question is arrogant, so size up the interviewer first and decide whether it would be an appropriate thing to ask.

D I remember one interview I attended with a company that makes ice cream and other dairy products. I didn't know much about the company, and it was brought home to me that I should have found out some basic facts. I turned up in a smart business suit and tie, only to find that my prospective employers were in jeans! They believed in being casual: no private offices, everyone ate in the same canteen, people all used first names with each other etc. I realised I should have done more research. Needless to say, I didn't get the job. On another occasion, at the end of an interview, I was asked if I had anything to say. I was so relieved that the interview was over that I just smiled and blurted out: 'No thanks!' I later realised this was a mistake. A candidate should decide in advance on at least ten things to ask the interviewer: it's not necessary to ask more than two or three questions, but you need to have some in reserve in case the question you wanted to ask is answered in the course of the interview.

E Preparation is of extreme importance; things like finding out what form the interview will have. Will there be any sort of written component, for instance, and will you be talking to one person or a panel? And of course, you need to prepare answers to those awkward questions designed to find out more about your character. For example, you might be asked about your most important achievement so far; don't answer this in a way that makes you seem swollen-headed or complacent as this will suggest that you don't learn easily. Actually, it's not so much what people say that makes them seem arrogant as the way they sit, how they hold their heads, whether they meet the interviewer's eye, so bear that in mind. Another question interviewers sometimes ask, to find out how well you work in a team, is about mistakes you have made. You should have an example ready and admit that you were at fault, otherwise it looks as though you are the kind of person who shifts the blame onto others. But you should also show that you learnt from the mistake and wouldn't make it again.

F Being nervous can make you forget things, so always take detailed notes with you to an interview, even about the simplest things – this will help you feel less nervous. I also think you have to strike the right balance between being too arrogant and too self-effacing. For example, if you are asked where you see yourself in five years' time, don't be diffident about showing that you are ambitious. You could even say you'd like to be doing the interviewer's job! Show that your ambition is the force that drives you – employers are happy to see this characteristic because it also suggests you will work hard. Take every opportunity to reinforce the impression that you are eager; one way is by asking questions about the job. This suggests that you will take it seriously. You could also ask what made the last person to fill the position you have applied for successful, or what you could accomplish in the job that would satisfy the interviewer. Naturally, the answers to questions like this are valuable in themselves, but frankly, the main reason for asking is to ensure you make the right impression.

1 You are the president of the student association at the college where you are studying. The principal of the college is planning an orientation weekend for new students at the beginning of the next academic year. She has asked you to come up with some ideas for the weekend, and you have invited students to send you their suggestions.

Read the principal's memo and the notes you have made on it. You should also read the suggestions you have received from other students, with your notes. Then, using all the information, write your **proposal**.

Memo

To: The President of the Student Association
From: The Principal
Re: Orientation Weekend

We have decided that the following events should be part of an orientation weekend for new students:

Saturday morning? → • a talk on college regulations

Saturday early afternoon? → • an introduction to using the library

Sunday morning? → • an introduction to using the computer room

I'd welcome your suggestion for a timetable which would incorporate these and more informal events over the weekend.

Alison Watson, Principal

Great idea! Saturday, early evening, followed by disco? → Why not ask the social organiser to give a talk about social events and social life in the town?

I remember my first week at the college – I didn't know where to buy food and what to cook for myself. Some helpful suggestions?

Show new students sports hall – late Saturday afternoon? → What about sports? Shouldn't new students be told about this side of college life?

Local volunteer groups and charities that students might want to become involved in?

Sunday afternoon, information stands of all college clubs in Main Hall? → Introduction to student societies such as the Drama Club?

Now write your **proposal** for the orientation weekend, explaining which events you would suggest, and why (approximately 250 words). You should use your own words as far as possible.

Choose one of the following writing tasks. Your answer should follow exactly the instructions given. Write approximately 250 words.

2   You read the following notice in a history magazine:

When is history interesting?

History becomes fascinating when it is related to personal experience. Write an article about a situation when you found the past of your region or country suddenly became relevant to you because of a personal or direct experience.

Write your **article**.

3   A friend of yours has seen the advertisement below. Your friend would like to apply for the job and has asked you to write a character reference.

Hands Across the Sea – Regional Organiser

Hands Across the Sea is an organisation that arranges high school and university student exchange programmes between Britain, the rest of Europe, the United States and Canada. We need a regional organiser for our Northern England and Scotland office. The successful applicant will have relevant business skills, experience in marketing and sales and the ability to work well in a team.

Write your **character reference**, explaining why your friend would be suitable for the position.

4   You have seen the following advertisement in a magazine on education:

Further Education

Every country needs well educated citizens, but a lot of youngsters still leave school as soon as they can. What are the benefits of further education? Why do many young people fail to appreciate these benefits? What could be done to motivate more youngsters to go on to college?

Write and tell us your ideas: the writer of the best entry will win a laptop computer!

Write your **competition entry**.

5   You work for a multinational company. The company is thinking of shutting down two smaller branches in other parts of the country and enlarging your own branch, making it the only one in the country. You have been asked by your branch manager to write a report indicating what advantages and disadvantages the proposed changes would bring. You should consider both short-term and long-term effects. You have also been asked to give your opinion on whether the plan should be implemented.

Write your **report**.

For questions **1–15**, read the text below and then decide which answer best fits each space. Put the letter you choose for each question in the correct box on your answer sheet. The exercise begins with an example (**0**).

Example:

0	D	0

Mountain Rescue

Last year over 200 climbers were rescued from the mountains of Scotland (**0**) ...... by local rescue teams, who go out in all (**1**) ...... to do whatever they can to help when disaster (**2**) .... These people are volunteers, giving their time and energy freely and, on (**3**) ...... , putting themselves in danger. They will risk life and (**4**) ...... in an emergency when they are (**5**) ...... on to rescue foolhardy or unlucky climbers.

A whole (**6**) ...... of things can go wrong up in the mountains. A storm can (**7**) ...... up without warning, reducing visibility to virtually zero. Then only the most experienced mountaineer could find their way back down to safety. And it is easy to come to (**8**) ...... , breaking a leg – or worse. Many climbers owe a huge (**9**) ...... of gratitude to the rescue teams!

While rescue teams work for no pay, there are considerable costs (**10**) ...... in maintaining an efficient service. Equipment such as ropes and stretchers is of (**11**) ...... importance, as are vehicles and radio communications devices. (**12**) ...... some of the costs are (**13**) ...... by the government, the rescue teams couldn't operate without donations from the public. Fortunately, fundraising for a good (**14**) ...... like this is not difficult; anyone who has ever been up in the mountains will gladly (**15**) ...... a contribution.

0	**A** apart	**B** even	**C** only	**D** alone
1	**A** times	**B** weathers	**C** factors	**D** states
2	**A** hits	**B** rises	**C** strikes	**D** arrives
3	**A** situation	**B** event	**C** moment	**D** occasion
4	**A** limb	**B** blood	**C** bone	**D** flesh
5	**A** brought	**B** called	**C** summoned	**D** beckoned
6	**A** scope	**B** extent	**C** range	**D** scale
7	**A** brew	**B** arise	**C** whip	**D** lash
8	**A** agony	**B** trouble	**C** problem	**D** grief
9	**A** recognition	**B** liability	**C** debt	**D** obligation
10	**A** implied	**B** involved	**C** featured	**D** connected
11	**A** lively	**B** vibrant	**C** essential	**D** vital
12	**A** Even	**B** Despite	**C** Though	**D** However
13	**A** borne	**B** held	**C** carried	**D** fulfilled
14	**A** effect	**B** cause	**C** reason	**D** exploit
15	**A** make	**B** take	**C** do	**D** hand

For questions **16–30**, complete the following article by writing each missing word in the correct box on your answer sheet. **Use only one word for each space.** The exercise begins with an example (**0**).

Example:

0	rest	0

The Ubiquitous Shopping Mall

It is a trend which started in the United States and is rapidly spreading to the (**0**) .... of the developed world. Many towns and cities do not really have a centre (**16**) .... more. Instead, a shopping mall somewhere (**17**) .... the outskirts serves some of the functions of an urban centre. Here, shops and banks are all crowded together, (**18**) .... is very convenient, especially (**19**) .... those people who use a car. You can park in the basement car park, (**20**) .... all your shopping inside the mall, and then load up the car and drive home. You don't even (**21**) .... to go outside, so it doesn't matter what the weather's (**22**) ....

So (**23**) .... should anyone possibly object to the growing number of shopping malls springing up around our cities? (**24**) .... fact, many people do object, (**25**) .... only urban planners and politicians, but environmentalists as well. (**26**) .... most shops are concentrated in malls, it leaves city and town centres deserted and (**27**) .... any life of their own. Furthermore, malls do not take into (**28**) .... people without cars, who simply can't get to them easily. Ultimately, perhaps, the most damaging criticism is that malls are virtually identical. (**29**) .... a result, our towns and cities are losing (**30**) .... character, which has been created over centuries.

In most lines of the following text, there is **either** a spelling **or** a punctuation error. For each numbered line **31–46**, write the correctly spelt word or show the correct punctuation in the box on your answer sheet. Some lines are correct. Indicate these lines with a (✓) in the box. The exercise begins with three examples (**0**), (**00**) and (**000**).

Example:

0	✓	0
00	*irreparable*	00
000	*water,*	000

Floods in Peter's City

0	The city of St Petersburg is facing the very real danger that floods
00	will cause irreperable damage over the coming decades. The city
000	has always had to battle with the water being constructed on marshes
31	where the River Neva enters the gulf of Finland, but the problem is
32	becoming increasingly serious. Experts agree, that flooding is now
33	a far more regular occurrance than was ever the case in the past. This
34	means a serious flood, like that of 1824, when the water rose by four
35	metres and 300 people lost their lives, could take place fairly soon
36	However, a major argument is rageing about the best way to protect
37	the city. Some people are covinced that a barrier stretching across
38	the banks of the Neva would be an answer. This would ensure that
39	water from high tide's could not cause a huge and catastrophic flood.
40	Opponents of the plan point out that the city produces a considrable
41	amount of sewage, most of which is carried safely out to see by the
42	tide. Anything that prevents the removal of this dirty water could
43	cause health problems for the city, including outbreaks off
44	disease. A decision has to be taken soon, but whathever the city
45	authorities decide to do, they will face critisicm that they are doing
46	the wrong thing and risking terrible damage.

For questions **47–61**, read the two texts below. Use the words in the boxes to the right of the texts to form one word that fits in the same numbered space in the text. Write the new word in the correct box on your answer sheet. The exercise begins with an example (**0**).

Example:

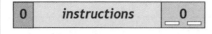

0	*instructions*	0

INFORMATION LEAFLET

The ADT 55 Printer

Please read these (**0**) .... carefully before using your new ADT 55 Printer for the first time.

Like other printers in the ADT range, the ADT 55 is (**47**) .... by its simple operating mode. At the same time, it displays a (**48**) .... that is otherwise only found on far more (**49**) .... devices. Consequently, the (**50**) .... of a wide range of tasks is possible. However, it is (**51**) .... to attempt to use the printer before you consult the manual and familiarise yourself with the controls and the operating system. This device is (**52**) .... a robust piece of equipment, but it is by no means (**53**) .... Therefore, never attempt to force any of the moving parts, and only approach an authorised representative for repairs and (**54**) ....

(0)	**INSTRUCT**
(47)	CHARACTER
(48)	VERSATILE
(49)	COST
(50)	EXECUTE
(51)	ADVISE
(52)	ESSENCE
(53)	DESTROY
(54)	MAINTAIN

EXTRACT FROM BOOK

Britain in the Nineteenth Century

The history of Britain in the nineteenth century is a tale of social upheaval; the (**55**) .... witnessed over this period were unlike anything that had gone before. These changes were linked to, and in some ways driven by, technological advances that turned the (**56**) .... rural society of the late eighteenth century into an industrial one that is (**57**) .... an early version of our own. (**58**) .... Britain had declined, and the process was (**59**) .... ; never again would farming be of such importance to the country. The economy would depend (**60**) .... on industrial production and the export of manufactured goods. One might say that the country's (**61**) .... of itself had changed: Britain now thought of itself as an industrialised land.

(55)	TRANSFORM
(56)	DOMINANT
(57)	RECOGNISE
(58)	AGRICULTURE
(59)	REVERSE
(60)	INCREASE
(61)	PERCEIVE

For questions **62–74**, read the notes from a meeting. Use the information in the notes to complete the numbered gaps in the formal letter. The words you need **do not occur** in the notes. **Use no more than two words for each gap**. The exercise begins with an example (**0**).

Example:

0	*assured*	**0**

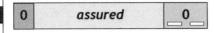

NOTES

John Henderson, Location Manager for Daytime Films, promised us that he would organise everything in advance for the 2 weeks of filming in Wales, but (1) there weren't enough places for the actors and crew to stay, (2) the police didn't work with us, (3) the historian hired didn't have specialised knowledge of the 1940s.

We wanted to shoot several scenes inside Ocean View Hotel, but (1) the manager didn't want to give us enough time, (2) the ballroom had been done up and it didn't look right any more, (3) we weren't given enough parking space for equipment vans.

Also, (1) there weren't enough cars, trucks and vans from the 1940s, (2) we couldn't connect to the Internet in the office rented for us, (3) the band for the ballroom scene arrived late and held up filming.

FORMAL LETTER

Dear Mr Henderson,

I am writing on behalf of Mr Mills, who was (**0**) .... by your firm that preparations had been made for the (**62**) .... we would spend in Wales, in line with our specifications. As Location Manager, you were responsible for the location arrangements while we were shooting *Hotel Heaven*. Unfortunately, we were not satisfied with your services.

The (**63**) .... provided for the actors and film crew was inadequate, and (**64**) .... from the police was not forthcoming. Moreover, the historian you employed on our behalf was not (**65**) .... on the 1940s.

We had stated that (**66**) .... of scenes would be shot inside the Ocean View Hotel, but the manager was (**67**) .... allow us sufficient time for this. In addition, the (**68**) .... of the ballroom had been changed, so it (**69**) .... looked appropriate. Furthermore, insufficient parking space was made (**70**) .... for our equipment vans.

We had specified that we wanted (**71**) .... from the 1940s for certain scenes, but too few were provided. There was no Internet (**72**) .... in the office, though again we had requested this. Finally, the band for the big ballroom scene was not (**73**) .... , with the result that filming (**74**) ....

For questions **75–80**, read the following text and then choose from the list **A–J** given below the best phrase to fill each of the spaces. Write one letter (**A–J**) in the correct box on your answer sheet. Each correct phrase may only be used once. **Some of the suggested answers do not fit at all**. The exercise begins with an example (**0**).

Example:

0	*J*	0

Don't Worry, Be Happy

An unusual hobby is becoming popular with young professional city dwellers who wish (**0**) .... All over the country beekeeping associations are reporting a rise of interest in what used to be considered an old person's hobby. These days people feel it is somehow sophisticated to be an expert on different types of honey; they feel this is similar (**75**) .... At the same time, keeping bees on the rooftop of your apartment confers the pleasant feeling that even if you are a city dweller, you can still take part in an activity that is related (**76**) .... In fact, there are practical benefits associated with keeping bees in cities. Urban bees are inclined (**77**) ...... than their country cousins. This is because they can harvest nectar from a wide variety of sources: anything from trees in the parks (**78**) .... And since these wonderful insects tend (**79**) ...... from their hives, country bees are generally confined to relatively few sources of nectar.

Moreover, average temperatures are higher in cities than in the surrounding countryside, and city bees are likely (**80**) ...... , which in turn means they produce more honey.

In fact, though, the practical advantages of beekeeping are probably less important to the new generation of beekeepers than the feeling that they are keeping in touch with nature through their peaceful and productive hobby.

A to produce a better quality of honey

B to everyone who might want one

C to the flowers in window boxes or public gardens

D to nature and the changing of the seasons

E to a much better life in the future

F to be more active as a result of this

G to be of any use in other situations

H to stray no more than about a mile

I to having a knowledge and appreciation of fine wines

J to bring nature closer to home

You will hear an astrobiologist talking about her work. For questions **1–8**, complete the sentences.

You will hear the recording twice.

What is Astrobiology?

It could be claimed that the science of astrobiology
has no [1]

However, astrobiologists are also concerned with how life evolved [2]

There are some popular misconceptions about what
[3] might look like.

For much of the Earth's history, single-celled [4]
were the only life forms in existence.

Multi-cellular life evolved during the [5]
known as the Cambrian.

Then, about [6] years ago,
human-like creatures evolved.

Life on other planets will probably be [7]
life on Earth.

Human beings might not have evolved if [8]
had not become extinct.

You will hear a fitness expert talking about different methods of keeping fit. For questions **9–16**, complete the notes.

Listen very carefully as you will hear the recording ONCE only.

Get Fit!

To get fit, [_____ **9**] essential.

Advertised on TV: [_____ **10**] machines.
Effective, but not by themselves.

Latest idea: machine that [_____ **11**] ,
strengthening muscles.

Drawback: effective only for [_____ **12**] people!

Some form of [_____ **13**] exercise recommended
four times a week.

For real fitness: [_____ **14**] training also necessary.

Good news: no need to join gym if you have [_____ **15**]
at home.

Bad news: must [_____ **16**] yourself!

You will hear part of a radio interview with Pete Birtwhistle, a playwright. For questions **17–22**, choose the correct answer **A, B, C** or **D**.

You will hear the recording twice.

17 What was Pete's attitude to the theatre before he started writing?
    A   He felt it had little relevance to his life.
    B   He didn't feel qualified to judge it.
    C   He thought it would be boring to watch a play.
    D   He preferred comedies to tragedies.

18 How did he feel about leaving his previous job?
    A   He felt very relieved.
    B   He was anxious about his health.
    C   He worried how others would see him.
    D   He was very depressed.

19 What was the most difficult aspect of writing his first play?
    A   disciplining himself to write every day
    B   coming up with a suitable story
    C   allowing the characters to develop
    D   finding an appropriate ending

20 What is the biggest impact that writing has had on Pete's life?
    A   It has made people respect him more.
    B   It has enabled him to express himself.
    C   It has opened up new professional opportunities.
    D   It has allowed him to appreciate other plays.

21 How does Pete choose the theme of a new play?
    A   He looks around for a challenging theme.
    B   He looks for a subject that is in the news.
    C   He looks for a theme that he understands.
    D   He thinks about issues that affect society.

22 How does Pete feel about writing for films?
    A   enthusiastic
    B   worried
    C   cautious
    D   intimidated

PAPER 1 Reading

PAPER 2 Writing

PAPER 3 English in Use

PAPER 4 Listening ▶

    Part 1
    Part 2
    Part 3
    Part 4

PAPER 5 Speaking

You will hear five short extracts in which different people talk about tracing their ancestors.

You will hear the recording twice. While you listen you must complete both tasks.

Task One

For questions **23–27**, match the extracts with what each person says about the discoveries he or she made, listed **A–H**.

A One of my ancestors did a great deal of humanitarian work.

B A relative ran away from home when he was young.

C I am descended from immigrants.

D A family tradition turned out not to be true.

E At one time the family was wealthy.

F My great-grandmother came from a rich family.

G A relative emigrated to Australia.

H My great-great-grandfather changed his name.

Speaker 1	23
Speaker 2	24
Speaker 3	25
Speaker 4	26
Speaker 5	27

Task Two

For questions **28–32**, match the extracts with the emotions aroused in each speaker by these discoveries, listed **A–H**.

A I hate the thought of their suffering.

B Learning the truth caused considerable bitterness.

C I have become more curious about the story.

D The whole thing made us feel quite embarrassed.

E I was delighted to make contact with my relatives.

F The story saddened me.

G I am very proud of my ancestor.

H I was disappointed at first.

Speaker 1	28
Speaker 2	29
Speaker 3	30
Speaker 4	31
Speaker 5	32

Part 1 (3 minutes)

The examiner will ask you a few questions about yourself and then ask you to talk to your partner. For example, the examiner may ask you:

- When and how did you start learning English?
- In what ways is knowing a foreign language useful to you now?
- How do you expect language skills to be important to you in the future?

Part 2 (4 minutes)

You will each be asked to talk for a minute without interruption. You will each be given a set of photographs in turn to talk about. After your partner has finished speaking, you will be asked a brief question connected with your partner's photographs.

Groups (compare, contrast and speculate)

Turn to pictures 1–2 on page **204**, which show people in groups.

Candidate A, compare and contrast these pictures and imagine how the members of these groups are feeling.

Candidate B, in which situations do you cooperate with others as part of a group?

Experience (compare, contrast and speculate)

Turn to pictures 1–2 on page **205**, which show people who have gained experience.

Candidate B, compare and contrast these two situations, saying what sort of experience you imagine each person has gained.

Candidate A, can you think of a situation where you learnt something by going through a difficult experience?

Part 3 (4 minutes)

Time management (discuss, evaluate and select)

Turn to the illustrations on page **206**, which show the need for time management.

Talk to each other about how these problems could be helped by better time management, and then decide which situation would benefit most and which would benefit least from better time management.

Part 4 (4 minutes)

The examiner will encourage you to develop the topic of your discussion in Part 3 by asking questions such as:

- Do you think it is a problem if someone is often late for appointments and meetings? Why (not)?
- Which aspects of modern life where time is managed badly do you find most annoying?
- Does modern life make us too anxious about punctuality? Why (not)?
- When was the last time you were late, and what caused you to be late?

Answer questions **1–16** by referring to the magazine article about lawyers involved in the theatre on page **125**.

Indicate your answers **on the separate answer sheet**.

For questions **1–16**, answer by choosing from the sections of the article **(A–D)**. Some of the choices may be required more than once.

Note: When more than one choice is required, these may be given **in any order**.

In which section of the article are the following mentioned?

an unexpected response to a new experience	**1** ....
the implication that acting is a disreputable profession	**2** ....
success that came early in life	**3** ....
lack of courage to take up a profession	**4** ....
empathy with people in the theatre	**5** ....
a dislike of the comparisons made between the law and acting	**6** ....
seeking professional assistance	**7** .... **8** ....
the desire to learn about another aspect of work in the theatre	**9** ....
limitations that come with age	**10** ....
the good luck to be financially independent	**11** ....
approaching a role in a different way	**12** ....
disapproval of acting as a profession	**13** ....
the ability to act in spite of a personal trait	**14** ....
the desire to be challenged	**15** ....
initial indifference to the theatre	**16** ....

Acting and the Law

Are the similarities between acting and the law the reason why some people make a career in both fields?

A Barrister Michaela Duncan has returned to the stage after an absence of twenty-five years. No longer young enough to play ingénue roles, as she herself admits, what induced her to give up the law in order to play the relatively unglamorous parts available to older women? 'All my life I've been stage struck,' she laughs. 'When I was at school, I used to sneak off to matinées instead of doing my homework and I enrolled in a drama school when I was eighteen.' Duncan made her first professional stage appearance shortly afterwards. She went on to enjoy a considerable measure of success, yet, rather unusually, she also felt she was not being stretched intellectually. 'My father was a lawyer, and I thought the law would probably suit me, too,' she says. She put herself through university and her acting career seemed to be over. In the years that followed, she proved herself as a barrister, eventually becoming a partner in a prestigious law firm. 'But I always maintained my stage contacts,' she remembers. Then one day she was asked for advice in a case involving Equity, the actors' union. 'Naturally, I was happy to help. I had worked as an actor, and I knew what it was like to struggle, to be unemployed. It was while I was working on the case that it suddenly struck me: I wanted to return to the stage! It's where I belong. It wasn't an easy decision to make, but at that point of my life, it was the right thing to do.'

B Harry Swithins is now building an acting career for himself after many successful years at the bar. He began shedding his legal persona six years ago because the lure of the footlights was too powerful to resist. 'I had taken part in amateur theatricals when I was younger,' he says, 'but acting was not a career that I dared to suggest for myself. I come from a long line of hard-headed Yorkshire businessmen, and my family would have thought that a stage career would be a waste of time and energy, not to mention money!' The change was not easy to make. 'I went to an agent and told her I was a lawyer but I wanted to become an actor. She looked incredulous and asked me if I had had a nervous breakdown. She simply couldn't conceive of anybody choosing to become an actor after making a living in a *proper* profession.' Swithins has managed to land a few small roles on television and in regional theatre, and he has also appeared in commercials. 'Fortunately, I have a private income and I don't have to depend on acting to earn a living,' he says. 'My whole life has changed radically, but I enjoy it. I'm working with my instincts more. Lawyers need to be analytical, but the great ones are also intuitive – about handling situations, resolving conflicts, anticipating reactions.'

C Alicia Bolton had no interest in the theatre, either at school or as a law student. Prior to taking her first acting classes five years ago, that is. 'I was pushed into enrolling,' she says. 'A friend wanted to attend some classes that were being given by a well-known actor, but she was too shy to go by herself. It's ironic, really. She dropped out after only three sessions – she suddenly lost interest – whereas I was smitten. I certainly wasn't prepared for the adrenalin rush I experienced', she says. 'One thing that continually surprises me is the fact that I do it at all, because deep down I'm a very shy and private person. However, I discovered that when it came to standing up and delivering my lines, another part of me took over. I suppose that's one positive outcome of having been a criminal lawyer: one gets accustomed to an audience, even though that audience is composed of a judge and jury!' Bolton is currently working with a small theatre troupe, and she is also keen to get to grips with the art of directing. 'Acting and the law are two very different worlds,' she says, 'with superficial similarities hiding fundamental differences. For one thing, acting is pure make-believe, while being a lawyer isn't: when I was addressing a judge and jury I was telling the truth in the real world. But acting is a hundred times more fun!'

D Why have these three successful people moved away from the law? 'We all have a picture of who and what we are,' says Duncan. 'I have always viewed myself as an actor.' And has their experience outside the theatre influenced them as actors? 'Acting for me is more of an organic process now,' comments Bolton. 'In earlier days my performances used to be slick. Now I spend a lot more time applying my lawyerly skills to uncover the real nature of the character I am impersonating.' Duncan concurs: 'I used to resent it if anybody said that lawyers lived in the real world, whereas actors were just acting. Now I feel that actors, to be compelling, have to be truthful – and real – in the self-contained universe brought into existence in the theatre.' And the influence works both ways, according to Swithins: 'There certainly are times when acting skills are useful to a lawyer. When you are arguing a case in court and trying to make an impression on a jury, dramatic training will be quite helpful.' And some essentials remain constant, according to Bolton: 'Like an actor, a lawyer has to be able to move people – whether it's a jury or an audience isn't so very different.'

PAPER 1	Reading	▶	Part 1
PAPER 2	Writing		Part 2
PAPER 3	English in Use		Part 3
PAPER 4	Listening		Part 4
PAPER 5	Speaking		

For questions **17–22**, choose which of the paragraphs **A–G** on page **127** fit into the numbered gaps in the following newspaper article. There is one extra paragraph which does not fit into any of the gaps.

Indicate your answers **on the separate answer sheet**.

Hybrid Homes

New building technologies are making nearly zero-energy houses a real possibility

Imagine a community for the deeply green. Walls nineteen inches thick keep temperatures comfortable year-round. Windows are triple-glazed. A wind-driven ventilation system feeds fresh air into each house – and grabs the heat from stale outgoing air. Outsize conservatories face south to trap the light and warmth of the sun. Solar panels provide enough power to run electric cars. The architecture is modish, and even the most modest apartment has its own garden.

17

In Europe and the United States buildings guzzle about forty percent of all energy – about ten percent more than transport – and create the same proportion of carbon dioxide emissions. BedZED and other initiatives show that trimming excess energy consumption needn't be difficult or even high tech – just a matter of intelligent design.

18

It's no wonder such ideas are gaining admirers. Over the past two years, BedZED has attracted thousands of visitors from as far away as India and China, and more zero-energy communities are under construction elsewhere in Britain as well as in the United States.

19

Major momentum for these changes has come from Europe, where governments are increasingly worried by threats to energy supplies and the need to meet energy-reduction goals agreed to under the Kyoto accords. Many are issuing grants and tax breaks for energy-efficient builders as well as tightening regulations. A European Union directive that takes effect at the end of next year will require house builders, landlords or sellers to show an energy-efficiency certificate setting out how well a building performs.

20

There's growing cooperation in this field between government, scientists and the environmental lobby. At the government-funded Lawrence Berkeley National Laboratory in California, Steve Selkowitz's windows-and-building-technology team has produced such innovations as dimmable windows that can minimise hot sunlight while preserving the view; the windows could save homeowners thousands of dollars a year in air-conditioning costs.

21

It's too early to know whether the public will embrace such measures fully. 'From the marketing point of view, energy efficiency is still a very hard sell,' says David Strong of Britain's Building Research Establishment. Who cares if warmth is leaking out through the roof when heating your home costs a relatively small amount?

22

'The technologies will be able to support each other,' says Thorne Amann. 'Solar panels, appliances, heat-pump water heaters – the synergy will improve the whole building.' And the outlook for world energy supplies.

A Much of the technology involved is not flashy, and could be used much more widely today. Things like triple-glazing windows to add extra insulation, tightening duct systems and using insulated panels in the construction of floors and walls are easy and cost-effective – and could cut the fuel consumption of the world's buildings by twenty percent before the end of the decade. 'You can accomplish a tremendous amount with the technologies that we have already,' says one official working on energy efficiency for the European Commission in Brussels.

B Still, as governments, scientists and builders continue to provide the 'market push' toward energy efficiency, the 'consumer pull' will be stimulated. Each new innovation will push us closer to what one might call the hybrid home, in which energy is conserved through a combination of increasingly efficient appliances and building techniques.

C The US government, too, has been doing its part. Through the Energy Star programme, it has set tough regulations on everything from home construction to major appliances and consumer electronics. 'Energy Star is transforming the market so that energy-efficient technologies become standard practice – and a money maker for companies, too,' says Jennifer Thorne Amann of the American Council for an Energy-Efficient Economy.

D Both of these regions still make every possible attempt to meet energy consumption guidelines as governments around the world attempt to come to grips with the threat of global warming. There seems every likelihood that this project could lead the way – one can only hope that others will follow.

E Even more exciting developments are creeping onto the market. Solar power is becoming more affordable, as are tankless water heaters, composting toilets and biomass heating systems like stoves that burn corn instead of declining resources like wood. In India, Development Alternatives, a New Delhi-based non-profit organisation devoted to sustainable development, has helped supply mini power stations fuelled by weeds and agricultural wastes to villages across the country. And beneath thousands of new houses in Sweden, a system of fluid-filled pipes taps the warmth of the surrounding earth to heat the home.

F This might sound like a high-tech oasis for the super-rich. But it's actually an 84-home development called BedZED on the site of a disused sewage treatment plant in an unfashionable patch of South London. Its residents aren't well-meaning ecology enthusiasts: many are tenants of a housing charity. But they are all at the forefront of a global trend toward reducing energy consumption in the home.

G The key is finding ways to maximise efficiency in the simplest ways possible: the 'ZED' in BedZED stands for 'zero energy'. Whatever little juice the London homes need after taking advantage of their built-in energy savers comes from an on-site power plant fuelled by waste timber. Simple also means cheap; build 5,000 ZEDHomes and the economies of scale mean the cost is no more than that of constructing a normal home: the price of components tumbles as production numbers rise.

TEST 6
CAE

Exam Essentials

PAPER 1	Reading	▶	Part 1
PAPER 2	Writing		Part 2
PAPER 3	English in Use		**Part 3**
PAPER 4	Listening		Part 4
PAPER 5	Speaking		

Read the following magazine article and answer questions 23–27 on page **129**. On your answer sheet, indicate the letter **A**, **B**, **C** or **D** against the number of each question. Give only one answer to each question.

Indicate your answers **on the separate answer sheet**.

Learning to Run

An article published recently in the prestigious scientific journal *Nature* is shedding new light on an important, but hitherto little appreciated, aspect of human evolution. In this article, Professors Dennis Bramble and Daniel Lieberman suggest that the ability to run was a crucial factor in the development of our species. According to the two scientists, humans possess a number of anatomical features that make them surprisingly good runners. 'We are very confident that strong selection for running – which came at the expense of the historical ability to live in trees – was instrumental in the origin of the modern human body form,' says Bramble, a biology professor at the University of Utah.

Traditional thinking up to now has been that the distinctive, upright body form of modern humans has come about as a result of the ability to walk, and that running is simply a by-product of walking. Furthermore, humans have usually been regarded as poor runners compared to such animals as dogs, horses or antelopes. However, this is only true if we consider fast running, or sprinting, over short distances. Even an Olympic athlete can hardly run as fast as a horse can gallop, and can only keep up a top speed for fifteen seconds or so. Horses, antelopes and greyhounds, on the other hand, can run at top speed for several minutes, clearly outperforming us in this respect. But when it comes to long-distance running, humans do astonishingly well. They can maintain a steady pace for miles, and their overall speed compares favourably with that of horses or dogs.

Bramble and Lieberman examined twenty-six anatomical features found in humans. One of the most interesting of these is the nuchal ligament, a band of tissue that extends from a ridge on the base of the skull to the spine. When we run, it is this ligament that prevents our head from pitching back and forth or from side to side. Therefore, we are able to run with steady heads, held high. The nuchal ligament is not found in any other surviving primates, although the fossil record shows that *Homo erectus*, an early human species that walked upright, much as we do, also had one. Then there are our Achilles tendons at the backs of our legs, which connect our calf muscles to our heel bones – and which have nothing to do with walking. When we run, these tendons behave like springs, helping to propel us forward. Furthermore, we have low, wide shoulders, virtually disconnected from our skulls, an anatomical adaptation which allows us to run more efficiently. Add to this our light forearms, which swing out of phase with the movement of our legs to assist balance, and one begins to appreciate the point that Bramble and Lieberman are trying to make.

But what evolutionary advantage is gained from being good long-distance runners? One hypothesis is that this ability may have permitted early humans to obtain food more effectively. 'What these features and fossil facts appear to be telling us is that running evolved in order for our direct ancestors to compete with other carnivores for access to the protein needed to grow the big brains that we enjoy today,' says Lieberman.

Some scientists speculate that early humans may have pursued animals for miles in order to exhaust them before killing them. Running would also have conferred an advantage before weapons were invented: early humans might have been scavengers, eating the meat and marrow left over from a kill by lions or other large predators. They may have been alerted to the existence of a freshly-killed carcass by vultures, and the faster they got to the scene of the kill, the better.

'Research on the history of human locomotion has traditionally been contentious,' says Lieberman. 'At the very least, I hope this theory will make many people have second thoughts about how humans learned to run and walk and why we are built the way we are.'

23 According to the text, the human ability to run
   A was only recently described in a scientific journal.
   B is now regarded as more important than the ability to climb trees.
   C played an important part in human evolution.
   D is surprising when we consider evolutionary trends.

24 According to the text, humans
   A are better runners than most other animals.
   B are not good at running short distances.
   C cannot run at top speed for long distances.
   D compare unfavourably with horses and dogs.

25 It appears that the nuchal ligament
   A is found only in modern primates.
   B is associated with the ability to run.
   C prevents the head from moving.
   D is a unique anatomical feature.

26 The text suggests that
   A we do not need calf muscles in order to walk.
   B without shoulders we could not run very fast.
   C the movement of our forearms is out of phase.
   D our Achilles tendons are an adaptation for running.

27 According to the text, early humans
   A killed animals by exhausting them.
   B may have evolved big brains for running.
   C competed with other animals for food.
   D could probably run before they could walk.

PAPER 1 Reading ▶
PAPER 2 Writing
PAPER 3 English in Use
PAPER 4 Listening
PAPER 5 Speaking

Part 1
Part 2
Part 3
Part 4

Answer questions **28–43** by referring to the newspaper article on pages **131–132**, in which people talk about setting up their own businesses late in life.

Indicate your answers **on the separate answer sheet**

For questions **28–43**, answer by choosing from the sections of the article **A–F**. Some of the choices may be required more than once.

Note: When more than one answer is required, these may be given **in any order**.

In which section of the article are the following mentioned?

the unexpected demands of the business	28 ....
a cautious approach to doing business	29 .... 30 ....
an established network of business contacts	31 ....
a prejudicial assessment of a person's value	32 ....
taking advantage of modern communications	33 ....
realising an ambition	34 ....
the cost of setting up a business	35 .... 36 ....
the confidence that comes with maturity	37 ....
plans to branch out	38 ....
a product that aims to help people fill in official forms	39 ....
the fact that few companies cater for a certain group of people	40 ....
the advantage of employing older people	41 ....
the competitive nature of a business	42 ....
self-imposed limits on growth	43 ....

STARTING OVER

*More and more people over fifty
are starting up in business for themselves.
What are their reasons – and why are so
many of them successful?*

A When I was fifty-three, I was made redundant almost literally overnight when the company I worked for was taken over by a multinational. The managing director called me into his office the following Monday and told me I was no longer on the payroll. It was a shock and I felt really depressed. I was also anxious about the future because we still had a mortgage to pay off on our house, and my husband's income couldn't cover our hefty monthly expenses. At the same time, I didn't feel I was ready for retirement, and to be honest, I was infuriated by the arrogance of the company, which appeared to believe I was too old to be useful any longer. So I gave some serious thought to starting up a business of my own. I'm an accountant, and for years I'd been advising friends about finances and helping them sort out their books, so I knew there were plenty of small businesses out there who would welcome the sort of services I could offer. The initial outlay for office equipment was pretty low, all things considered. So I set up as a consultant to people who want to branch out on their own, like me, and I find it extremely rewarding.

B About seven years ago, after being more or less forced to take early retirement, I looked around for an occupation to fill up my days and eventually decided I'd set up a company specialising in all-inclusive trips for retired people to domestic UK resorts. There seemed to be a dearth of companies catering for the over sixties, which is ironic because they're the ones who often have the leisure and the income to take advantage of opportunities for travel. I'd say someone like me has certain advantages when it comes to setting up in business. I spent years running a travel agency and I know a lot of people in the industry. They have been great, offering advice as well as concrete help. At first, there was a lot of work involved and I had to travel around the country a great deal making new contacts, but now I don't have to be away from home very often at all. I enjoy what I do, especially because I've always worked with people, and without the daily contact I'd go mad!

C Three years ago I decided I'd had enough of being a teacher, so I retired and started a pottery business. Now we've got a fair-sized factory, and we're about to expand into glassware as well. Most of the people who work for me are more or less my generation. I find they tend to be more loyal; they don't rush off if they think they can see a better prospect elsewhere. It's also good for the economy when some of these older workers return to employment. It seems to me that people who start up businesses at my age are realistic: they don't aim to be millionaires, and they are less inclined to take unnecessary risks. So I'd guess that fewer businesses started by older people go bust in the first few years. As for me, I must admit I miss teaching at times, but we now have a few apprentices, and working with them is rather like being a teacher in some ways. Of course, running a business is a responsibility, especially since I know the people who work for me rely on the income from their jobs, but it's also a very stimulating, challenging experience.

D When I left the company I'd been with for twenty-five years, they gave me a rather good retirement package, which meant I had a reasonable amount of cash to invest in my own company. It was something I'd longed to do for years. I've always been a keen gardener, you see, so I started a landscape gardening company. All the physical work involved means I'm fitter than I have been for years! One thing that did surprise me at the start was how much official paperwork I have to deal with. It's exhausting filling in all those forms, but apart from that, I find the work itself rewarding. As for the future, who knows? Obviously, I wouldn't want to be travelling around the country and working outdoors as much when I'm over seventy, although on the other hand, I firmly believe that working has kept me active and alert, so why should I give it up until I really have to?

E My career was in accounting, and I knew that there was shortly going to be a change in the way self-employed people fill in tax returns. So when I was made redundant, I thought it would be a good idea to produce software showing people exactly how to go about it, and that was the first item my company put on the market. With my experience it was relatively easy to come up with the material – I wrote it all myself – and then I got together with a software producer to make the CD-ROMs. My wife's first reaction was that I should try something completely different from what I'd been doing all my working life, but I figured I'd be better off sticking to what I know. Things are going well, although I've deliberately not tried to expand the business – it can be stressful for a boss when a company expands fast, and I prefer to take things easy and enjoy what I do. Of course, there have been some tricky moments, but I can honestly say I've never regretted starting my own firm. I'm sure I wouldn't have had the nerve to do it when I was younger, but I'm very glad I did.

F I was in advertising for almost thirty years, but it's a very cut-throat business, and when we got a new boss he decided to make his mark by sacking quite a few people. It was particularly painful for me because I love advertising; it's a very creative line of work. So once I got my breath back, I decided to start working freelance. It occurred to me that a lot of companies need not only an advertising campaign but also a consultant, an independent expert to give them an honest view of their situation. I do almost all my work from home, using my PC for e-mails and video conferencing, and it's extremely satisfying as well as being financially rewarding. I believe older entrepreneurs like us play a vital though unsung role in the economy because we're not only generating money, we're also saving the country money by not claiming our pensions. Since I started my company, I've come into contact with a fair number of people in a similar position to me – older people who have set up by themselves – and if I have the choice, I prefer to do business with older people. We're so much more reliable!

PAPER 1 Reading

PAPER 2 Writing ▶ | Part 1 | Part 2

PAPER 3 English in Use

PAPER 4 Listening

PAPER 5 Speaking

1 You have recently received a letter from a friend who wants to go to Britain to improve his/her English. Read the extract from the letter and an advertisement your friend has sent you for a study holiday in Britain, on which you have made some notes. Then, **using the information carefully**, write a **letter** to your friend.

> You've studied English and you know a lot about Britain, so could you tell me what you think of the Kingland School programme? I need to improve my English – you know I'm taking an important exam next year – but I'd also like to get some experience of British life and culture, and to practise conversational English. I hope I can learn about typical British sports, too! And of course, I'd like to enjoy myself: go to some concerts and films, and so on. I'd like to write to Kingland School for more information. What should I ask them?

KINGLAND SCHOOL STUDY HOLIDAYS IN BRITAIN

Come and learn English in one of the most exciting cities in the world!

Kingland School has many years' experience in organising summer study holidays for students wishing to improve their English and enjoy life in Britain at the same time.

By train? Exact location? →

Located just half an hour from London, Kingland School provides simple but comfortable accommodation for students.

← *With families? Or what?*

What size? What level? →

Classes are small, with a friendly atmosphere, and students have plenty of time to themselves. And of course, there are numerous recreational facilities in the area!

How much? Class hours per week? →

What sort? Sports? Cinema? Music?

For full details, contact us at:
Kingland School

Now write a **letter** to your friend, giving your views on the suitability of the study holiday he/she is considering and suggesting what further information he/she should request before making a final decision (approximately 250 words). You should use your own words as far as possible. You do not need to include postal addresses.

Choose one of the following writing tasks. Your answer should follow exactly the instructions given. Write approximately 250 words.

2 You see the following announcement in a magazine called *Education World*:

> ### What sort of secondary education do young people really need?
>
> Is it better to specialise at an early age with a view to becoming an expert in one field, or should young people have as broad an education as possible? What do employers want from someone they hire?
>
> Send us an article expressing your views and the reasoning behind them.

Write your **article**.

3 You have seen the following advertisement in an in-flight magazine:

> ### Competition
>
> We are bombarded on all sides by information: from TV and radio, the Internet and mobile phones, newspapers and magazines. Are we in danger of suffering information overload? Is there a danger that people will switch off completely and not want to know anything about the world around them?
>
> Write and tell us your views. We will publish the best entry.

Write your **competition entry**.

4 The tourist board of your country is planning to publish a travel guide aimed at young visitors from abroad. You have been asked to write a short contribution describing the attractions and popular features of your region that young people aged 16–25 might find particularly interesting.

Write your **contribution** for the travel guide.

5 You see this announcement on your company notice board:

> In order to increase local awareness of the company and its activities, we are planning to sponsor a cultural event, preferably with a traditional flavour. If you have any ideas to put forward, send us a proposal including:
> • a description of the event in question
> • an explanation of why it is a suitable event for the company to sponsor
> • suggestions as to how we could publicise our involvement (in the local media etc.)

Write your **proposal**.

PAPER 1 Reading

PAPER 2 Writing

PAPER 3 English in Use ▶ Part 1

PAPER 4 Listening   Part 2

PAPER 5 Speaking   Part 3
                            Part 4
                            Part 5
                            Part 6

For questions **1–15**, read the text below and then decide which answer best fits each space. Put the letter you choose for each question in the correct box on your answer sheet. The exercise begins with an example (**0**).

Example:

0	C	0

A new look at the Middle Ages

The Institute for Medieval Studies is holding a series of lectures to (**0**) ...... interest in a period of history which is all too often (**1**) .... It is hoped that these lectures will (**2**) ...... some of the misconceptions that (**3**) ...... to this day about the long and eventful span of time between the crowning of Charlemagne and the Renaissance.

It is true that Europe was (**4**) ...... by the plague in the latter part of the fourteenth century, while the terrors of the Inquisition cast a grim (**5**) ...... over the continent. Living (**6**) ...... for the majority of people were appalling by modern standards, and life (**7**) ...... was low. The peasants suffered under a brutal feudal system and the (**8**) ...... of learning was open only to the clergy and the small minority who were literate.

However, these (**9**) ...... negative aspects of medieval life cannot be properly evaluated unless they are viewed in the broader (**10**) .... The Middle Ages saw the construction of the magnificent cathedrals that (**11**) ...... so many European cities and the (**12**) ...... of a middle class. Many institutions we think of as modern were a(n) (**13**) ...... part of medieval life. Progress was being made in science and technology, and artists were (**14**) ...... styles that had a powerful and (**15**) ...... influence on subsequent centuries.

0	**A** define	**B** adopt	**C** generate	**D** cause
1	**A** neglected	**B** abandoned	**C** subdued	**D** deserted
2	**A** respond	**B** refuse	**C** rectify	**D** revive
3	**A** insist	**B** persist	**C** consist	**D** desist
4	**A** injured	**B** eliminated	**C** wounded	**D** ravaged
5	**A** shade	**B** shadow	**C** eclipse	**D** twilight
6	**A** states	**B** circumstances	**C** conditions	**D** situations
7	**A** estimate	**B** forecast	**C** prediction	**D** expectancy
8	**A** pursuit	**B** chase	**C** desire	**D** quest
9	**A** comprehensively	**B** admittedly	**C** dubiously	**D** potentially
10	**A** background	**B** setting	**C** context	**D** environment
11	**A** grace	**B** delight	**C** decorate	**D** illuminate
12	**A** debut	**B** invention	**C** introduction	**D** rise
13	**A** total	**B** entire	**C** seamless	**D** integral
14	**A** etching	**B** welding	**C** forging	**D** carving
15	**A** maintaining	**B** enduring	**C** remaining	**D** sustaining

For questions **16–30**, complete the following article by writing each missing word in the correct box on your answer sheet. **Use only one word for each space.** The exercise begins with an example (**0**).

Example:

0	*can*	0

Speed limit

A recent proposal to limit the speed cars (**0**) .... reach is proving controversial. The idea, put (**16**) .... by the Institute for Road Safety, involves fitting vehicles with a communications box containing a digital map of the road network. (**17**) .... a car is in motion, the communications box – which knows (**18**) .... fast the vehicle is legally permitted to travel on a particular section of road – automatically regulates the car's speed. (**19**) .... therefore becomes impossible for a vehicle fitted with (**20**) .... a device to exceed the speed limit.

There are plans (**21**) .... charge motorists to drive into the centre of major cities, and a communications box could be used to identify vehicles that enter this zone. At present, (**22**) .... time a vehicle does so, its number plate is photographed. (**23**) .... the number is compared against a list of authorised vehicles, but this system is costly and (**24**) .... from foolproof.

The system (**25**) .... be put in place quickly if the government wished as part (**26**) .... the technology has already been developed for another purpose. Electronic vehicle identification is unpopular with some people, who regard it (**27**) .... an infringement of their rights. (**28**) .... would certainly object to the plan to restrict the speed of their cars, (**29**) .... may make the government hesitate to go through with it. But by forcing drivers to slow (**30**) .... , the scheme would save lives, and this is likely to be popular with the general public.

In most lines of the following text, there is one unnecessary word. It is **either** grammatically incorrect **or** does not fit in with the sense of the text. For each numbered line **31–46**, find the unnecessary word and then write it in the box on your answer sheet. Some lines are correct. Indicate these lines with a (✓) in the box. The exercise begins with two examples (**0**) and (**00**).

Example:

0	✓	▭ 0 ▭
00	*they*	▭ 00 ▭

More Only Children

0	A recent survey of families in Britain has established not only that
00	the birth rate is declining steadily but also that families they are
31	getting smaller. More people are limiting themselves down to one
32	child than was the same case just a generation ago. It is not entirely
33	clear what has made this change to come about. There is, though,
34	some evidence to suggest that more women are unwilling to take
35	more than a year or so off work, in particularly those with successful
36	careers. In an addition, a significant number of women prefer to
37	delay having children until they feel secure in the professions they
38	have chosen. This may then mean they have been left it too late to
39	have more than one child. Whatever are the reasons, the tendency to
40	have smaller families is evident all throughout the country. Ann
41	Winters, is a lecturer in demographics at Winchester University,
42	feels the government should make it easier for mothers. 'Many
43	women would very much like to have had at least two children, but
44	they simply can't. Their careers don't give them enough of time.
45	And it just isn't possible to combine together work and children.
46	So women have to make a choice that is fundamentally unfair.

PAPER 1 Reading

PAPER 2 Writing

PAPER 3 English in Use ▶ | Part 1 | Part 2 | Part 3 | **Part 4** | Part 5 | Part 6

PAPER 4 Listening

PAPER 5 Speaking

For questions **47–61**, read the two texts below. Use the words in the boxes to the right of the texts to form one word that fits in the same numbered space in the text. Write the new word in the correct box on your answer sheet. The exercise begins with an example (**0**).

Example:

| 0 | *fashionable* | 0 __ __ |

RESTAURANT REVIEW

> ## Speak Easy
>
> The owner of the most (**0**) .... restaurant in town, Speak Easy in Brook Street, has (**47**) .... recreated the mood of an American diner from the 1950s. It's all there, from the neon sign outside in a garish and rather (**48**) .... shade of pink, stretching across the entire (**49**) .... of the building, to the authentic 1950s records on the juke box. Nothing has been (**50**) .... in this fond homage to the America of days gone by. The food is far healthier than the surroundings might suggest, however, with (**51**) .... fresh vegetables and salads, meals that are not in the fast food spirit, despite the (**52**) .... Definitely a place for (**53**) .... youngsters who prize atmosphere.

(0)	**FASHION**
(47)	FAITH
(48)	REVOLT
(49)	WIDE
(50)	LOOK
(51)	WHOLE
(52)	SET
(53)	AGE

EXTRACT FROM BOOK

> ### Video Recorders
>
> The (**54**) .... of home video recorders is so great that it can hardly be exaggerated. While there have been other changes in the way we watch television, the advent of the video recorder caused a fundamental shift in the (**55**) .... between viewers and televising schedules. For many (**56**) .... , life without a video recorder is (**57**) .... Until the 1980s, if you wanted to watch a television programme, you had to be at home – or engage in delicate (**58**) .... with friends so you could watch it on their set. If you missed some (**59**) .... , there was nothing you could do about it. But then along came video recorders, which made television programmes more (**60**) .... than films showing at the cinema. However, they also signalled the end of a common TV culture, beginning the (**61**) .... of television viewing that has continued with satellite TV.

(54)	IMPORTANT
(55)	RELATE
(56)	ADOLESCENCE
(57)	IMAGINE
(58)	NEGOTIATE
(59)	MASTER
(60)	ACCESS
(61)	FRAGMENT

PAPER 1 Reading

PAPER 2 Writing

PAPER 3 English in Use ▶
- Part 1
- Part 2
- Part 3
- Part 4
- **Part 5**
- Part 6

PAPER 4 Listening

PAPER 5 Speaking

For questions **62–74**, read the notes for a leaflet for first-year students at a college. Use the information in the notes to complete the numbered gaps in the formal leaflet. The words you need **do not occur** in the memo. **Use no more than two words for each gap**. The exercise begins with an example (**0**).

Example:

| 0 | *daily* | 0 |

NOTES

Pete,

Please write up these notes so we can print leaflets for new students. Thanks!

- Gates open 8 am to 10 pm every day; otherwise get in through porter's lodge (only those with student ID cards allowed in after hours).

- Eating isn't allowed in computer lab. If students have problems logging on to Internet, they must let supervisor know. Check with an assistant before trying to print off documents.

- Students need library card to take out books (go to librarian's office to get one).

- Very few spaces in car park for students. It costs £120 a year for a space.

- Students who eat at canteen three times a week or more can get catering card – it costs less to eat there if you have one. Students on a special diet should tell the canteen people.

LEAFLET

College Building: The college is open from 8.00 to 22.00 (**0**) .... At other times (**62**) .... is via the porter's lodge, but is (**63**) .... to holders of student identity cards.

Computer Lab: It is strictly (**64**) .... consume food in the lab. Please (**65**) .... the supervisor if you experience difficulties connecting to the Internet. Always (**66**) .... an assistant before you (**67**) .... to print documents.

Library: Students cannot (**68**) .... books without a library card. This can be (**69**) .... from the librarian's office.

Car Park: There is only a limited (**70**) .... spaces available for students. The (**71**) .... for reserving a space is £120 a year.

Canteen: Students who use the canteen (**72**) .... three times a week are (**73**) .... to a catering card. The canteen's prices are lower for card holders. Students with particular dietary (**74**) .... should report to the chief caterer.

TEST 6 CAE

Exam Essentials

PAPER 1 Reading

PAPER 2 Writing

PAPER 3 English in Use ▸

PAPER 4 Listening

PAPER 5 Speaking

Part 1
Part 2
Part 3
Part 4
Part 5
Part 6

For questions **75–80**, read the following text and then choose from the list **A–J** given below the best phrase to fill each of the spaces. Write one letter (**A–J**) in the correct box on your answer sheet. Each correct phrase may only be used once. **Some of the suggested answers do not fit at all**. The exercise begins with an example (**0**).

Example:

0	J	0

PEDAL POWER

If you are trying to get around central London when the traffic is bad and you can't find a taxi, (**0**) ...... : pedal-powered rickshaws are becoming increasingly popular in the capital. In fact, (**75**) ...... , though there is no official licensing procedure for these diminutive vehicles, so precise numbers are not available. And this is exactly the problem, it is claimed by residents' associations and taxi drivers. Since rickshaws are not subject to the same regulations as other vehicles, (**76**) .... Consequently, the areas around popular tourist sights are sometimes packed with stationary pedicabs, as the rickshaws are also known. And (**77**) ...... , as no specific law is being broken.

On the other hand, (**78**) ...... , which naturally get stuck in traffic jams like any other motor vehicle. And unlike traditional London cabs, pedal-powered rickshaws cause no pollution whatsoever. Many tourists like them because they are an amusing, unusual way to get around. But are they potentially dangerous? Well, (**79**) .... Some taxi drivers claim the three-wheeled vehicles are inherently unstable and may tip over if the driver takes a corner too quickly. Rickshaw drivers insist that they drive almost exclusively in the narrow streets of the city centre, where (**80**) .... There has as yet been no serious accident involving a pedicab, but the government is considering some form of regulation just to be on the safe side.

A it could hardly be any different in this context

B it is difficult for traffic police to do anything about them

C it never seems to cause too much inconvenience

D it is estimated that 350 of them now cruise the streets

E it very much depends who you talk to

F it annoys pedestrians as much as motorists

G it is clear that there is a need for an alternative to taxis

H it is impossible to gain enough speed for this to be a problem

I it is not clear whether they are subject to parking restrictions

J it is tempting to try an alternative

You will hear an archaeologist talking about an experience he had in South America. For questions **1–8**, complete the sentences.

You will hear the recording twice.

An Unpleasant Adventure

The archaeologist's original task was to [_____ 1] the ruined city and the area around it.

He was then asked to suggest ways to [_____ 2]

It appears that the [_____ 3] air exhaled by visitors is damaging the walls.

The archaeologist wanted to survey a tomb near the site of a proposed [_____ 4]

Unfortunately, the tomb had been damaged by flood water from [_____ 5]

The archaeologist lost his footing on some [_____ 6]

As he fell, he broke his [_____ 7]

He was found when a [_____ 8] heard his shouts for help.

You will hear a talk on the subject of salt. For questions **9–16**, complete the sentences.

Listen very carefully as you will hear the recording ONCE only.

Salt of the Earth

Salt had a vital role to play in the development of

| | **9** |

In the past salt was as precious as | | **10** |

Today most of the salt we consume comes from

| | **11** |

Salt retains water, which is one reason why

| | **12** | adds it to many foods.

Too much salt in the diet can lead to high | | **13** |

People who suffer from hypertension risk having

| | **14** | or strokes.

A | | **15** | of the population

could lower their blood pressure if they consumed less salt.

Salt manufacturers in the UK sell more salt for use on

| | **16** | than in foods.

PAPER 1 Reading

PAPER 2 Writing

PAPER 3 English in Use

PAPER 4 Listening ▶

PAPER 5 Speaking

Part 1
Part 2
Part 3
Part 4

You will hear part of an interview with Professor Hector Williams, a linguist. For questions **17–22**, choose the correct answer **A**, **B**, **C** or **D**.

You will hear the recording twice.

17 What was the assumption behind medieval interest in an artificial language?
   A It would be easy to learn a logical language.
   B The language would be more suited to classification.
   C The universe was constructed on linguistic principles.
   D The language would be a key to understanding the universe.

18 The artificial language based on the names of the notes in the scale
   A had a vocabulary of single-syllable words.
   B could be understood by people in the west.
   C simplified the task of reading music.
   D was intended to be easy to learn and understand.

19 How did Professor Williams feel when he first heard Esperanto spoken?
   A He thought it was a dialect of Italian.
   B He felt it had a pleasant sound.
   C He considered it was successful in its aims.
   D He wanted to know the logic behind it.

20 According to Professor Williams, what is the main objection to an artificial language?
   A It is not very expressive.
   B It cannot be used to talk about the past.
   C It does not have any native speakers.
   D It has a limited vocabulary.

21 What characteristic of Esperanto speakers does Professor Williams find most striking?
   A their optimism
   B their naivety
   C their dedication
   D their elitism

22 Professor Williams considers that no artificial language will ever become universal because
   A the language instinct is fundamental in all human beings.
   B identity and language are strongly linked for most people.
   C it is impossible to invent a completely artificial language.
   D too few people would ever consider learning one.

You will hear five short extracts in which different people talk about the Internet.

You will hear the recording twice. While you listen you must complete both tasks.

Task One

For questions **23–27**, match the extracts with what each person says about starting to use the Internet, listed **A–H**.

A I first used it when I needed some historical information.

B I was obliged to start using it in my job.

C I first began using it for academic purposes.

D I wanted to buy books online.

E I first learnt to use it for recreation.

F I was put off by my initial experiences of using it.

G The commercial potential attracted me in the first place.

H I've always taken it for granted.

Speaker 1	23
Speaker 2	24
Speaker 3	25
Speaker 4	26
Speaker 5	27

Task Two

For questions **28–32**, match the extracts with the views each speaker expresses about the influence of the Internet, listed **A–H**.

A It is a source of information about current affairs.

B It threatens the security of our society.

C Lack of access to the Internet can perpetuate inequalities.

D Online games will come to dominate the leisure industry.

E Our reading habits will be transformed.

F Standards of literacy will decline still further.

G It may one day replace interpersonal communication.

H There are considerable temptations attached.

Speaker 1	28
Speaker 2	29
Speaker 3	30
Speaker 4	31
Speaker 5	32

Part 1 (3 minutes)

The examiner will ask you a few questions about yourself and then ask you to talk to your partner. For example, the examiner may ask you:

* What means of transport did you use to get here today?
* What sort of public transport is available in this area?
* Which forms of transport do you prefer, and which do you dislike?

Part 2 (4 minutes)

You will each be asked to talk for a minute without interruption. You will each be given a set of photographs in turn to talk about. After your partner has finished speaking, you will be asked a brief question connected with your partner's photographs.

Anxiety (compare, contrast and speculate)

Turn to pictures 1–4 on page **207**, which show people feeling anxious.

Candidate A, compare and contrast these pictures and imagine what these people could be thinking about that is making them anxious.

Candidate B, what sort of thing do you find most worrying?

Achievement (compare, contrast and speculate)

Turn to pictures 1–4 on page **208**, which show people who have achieved something.

Candidate B, compare and contrast these situations, saying how you think the people might be feeling.

Candidate A, in what situations do you find a sense of achievement most satisfying?

Part 3 (4 minutes)

Appearance (discuss, evaluate and select)

Turn to the pictures on page **209**, which show examples of the outward appearance people present to the world.

Talk to each other about what each person is expressing by his or her appearance, and then decide which two pictures you would choose to demonstrate the wide variety of messages that appearance can give out.

Part 4 (4 minutes)

The examiner will encourage you to develop the topic of your discussion in Part 3 by asking questions such as:

* In what sort of situations do you think someone's appearance is most important?
* Do you think it is possible to ignore fashion? Why (not)?
* To what extent do you judge a person by his or her appearance?
* How important is appearance to someone who cares what other people think of them?

Answer questions **1–14** by referring to the magazine article about taking part in marathon races on page **147**.

Indicate your answers **on the separate answer sheet**.

For questions **1–14**, answer by choosing from the sections of the article (**A–D**). Some of the choices may be required more than once.

In which section of the article are the following mentioned?

the place of someone's permanent residence	**1** ....
a river that flows through a city	**2** ....
the festive atmosphere in a certain city	**3** ....
a dislike of travelling somewhere with no particular aim	**4** ....
a more economical way to organise a trip	**5** ....
the fear of being forced to abandon a race	**6** ....
combining work and pleasure	**7** ....
stretches of a course that involve running uphill	**8** ....
a means of expressing gratitude	**9** ....
the worry that one might arrive late	**10** ....
the result of following medical advice	**11** ....
taking precautions in case of accidents	**12** ....
an affinity for a type of music	**13** ....
the opinion that running a marathon is a fundamentally irrational activity	**14** ....

Running for Fun

Four marathon runners explain what makes their sport so attractive

A I would say running has become an important part of my life. More and more people take it up every year, and part of its appeal has to do with the fact that it requires very little in the way of gear or equipment. I particularly enjoy running in marathons and whenever I can, I plan trips to places where I can take part in a race while my family can quite simply have a fabulous holiday. After months of the gruelling and solitary training necessary to run 26.2 miles, I can finally compensate my nearest and dearest for all those Sundays I went missing for the better part of the day.

I recently ran the marathon in Berlin, which hosts one of the world's best marathons. My family loved it. The city is of huge historical interest, and my son is studying history at university. My wife loves jazz, and since the 1930s Berlin has had a thriving jazz scene, featuring everything from Dixieland to the most modern, free-form music you can imagine. I would recommend a trip to Berlin for the marathon to any serious runner. One tip: it makes sense to plan a trip like this well in advance since important marathons frequently have arrangements with airlines and hotels for special rates.

B I've always liked travelling, especially when there's a point to it, so a long weekend away with a marathon in the middle is a great idea. You turn up in a fascinating city, relieved you are not there to wander aimlessly and get bored; you're there to run in the streets – the best way to get a feel for a place. Over the past four years my husband and I have made a lot of trips like this. It all started when I became interested in running the marathon in London, our home town, after a back injury. My physiotherapist suggested some regular exercise, so I took up jogging and soon became very keen on running.

So far we've been to eight cities around the world to run the marathon. Two years ago we went to northern California, saw the world from the Golden Gate Bridge in San Francisco and ran the Big Sur International Marathon in Monterey. I think that has been my favourite event so far. There are stunning views of the Pacific Ocean – in fact, part of the course takes you along the ocean, so close that you can practically hear the surf – though it's a difficult course. There are some steep gradients, which means that runners who keep track of their times should expect to take considerably longer for this event than their average. But we had an unforgettable holiday and ran a great marathon as well.

C I have to see clients abroad as part of my job, but fortunately, my schedule of visits is pretty flexible, and I often manage to arrange business trips so that my stay in a city coincides with a marathon. Last year I was able to do that four times!

The marathon I enjoy most is the London Marathon, and I like to make sure I have reasons for being in London around the time when it takes place. It has become one of the biggest events in the world, and in purely physical terms it is not too gruelling. London has a real carnival atmosphere for the marathon, and I love the feeling of participating in something so exciting. People seem glad to see you there.

My advice to anyone visiting London for the marathon would be to get to the city a few days in advance, because London traffic is notorious, and you will need more time than you might normally allow if you want to examine the route. Of course, there's so much to do in London that you might want to stick around for a few days afterwards and take in the sights. I'd also suggest that you check your insurance before each event to make sure you're covered in case of mishaps. Naturally, you never think anything will happen to you – but it can!

D About two years ago I was persuaded by my girlfriend to go to Paris with her so she could run the marathon. At least, that was the idea initially. But then I started wondering if I could run the marathon with her, so I began a fairly intensive training programme. Luckily, I was already fairly fit, and it wasn't too hard for me to prepare for the race. It was an amazing experience. The planners who designed the course appear to have made sure it goes past every major sight in the city, including the Arc de Triomphe and the Louvre. The second half of the route also takes you past Notre Dame and the Eiffel Tower, along the banks of the Seine – it's hard to concentrate on running when you have such magnificent distractions!

Three-quarters of the way through the marathon, I started to get tired and I was rather dubious about completing it. But then I reminded myself that there wasn't much further to go, and the thought of finishing gave me an extra spurt of energy. I've decided that the appealing thing about running a marathon is that it's basically an illogical thing to do, but you share it with literally thousands of other people, and you are cheered on by enthusiastic spectators. As far as the practicalities are concerned, we discovered how important it is to find a hotel near the start line. That eliminates race-day nerves about getting there on time.

PAPER 1 Reading	▶	Part 1
PAPER 2 Writing		**Part 2**
PAPER 3 English in Use		Part 3
		Part 4
PAPER 4 Listening		
PAPER 5 Speaking		

For questions **15–20**, choose which of the paragraphs **A–G** on page **149** fit into the numbered gaps in the following magazine article. There is one extra paragraph which does not fit into any of the gaps.

Indicate your answers **on the separate answer sheet**.

All This Jazz

What makes someone give up a stable career for the uncertainty of playing the saxophone in a jazz band? Walter Williams finds out.

Marjorie Anderson is terrified. We're sitting backstage in a small theatre that constitutes one of the few amenities the tiny French town of Villeneuf can boast of. In a few minutes she will walk on stage with the jazz band she plays with, Les Jazzistes. They have been together for two years now, slowly but steadily building up a loyal following, and there is little doubt that tonight's gig will be a success. An enviable position to be in, especially for someone who, like Marjorie, has managed to make a living in a notoriously precarious profession, and in a foreign country to boot.

15

Marjorie lives in France and does little else other than play the sax professionally. She has a distinctive technique, honed to perfection by hours of practice and, some would claim, plays with added passion by virtue of the fact that she has made huge sacrifices in order to devote herself to jazz. In addition to being a fine musician, she's a vet by training: an extraordinary combination.

16

She grew up in Sydney and was something of a child prodigy – as a flautist. She studied with a distinguished teacher and played with a youth orchestra, but then she abruptly decided that music was not for her. What happened? 'I auditioned for a prestigious orchestra, but nothing came of it.' Her sense of rejection at the time was overwhelming, but perhaps her failure was due to her attitude. 'I was abrasive

in the interview,' Marjorie admits. 'I was very thin-skinned in those days. I felt threatened every time someone commented on my playing or my technique.'

17

However, it emerged a decade later that contentment of this sort was not what Marjorie really yearned for. Her brother treated her to a week in Paris for her thirty-fifth birthday, and on the final evening they went to a club whose lively jazz scene has been attracting a demanding clientele for over seventy years. The effect on Marjorie was immediate; it was as if she was hearing music for the first time.

18

'I moved here because it hit me that for thirty-five years, I had never been in touch with my inner self, with my needs and desires,' she told me. 'Oddly enough, I didn't consider taking up the flute again. It was the saxophone that grabbed my attention. It was so much more expressive in terms of my own essential being.'

19

I ask her if she has any regrets about dropping out to follow her dreams. She says no, but that she feels a bit guilty. 'I realise playing the sax in a band isn't saving the world. Sometimes I feel I ought to be doing something more useful.'

20

There seems a good chance that her latest project will provide what's missing. Marjorie has decided to reinvent herself yet again – as a writer this time. She has just finished her autobiography, entitled *Why Not Try It*? It's a question many readers, envious of her courage, will find uncomfortable.

A Yet she is clutching her saxophone like a petrified child. 'I'm scared of the audience,' she says. 'You've got to be kidding,' I tell her. 'No,' she says with a snort. 'I freeze up when I look at them.' With a slightly shamefaced expression she reaches for her sunglasses. Wearing them throughout her appearance in front of this small crowd – maybe 250 people – is one of the methods she uses to control her nerves.

B Marjorie works hard, but being a musician, even a respected one, leaves her little opportunity to feed her brain in other ways. She's frustrated that her French isn't good enough to allow her to communicate at a depth she's accustomed to. And sitting around her tiny apartment reading books only goes a small way towards intellectual fulfilment.

C Marjorie refused to let such a minor problem daunt her. Soon she was playing music again, this time with renewed determination to be one of the best sax players in the world. Then, without any warning, she developed a fear of performing in public that nearly paralysed her the first time it struck. It was time to take action.

D 'I thought I'd gone to heaven,' she says. 'It was a turning point. The experience told me I had to play more music, hear more music and really live before it was too late.' This was the moment when she decided to make a radical change in her life.

E As if this weren't unusual enough, five years ago, seemingly on a whim, she suddenly decided to sell her thriving veterinary practice in Australia and moved to Villeneuf – without knowing a single word of French or how long she might stay. What would make someone abandon her entire life and take up playing music with a bunch of amateurs at the age of thirty-five?

F Her new-found stagefright was the other curious factor about this return to public performance. Marjorie believes her terror is related to the sense that she is baring her soul when she performs. 'The other thing I do to make myself less scared is stand completely still on stage,' she explains. 'Paradoxically enough, this seems to get me more attention!'

G So she went to college instead, and trained as a vet. She threw herself into her profession, channelling her energy into building up a practice. 'I became stronger psychologically because I was successful in my career,' she says. 'I see it as a positive thing. I was satisfied with my life.'

PAPER 1	Reading	▶	Part 1
PAPER 2	Writing		Part 2
PAPER 3	English in Use		Part 3
PAPER 4	Listening		Part 4
PAPER 5	Speaking		

Read the following magazine article and answer questions **21–25** on page **151**. On your answer sheet, indicate the letter **A**, **B**, **C** or **D** against the number of each question. Give only one answer to each question.

Indicate your answers **on the separate answer sheet**.

Saving the Big Birds

At first glance, why anyone would want to save California condors is not entirely clear. Unlike the closely related Andean condors with their white neck fluff or king vultures with their brilliant black-and-white colouring, California condors are not much to see. Their dull black colour – even when contrasted with white underwings – featherless head and neck, oversized feet and blunt talons are hardly signs of beauty or strength. Their appeal begins to become evident when they take flight. With nine-and-a-half-foot wingspans and weights up to twenty-eight pounds, California condors are North America's largest fully flighted birds. In the Americas, only Andean condors are bigger. California condors can soar almost effortlessly for hours, often covering hundreds of miles a day – far more than other creatures of the air. Only occasionally do they need to flap their wings – to take off, change direction or find a band of warm air known as a thermal to carry them higher.

When it was discovered that the condor population was becoming dangerously small, scientists and zookeepers sought to increase condor numbers quickly to preserve as much of the species' genetic diversity as possible. From studying wild condors, they already knew that if a pair lost an egg, the birds would often produce another. So the first and sometimes second eggs laid by each female in captivity were removed, artificially incubated, and the chicks raised using hand-held puppets made to look like adult condors. Such techniques quickly proved effective.

Despite these successes, the effort to save California condors continues to have problems, evoke criticisms and generate controversy. Captive-hatched condors released to the wild have died at what to some people are alarmingly high rates. Others have had to be recaptured after they acted foolishly or became ill. As a result, the scientists, zookeepers and conservationists who are concerned about condors have bickered among themselves over the best ways to rear and release the birds.

Some of the odd behaviour on the part of these re-released birds is hard to explain. At times they landed on people's houses and garages, walked across roads and airport runways, sauntered into park visitor centres and fast food restaurants, and took food offered by picnickers and fishermen. None are known to have died by doing so, though. More seriously, one condor died from drinking what was probably antifreeze. Others died in collisions with overhead electrical transmission wires, drowned in natural pools of water, or were killed by golden eagles and coyotes. Still others were shot by hunters and killed or made seriously ill from lead poisoning. Some just disappeared. Most recently, some of the first chicks hatched in the wild died after their parents fed them bottle caps, glass shards, pieces of plastic and other man-made objects that fatally perforated or blocked their intestines. These deaths may be due to the chicks' parents mistaking man-made objects for bone chips eaten for their calcium content.

Mike Wallace, a wildlife specialist at the San Diego Zoo, has suggested that some of the condors' problems represent natural behaviour that helps them survive as carrion eaters. The real key to successful condor reintroduction, he believes, lies in properly socialising young condors as members of a group that follow and learn from older, preferably adult birds. That, he argues, was missing from earlier condor releases to the wild. Typically, condors hatched in the spring were released to the wild that autumn or winter, when they were still less than a year old. Especially in the early releases, the young condors had no adults or even older juveniles to learn from and keep them in their place. Instead, the only other condors they saw in captivity and the wild were ones their own age. Now, condor chicks at several zoos are raised in cave-like nest boxes. The chicks can see older condors in a large flight pen outside their box but cannot interact with them until they are about five months old. Then the chicks are gradually released into the pen and the company of the social group. The group includes adult and older juvenile condors that act as mentors for younger ones. It is hoped that this socialisation programme will help the birds adapt to the wild when they are released.

21 According to the writer, the most impressive feature of the California condor is

    A its resemblance to the Andean condor.

    B its ability to glide.

    C its colourful plumage.

    D its blunt talons.

22 In the first stage of the conservation programme,

    A eggs were removed from the nests of wild condors.

    B female condors were captured and studied carefully.

    C scientists and zookeepers tried to create genetic diversity.

    D condors were induced to lay more than one egg.

23 What are we told about the attempts to save these birds from extinction?

    A There is disagreement about the methods employed.

    B The majority of condors released into the wild have died.

    C Attempts to breed condors in captivity have failed.

    D Condors reintroduced into the wild are unable to hunt.

24 Some chicks hatched by condors released into the wild died because

    A they fell into pools of water.

    B they fell prey to other animals.

    C they had odd drinking habits.

    D they swallowed dangerous objects.

25 According to Mike Wallace, there will be fewer problems

    A if young condors are taught not to eat so much carrion.

    B if the chicks are kept in cave-like nest boxes for five months.

    C if young condors are taught appropriate behaviour by older birds.

    D if the chicks are in the company of older birds when they hatch.

Answer questions **26–40** by referring to the magazine article about choosing a camera on pages **153–154**.

Indicate your answers **on the separate answer sheet**.

For questions **26–35**, answer by choosing from the sections of the article **A–D** on page **153**. Some of the choices may be required more than once.

In which sections of the article (A–D) are the following mentioned?

hidden costs   **26** ....

adding data to images   **27** ....

taking pictures from a particular distance   **28** ....

developing technical skills   **29** ....

the compatibility of component parts   **30** ....

the danger that you will not be able to
access your photos   **31** ....

protecting fragile items   **32** ....

a joint venture   **33** ....

the loss of quality that comes with enlargement **34** ....

similar quality for less money   **35** ....

For questions **36–40**, answer by choosing from the sections of the article **E–H** on page **154**. Some of the choices may be required more than once.

Which person (E–H) mentions the following?

taking people unawares   **36** ....

the tendency of some devices to develop faults   **37** ....

the views of others   **38** ....

evaluating one's work   **39** ....

difficulties in obtaining supplies   **40** ....

Buying Your First Camera

With so many different cameras on the market nowadays, how can you choose what to buy? We describe the four main types and ask a group of experts which one they would recommend to a beginner with £400 to spend.

The Cameras

A Compact/Point-and-shoot

These cameras are small and simple, making them ideal for use on holidays or taking snaps when you are out and about. There are no adjustments to be made, no settings to check: you simply aim the camera and press the button. And since they have a built-in flash as well as automatic focus, you get a good, clear image every time you press that button. On the other hand, the flash will probably be of poor quality, with an effective range of only about four metres. This means that even with 400 ASA film (the kind that needs least light), you will be unable to get a reasonable picture of anything further away. Another disadvantage is that the lens is not very good: the image will not be clear if you blow up the picture bigger than 15cm x 21cm. If you buy one of these cameras, it should have red-eye reduction for the flash so that people in your pictures do not have red dots in their eyes. Also, the larger and clearer the viewfinder, the better. Bear in mind that you will not be able to control the settings, so if you want pictures that look at all unusual (by being deliberately out of focus, for example), you won't be able to take them.

B APS

The Advanced Photo System (APS) was launched in 1996 by several manufacturers who established a common standard. Instead of the 35mm film used by compacts and Single Lens Reflex (SLR) cameras, APS cameras use little film cartridges. Consequently, APS cameras can be extremely small. And this isn't the only advantage: you can put your own information on each picture you take, such as the time, day and place where it was taken. The cartridges are easier to insert into the camera than normal film, and you can take one out before it's finished and use it again later. On the other hand, you don't have much choice about the texture of the picture – it has to be gloss, and it more or less has to be colour, since black and white cartridges are hard to find. While APS cameras are new, and some people feel it is best to stick to famous brand names for new technology, remember that – as with most types of camera – these famous names have their cameras made by the same factories that produce cameras for lesser-known brands. These often offer comparable features, build qualities and guarantees for a lower price.

C SLR

Single Lens Reflex (SLR) cameras are the oldest and simplest type of camera discussed here, with a comparatively large body and lenses that screw on to the front. The old-fashioned type had no electronic components at all, though now many SLR cameras have automatic features; one advantage here is that they can be turned off, in contrast to compact cameras. With SLRs you must make sure the lens and body will fit together since they come in different sizes. It is also worth thinking carefully about whether to buy a camera with an automatic focus lens. Naturally, this lets you take photographs quickly, without having to adjust anything yourself, but this is not always the advantage it may seem. Firstly, an automatic focus lens does not always produce the same quality of picture as a manual focus lens. Furthermore, the fact that an automatic focus lens is so easy to use will also encourage you to take far more photographs. So learning how to use a manual focus lens will not only save on film, your camera will work out to be less expensive altogether because manual focus lenses are cheaper – and you will learn how to make all the adjustments yourself, for different types of light etc. Get a camera with a metal body – some are made of plastic – because metal is far more sturdy, and delicate lenses are less likely to come to grief.

D Digital

Digital cameras don't need film: the picture you take is stored on a computer memory card, and then you can delete it, give it to a shop to print or print it on your own computer printer. You can even edit the picture yourself. These new and popular cameras are ideal if you just want to use them for basic holiday and home snaps that you intend to e-mail to others, post on a website or play around with on a computer. However, the lenses are not as good as SLR lenses, except on the most expensive cameras, and storing images can be a problem. You will have to store your photos on your computer, which can quickly get full, and what happens if it breaks down or you decide to get a new one? And though manufacturers stress the saving on film, they may fail to mention that you need expensive memory cards. What's more, some digital cameras use up batteries at an alarming rate. Depending on the printer you normally use, you may need to invest in special paper and ink, too.

The Experts

E I'd say a beginner should go for the best digital camera he or she can afford. You develop as a photographer by taking lots of shots, studying them and throwing away the vast majority; this is how you learn what makes a good picture. Digitals let you do this more easily than any other type, and some have software that enables you to do very sophisticated things on your computer in the way of editing. Plus you can always get normal prints if you want.

F A beginner who wants to become a good amateur, and maybe join an amateur photography club, needs an SLR. The basic technology is fairly old, but it's very reliable, and since they've been making these cameras for years, there are lots of second-hand models on the market. You learn better without the modern electronic gadgetry, which will probably break down in a couple of years anyway. Nobody will take you seriously as a photographer with anything other than an SLR.

G Spend around £400 on a good compact. You can take it everywhere with you and photograph interesting or amusing incidents that simply crop up in everyday life. That's what professionals do. You know you'll get a good picture every time, so you never waste film. Unlike APS and digital cameras, you can use any 35mm film with a compact – a definite advantage when you're in some tiny village where shops only have normal films.

H Get the best APS camera you can – that's my advice. It's tiny, so you can have it in your pocket or handbag and get those special shots without anyone realising they're being captured on film. You have a lot more control over the pictures than with compacts. You can choose the size of the print format, and you can change the print format at a later date.

1 You are a member of the student council at Whitewall College. You recently received a memo from the principal announcing changes to the college library. The student council is opposed to these changes and has produced the leaflet below.

You have offered to write an article for the college newsletter to inform students about the planned changes and to get their support. You have also been asked to reply to the principal's memo, explaining the student council's opposition to the plans.

Read the leaflet and the principal's memo, to which you have added your comments. Then, **using the information carefully**, write the **article** and **letter** as instructed.

Save Our Library!

Do you realise that the college plans ...
- to merge our library with the Technical College library?
- to house both libraries in the Tech College library building?
- to introduce charges for borrowing?

Is this what _you_ want?
The overwhelming majority of people surveyed is opposed to this idea:
- 78% of Whitewall students
- 67% of Technical College students
- 83% of lecturers at both colleges

Let's fight these plans together!
Come to the student council meeting
Date: Friday 24th February
Time: 18.00
Place: Junior Common Room

Memo

To: The Student Council
From: The Principal
Re: Whitehall College Library

We weren't → <u>You will all be aware</u> that we have been reviewing college facilities to find ways of reducing costs, and <u>it has been decided</u> to reform our library facilities. ← *Why no discussion?*

But Tech College has no humanities books! → Since there is <u>considerable overlap</u> between our library and the Technical College library, the two will be merged. The new library will be housed in the present Technical College library building, <u>which will be enlarged in due course</u>. ← *When?*

Will lead to overcrowding! → It has also been decided to levy <u>a small charge</u> for use of the library, which will be <u>open to members of the public</u> as well. ← *How much? Unfair to poor students!*

I am sure you will appreciate the need for these measures.

David Wingard, Principal

Now use this information to write:
- an **article** for the college newspaper (approximately 150 words).
- a **letter** to the principal with your reaction to the plans (approximately 100 words).

You do not need to include postal addresses. You should use your own words as far as possible.

Choose one of the following writing tasks. Your answer should follow exactly the instructions given. Write approximately 250 words.

2 You have seen the following advertisement in a magazine on books:

Long Live Books!

In the not too distant future most books will be available online for people to download and read on their computer screens. Will this mean the end of books as we know them?

Write and tell us why the printed book will never die! The best entry will win a complete set of the novels of Charles Dickens!

Write your **competition entry**.

3 You see the following notice in a magazine called *International Restaurants*:

Do young people care about good food?
Does it matter to youngsters today if food is tasty and made from fresh ingredients – or do they prefer fast food? What could school and college canteens do to encourage an interest in the art of cooking?

Write an article for the magazine giving your views.

Write your **article**.

4 This is an extract from a letter you received from a magazine called *Family Matters*:

We are very interested in finding out how the family is perceived in different parts of the world. Please write a report for us describing the importance of both the nuclear and extended family in your country, and how family relationships might evolve in the foreseeable future.

Write your **report**.

5 You have been asked to write about your company's relevance to the local economy for inclusion in an information leaflet about the company. You should give a brief outline of the structure and character of the company, followed by an account of its place in the local economy in terms of workforce, sales etc. You should also mention any other points that you think are important.

Write the **text** for the leaflet.

For questions **1–15**, read the text below and then decide which answer best fits each space. Put the letter you choose for each question in the correct box on your answer sheet. The exercise begins with an example (**0**).

Example:

0	A	0

Vanilla Surprise

Vanilla is such a(n) (**0**) ...... flavour that it comes as a surprise to learn that it is also one of the world's most expensive spices. The vanilla plant is a(n) (**1**) ...... of the Americas. Its flowers grow in (**2**) ...... , and in nature they are pollinated by hummingbirds and bees. The (**3**) ...... seed pods resemble oversized French beans, and develop their (**4**) ...... flavour and fragrance during the curing process. After harvesting, the beans are (**5**) ...... with heat or hot water and are placed in the sun every day for many weeks. When they have (**6**) ...... to a fifth of their original size, they are (**7**) ...... according to size and quality.

Like other spices that we (**8**) ...... for granted today, vanilla has a fascinating history. In the sixteenth century, the Spanish imported the spice to Europe. However, attempts to grow vanilla in other locations (**9**) ...... with failure: the plants would not produce pods, and it was only when a way was found to pollinate the flowers artificially that the commercial exploitation of this valuable crop (**10**) ...... under way.

Today vanilla is used in the manufacture of perfumes and cosmetics, as well as in the (**11**) ...... arts, where it is often a(n) (**12**) ...... of puddings. Recently, it has also been used in more (**13**) ...... ways. Lobster and vanilla is now a popular (**14**) ...... in certain restaurants – proving that chefs can (**15**) ...... up with amazing ideas to tickle the taste buds.

0	**A** common	**B** expected	**C** usual	**D** normal
1	**A** resident	**B** aborigine	**C** native	**D** inhabitant
2	**A** groups	**B** bouquets	**C** teams	**D** bunches
3	**A** deriving	**B** resulting	**C** producing	**D** arising
4	**A** distinctive	**B** appetising	**C** tasteful	**D** potential
5	**A** processed	**B** passed	**C** treated	**D** immersed
6	**A** reduced	**B** shrunk	**C** diminished	**D** lessened
7	**A** classed	**B** split	**C** divided	**D** sorted
8	**A** consider	**B** do	**C** make	**D** take
9	**A** resulted	**B** ended	**C** met	**D** finished
10	**A** got	**B** went	**C** came	**D** began
11	**A** cooking	**B** culinary	**C** cuisine	**D** kitchen
12	**A** substance	**B** element	**C** additive	**D** ingredient
13	**A** imaginative	**B** fabulous	**C** unimaginable	**D** different
14	**A** portion	**B** plate	**C** dish	**D** platter
15	**A** get	**B** come	**C** make	**D** run

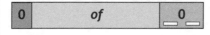
For questions **16–30**, complete the following article by writing each missing word in the correct box on your answer sheet. **Use only one word for each space**. The exercise begins with an example (**0**).

Example:

0	*of*	0

The First Cartoons

The technique of telling a story through a sequence (**0**) .... pictures, though associated with modern cartoons, was (**16**) .... fact in use about 500 years ago. Some wonderful examples of these early cartoons can now be seen at an exhibition in London, all of (**17**) .... were produced to order for wealthy clients. (**18**) .... makes this art form so interesting is that it flourished in one small part of Europe – Flanders, today a region of northern Belgium – (**19**) .... to die out as printing was developed.

Many of the tiny pictures were (**20**) .... larger than a postage stamp. They (**21**) .... painted by hand in books about (**22**) .... size of a modern paperback. The artists, whose skills were rewarded by high salaries, worked slowly, and the buyers sometimes (**23**) .... to wait years for the work to be completed. In the (**24**) .... of one four-volume example, the buyer waited for (**25**) .... than a decade.

(**26**) .... the majority of these cartoons depict religious stories, other subjects are illustrated, (**27**) .... Episodes from history were popular, (**28**) .... were fairy tales. And yet the artists had a visual style that seems oddly modern. (**29**) .... made full use of perspective and techniques familiar to us today from films, such as following a long shot (**30**) .... a dramatic close-up.

In most lines of the following text, there is **either** a spelling **or** a punctuation error. For each numbered line **31–46**, write the correctly spelt word or show the correct punctuation in the box on your answer sheet. Some lines are correct. Indicate these lines with a (✓) in the box. The exercise begins with three examples (**0**), (**00**) and (**000**).

Example:

0	*possibility*	__ 0 __
00	*future.*	__ 00 __
000	✓	__ 000 __

The Thinking Computer

0   Scientists exploring the possibilty of making a computer that can

00   think for itself have concluded this is unlikely in the foreseeable future

000 The government-sponsored Intelligent Systems Project was set up

31   to predict were technology would lead us in the next few decades.

32   The report just issued by the investigators says, that computers are

33   certain to play an even bigger roll in our lives in the years to come.

34   We already use computing devices when we book cinema tickets over

35   the phone, search the web or use mobile phones. The computers that

36   are part of these systems will become more efficient,' forecasts Dr

37   Bevan of Winchester university, who was involved in this project.

38   And more sophisticated machines that can moniter a sick person and

39   summon help if required, for instance, will probably be developed

40   soon. 'However, computers like that still wont be thinking,' admits

41   Dr Bevan. 'They will just be reacting to the input they receive in the

42   way they have been taught to.' Thinking involves seperate processes:

43   understanding information from the out-side world first, and then

44   makeing a decision about how to react. And at present there is no

45   way a computer can decide anythink; all it can do is respond. This

46   is not what goes on in a persons mind when he or she is thinking.

PAPER 1 Reading
PAPER 2 Writing
PAPER 3 English in Use ▸
    Part 1
    Part 2
    Part 3
    Part 4
    Part 5
    Part 6
PAPER 4 Listening
PAPER 5 Speaking

For questions **47–61**, read the two texts below. Use the words in the boxes to the right of the texts to form one word that fits in the same numbered space in the text. Write the new word in the correct box on your answer sheet. The exercise begins with an example (**0**).

Example:

0	*registration*	0

NEWSLETTER

News in Brief

The Annual General Meeting of the Literary Society will be held on 29ᵗʰ November. Members should fill in a (**0**) ………………….. card if they plan to attend.

The online database of members is now in place. Any (**47**) ………………….. have to be made soon, so please contact the secretary if you would like anything altered.

Ms Emily Wilson has finished her history of the Society. It is (**48**) …………………..
A Society for Everyone. The date of (**49**) ………………….. is not yet known.

This year's social evening will be held on 5ᵗʰ December. There is a charge of £5 for
(**50**) ………………….. , and there will be (**51**) ………………….. snacks.

The first event of next year is a talk by Robert McWilliam, *Hopelessness in the Novels of F. Scott Fitzgerald*, which focuses on the melancholy mood of (**52**) ………………….. desire in Fitzgerald's works. Further details will be (**53**) ………………….. .

(0)	**REGISTER**
(47)	MODIFY
(48)	TITLE
(49)	PUBLISH
(50)	ADMIT
(51)	COMPLIMENT
(52)	FULFIL
(53)	FORTH

EXTRACT FROM ARTICLE

Edison's Eccentric Project

When businessman Sam Edison decided he would design his new house himself, the fact that he had no (**54**) ………………….. experience whatsoever was not a
(**55**) ………………….. . Sam has always approached challenges (**56**) ………………….. ,
and he believes in the old (**57**) ………………….. that you can do anything if you put your mind to it. He recalls how his efforts were greeted by the men who were going to build the house. 'When I showed the foreman my plans, what little (**58**) ………………….. I may have had as a boss evaporated. He stared at me in (**59**) ………………….. . My lack of
(**60**) ………………….. about building must have been all too (**61**) ………………….. ,'
Fortunately, the foreman took matters in hand, and the house was eventually finished. It is an absolute triumph.

(54)	ARCHITECT
(55)	DETER
(56)	CONFIDENCE
(57)	SAY
(58)	CREDIBLE
(59)	BELIEVE
(60)	KNOW
(61)	APPEAR

For questions **62–74**, read the extract from a public transport leaflet. Use the information in the leaflet to complete the numbered gaps in the informal letter. The words you need **do not occur** in the leaflet. **Use no more than two words for each gap.** The exercise begins with an example (**0**).

Example:

0	*buy*	0

PUBLIC TRANSPORT LEAFLET

Public Transport in Prague

Multi-purpose tickets for travelling on metro, tram and bus routes can be purchased from metro stations and certain commercial outlets. The ticket must be inserted into the yellow validation machine before boarding, ensuring its validity for 60 minutes from the marked time and date. Passengers must display their tickets to authorised officials.

Bus and tram operating schedules at each stop indicate the expected time of arrival of the vehicle, while the number adjacent to each stop in the list of stops for that line indicates the time in minutes required for the bus or tram to reach the subsequent stop.

Metro trains run at intervals of 4–6 minutes from 0800 to 1800 hours on weekdays and at longer intervals at other times. An illuminated digital clock at the end of the platform in every station indicates the time that has elapsed since the departure of the previous train.

INFORMAL LETTER

You can (**0**) .... tickets that allow you to travel on all underground trains, buses and trams from metro stations. Lots of (**62**) .... sell them, too. When you get on a bus or other means of transport, you (**63**) .... the ticket into a yellow machine and it (**64**) .... the time and date on it. You can (**65**) .... of the ticket for an hour after that. If you are stopped by (**66**) .... , you have to let him or her have (**67**) .... at your ticket.

For buses and trams there's (**68**) .... at every stop showing when the bus or tram is (**69**) .... , and there's also a list of all the stops on the line showing how long it (**70**) .... to get to the (**71**) .... stop.

The metro trains come along (**72**) .... every five minutes during the day, and a bit less (**73**) .... in the evenings and at weekends. There's a clock on each platform that shows (**74**) .... it's been since the last train left.

For questions **75–80**, read the following text and then choose from the list **A–J** given below the best phrase to fill each of the spaces. Write one letter (**A–J**) in the correct box on your answer sheet. Each correct phrase may only be used once. **Some of the suggested answers do not fit at all.** The exercise begins with an example (**0**).

Example:

0	J	0

The Rise of the Polytunnel

Almost 80% of British summer fruit is grown inside plastic tunnels to protect it from the weather. Over the last five years polytunnels, as these plastic tunnels are known, have become hugely popular among farmers, (**0**) ....

The efficiency of the system is beyond question. These tunnels make it possible to harvest strawberries, for instance, from April until November, (**75**) .... The tunnels are made of lightweight steel frames, with plastic sheets pulled taut across the frame. Thus sunlight is allowed in, while the plastic keeps off the rain, (**76**) ....

The argument about the environmental impact of these poytunnels is a bitter one. Perhaps their most vocal opponents are people who have moved to the countryside from big cities, eager for a view of nature at its best, (**77**) .... The fact that farmers do not even need planning permission to put up these tunnels, (**78**) ...... , is particularly galling to the protestors. However, farmers point out that increased yields from British farms means a healthier agricultural sector, (**79**) .... And since the big supermarkets are now able to stock British strawberries rather than imported fruit, there is some benefit to the environment (**80**) ....

There is now a possibility that crops other than summer fruit will be grown in polytunnels, which could see even more of the countryside covered in plastic sheets. The prospect is hardly likely to please those local residents who are already disenchanted with the situation as it is.

A which benefits the economy as a whole

B although it would be in the country's best interests

C and helps retain heat for a long time after dark

D despite having no official permission to do so

E whereas previously they could only be picked in midsummer

F because there is less pollution caused by planes bringing these imports into the country

G which are more resistant to the cold

H only to find these giant white structures on their doorsteps

I since they are classified as temporary structures

J though many rural residents object strenuously to them

PAPER 5 Speaking

You will hear part of a talk by a writer who has written a book about bread. For questions **1–8**, complete the sentences.

You will hear the recording twice.

Our Daily Bread

Supermarket [1] believe that baking bread on the premises attracts customers.

About [2] of bread in Britain is no longer baked in the old-fashioned way.

In the past, it took [3] for the yeast to ferment.

Nowadays, the fermentation process is faster, and less [4] is used.

Unless salt is added, bread baked in the modern way is [5]

Calcium propionate can be sprayed on the bread to prevent it from going [6]

The speaker believes certain [7] may be caused by modern bread-making methods.

Supermarkets [8] on the sale of bread.

You will hear an archaeologist talking about an important discovery. For questions **9–16**, complete the notes.

Listen very carefully as you will hear the recording ONCE only.

The Pharaoh's Sons

Survey took long time:
tomb construction more [**9**] than expected.

For example, when measured,
some corners did not form a [**10**]

KX5 full of rubble and originally considered [**11**]

Weeks and his team noticed
names [**12**] of chamber.

Names were sons of Rameses II,
who reigned for [**13**] years.

Archaeologists eventually discovered many [**14**]
leading to 130 chambers.

Rameses was made [**15**] during his lifetime.

His sons performed [**16**] in place of their father.

You will hear part of a discussion between Velma Andrews, a lawyer, and Sergeant William Bailey, a police officer. For questions **17–22**, choose the correct answer **A, B, C** or **D**.

You will hear the recording twice.

___

17 How did William feel the first time he gave evidence in court?
   A humiliated
   B nervous
   C furious
   D indifferent

18 Velma suggests that police officers giving evidence should
   A study the evidence more carefully.
   B ignore the lawyer for the defence.
   C not take comments personally.
   D demonstrate that they are honest and reliable.

19 Velma compares a police officer's evidence to a piece in a jigsaw puzzle because
   A it is unimportant unless it is part of a bigger picture.
   B it may not fit in with the rest of the evidence.
   C the defence lawyer will try to destroy it.
   D the police officer should only talk about his or her evidence.

20 William suggests that lawyers
   A adopt a special manner in the courtroom.
   B can be detached about a case.
   C might actually be close friends.
   D do not take their work seriously.

21 Velma's advice suggests that police officers should
   A never volunteer a personal opinion.
   B not answer a question unless they are sure of the answer.
   C remember they are not really addressing the lawyer.
   D not get into an argument with the judge.

22 William's main concern is that
   A a criminal could get away with his or her crime.
   B a court case could be confusing.
   C young police officers find courts terrifying.
   D police officers might argue with the lawyer.

You will hear five short extracts in which different people talk about wind power. Each extract has two questions. For questions **23–32**, choose the best answer **A**, **B** or **C**.

You will hear the recording twice.

---

23 The first speaker mentions a wind farm started by people who
    A   wanted to take advantage of a government subsidy.
    B   had already earned considerable sums of money.
    C   were seeking an alternative source of income.

24 What does she believe was the reason for opposition to this project?
    A   prejudice against wind power
    B   jealousy of another's success
    C   aesthetic considerations

25 What does the second speaker see as the main problem with wind farms?
    A   the visual impact on the landscape
    B   the inefficiency of wind turbines
    C   the need for an alternative source of energy

26 He implies that small communities who start their own wind farms are
    A   altruistic.
    B   greedy.
    C   misguided.

27 Where does the third speaker think wind farms should be constructed?
    A   out at sea
    B   along coastlines
    C   along main shipping routes

28 Which other method of generating power does she think should be encouraged?
    A   other renewable energy sources
    B   nuclear power
    C   coal- and oil-powered generators

29 The fourth speaker disagrees on principle with wind power because
    A   the erection of wind turbines is a threat to wildlife.
    B   the turbines cannot generate sufficient energy.
    C   most industries cannot take advantage of it.

30 What example does he give of how to conserve energy?
    A   reducing heat loss
    B   reducing industrial output
    C   improving power stations

31 The fifth speaker feels the danger posed by wind farms to wildlife is
    A   considerable.
    B   exaggerated.
    C   acute.

32 She believes that wind power
    A   has a place in future energy policy.
    B   can never be a reliable source of energy.
    C   has few prospects in the future.

Part 1 (3 minutes)

The examiner will ask you a few questions about yourself and then ask you to talk to your partner. For example, the examiner may ask you:

- What job do you do, or what job would you like to do?
- What kind of working environment would suit you best?
- What sort of job would you dislike, and what working conditions would not appeal to you?

Part 2 (4 minutes)

You will each be asked to talk for a minute without interruption. You will each be given a set of photographs in turn to talk about. After your partner has finished speaking, you will be asked a brief question connected with your partner's photographs.

Respect (compare, contrast and speculate)

Turn to pictures 1–3 on page **210**, which show people expressing respect.

Candidate A, compare and contrast these pictures and imagine what could be prompting people to display respect in these situations.

Candidate B, what sort of people do you respect?

Partnership (compare, contrast and speculate)

Turn to pictures 1–3 on page **211**, which show people in partnerships.

Candidate B, compare and contrast these situations, saying how you think the partners in each case might feel about each other.

Candidate A, would you prefer to work with a partner or on your own?

Part 3 (4 minutes)

Recreation (discuss, evaluate and select)

Turn to the pictures on page **212**, which show different forms of recreation.

Talk to each other about the wide variety of activities people can do in order to relax, and then decide which two pictures best illustrate this diversity.

Part 4 (4 minutes)

The examiner will encourage you to develop the topic of your discussion in Part 3 by asking questions such as:

- Why do you think some people choose to do dangerous recreational activities like mountain climbing?
- Do you think everyone needs some sort of recreational activity? Why (not)?
- Would it be possible to encourage more children to take up recreational activities other than sports: hobbies such as collecting stamps or gardening?
- Which recreational activities are more beneficial: those that exercise the mind or those that exercise the body?

PAPER 1 Reading	▶	Part 1
PAPER 2 Writing		Part 2
PAPER 3 English in Use		Part 3
PAPER 4 Listening		Part 4
PAPER 5 Speaking		

Answer questions **1–16** by referring to the newspaper article on page **169** which reviews a number of hotels.

Indicate your answers **on the separate answer sheet**.

For questions **1–16**, answer by choosing from the sections of the article (**A–F**). Some of the choices may be required more than once.

Note: When more than one answer is required, these may be given **in any order**.

In which section of the article are the following stated?

The area is famous for its local cuisine.	**1**	
The owner makes guests feel welcome.	**2**	
The people in this region are generally hospitable.	**3**	
The hotel is close to the sea.	**4**	**5** ....
Standards of service in hotels have dropped recently.	**6**	
Care has been taken to show modern art off to advantage.	**7**	
A range of different restaurants can be found within walking distance.	**8**	
There is a successful mixture of styles.	**9**	
The meals served at the hotel are different every night.	**10**	
The exterior does not prepare guests for the style of the interior.	**11**	
It is possible to listen to old records here.	**12**	
The décor of the rooms may not appeal to everyone.	**13**	
One part of the hotel is very large.	**14**	
Local specialities are served at the hotel.	**15**	
Young people will find amusements nearby.	**16**	

Weekend breaks

A selection of hotels you might like to try for a weekend away

A Bark Park Hotel, Timberley

<u>General impressions:</u> A honey-coloured, wisteria-clad mansion overlooking the shimmering river Exe.

<u>What are the rooms like?</u> Large, comfortable and charming.

<u>The bathrooms:</u> Plain, but pleasant and light, properly equipped.

<u>The restaurant:</u> Adventurous gourmet dinner menus, changing nightly (about £25 per person). Even if you get up late, you'll find it easy to get breakfast, which is the kind of service found only rarely these days.

<u>What can you do nearby?</u> In this part of the south-west, with Exmoor a few miles north, there is no shortage of good walking country. Or just stroll in the hotel gardens or along the river.

<u>The price:</u> From £79.50 per person per night.

B Sinclair House, Bleverton

<u>General impressions:</u> Sinclair House recalls childhood holidays in terraced Victorian B&Bs – except that the blend of modern and traditional design in this townhouse hotel is far more stylish.

<u>What are the rooms like?</u> Airy and elegantly decorated. There are leather sofas, widescreen TVs and tremendous views. You can leave the windows open at night and listen to the sounds of the harbour.

<u>The bathrooms:</u> Plain but elegant, with free-standing bath, good shower, fluffy towels, bathrobes and hand-made soaps.

<u>The restaurant:</u> There is no restaurant although there are some good options in the area. An excellent breakfast is provided in the lounge. There is no bar, either, but drinks are available in the lounge, which gives you a chance to enjoy the hotel's excellent collection of 70s and 80s rock on the original vinyl.

<u>What can you do nearby?</u> Walk four miles to explore one of the most beautiful parts of Wales and then take the train back; go hiking in nearby Snowdonia National Park.

<u>The price:</u> £68–80 per night for a double room.

C Harper's House, London

<u>General impressions:</u> A nondescript front door opens to reveal a magnificent staircase, which is lit by candles in sconces in the evenings.

<u>What are the rooms like?</u> There are six rooms and two suites, all named after Romantic poets. The suites (Wordsworth and Keats) are delightful. The Byron room is popular, but my favourite is the Coleridge: dark red, silky and plush.

<u>The bathrooms:</u> Compared with the rooms, a bit of a let-down, plain and white. The bathrooms of the more expensive suites have a dash of colour.

<u>The restaurant:</u> There is no restaurant although a continental breakfast is served, but a leisurely stroll brings you to Westbourne Grove, which has a whole gamut of restaurants specialising in ethnic cuisines. Tom Conran's The Cow Dining Room is also nearby. There is a free bar in the drawing room, and obscure liqueurs are a speciality.

<u>What can you do nearby?</u> Enjoy the boutiques and stalls of Portobello Road, then dine in Notting Hill. Holland Park is for quiet reflection.

<u>The price:</u> From £150 per night.

D Argyl Hotel, Oban, Scotland

<u>General impressions:</u> Splendidly isolated, this fine Edwardian hotel is in beautiful grounds with tremendous views across Ardmucknish Bay to the Isle of Mull. The cavernous main hall is rather intimidating and encourages conversation in hushed whispers.

<u>What are the rooms like?</u> As large and airy as one might expect, though a touch on the austere side.

<u>The bathrooms:</u> Power showers, good-sized baths, fluffy bathrobes and luxury toiletries.

<u>The restaurant:</u> The breakfast lounge offers a wide range of delicious breakfast dishes, including potato scones, kedgeree and smoked haddock with poached eggs. No evening meals, but ten minutes' drive away is Oban's Eeusk, a fabulous restaurant specialising in seafood for which the region is renowned. There is no bar, but The Ferryman in Connel village, five minutes away by car, prides itself on its ales, malts, fiddlers and the warm welcome so typical of the entire area.

<u>What can you do nearby?</u> Ferry day trips to Mull; mountain-biking at Glen Nevis; superb walks up Ben Lora and Ben Cruachan

<u>The price:</u> £45–£60 per night for a double room. £40–50 for a single.

E Gate Inn, near Canterbury

<u>General impressions:</u> Set in the hills of Kent, with orchards and market gardens just over the horizon, this is a converted oasthouse.

<u>What are the rooms like?</u> Underlining its claim to be one of the county's best boutique hotels, there's a restored fireplace in every one of the cool, whitewashed bedrooms, which also have CD/DVD players. There are low-slung pine beds with fresh-coloured linen and tasteful cushions, which nicely set off the austere but interesting contemporary prints on the walls.

<u>The bathrooms:</u> Adequate, though some are on the small side.

<u>The restaurant:</u> Excellent variety of international cuisine, with Italian dishes given special prominence.

<u>What can you do nearby?</u> Sefton Peaks Theme Park is just minutes away, with attractions for all ages, though especially good for teenagers.

<u>The price:</u> From £49.50 per person per night.

F Rowe House, near Bristol

<u>General impressions:</u> A man bounces out the door to take our bags. It emerges that he is the proprietor, Walter, and he remains courteous and helpful throughout our stay, exuding a genuine pleasure in having guests. The reception rooms are oddly bland, so it's a good thing the atmosphere is brightened by the hotel's cheerful owners.

<u>What are the rooms like?</u> Decorated with a genuine sense of enjoyment in colour, which may be overpowering for some tastes.

<u>The bathrooms:</u> A nice touch here is having old-fashioned baths, polished until they gleam, though with lashings of hot water.

<u>The restaurant:</u> No restaurant as such for evening meals, but a delicious breakfast is provided, featuring delicacies of the region, such as goat's cheese and smoked salmon.

<u>What can you do nearby?</u> Enjoy the vibrant city of Bristol with its museums and rich cultural life.

<u>The price:</u> From £55 per person per night.

PAPER 1 Reading   ▶   Part 1
PAPER 2 Writing   Part 2
PAPER 3 English in Use   Part 3
PAPER 4 Listening   Part 4
PAPER 5 Speaking

For questions **17–22**, choose which of the paragraphs **A–G** on page **171** fit into the numbered gaps in the following magazine article. There is one extra paragraph which does not fit into any of the gaps.

Indicate your answers **on the separate answer sheet**.

Close Encounters of the Wild Kind

The rise of the wildlife-watching experience

Wildlife observation has always proved inspirational for humans. It led Charles Darwin to provide us with a better understanding of how we evolved and inspired such everyday innovations as Velcro. US author Peter Matthiessen wrote: 'The variety of life in nature can be compared to a vast library of unread books, and the plundering of nature is comparable to the random discarding of whole volumes without having opened them and learned from them.' While there is indeed much to learn from many species not yet known to science, it's the already opened 'books' that attract the majority of us – in ever increasing numbers.

17

Awareness and understanding of the state of the planet and its wildlife has been spurred on by the efforts of conservation groups and natural history television. This, in turn, has led to an increased demand for wildlife tours or the addition of a wildlife-watching component to traditional holidays. It seems people want to discover nature for themselves.

18

Although the term is overused, 'ecotourism' allows tourists both to see and help wildlife. This encouraging development within the wildlife-tourism industry offers an added hope for the future of many endangered species, as money from clients is often given directly to conservation organisations. Tour operators who are listed with independent bodies such as Responsibletravel.com have ethical policies in place to ensure that proper procedures are followed. They use the services of local communities, train local guides and have close ties to conservation projects.

19

Conservation organisations have also realised that tourism can help educate people and provide a valuable source of revenue and even manpower. The World Wildlife Fund, for example, runs trips that give donors the chance to see for themselves how their financial aid is assisting conservation projects in the field. But not all wildlife watching trips are so hands-off. Some offer the opportunity to participate in research and conservation.

20

Similarly, Biosphere Expeditions takes about 200 people every year on what its field operations director, Dr Matthias Hammer, calls an 'adventure with a conscience'. Volunteers can visit six destinations around the world and take part in various activities including snow leopard, wolf and bear surveys and whale and dolphin research.

21

Of course, to go in search of wildlife doesn't always mean you will find it. That sightings of animals in large wild areas don't come on tap is simply a fact of life. Although potentially frustrating, it makes sightings all the more rewarding when they are made.

22

Indeed, some of the best wildlife-watching opportunities on offer are on our doorstep, according to author and ornithologist Malcolm Tait. 'People assume you have to go a long way to do it, which is simply not the case – your garden or even a railway cutting can bring constant surprises.'

A 'If done properly, wildlife-watching tourism can be a win-win situation,' says Hammer. 'People have a unique experience while contributing to conservation directly. Local people and habitats benefit through job creation, research and an alternative income. Local wildlife benefits from our conservation and research work.'

B 'What is interesting is how much people are willing to pay to be in a wilderness environment,' says Julian Matthews, director of Discovery Initiatives, which takes people on small group trips to more than thirty-five countries and works directly with conservation organisations such as the Orang-utan Foundation. 'It's still a small part of the tourism industry – maybe four or five percent of the whole – but it's undoubtedly expanding. There are definitely more and more people seeking wildlife experiences now.'

C A comparable problem is found in various parts of East Africa, though government intervention has, in these cases, done little to alleviate the hardships. Would it be possible for ethical tourism to play a role in the future of this region? Ken Logan, Director of the African Wildlife Association, is not optimistic about the chances.

D 'There's no way to compare seeing an animal in the wild with watching one on TV,' says Matthews. 'While a filmmaker may spend six months shooting an animal and will get closer to it than you will when watching it in the wild, there's no greater pleasure than seeing an animal in its own environment. On film, you're only getting the visuals and the sound. As impressive as they may be, it's not the real McCoy and misses other aspects that you can appreciate only by being there.'

E Earthwatch is a nonprofit international environmental group that does just that. 'Participation in an Earthwatch project is a positive alternative to wildlife-watching expeditions, as we offer members of the public the opportunity to be on the front line, not the sidelines, of conservation,' says Claudia Eckardt, Earthwatch volunteer programme manager.

F Wildlife covers all wild creatures, not just those that are big, dangerous or exotic. As people are able to travel to more extreme places in search of the ultimate wildlife experience, it's worth remembering that you don't have to go to the ends of the Earth to catch rewarding glimpses of animals.

G Thus tour operator Rekero has established its own school – the Koyiaki Guide School and Wilderness Camp – for young Maasai in Kenya. Maasai have largely been excluded from the benefits brought to the region by tourism; they make up just fifteen percent of employees in tourist camps. 'It is a concerted effort to put the running of the reserve into the hands of indigenous people,' says Ron Beaton, founder of the school.

| PAPER 1 Reading |
| PAPER 2 Writing |
| PAPER 3 English in Use |
| PAPER 4 Listening |
| PAPER 5 Speaking |

Part 1
Part 2
Part 3
Part 4

Read the following newspaper article and answer questions **23–28** on page **173**. On your answer sheet, indicate the letter **A, B, C** or **D** against the number of each question. Give only one answer to each question.

Indicate your answers **on the separate answer sheet**.

Are you a slumper?

Ashley Seager was, but cured bad posture – and her chronic back pain – with the Alexander technique

Many people will have heard of the Alexander technique but have only a vague idea what it is about. Until earlier this year, I didn't have the faintest idea about it. But, hunched over a computer screen one day, I noticed that the neck- and backache I regularly suffered were more painful than usual. I consulted an osteopath, who said: 'I can treat the symptoms by massaging your neck and upper back. But you actually have bad posture. That is what you need to get sorted out. Go off and learn the Alexander technique.'

I had regularly been told by friends and family that I tend to slouch in chairs but had thought bad posture was something one was born with and could do nothing about. That is not true. Dentists and car mechanics, among others, tend to develop bad posture from leaning over patients or engine bays. Mothers often stress and strain their necks and backs lifting and carrying children, and those of us who sit in front of computers all day are almost certainly not doing our bodies any favours.

A few clicks on the web and I found an Alexander technique teacher, Tanya Shoop, in my area of south London and booked a first appointment. Three months later I am walking straighter and sitting better, while my neck and back pain are things of the past. I feel taller, too, which I may be imagining, but the technique can increase your height by up to five centimetres if you were badly slumped beforehand.

The teaching centres on the neck, head and back. It trains you to use your body less harshly and to perform familiar movements and actions with less effort. There is very little effort in the lessons themselves, which sets apart the Alexander technique from pilates or yoga, which are exercise-based.

A typical lesson involves standing in front of a chair and learning to sit and stand with minimal effort. You spend some time lying on a bench with your knees bent to straighten the spine and relax your body while the teacher moves your arms and legs to train you to move them correctly.

The key is learning to break the bad habits accumulated over years. Try, for example, folding your arms the opposite way to normal. It feels odd, doesn't it? This is an example of a habit the body has formed which can be hard to break. Many of us carry our heads too far back and tilted skywards. The technique teaches you to let go of the muscles holding the head back, allowing it to resume its natural place on the summit of our spines. The head weighs four to six kilos, so any misalignment can cause problems for the neck and body.

The Alexander technique teaches you to think of the space above your head. This may sound daft, but it is an important element in the process of learning to hold yourself upright. You learn to observe how you use your body and how others use theirs – usually badly. Look how a colleague slumps back in a chair with his or her legs crossed. That puts all sorts of stresses and strains on the body. Even swimming can harm the neck. The Alexander technique can teach you to swim better, concentrating on technique rather than clocking up lengths. 'In too many of our activities we concentrate on how we get to a destination rather than the means or way of getting there,' says Shoop.

So who was Alexander and how did he come up with the technique? Frederick Matthias Alexander, an Australian theatrical orator born in 1869, found in his youth that his voice was failing during performances. He analysed himself and realised his posture was bad. He worked on improving it, with dramatic results. He brought his technique to London 100 years ago and quickly gathered a following that included some very famous people. He died in 1955, having established a teacher-training school in London, which is thriving today.

So if you are slouching along the road one day, feeling weighed down by your troubles, give a thought to the Alexander technique. It could help you walk tall again.

23 The writer learnt about the Alexander technique
   A after consulting someone about her problems.
   B when she suddenly developed a bad back.
   C when massage failed to alleviate her back pain.
   D while she was browsing the Internet.

24 The Alexander technique teaches that familiar movements
   A have been learnt by incorrect methods.
   B need more energy and effort than we think.
   C do not have to be performed so strenuously.
   D are the most common cause of backache.

25 It appears that the body forms habits that
   A inevitably cause physical pain.
   B can be difficult to change.
   C are a consequence of actions we perform.
   D develop in early childhood.

26 The Alexander technique
   A makes you aware of other people's faults.
   B has immediate and dramatic results.
   C helps athletes perform better.
   D brings about a change in body posture.

27 It is suggested that Frederick Alexander
   A believed in the benefits of exercise.
   B invented an alternative to yoga.
   C developed a form of exercise for actors.
   D recovered his vocal powers.

28 What is the writer's main purpose in the article?
   A to recommend regular physical exercise
   B to explain how debilitating backache can be
   C to suggest that back problems can be remedied
   D to explain the widespread occurrence of back pain

PAPER 1 Reading ▶ Part 1
PAPER 2 Writing   Part 2
PAPER 3 English in Use   Part 3
PAPER 4 Listening   Part 4
PAPER 5 Speaking

Answer questions **29–42** by referring to the newspaper article on pages **175–176**, which discusses alternative power systems for vehicles.

Indicate your answers **on the separate answer sheet**.

For questions **29–42**, answer by choosing from the sections of the article **A–F**. Some of the choices may be required more than once.

In which section of the article are the following mentioned?

the advantages of conventional cars	**29** ....
a more compact version of existing technology	**30** ....
a willingness to invest in new technologies	**31** ....
limitations concerning where a vehicle can be used	**32** ....
a power source associated with a space programme	**33** ....
recycling waste products	**34** ....
a negative aesthetic impression	**35** ....
laws that encourage the development of new technologies	**36** ....
the inability to transport many people	**37** ....
devices that function best when conditions are constant	**38** ....
the rate of acceleration of a vehicle	**39** ....
the possibility of returning to a source of power used in the past	**40** ....
the existence of a market for a certain type of vehicle	**41** ....
the ability to switch from one power source to another	**42** ....

Vehicles of the Future

A The motor industry is finally showing some serious interest in developing cost-effective and environmentally-friendly technologies to power vehicles, as can be seen by the amount of money they are spending on research and development. There are some sound reasons for this: nowadays a significant number of people would prefer to buy a vehicle that did not emit greenhouse gases into the atmosphere or pollute the environment in other ways. But there are other forces at work in the industry as well. Governments throughout the world are demanding restrictions on gas emissions, and the goals they have set can only be met in the long run if conventional cars with internal combustion engines are phased out and replaced by vehicles that run on alternative power sources. Naturally, public opinion is ultimately behind legislation like this, which is aimed at protecting the environment. Governments, after all, need to respond to the wishes of their voters.

B For the last few decades innovators have been coming up with ideas for alternative power sources for automobiles, though so far none has had a significant appeal for consumers. The alternative technologies we have at present are lagging far behind the petrol-guzzling internal combustion engine in terms of speed and the distance that can be travelled before refuelling. But what does the future hold? At present a hybrid car propelled by a combination of an electric motor and petrol engine may be the best compromise for those who want to help save the planet and still have the convenience of a car. When you start the hybrid car and when you are driving normally, power is provided by the electric motor, which works with a battery. However, when the battery starts to go flat, the petrol engine starts automatically and drives a generator to recharge the battery. Similarly, when the car needs extra power – in order to accelerate, for instance – the petrol engine provides that power. This vehicle performs respectably, though not spectacularly: it can go from 0 to about 100 kph in around 10 seconds, has a top speed of 165 kph, and below average fuel consumption.

C And what of cars powered solely by electricity? Here the main stumbling block has always been storing the electricity: batteries may have come a long way, but they are still bulky and have to be charged for long periods. The latest completely electric car, for example, has a top speed of 60 kph and a range of 60 kilometres. It takes 6 hours to charge the battery fully. But the makers claim this is perfectly acceptable for city driving, when people are unable to go much faster or further in any case. Many cities provide benefits such as free parking for drivers of electric cars. But these vehicles are virtually confined to urban settings, which is off-putting, and most people find electric cars have a toy-like appearance which is definitely not appealing. Moreover, environmentalists point out that while the car itself may not emit poisonous fumes, as is the case with petrol-driven vehicles, this is of little real benefit to the environment if the electricity used to drive the car has been generated by coal or oil power stations, as is generally the case.

D First developed for use in missions to the moon, fuel cells appear to be the most serious challenger to the internal combustion engine as an alternative source of energy for both mobile and stationary applications. A fuel cell uses relatively straightforward technology that converts chemical energy into electrical energy with benign by-products. In fact, the only by-products are water, which is harmless, and heat. The other advantage is that fuel cells have no complex moving parts that need to be cooled or lubricated. But rather than replacing the internal combustion engine as the source of power for the vehicle itself, the fuel cell – in the view of some manufacturers – will only replace the battery and alternator, supplying electricity to vehicle systems, operating independently of the engine. The actual drive power for the vehicle itself would still be provided by the combustion engine. However, while fuel cells certainly hold a great deal of promise, there are some drawbacks. They need a steady supply of hydrogen, which needs to be extracted from some source, such as methanol gas, and this process can be cumbersome. In one model that uses fuel cells, the reformer required to extract the hydrogen from methanol takes up so much space that the vehicle can only seat the driver and one passenger.

E Another possibility is represented by turbines. Gas turbines have long been considered a possible mobile and smaller stationary power source, but their use has been limited for a variety of reasons, including cost, complexity and size. These large turbines shine when in steady-state applications but are not as efficient when speed and load are continually changing. However, a new generation of turbines – microturbines – has been developed in large measure for use in vehicles. They are small, high-speed engine systems that typically include the turbine, compressor and generator in a single unit with all the other vital components and control electronics. A different possibility in terms of energy supply for cars is household gas. A special device installed in a garage can compress the gas, which is then fed into the car. A gas car is cheaper to run, as well as being cleaner than a conventional car. On the other hand, the vehicle itself is expensive because the technology is new, and environmentalists argue that a gas car will produce only a little less carbon dioxide than petrol-driven vehicles.

F In the meantime, various compromises are being employed as temporary measures. For example, most diesel cars can now be converted to run on biodiesel fuel, which is made from used vegetable oils and animal fats. However, the environment lobby is not convinced that biodiesel helps cut local air pollution by any significant amount. Many experts believe that the ultimate solution to the problem of reducing dangerous emissions ultimately lies with electric vehicles once the battery technology has improved. Some experts even believe that the future may lie with steam cars, and since the first genuine 'automobile' – a vehicle capable of moving itself – was powered by steam more than two centuries ago, it could be that the wheel is coming full circle.

1 You are the secretary of the student council at the college where you are studying. Recently you came up with the idea of having a career day, when companies can send representatives to talk to students and help them plan their careers. You mentioned the idea to the principal of the college, and as a result, he sent you a memo supporting the idea and asking for a more detailed proposal.

You have also received some suggestions from former students at the college who are now working for large companies.

Read the principal's memo and the suggestions from former students, as well as the notes you have made on them. Then, using all the information, write your **proposal**.

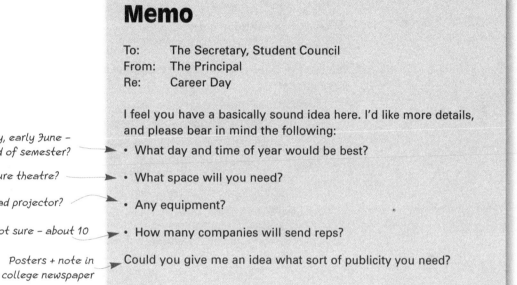

Memo

To: The Secretary, Student Council
From: The Principal
Re: Career Day

I feel you have a basically sound idea here. I'd like more details, and please bear in mind the following:

Friday, early June – end of semester? → • What day and time of year would be best?

Large lecture theatre? → • What space will you need?

Overhead projector? → • Any equipment?

Not sure – about 10 → • How many companies will send reps?

Posters + note in college newspaper → Could you give me an idea what sort of publicity you need?

Thanks,

David Oliphant, Principal

Yes! → I'd suggest setting out a desk for each company so students can go and talk to them 2 or 3 at a time.

Good idea – could Dr Jones from Business School do it? → What about a short talk to all students on planning a career?

Maybe. Have leaflets on CV writing available in college office? → What about information on writing CVs?

Will write to 15 big local companies → Get companies to give you a firm yes or no: give them until a fortnight before career day to reply!

Now write your **proposal** for the career day, explaining what you envisage could happen on that day (approximately 250 words). You should use your own words as far as possible.

Choose one of the following writing tasks. Your answer should follow exactly the instructions given. Write approximately 250 words.

2 You see the following announcement in a magazine called *Leisure Today* and decide to enter the competition.

> **DO YOU HAVE AN INTERESTING OR UNUSUAL INDOOR LEISURE ACTIVITY?**
>
> It could be anything from calligraphy to making models or embroidery! If so, write and tell us about the activity, explaining its attraction. The writer of the best entry will win £250.

Write your **competition entry**.

3 You see the following notice in a magazine called *Career Management International*:

> **'Soon nobody will spend all their working lives with the same employer – or even in one single type of work.'**
>
> What do young people today feel about the necessity of having a range of skills and qualifications rather than knowledge of one specialised field? Are they stimulated or disconcerted by the prospect of performing a range of professional activities? Would they miss the security of a job for life – or see the alternative as a challenge?

Write your **article**.

4 You are a regular contributor to a magazine for young people called *Film Scene*. You have been asked to write a review of two films which you saw recently, and of which most people had great expectations. You enjoyed one of the films, but found the other one very disappointing.

Write your **review**.

5 You work in the human resources department of a large multinational company. Over the last year your company has been operating a recruitment programme for university graduates. Your managing director has asked for a report describing how effective the programme has been, including information on the following:

- the activities involved in the programme (e.g. visiting universities etc.)
- direct benefits for the company (e.g. hiring new staff)
- indirect benefits for the company (e.g. raising the company's profile among students)

Write your **report**.

TEST 8

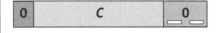

PAPER 1 Reading

PAPER 2 Writing

PAPER 3 English in Use ▸ Part 1

PAPER 4 Listening

PAPER 5 Speaking

Part 1
Part 2
Part 3
Part 4
Part 5
Part 6

For questions **1–15**, read the text below and then decide which answer best fits each space. Put the letter you choose for each question in the correct box on your answer sheet. The exercise begins with an example (**0**).

Example:

0	C	0

Raising Awareness

In cities around the world a wide (**0**) ...... of schemes is being instigated to (**1**) ...... environmental awareness. 'It's just as easy to (**2**) ...... of litter properly as it is to drop it on the streets,' says city councillor Mike Edwards, who has (**3**) ...... on the government to mount a concerted (**4**) ...... to deal with the problem of litter. 'It's just a matter of encouraging people to do so as a (**5**) ...... of course. Once the habit is ingrained, they won't even (**6**) ...... they are doing it. After all, think what we have achieved with recyclable waste in the home. Sorting paper, glass, aluminium and plastic waste and then depositing it in the appropriate container outside is (**7**) ...... a great chore any more. People have become accustomed to doing this, so it doesn't (**8**) ...... to them that they are spending any additional time in the process. Only if they have to carry this waste for some (**9**) ...... distance to find a suitable container do they feel they are (**10**) ....'

Most people know they should behave in a responsible way and just need (**11**) ...... to do so. So a quirky, (**12**) ...... gimmick might be enough to change behaviour. With this in (**13**) ...... , the city of Berlin is introducing rubbish bins that say 'danke', 'thank you' and 'merci' – Berlin is a(n) (**14**) ...... city – when someone drops an item of rubbish into them. It might just (**15**) ...... the trick in this city, too.

0	**A** band	**B** scale	**C** range	**D** scope
1	**A** market	**B** advertise	**C** promote	**D** launch
2	**A** dispose	**B** discard	**C** jettison	**D** throw
3	**A** appealed	**B** called	**C** approached	**D** urged
4	**A** plan	**B** trial	**C** campaign	**D** tactic
5	**A** principle	**B** system	**C** matter	**D** duty
6	**A** notice	**B** remark	**C** comprehend	**D** appreciate
7	**A** almost	**B** barely	**C** virtually	**D** hardly
8	**A** concern	**B** occur	**C** impress	**D** strike
9	**A** estimated	**B** remarkable	**C** appreciable	**D** visible
10	**A** inconvenienced	**B** sacrificed	**C** complicated	**D** imposed
11	**A** ordering	**B** prompting	**C** forcing	**D** obliging
12	**A** lighthearted	**B** mundane	**C** subjective	**D** intense
13	**A** context	**B** thought	**C** spirit	**D** mind
14	**A** worldly	**B** mixed	**C** cosmopolitan	**D** international
15	**A** serve	**B** do	**C** make	**D** play

TEST 8
CAE

Exam Essentials

PAPER 1 Reading
PAPER 2 Writing
PAPER 3 English in Use ▶ | Part 1
PAPER 4 Listening | Part 2
PAPER 5 Speaking | Part 3
                     | Part 4
                     | Part 5
                     | Part 6

For questions **16–30**, complete the following article by writing each missing word in the correct box on your answer sheet. Use only one word for each space. The exercise begins with an example (**0**).

Example:

0	*These*	0

Flying in Style

(0) .... days commercial airliners are becoming larger, (16) .... makes flying cheaper but in many ways more impersonal. Perhaps (17) .... a response to this, a more old-fashioned way of taking to the air is gaining popularity in Britain. (18) .... number of companies today offer charter flights in small aircraft. You hire the plane and pilot, just as you might hire a chauffeur-driven car, and (19) .... are yours for the day.

If you are flying on a short trip (20) .... Britain to the continent, a light plane can get you (21) .... almost as quickly as a jet airliner. In fact, the whole journey takes far (22) .... time, since you don't need to be at the airport hours (23) .... advance. And if you share the cost with friends, it can be cheaper than a scheduled flight.

The atmosphere (24) .... board is relaxed and friendly, with formalities (25) .... passport control and customs, if not entirely eliminated, at least kept (26) .... a minimum. Instead of walking for (27) .... seems like miles through a vast airport terminal, (28) .... it's time to take off, you simply stroll over and ease (29) .... into the plane. Even the flight itself is more fun, as (30) .... as the weather is fine. And if you want to descend and take a closer look at something on the ground, just ask the pilot; you're the boss!

In most lines of the following text, there is **either** a spelling **or** a punctuation error. For each numbered line **31–46**, write the correctly spelt word or show the correct punctuation in the box on your answer sheet. Some lines are correct. Indicate these lines with a (✓) in the box. The exercise begins with three examples (**0**), (**00**) and (**000**).

Example:

0	*composer's*	0
00	✓	00
000	*especially*	000

The Sound of Music

0	Music appears to mimic the intonation of its composers language,
00	according to experts who have been studying music from different
000	countries – especialy music by British and French composers – in an
31	attemt to establish whether there is a link between the sound of pure
32	music (as opposed to songs) and language. The first step, was to make
33	an analysis of sentences spoken in English and French, recording the
34	rythm and intonation used by the speakers. It was found that English
35	had more of a swing to it than French, which quiet astonished the
36	experts. 'We hadnt expected English to be so musical,' admitted
37	Dr Helen Crosby. 'Perhaps this phenomonon is due to the tendency
38	to cut some vowels short while stressing others.' When the team
39	peformed a similar breakdown of the pitch and melody of popular
40	works of music, they found staggering similarities This leads them to
41	conclude that composers mimic the sound of language to a suprising
42	degree. 'I don't imagine that the composers are aware of what their
43	doing,' said Dr Crosby. Even if they are not conscious of this, the
44	tendency of composers to mimic linguistic patterns is pronounsed.
45	Farther research has indicated that it is more apparent in music
46	composed since the early ninteenth century than in earlier music.

PAPER 1 Reading

PAPER 2 Writing

PAPER 3 English in Use ▶

PAPER 4 Listening

PAPER 5 Speaking

Part 1
Part 2
Part 3
Part 4
Part 5
Part 6

For questions **47–61**, read the two texts below. Use the words in the boxes to the right of the texts to form one word that fits in the same numbered space in the text. Write the new word in the correct box on your answer sheet. The exercise begins with an example (**0**).

Example:

0	*unlike*	0

BOOK REVIEW

A Boy for Turning

Hamish Middleton's latest novel *A Boy for Turning* is (**0**) .... any of his earlier

works. The plot is (**47**) .... complex, with (**48**) .... characters

– far more than the reader can readily remember – which is a new (**49**) ....

for him. And while his previous novels have been notable for their sparse prose, here the

language is (**50**) .... rich in texture. But some things have not changed.

Middleton has the (**51**) .... ability to capture the rhythms of everyday speech,

and the dialogue here is impressive in its (**52**) .... And his attitude towards

those who strive to assert their independence from the forces tying them down is as

(**53**) .... as ever.

(**0**)	**LIKE**
(**47**)	ASTONISH
(**48**)	NUMBER
(**49**)	DEPART
(**50**)	PHENOMENON
(**51**)	ADMIRE
(**52**)	AUTHENTIC
(**53**)	COMPASSION

JOB ADVERTISEMENT

Sales Manager

Wallymart, a (**54**) .... importer of fashion clothing and related items, has

expanded (**55**) .... over recent years. We are now in need of a Sales

Manager, (**56**) .... , but not necessarily, someone with experience in the

garment industry. In a sector that must be (**57**) .... to the requirements of its

clients, we need a person who can bring (**58**) .... and creativity to the

position. Our head office is in Reading, but we also have offices in Manchester, Edinburgh

and Cardiff. The successful candidate will receive an excellent salary and fringe benefits,

including a relocation bonus if applicable. Wallymart is an equal (**59**) ....

employer. We hereby give our solemn (**60**) .... that every applicant will be

assessed purely on merit, (**61**) .... of gender or race.

(**54**)	LEAD
(**55**)	STEADY
(**56**)	PREFER
(**57**)	RESPONSE
(**58**)	ADAPT
(**59**)	OPPORTUNE
(**60**)	ASSURE
(**61**)	RESPECT

PAPER 1 Reading

PAPER 2 Writing

PAPER 3 English in Use ▸

PAPER 4 Listening

PAPER 5 Speaking

Part 1
Part 2
Part 3
Part 4
Part 5
Part 6

For questions **62–74**, read the notes about a grant for young artists. Use the information in the notes to complete the numbered gaps in the formal leaflet. The words you need **do not occur** in the notes. **Use no more than two words for each gap.** The exercise begins with an example (**0**).

Example:

| 0 | *between the* | 0 __ __ |

NOTES

- Haley Watt Grant is for young artists.

- It's open to anyone 16–22 who lives in UK.

- Anyone who wants to apply for a grant has to send an original work of art.

- They also have to write an article saying why, in their opinion, art matters to society – 500 words.

- We will decide on the winners and send them a letter some time in January.

- Five people get the grant every year. They will be given £2000, paid out over a year (£500 every 3 months).

- They can do whatever they like with the money, but we want them all to take part in the exhibition that will take place at the end of the year in which they receive the grant.

LEAFLET

The Haley Watt Grant

The Haley Watt Grant is open to young people (**0**) .... ages of 16 and 22 who (**62**) .... of the UK.

In order to be (**63**) .... for the grant, applicants must (**64**) .... one original work of art. (**65**) .... , they are required to write a short article (**66**) .... their views on the subject of (**67**) .... of art in society (approximately 500 words).

The grant committee will make its (**68**) .... from the applications received, and the winners will be (**69**) .... letter in January. The five recipients of the grant will each be (**70**) .... the sum of £2,000, which will be paid in four equal instalments of £500 at three-monthly (**71**) ....

Winners are (**72**) .... to use the money as they wish, but they are expected to (**73**) .... in an exhibition which will be (**74**) .... at the end of the calendar year in which they receive the grant.

For questions **75–80**, read the following text and then choose from the list **A–J** given below the best phrase to fill each of the spaces. Write one letter (**A–J**) in the correct box on your answer sheet. Each correct phrase may only be used once. **Some of the suggested answers do not fit at all**. The exercise begins with an example (**0**).

Example:

0	J	0

What causes volcanic eruptions?

The largest volcanic eruption of the last thousand years took place in 1815, when Tambora in Indonesia exploded. (**0**) .... It is believed that 92,000 people died, 10,000 of whom were killed as a direct result of the eruption. (**75**) .... That year minimum temperatures were lower than usual in the northern hemisphere and people starved when crops failed.

It has long been known that volcanic eruptions like that of Tambora can have a dramatic effect on the environment, but does it work the other way round as well? Does the environment have an effect on volcanic activity? (**76**) .... Records of volcanic eruptions over the last three hundred years show that these eruptions did not occur randomly throughout the year. (**77**) .... This indicates that changes in the weather, climate and sea level may exert as great an influence on volcanoes as volcanoes do on the environment. (**78**) ....

Evidence suggests that at the end of the last ice age, when the ice melted, magma that had previously been suppressed by the weight of ice was able to move. (**79**) .... Rising and falling sea levels also seem to have played a major role, which is not surprising considering the pressures exerted by trillions of tons of water on the Earth's crust. For the past few millennia, sea levels have not changed much, but still, unimaginably vast volumes of water move around every year as a result of seasonal changes. (**80**) .... Some scientists now fear that with global warming melting the ice caps, we are going to see an increase in volcanic activity. In an already disturbed environment, it is safe to say that the consequences of this are likely to be unpredictable.

A However, what is less clear is exactly how the environment triggers volcanic eruptions

B A further 82,000 succumbed to disease and hunger in the aftermath

C Of course, a tsunami can also have a devastating effect on coastal areas.

D Volcanoes appear to be more active when sea levels change

E Instead, they occurred more often between the months of November and March

F As a result, there was an increase in volcanic activity

G Recent research suggests that this can and does happen

H The chances are that we will never really know exactly what happened

I This may well be enough to trigger volcanic eruptions

J An estimated 150 cubic kilometres of ash were released into the atmosphere

You will hear part of a talk by the director of a sports academy. For questions **1–8**, complete the sentences.

You will hear the recording twice.

The Waterman Sports Academy

The Waterman Sports Academy offers training in several sports,
including swimming and [_____ **1**]

Helen coached a girl
who wanted to compete in the [_____ **2**]

Her interest in sports medicine dates back to the time
when her [_____ **3**] suffered a back injury.

To be successful in a particular sport,
an athlete must have the right [_____ **4**]

Helen says that fitness is important,
even in sports like [_____ **5**]

She stresses that a [_____ **6**]
is vital in physical development.

Athletes who do not have the latest [_____ **7**]
are handicapped in competitions.

In Helen's opinion, the most important factor for success is having
the right [_____ **8**]

You will hear a talk about the popular fictional character, Aladdin. For questions **9–16**, complete the sentences.

Listen very carefully as you will hear the recording ONCE only.

The Appeal of Aladdin

Although his father is only [_____ 9] ,

Aladdin eventually marries the king's daughter.

Aladdin was probably not one of the [_____ 10] tales

in *The Thousand and One Nights*.

The French translator of this collection may have written the Aladdin story in

[_____ 11]

The story has been particularly popular

in periods of limited [_____ 12]

The speaker implies that [_____ 13] of this story

are not crucial to its success.

Films made in Hollywood

do not depict [_____ 14] accurately.

We are told that people enjoy films set in

[_____ 15] locations.

Aladdin is popular with theatre companies that have

a limited [_____ 16]

You will hear part of an interview with Harold Mackenzie, who has written a book about early adolescence. For questions **17–22**, choose the correct answer **A**, **B**, **C** or **D**.

You will hear the recording twice.

---

17 According to Harold, what is the main reason pre-teens are receiving more publicity?
  A Psychologists now understand the importance of the pre-teen years.
  B A great deal of research is being done into the way children develop.
  C Pre-teens are now demanding more attention from the media.
  D People now realise pre-teens have economic power.

18 Harold suggests that pre-teens
  A cannot keep up with their peers.
  B start to choose their own clothes.
  C develop unusual tastes.
  D become more aware of their image.

19 Harold claims friendships are important to pre-teens because
  A these relationships help them establish their identities.
  B the children are beginning to rebel against their families.
  C friends are starting to replace family members.
  D the children are now capable of reacting to other people.

20 He suggests that an alternative method of academic evaluation would
  A enable parents to be more supportive.
  B be more effective than examinations.
  C mean less stress for pre-teens.
  D delay the onset of tension in adolescence.

21 How does he suggest parents can help pre-teens develop confidence?
  A by allowing them to buy whatever they like
  B by allowing them a certain degree of independence
  C by allowing them to make decisions about their spare time
  D by allowing them to control unimportant aspects of their lives

22 According to Harold, what is the greatest challenge facing parents of pre-teens?
  A deciding what kinds of toys to buy for their children
  B developing the correct approach to material possessions
  C establishing a way of communicating effectively with their children
  D discovering what kind of help their children really need

PAPER 1 Reading

PAPER 2 Writing

PAPER 3 English in Use

PAPER 4 Listening ▶ Part 1

PAPER 5 Speaking Part 2

Part 3

Part 4

You will hear five short extracts in which different people talk about their experiences at the theatre.

You will hear the recording twice. While you listen you must complete both tasks.

Task One

For questions **23–27**, match the extracts with what each person says about the show he or she enjoyed most, listed **A–H**.

A The atmosphere was intimate.

B I loved the period costumes.

C The play was very moving.

D I saw the play a couple of times.

E The play had a large cast.

F I went along reluctantly.

G The star of the show was very talented.

H The show was performed by a foreign company.

Speaker 1	23
Speaker 2	24
Speaker 3	25
Speaker 4	26
Speaker 5	27

Task Two

For questions **28–32**, match the extracts with the views each speaker has about why theatre is an interesting medium, listed **A–H**.

A The thrill of watching big stars is unforgettable.

B You can get carried away by the performance.

C The theatre can be a communal experience.

D It's interesting to learn from the cast.

E Ideas can be conveyed with stunning force.

F Each performance is a unique experience.

G You sometimes feel transported to a different era.

H The theatre can surprise and stimulate the audience.

Speaker 1	28
Speaker 2	29
Speaker 3	30
Speaker 4	31
Speaker 5	32

Part 1 (3 minutes)

The examiner will ask you a few questions about yourself and then ask you to talk to your partner. For example, the examiner may ask you:

- How popular are the cinema and theatre in your town or region?
- Which do you prefer, going to the cinema or watching films on television?
- What was the last film that you enjoyed?

Part 2 (4 minutes)

You will each be asked to talk for a minute without interruption. You will each be given a set of photographs in turn to talk about. After your partner has finished speaking, you will be asked a brief question connected with your partner's photographs.

Stress (compare, contrast and speculate)

Turn to pictures 1–4 on page **213**, which show people in stressful situations.

Candidate A, compare and contrast these pictures and say what you think they show about stress.

Candidate B, what sort of situation causes you the greatest amount of stress?

Struggling against the elements (compare, contrast and speculate)

Turn to pictures 1–2 on page **214**, which show people who have to struggle against the elements.

Candidate B, compare and contrast these two situations, saying how you think the people might have got into the situation and could be feeling now.

Candidate A, what sort of struggle against the elements would you find most difficult?

Part 3 (4 minutes)

Creativity (discuss, evaluate and select)

Turn to the illustrations on page **215**, which show different forms of creativity.

Talk to each other about the type of creativity in each of these situations and then decide which illustration best shows the rewards of being creative.

Part 4 (4 minutes)

The examiner will encourage you to develop the topic of your discussion in Part 3 by asking questions such as:

- How important is it to people to feel they are creative in some way?
- Do you feel people get a similar sense of satisfaction from other activities?
- It is sometimes said that everyone has the potential to be creative in some way. Do you agree? Why (not)?
- Does modern society encourage people to be creative more or less than was the case in previous times?

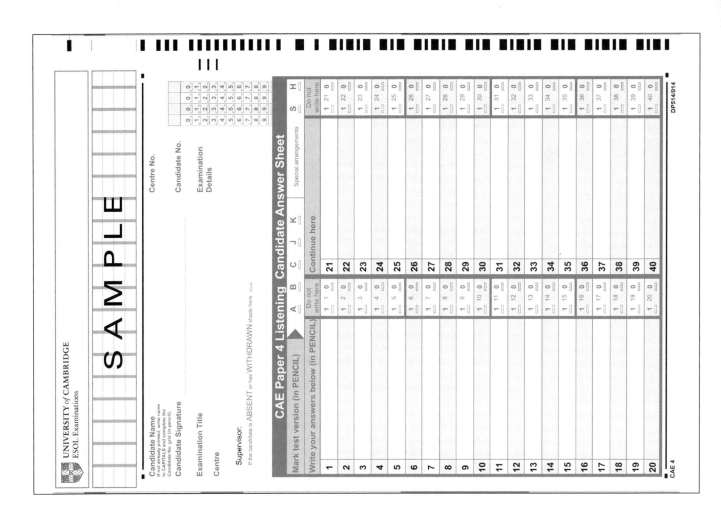

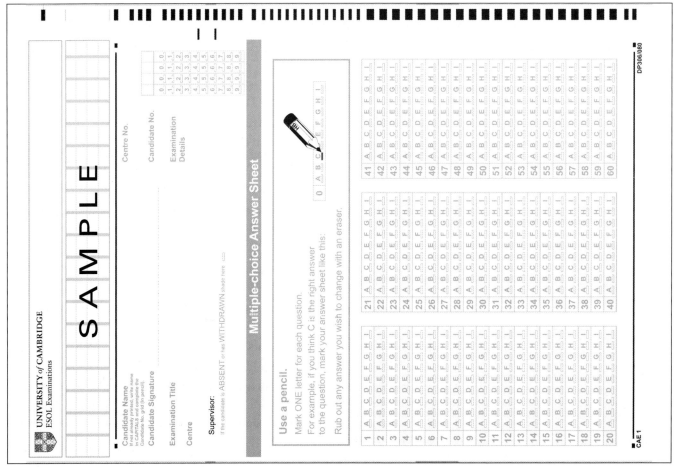

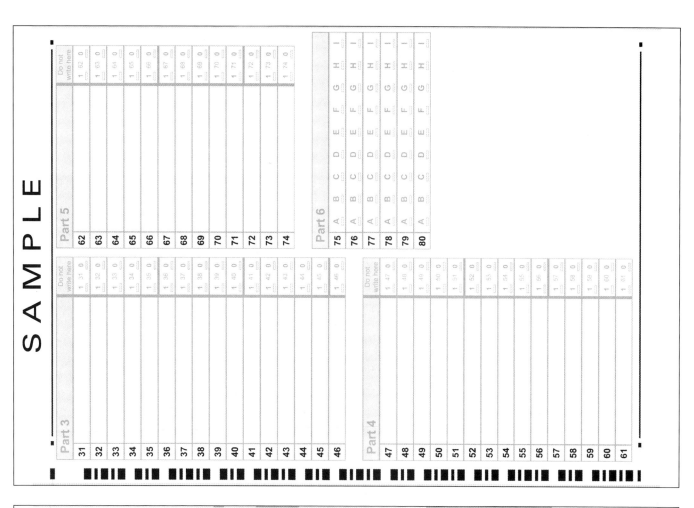

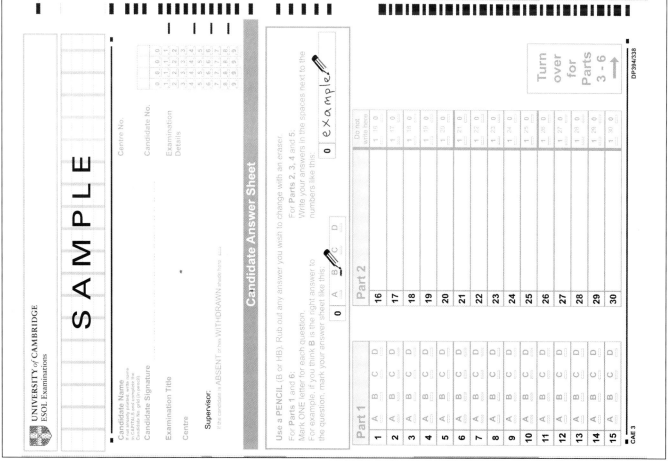

TEST 1

▶▶ **PART 2**

Candidate A

Language bank

These people could be ...

They seem to be ...

I imagine ...

I suppose ...

I'm fairly sure ...

I'd say they're probably ...

Apparently, ...

Judging by the fact that ...

Similarly, ...

I can't tell who/where/what ...

actors
amateur
annual tradition
bow to the audience
brightly coloured costumes and
    masks
clown in a circus
curtain call
folk costumes of some sort
on the stage
pastime/hobby
perform a folk dance
professional
put on a performance
revellers
street party
take part in a festival/carnival/
    performance/play
well-equipped theatre

▶▶ **PART 2**

Candidate B

Language bank

The picture shows/depicts ...

They must be ...

It might/could be ...

He/She seems to be ...

In contrast to ...

As in the previous picture, ...

There are a number of advantages/
disadvantages to working ...

One advantage/disadvantage would
be ...

I imagine it's very satisfying to ...

agricultural workers
cheap labour
craft
create something with your hands
cut off from contact with the outside
   world
deal with students
discipline
executive
exhausting
field on a hillside
highly-paid/badly paid
indoors/outdoors
job satisfaction
make objects from clay
manual labour
mentally/physically exhausting
potter
sophisticated modern office
spectacular view of the city
stressful
suffer from the heat/stress
well-behaved
well-equipped office

Candidates A and B

Language bank

The benefits/drawbacks of ... are obvious, I think.

What about the advantages/disadvantages, in your view?

Do the disadvantages outweigh the advantages in your opinion?

It's easy to see the benefits of laptop computers, don't you think?

Mobile phones certainly make it easier to keep in touch, wouldn't you say?

I don't think anyone would disagree about the benefits of modern communications.

It's undoubtedly easier for the average person to travel these days, but what about the air pollution caused by commercial aircraft?

I'm not sure whether there are any health risks associated with cooking food in a microwave oven. What do you think?

It's usually more convenient to drive somewhere than to take public transport, but surely the pollution caused by cars is too high a price to pay?

I'd find it difficult to think of any disadvantages connected with electricity.

Perhaps we have to distinguish between electricity itself and the means of generating it.

Is this a nuclear power station?

I'm not sure whether this photo is meant to illustrate modern western medicine in general or operations in particular.

commercial plane	microwave oven meal	telecommunications satellite
laptop computer	operating theatre	satellite dish power station

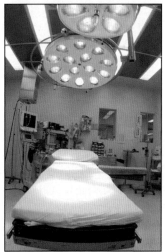

▸▸ **PART 2**

Candidate A

Language bank

I guess/I imagine ...

They appear to be ...

He/She may be ...

He/She looks as though ...

On the other hand, he/she might be ...

To judge from the clothes they're wearing, ...

To judge from his/her posture, ...

about to dive
apprehensive
bathing trunks
business lunch
business suit
concentrate on what you are about to do
decide/make up your mind
diving board
interview for a job
look at the menu
miss your cue
nervous
order a meal
overcome your fears
have your arms outstretched
wait in the wings

▸ **2**

▸ **3**

▸ **1**

▸ **4**

Language bank

I can't tell whether the person is a man or a woman.

It looks as if/though ...

I can't see the expression on his/her face, but I think he/she must be ...

Perhaps he/she feels ...

It's also possible that he/she ...

If I were him/her, I'd probably feel ...

The landscape/room might make me feel ...

The sun appears to be setting because the scene is bathed in red light.

The person is dwarfed by the landscape.

Perhaps she's waiting ...

She might simply be looking at something outside.

alone	long shadows
depressing atmosphere	peer through the curtains
dry grass	remote
elderly lady	rugged
formal clothes	spectacular
insignificant	suffer from loneliness
inspiring	tracksuit
lonely	uplifting

▶ 1

▶ 2

▶▶ **PART 3**

Candidates A and B

Language bank

I'd imagine that anyone who wishes to ... would have to be motivated.

He/She's probably motivated by ...

He/She must be motivated by ...

People can be motivated to excel/overcome difficulties.

Judging by ... , I imagine he/she works very hard.

A powerful sense of motivation could be negative if a person became obsessed with his/her goals.

Do you think such people might put others at risk?

Surely this sort of motivation is the most harmful type that we have seen?

depressed
discouraged/encouraged
inspired
jealous
miss out on other aspects of life
overcome physical hardships
personal ambition
push yourself to achieve a goal
ruthless and unfeeling
single-minded
the desire for knowledge
the desire to acquire material possessions
the desire to be admired by your colleagues
the desire to be the first
the desire to excel
the desire to gain the approval of others
the desire to impress others
the desire to overcome hardship/difficulties
the desire to pursue a career

Language bank

It looks as if/though ...

They appear to be ...

They must be ...

I would say he/she's probably ...

Perhaps they're going somewhere on holiday.

They're about to leave on a holiday, not a business trip.

Like the man in the second picture, ...

Unlike the man in the second picture, these people are ...

The mode of transport in this case is very different.

about to board a spaceship
about to set off
boot of the car
briefcase
business trip
casual clothes
crew of a spaceship
embark on a journey/mission
family car
intercity train
load the luggage
members of a family
space mission
spacesuit
station platform
suit and tie
suitcase on wheels

▶▶ **PART 2**

Candidate B

Language bank

He/She looks very tired.

He/She must be feeling exhausted.

This makes me think he/she's been working ...

In all likelihood, ...

Of course, it's also possible that ...

I suppose they feel satisfied as well as exhausted.

In contrast to the previous two images, this picture shows ...

excited by the prospect of (doing something)
look after a young child
loosen your tie
mental/physical work
renovate a house
rest your head on your hand
stare at a computer screen
stiff muscles
wear a shirt and tie

▶▶ **PART 3**

Candidates A and B

Language bank

They seem very proud of ...

Judging by their expression, ...

He/She's probably proud of his/her achievement.

Naturally, he/she must be proud of this accomplishment.

This kind of pride is very natural.

I'd say he/she's probably a ... .

Is his/her pride due solely to the fact that he/she ... ?

Obviously, he/she's just ...

cheer
dedicate yourself to achieving your
    goal
delighted
justifiably proud
lean against the car
own an impressive car
parental pride
politician
proud of your child/offspring
public acclaim
push a stroller
satisfied with yourself
trophy
victory
vote for someone
win an election
work and save in order to buy
    something

▶▶ **PART 2**

Candidate A

Language bank

Presumably, this sport appeals to people who ...

It attracts people who are ...

People who are ... are inclined to do this sport.

People who want to excel in this sport must be ...

This sport does not demand the same level of fitness as ...

In contrast to ... , this sport ...

aim
archer
archery
bow and arrow
bull's eye
concentration
co-ordination and balance
good sense of rhythm
gymnastics
head a ball
hit the target
individual/team sport
pole
pole vault
powerful physique
take part in
score a goal
training and practice
weightlifting

Language bank

I should think a house like this would be ...

In contrast to the other buildings, this house ...

The house seems to be made of ...

One advantage/disadvantage of a home like this would be ...

Its location would be a disadvantage in case of illness or other emergencies.

The house itself would be expensive to keep up because ...

It would require a large staff to look after a house like this.

Some people may dislike feeling that their house is just like all the rest.

Privacy might be a problem in a home like this.

The house might be damp because it's so close to the water.

The houses are standing on stilts in a lake or river.

(lack of) privacy
damp
cut off from civilisation
flats in a high-rise block
high heating and maintenance costs
insulation
isolated
log cabin
mansion
rural/urban environment
stately home
suburban environment
terraced houses
unsuitable for domestic purposes
wooden house on stilts

▸▸ **PART 3**

Candidates A and B

Language bank

Why couldn't we use this picture to show an interesting aspect of the city?

I think ferries are an interesting means of transport, don't you?

I'd say it shows the city is concerned about the environment.

I hardly feel buses are interesting enough to feature on a brochure.

I completely agree with you about that.

I think you're absolutely right about that.

I take your point.

I agree with you up to a point, but I think there are other factors to be taken into consideration.

I'm afraid I have to disagree with you on that point.

cause less pollution than other
  forms of transport
cycle path
efficient
extensive transport system
ferry
highway
lane
tram
underground train

Language bank

These people are wearing some sort of uniform ...

They're wearing white shirts and dark trousers.

They're all looking in the same direction and saluting.

They look as if they're in the army or some branch of the armed forces.

They look as if they're parading.

They're musicians in an orchestra.

Clearly, they feel part of a group because ...

As far as I can tell, the orchestra is made up of people of different ages.

Presumably, the sense of belonging to a group comes from their shared interest in music.

They may be amateur musicians, but they might also be professionals.

belt
blue and white helmet
brass instrument
bright red jacket
conductor
military uniform
music stand
officer
sense of shared danger
wind instrument

▶ 1

▶ 2

▶▶ **PART 2**

Candidate B

Language bank

The farmer appears to be examining his crops.

Although the plants look healthy to me, it's possible that the harvest won't be as good as he had hoped.

His experience may allow him to predict how good the harvest will be.

It's not entirely clear from his expression how he feels about ...

Perhaps the crop has been attacked by insects or other pests.

The maize may be infected with some kind of disease.

He seems to be a teacher.

He may be demonstrating something to his pupils.

Perhaps his experience has led him to conclude that ...

I suppose he's learnt how to use discipline in a class/gain the respect of the children he's teaching.

▶ **1**

▶ **2**

▸▸ **PART 3**

Candidates A and B

Language bank

Do we agree that better time management is necessary?

Would you say he/she's managed his/her time badly?

It's very obvious that ...

Maybe he/she should/shouldn't ...

If this situation occurs regularly, I think he/she needs to manage his/her time better.

This illustrates one of the problems connected with bad time management.

It must be frustrating to be in this situation.

I can imagine exactly how he/she feels.

Maybe he/she has no choice but to ...

badly organised
chat idly
deliver stationery supplies
ensure you get to the bus stop on time
have too much time on your hands
inefficient
miss the bus
point at your watch
queue at a post office counter
run to catch a bus
the baby in the high chair is screaming
the child is tugging at her dress
waste time

▶▶ **PART 2**

Candidate A

Language bank

I imagine he/she's anxious about ...

My impression is that he/she ...

My guess would be that he/she ...

Maybe he/she's already ... and is now ...

Whereas the first picture shows someone worried about a medical matter, this picture depicts someone in a state of anxiety about work.

The person's facial expression shows he/she's anxious or worried.

deal with a problem
exam results
frown
notice board
patient
physician
possible treatment.
talk about the prognosis
work-related stress

Language bank

It's obvious that he/she ...

I suppose he/she's pleased/relieved that ...

He/She's probably feeling pleased because ...

He/She's happy because he/she's finally managed (to do something).

I would guess that he/she ... for the first time, and he/she's delighted that he/she's achieved this.

He/She's expressing his/her pleasure at this achievement.

It's not entirely clear what/who ...

academic gown
bicycle fitted with outriders
congratulate someone on his/her
   promotion
degree/diploma
designer
dressmaker
dressmaker's dummy
sense of elation
give the 'thumbs-up' sign
graduate from college/university
sign a mutually beneficial business
   deal
successful negotiation
take pleasure in creating something

▶ 1

▶ 2

▶ 3

▶ 4

▶▶ **PART 3**

Candidates A and B

Language bank

The clothes he/she's wearing give the impression that he/she's ...

Perhaps he/she intends his/her appearance as some sort of statement.

Surely his/her appearance is a symbol of what he/she's attained/what he/she believes?

Don't you think he/she's trying to show the world ... ?

He/She doesn't seem to care about convention/fashion.

Would you say his/her appearance shows ... ?

He/She's wearing what looks like ...

He/She comes across as ...

anti-establishment
arrogant
capable
catwalk
cloak trimmed with fur
coat/gown with a large fur collar
conservative
diamond necklace
efficient
extravagant clothes
fashion victim
formal event
haughty
loose-fitting
member of the armed forces
rank
scruffy
three-piece suit
unorthodox clothes
veil

Language bank

She might be his grandmother.

He/She's looking at ... with a friendly but respectful expression.

He/She may respect ... for several reasons.

He/She may have been brought up to behave respectfully towards older people.

He/She appears to have made a speech.

I expect an audience is obliged to applaud a speaker out of politeness, but the facial expressions of these men suggest that their respect is genuine.

I know he's a famous politician, but I can't remember his name.

I think the man in the photo is Nelson Mandela, but I'm not sure.

applaud
bow to someone
express your respect and
   admiration
honour someone for his/her
   achievements
make a speech
politeness/courtesy is important in
   this culture
politician
(regrettable lack of) respect for old
   people
respect for your elders
statesman
western society

Candidate B

Language bank

There's no way of telling whether they're the architects or the owners.

In all likelihood, they're colleagues.

They're wearing ... , so they're probably ...

An undertaking like this must involve working closely with other people, all of whom have different skills to contribute.

If they're partners, they must have a great deal of confidence in one another.

Trust would be the basis of their working relationship, I imagine.

In this kind of partnership, I imagine respect for the other person's ability must be crucial.

architect
building site
collaboration
colleague
contribution
co-operation
engineer
hard hat
have confidence in someone
intellectual ability
lab technician
laboratory
mutual trust
rely on your colleague
street musician
white lab coat

▶▶ **PART 3**

  Candidates A and B

Language bank

This is a physically taxing activity, but I suppose it represents a way of relaxing for some people.

I imagine there's some danger involved as well.

Personally, I don't understand why people would choose to ...

This game usually requires a partner, but it's also possible to play against a computer program.

This is a solitary/creative/exciting pastime.

Gardening is a very popular hobby, especially with older people.

battle of wits
chess
competitive
croquet
croquet mallet
danger of dehydration
easel
lawn
recreation
rucksack
sand dune
weed the flower bed

▶▶ **PART 2**

Candidate A

Language bank

I can't see exactly what they're doing, but I think they're ...

It looks as though they're under a lot of stress.

I'd say this kind of stress is due partly to ... and partly to ...

There's a certain amount of danger involved in work like this.

Serious accidents can happen all too easily if people are not careful.

There's always the danger that something could go wrong.

I think most performers feel nervous before going on stage, and this could be a cause of stress.

assembly line
boring and repetitive
buy/sell shares
conjuror
construction site
construction worker
fall behind
fatal accident
high levels of noise
investor
make/lose a fortune
price of shares
stock exchange
stockbroker
there's a lot at stake

▶1

▶2

▶3

▶4

▶▶ **PART 2**

Candidate B

Language bank

The people in the boat are probably there from choice.

Probably they feel exhilarated, even though there are dangers involved.

They may not have realised how dangerous the situation would be.

They might regret ...

In contrast, the man probably has no alternative but to do battle against the elements.

He might be facing starvation.

coastline
drown
in danger of capsizing
rough sea
scorching heat
scratch a living from the land
skinny cow
sparse vegetation
starve
subsistence farmer
suffer from drought
survive
take part in a race/regatta
the soil is parched
water shortage

▶▶ **PART 3**

Candidates A and B

Language bank

Do you feel this is a good illustration of the rewards that creativity can bring?

Talent is not enough; you have to work at your craft.

Many people believe they could write a novel, but I think creative writing requires talent.

Is composing music one of the most rewarding forms of creativity? After all, everyone can appreciate music.

Carpenters are not generally regarded as being creative.

It must be immensely rewarding to know that people live and work in a building you've designed.

Top designers are often in the public eye.

architect
carpenter
composer
craft
fine craftsmanship
functional as well as aesthetically
    pleasing
invent
landscape gardener
prune a bush/tree/shrub
social status
sturdily built
take pride in your work
topiary

1 Formal letter

▶▶ **Exam task**

A colleague of yours, Alice Watson, has applied for a job in the public relations department of a large charity, Poverty Action. You have been asked to write a letter providing a character reference for her. Indicate how long and in what capacity you have worked with her, and how her personal characteristics would make her suited for the job. Here is part of the letter you received from Poverty Action:

> The job of Public Relations Co-ordinator consists mainly of supervising PR work, and entails travelling around the country and working with various people in our large organisation. The successful applicant will need good managerial skills and be committed to the philosophy of our charity.

Write your **letter**.

▶▶ **Approach**

▶ A character reference is almost always addressed to the organisation where someone has applied for a job or a place to study. Generally, you should use the heading line 'To whom it may concern', rather than writing to a specific person. If the exam question asks you to refer to certain characteristics of a person, make sure you do so. You should also imagine what other information may be required, bearing in mind the position the person has applied for.

▶ All character references are formal in style. Generally, you should write at least three paragraphs: introduction, main body and conclusion.

Useful phrases

Introduction
To whom it may concern

I have been asked to write this reference for (Ms Watson).

With reference to your letter of (3rd March), ...

I have known (Ms Watson) for the last (four) years ...

I was her supervisor/superior in (the publicity department of Children in Need) ...

Main body
(Ms Watson) has always shown great dedication/commitment to her work.

She has (excellent managerial skills) ...

Her duties/tasks here included ...

She proved to be ...

competent

dependable

efficient

popular with colleagues

trustworthy

Conclusion
I understand that (Ms Watson) has applied for ...

I am certain that (Ms Watson) would be extremely capable ...

I have no hesitation in recommending her for ...

I should be very happy to supply any further information.

Please do not hesitate to contact me ...

This is the standard heading for character references.

To whom it may concern

State the name of the person for whom you are writing the reference.

Ms Alice Watson

I have been asked to write this reference for Ms Alice Watson, who worked with me for almost four years in the Head Office of the charity Children in Need. I was her immediate superior in the publicity department of that organisation, so I was able to observe her work at close quarters and feel qualified to evaluate her suitability for similar positions.

Say how you know the person and explain in what way you worked together.

Explain what sort of jobs the person did, and describe the positive characteristics she showed.

Ms Watson was extremely committed to her work and always performed to the highest standard. Her tasks included checking press releases and writing letters to a wide variety of recipients, and she displayed first-class communication skills. The executives of the organisation found her entirely trustworthy, and she always carried out her work cheerfully and efficiently. At various times of the year our department employed a number of temporary staff in order to send out appeals for donations, and in her dealings with these people Ms Watson exhibited very good managerial skills. She was also popular with the permanent staff, though she never allowed this to interfere with the work that had to be done.

I understand that Ms Watson has applied for the position of Public Relations Co-ordinator, which I imagine entails considerable responsibility. I have no hesitation in recommending her for this position, and I am certain she will prove an excellent and hard-working member of your organisation. Naturally, I would be very happy to supply any further information, so please do not hesitate to contact me if this should be required.

Refer to the person's suitability for the tasks involved in the new job.

End the letter formally.

Yours faithfully,

Emma Lyons
Public Relations Officer
Children in Need

2 Informal letter

▶▶ **Exam task**

You have recently received a letter from your penfriend, Antonio, who wants to visit Britain to learn more about the culture and history of the country. Read his letter and the advertisement he has sent you for a study holiday in Britain, on which you have made some notes. Then, using the information carefully, write a letter to Antonio.

> I have a place at university to study British History next year, and I think it would be good to get to know more about the culture and history of the country before I start. Now you've lived in Britain, so could you give me your opinion of this study holiday? I plan to go in the spring for a few weeks. Do you think the programme sounds reasonable? Would it give me a good general background to the arts, sports, way of life, traditions and history of Britain? I realise I can't learn much in three weeks, but I'd like to get as much as I can!

How close?
Public transport to Oxford itself?

What activities exactly?

What kind and where?
Included in price?

QUEENSBRIDGE HERITAGE Study Holidays

<u>Situated near Oxford</u>, Queensbridge Heritage has been offering cultural study holidays to visitors from abroad since 1974. These holidays combine fascinating lectures and stimulating <u>classroom activities</u> with <u>field trips</u> to sites of interest all around the country.

Qualified experts provide detailed summaries of the key aspects of British artistic and cultural life, including notes on the major historical periods such as Victorian Britain and the Swinging Sixties.

<u>Programmes start in late spring and early summer</u>.

<u>Suitable accommodation is provided</u>.

Fees from £500 per week.

Write or email for full details to:

Included in price?
Or extra?

Exact dates?

Now write a **letter** to Antonio, giving your views on the suitability of the study holiday he is considering and suggesting what further information he should request before making a final decision (approximately 250 words). You should use your own words as far as possible. You do not need to include postal addresses.

▶▶ **Approach**

▶ Be careful you understand exactly who you are writing to, and what you must include in your letter. Here you are writing to a penfriend, giving him your views about a study holiday he is planning. You must answer all your friend's questions and mention all the notes you have made on the advertisement. For example, in his letter, Antonio mentions sports, which are not mentioned either in the advertisement or your notes – but you must mention sports in your letter.

▶ You are writing to a penfriend, so the register should be informal or semi-formal.

Useful phrases

▶▶ **Model answer**

Begin with a brief reaction to your friend's letter. In a few words, express your opinion of his idea, and link to the main body of the letter by indicating what you are going to say next.

Use your own words to express the points mentioned in the input material. For example, you can talk about 'hidden extras' instead of 'Included in price?'

End by summarising the main ideas in your letter.

As this is a letter to a friend, you can end informally.

Dear Antonio,

Thanks for your letter last week. I was delighted to hear you're going to study British History – congratulations on getting a place at university! I think getting some background knowledge first would be a great help, but I feel you need more information about Queensbridge Heritage Study Holidays. The advertisement doesn't go into much detail, and there are some fundamental questions that need to be answered.

It seems to me that the advertisement isn't very clear about the price. You should find out if there are any hidden extras, such as charges for accommodation and field trips, which may not be included in the basic price. To be perfectly honest, I think £500 per week is rather inexpensive, so this might not include everything. In addition, if I were you, I would establish exactly what sort of accommodation they offer, and whether you might be expected to share a room. You should also find out exactly where the school is, what facilities it has, and what sort of public transport is available to the centre of the city.

On balance, I think this holiday might be very good, but it's impossible to say until you get more information. And you might find it doesn't give as broad a background in culture as you want; it seems to focus mainly on academic subjects, but sports aren't mentioned at all in the advertisement.

I hope I've been some use. Don't forget to write and tell me what you decide in the end.

Take care of yourself.

Alan

3 Article (1)

▶▶ Exam task

You see the following notice in a tourism magazine:

What was the most frightening journey you ever made?

Write an article for us, describing what happened and explaining what you learnt from the experience.

The best article will win a prize of two free air tickets!

Write your **article**.

▶▶ Approach

▶ There are often similarities between an article, a competition entry and a contribution to a guidebook in Part 2 of the Writing Paper. In fact, most competition entries and guidebook contributions can be considered a type of article in terms of content. In all cases, however, you will need to think carefully about the function of your writing. A typical question may ask you to describe something or someone, or give an account of what happened on a certain occasion – to narrate a story, in other words. But it is unlikely that that is all the question will ask you to do. You will usually also be asked to expand on your description or account, or add to it – by expressing an opinion, for example. In this question, you first have to narrate something that happened to you, and then explain what you learnt from your experience. You must also think carefully about the type of language required. For example, when you narrate something that has happened, remember to use appropriate past tenses (past continuous, past simple and past perfect).

▶ Think carefully about your target reader and make sure you write in an appropriate style. If your article, competition entry or contribution is for a fairly serious magazine, newspaper or book, a neutral or formal register may be suitable, but if you are writing for a young people's magazine, a more relaxed and informal style may be better. Whatever the style, however, your writing should be organised in clear paragraphs.

Useful phrases

Introduction

I had a rather frightening experience several years ago when ...

I'll never forget a journey I made a few years ago.

Several years ago, when I was ...

It turned out to be a scary/ frightening/terrifying experience.

Main body

All of a sudden, ...

a problem with the engine

flat tyre

run out of fuel

the car rolled to a standstill/came to a halt

Just as I was starting to worry, ...

Conclusion

Ever since that day ...

That event/accident/experience changed my view/opinion/outlook ...

The event/accident/whole episode taught me ...

▶▶ **Model answer**

Think of a suitable title for your article.

A Winter Journey

Several years ago, when I was a homesick first-year university student, I decided I was not going to join my friends on a skiing trip: I was going to spend Christmas with my parents instead. There was no convenient train or bus I could take, so I thought I would drive home to our rather isolated farm in my car. Although the journey was only about 200 miles, it turned out to be a scary experience, mainly because my ancient jalopy had a mind of its own.

Show you can use tenses correctly to describe the event.

I was about three-quarters of the way home, when all of a sudden, there was a deafening bang from the engine, and the car gently rolled to a standstill. I reluctantly decided to walk back to the town I had just passed, about five miles away. Unfortunately, it had started to snow and it was getting dark, so I didn't see the pothole until I fell into it and sprained my ankle! The pain was excruciating and I couldn't walk. And then, as I was starting to worry I might freeze to death, I heard a cheerful voice saying: 'Well, well! Need any help?'

Use adjectives and adverbs to make your story interesting. Use direct speech to make your story more dramatic. Think of interesting ways of expressing yourself. For example: 'gently rolled to a standstill' rather than 'stopped'.

The voice belonged to an old man, who took me home, bandaged my ankle, and made me comfortable in his spare room. The following morning, he called a mechanic to come and fix my car. He was very kind to me and made sure I got home safely.

The whole episode taught me that you should never give up hope, even if things look bad. I also learnt that ordinary people are basically decent and kind. And ever since that day, I take a mobile phone with me on every journey.

Answer the question fully and explain what you learnt from the experience.

4 Article (2)

▶▶ **Exam task**

You are a student at Whitebridge College, which recently held a party for the elderly people who live in the area. An article in the local newspaper was critical of the party, and when you phoned the editor of the newspaper to express your disagreement, she suggested you write an article expressing your own views.

You have made some notes in response to the first article, and you have also received some comments from a director of an old people's home who accompanied several elderly people to the party.

Good intentions, but college party could have been better!

While Whitebridge College deserves top marks for its good intentions, the party it held for old folk last Saturday did not live up to expectations. It was obvious that too little preparation had gone into the event: publicity was sadly lacking, and as a result, the party was not well attended.

Publicity aimed at old people's homes, not general public

One problem was obvious from the start, with the opening address by the mayor timed to begin at 11.30, when coaches bringing guests to the party were still arriving.

OK, bad timing

Several letters praising Jones

Some entertainment was provided in the person of stand-up comedian Jimmy Jones, although his peculiar brand of humour did not get many laughs. There was also swing music from the Walt Mitty Jazz Band, but surely the organisers must have realised jazz is too energetic and loud for an elderly audience!

Many elderly people love jazz!

Chicken dish clearly described as curry!

Lunch included 'a range of options', but at least one of the guests, Mrs Nelly Allbridge (82), complained that the chicken dish was 'too spicy by half' for her taste.

Let's hope the college does better in the future!

Please pass on my thanks to all the students who helped out. I know the people I accompanied had a fine time. As you requested, I talked to them afterwards, and below are some of their comments. Let's hope you can organise something similar next year!

Comments

'Great entertainment! The music took me back to my youth!' (Daniel Evans, 81)
The music was popular, though some people couldn't hear the comedian properly.

'Pity we missed the mayor's speech.' (Emma Perkins, 76)
More time could have been allowed to allow people to settle in?

'Nice refreshments.' (Bill White, 89)
People loved the food!

Now use this information to write an **article** for the newspaper, responding to the criticism in the first article, and expressing your own views of the party (approximately 250 words).

▶ When you write in response to an article, you should refer to all the points made in that article. You also need to include information from the other input material, in this case, the comments made by guests as well as the notes 'you' have made.

▶ You are asked to write an article for a local newspaper, so the register should be neutral or formal.

Useful phrases

Introduction
In last week's edition, you published an article that ...

I am writing on behalf of my fellow students ...

I would like to refer/respond to the article in last week's edition ...

Main body
The article suggested/stated that ...

The article was unfairly critical of ...

On the contrary, ...

Conclusion
In conclusion/To summarise, ...

There can be little doubt that ...

I hope I have succeeded in putting the record straight.

▶▶ **Model answer**

Whitebridge College Party for the Elderly

In last week's edition, you published an article that was unfairly critical about the Whitebridge College Summer Party for the Elderly. As a student who was actively involved in planning the party, I should like to respond to the points made in the article: your readers may have got the impression that the party was a dismal failure. In fact, the party was a great success, and we have been urged to repeat the event next year!

In your introduction, refer to the first article and say who you are and why you are writing.

Your correspondent suggests that too little effort had been put into organising the party. On the contrary, we had extensive discussions with residents at old people's homes in order to find out exactly what would be popular. Since the event was for the people in these homes, on what grounds does the writer of the article claim that 'publicity was sadly lacking'?

Respond to specific points in the previous article.

Secondly, we have been assured that guests enjoyed the entertainment provided. Mr Jones, the comedian was very popular, though admittedly, he was not audible at all times. However, the music was neither too energetic nor too loud. Many elderly people love jazz, and one guest said: 'The music took me back to my youth!' Thirdly, the majority of people commented favourably about the food, and we went to a great deal of trouble to cater for most tastes.

Use quotations to support your argument.

I have to agree, however, that the timing of events could have been improved: we had not realised how long it would take for all the guests to arrive. We shall certainly learn from this mistake and do better next year. In the meantime, I hope I have succeeded in putting the record straight.

It is a good idea to admit there were mistakes, as long as you stress that these mistakes will not be repeated.

5 Report

▶▶ **Exam task**

An international magazine is investigating tourism in various areas around the world. You have been asked to write a report for the magazine's editors, addressing the following questions:

- How has tourism in your region changed over the last decade?

- What are the reasons for these changes?

- What problems exist and can anything being done to solve them?

Write your **report**.

▶▶ **Approach**

▶ Read the question carefully to see whether you should include your own opinions in the report, and if this is the case, make it clear in the report when you are describing objective facts and when you are giving your interpretation. Depending on the task, you may need to describe something, give an account or narrate an event, express an opinion, and possibly compare and contrast.

▶ You can use headings and possibly bullet points or numbered lists to make it easier for the reader to find information quickly. The introduction and conclusion can be short. You are usually asked to write a report for some sort of organisation or publication, so the language you use should be semi-formal or formal. Even if you use bullet points or numbered lists, you should write complete sentences, not just notes. Remember that in formal writing we often use the passive voice.

Useful phrases

Introduction
The following report evaluates/describes/presents/provides an account of ...
This report aims to provide an overall view of the situation.
I shall describe the situation below.

Main body
a popular destination
easy to reach by rail/road/air
holidays to (Prague) are widely advertised
overcharge

service in hotels
It is generally accepted that ...
The vast majority of visitors ...
This is probably due to the fact that ...
While data is hard to come by, it is thought that ...

Conclusion
One measure which may improve the situation would be to introduce ...
I am of the opinion that ...
It is my view/opinion that ...
On balance, it appears that ...

▶▶ **Model answer**

Give your report a suitable title.

Tourism in Prague

Introduction
The last decade has seen a dramatic increase in the number of tourists visiting the Czech Republic in general and Prague in particular. The following report presents a brief overview.

Write a brief introduction that provides a few important facts and summarises what your report is about.

Background
Until 1989, Prague was not a popular destination for tourists from western Europe due to a number of factors:

Use bullet points to provide a list, but make sure each point is grammatically the same; here each point is a complete sentence.

▶ The city was difficult to reach; visitors often had to wait for long periods at border crossings.
▶ There was little information about trips to Prague in foreign travel agencies.
▶ Some people felt nervous about trips to countries in central and eastern Europe.

Changes
All the above factors have changed dramatically: Prague is now easy to reach by road, rail and air; trips to Prague are widely advertised in western countries; few visitors feel nervous about visiting a country in eastern Europe any more.

You can use semi-colons to separate items in a list, but as with bullet points, make sure each item is the same grammatically.

Criticisms
The majority of visitors to Prague are extremely satisfied on the whole; however, there are a few complaints about two specific areas:
▶ taxi drivers acting in a rude manner and, in many cases, overcharging.
▶ hotels providing less than adequate service.

Future development
The city council is at present considering stricter laws relating to taxi drivers. Moreover, the local tourist authority is reclassifying the hotels in the city.

Conclusion
While Prague can offer visitors a generally positive experience, there are some issues which need to be addressed. I am of the opinion that better regulation of taxi drivers and hotels will solve these problems.

Make sure each section is clearly separated from the others.

6 Proposal

▶▶ **Exam task**

Each summer for the past few years you have had students from abroad staying with your family for a month in the summer while they attend language lessons in your town or city. The organisation that arranges these summer study holidays wants to hold an introductory weekend for the foreign students. You have been asked to suggest what should be on the programme.

Write your **proposal**.

▶▶ **Approach**

▶ Since a proposal is, by definition, a piece of writing that makes suggestions, you will often need to use conditional sentences and structures. Read the question carefully and make sure everything you suggest fits in with the information you are given about who and what the proposal refers to.

▶ Your ideas should be clearly presented, and the use of headings will assist in this. Generally, bullet points are not required, since you do not need to go into much detail, and you do not have much space to do so in any case. The introduction and conclusion can be short. As with a report, you are usually asked to write a proposal for some sort of organisation or publication, so the language should be semi-formal or formal.

Useful phrases

Introduction
In view of the fact that ...
Considering the fact that ...
At present, the situation is that ...
My experience suggests that ...

Main body
It would be helpful to students to be told ...
It would be of great benefit to students if ...
One possible solution would be to ...
Providing the event is properly organised, it could be of great assistance to students.
Students could also be ...

You might also like to consider ...
In all likelihood, ...
The chances are ...

Conclusion
Any teething troubles could quickly be overcome ...
In conclusion, I feel (quite) strongly that this is the best way to ...
In spite of/Despite the effort required, this would be a worthwhile step ...

Think of a suitable
title for your proposal.

Introductory Weekend for Foreign Students

Considering the fact that the vast majority of foreign students
who come here for language courses have not visited this
country before, some introduction to the way of life here would
be very beneficial. After a great deal of experience with these
students and the difficulties they encounter, I would suggest
that an introductory weekend should include the following
features.

In the introduction,
briefly outline the
situation and indicate
your position.

Refer to two or three
examples or ideas
under each heading.

Social life
It would be helpful to explain to foreign students what they can
expect to be served in pubs, cafés and restaurants so they do
not, for example, go to a restaurant and ask for just a cup of
coffee. They could also be provided with information about
local cinemas, sports facilities etc.

Public transport
The system of tickets for buses and local trains is quite
complicated, and visitors often become confused. One possible
solution would be to devote some time to explaining the system
to them. Students might also like some advice about their own
special transport needs. Another good idea would be to discuss
interesting places outside the city that are easily accessible by
bus or train for a day's outing.

Use a variety of
structures to make
suggestions. For
example: 'would be'
and 'might also be'.

Politeness and courtesy
A brief summary of everyday polite and friendly ways of
greeting people would be of great help to visitors. In all
likelihood, they have not been taught the current expressions
used in these situations.

In conclusion, I feel strongly that an introductory weekend
should be interesting and enjoyable for students. They are, after
all, coming here to have a holiday as well as to improve their
language skills. I would be glad to explain my ideas in more
detail if required.

In your conclusion, offer
to help in other ways if
required.

7 Leaflet

▶▶ **Exam task**

You are the secretary of the student council at the college where you are studying. The college is about to hold its first career day, when companies send representatives to talk to students and help them plan their future careers. You have been asked to write the text for a leaflet for students explaining what a career day is, why they should attend, and any other points you think necessary.

Write your **text for the leaflet**.

▶▶ **Approach**

▶ Your leaflet must deal with the points mentioned in the question, but it is also important to provide additional information from your own experience or imagination. Your writing needs to be organised clearly, and a layout that enables the reader to find information easily is also important. As with reports and proposals, you can use headings and bullet points or numbered points.

▶ In general, there are two types of leaflet for which you might be asked to write the text: those that give information (about a company, for example, or a place such as a museum), and those that try to motivate the reader (such as advertising leaflets). The use of headings and bullets or numbered points is particularly advised for leaflets that give information.

▶ The tone and register will depend on the target audience for your leaflet, so think carefully about who will be reading it. A clear and effective title and introduction are useful; you might want to use a rhetorical question if your leaflet is advertising something or trying to encourage the reader to do something. It is also important to have a good conclusion, perhaps summarising the main ideas in the leaflet.

Useful phrases

Introduction

Why should you ... ? Because ... !

Wouldn't you like to ... ?

Have you ever wanted to ... ? Now is your chance!

Come to ... for the time of your life!

Main body

If you want to ... , you will need ...

Please bear in mind that ...

You may be interested to know that ...

Take this opportunity/chance to ...

Conclusion

Don't forget to ...

We are sure you will find (the experience) a useful one.

Give your text a title that will attract the reader's attention.

The introduction should be short and clear.

Headings can ask questions which you then answer.

Career Day – A Chance You Shouldn't Miss!

On 12ᵗʰ June St Mary's College is organising its first Career Day. Why should you attend? Because you need to start thinking about a career now. It's never too soon to take your future seriously!

What is a Career Day?
At a Career Day you have the opportunity to speak to Human Resources Managers from big companies about your possible future with them, and about planning your career in general. We have invited over 30 companies, many of them major international companies, to send representatives. Each company will have a desk in the Main Hall, and students will have the chance to talk to representatives face to face.

Why should I be there?
Even if you have no clear idea what sort of career you would like in the future, talking to people from major companies will help you clarify what options are open to you. And if you do feel fairly sure about the type of career you want, this is a perfect opportunity to ask for advice on how to achieve your goals.

What should I bring?
You don't really need to bring anything, apart from a notebook and pencil to keep notes. If you are graduating soon and are interested in a job with one of these companies in the near future, then it's a good idea to bring several copies of your curriculum vitae with you, describing your education, past employment, interests etc.

Don't forget: June 12ᵗʰ is Career Day. Make sure you are there!

The conclusion can be short and should leave the reader with a clear idea of what has been described or discussed.

Preparing, planning and checking

▶▶ Preparing for the Writing Paper

Producing a piece of writing that fulfils a certain function is a difficult task for anybody, even in their native language. To prepare for the Writing Paper, it goes without saying that you need to have read widely. Then, you need to have studied all the basic text types you may be asked to produce, and understood the basic features that characterise them: layout, organisation, style and register. You should also practise completing writing tasks in the time allowed in the exam. Remember the criteria the examiners will use in awarding marks:

- Has the candidate achieved the purpose stated in the instructions?
- Does the text have a positive general effect on the target reader?
- Does the text cover all the content points?
- Is the text well organised and are ideas linked appropriately?
- Has language been used accurately?
- Does the text exhibit a good range of vocabulary and grammatical structures?
- Is the register appropriate for the task?
- Is the layout appropriate?

Ideally, the pieces of writing you produce should be checked by an experienced teacher who can provide useful feedback. Such feedback can help you compile a list of useful expressions, such as the useful phrases you find with the model answers in this section. You can also learn what sort of mistakes you make habitually so you can avoid them. For instance, if you find that you frequently make mistakes with a certain tense, you should consult a good grammar guide to clear up your confusion.

▶▶ Planning your answer

Perhaps the most useful lesson that experienced writers learn is the importance of planning what to write before they actually begin writing. Most good writers usually write several drafts of a text before they are satisfied with the result. Unfortunately, in the exam you do not have time to produce several drafts, and it would be a serious mistake to try: you only have time for a single draft. But you do have time to make a plan.

Always read the question carefully and make sure you understand the following:

- Who are you writing for?
- What are the points you must include in your answer?
- Does the text type have any particular layout requirements?
- Do you have the necessary vocabulary to answer the question?

Then prepare a plan or outline of what you are going to write. Its purpose is to help you, so it doesn't matter if you change it or cross things out – nobody else is going to read it. But it has to show clearly the different sections of your writing and what points you must include in which section. When you look at the plan closely, you might want to change it; for instance, something might be better in a different paragraph, or you might realise you will be repeating yourself. When you are satisfied with your outline, you will find it much easier to write your text. Planning takes time, so allow a minimum of fifteen minutes for it.

▶▶ Checking

Most people make more mistakes than normal under exam conditions, so always allow at least ten minutes at the end to read through your work. Think of your task here as having two parts. First, check that you have answered the question correctly and that you have included all the information that was required. Secondly, check for mistakes in grammar, spelling, punctuation etc. You should by now have had enough experience to know where you often make mistakes – the spelling of certain words, for instance, or a particular type of punctuation.

If you need to correct something, make the correction neatly and legibly. If you need to cross out something you have written, just put one line through the word or words.

TEST 1

PAPER 1 Reading

▶▶ PART 1

evolve (v) to develop; to change

crucial (adj) extremely important

fluctuation (n) a change in a level

emission (n) electromagnetic waves radiated by an antenna or a celestial body

sentient (adj) having sense perception; conscious

criterion (n) a standard that one uses to judge something

sustain (v) to keep in existence by providing support, strength or necessities

elliptical (adj) rounded like an egg

revolution (n) a circular movement around something

constituent (adj) serving as part of a whole

window of opportunity (phr) a short period of time that is available for a particular activity

cosmic rays (n) radiation reaching the Earth from space

promising (adj) presenting hope or success for the future

erosion (n) the process by which rock or soil is gradually destroyed by wind, rain or the sea

fluid (n) a liquid

inconclusive (adj) not leading to a sure result; not complete enough

ascertain (v) to determine; to find out (facts)

proximity (n) nearness; closeness

preclude (v) to prevent; to make impossible

rule out (phr v) to decide something is not possible

pinpoint (v) to locate exactly

train (v) to aim

spot (v) to find with the eye; to see

fundamental (adj) of central importance

educated guess (phr) a guess based on knowledge and experience, making it more likely to be correct

refine (v) to improve something

sole (adj) the sole person, thing etc. is the only one

▶▶ PART 2

contemplate (v) to think about something that might happen in the future

verdict (n) someone's opinion about something

naive (adj) inexperienced and believing only good things will happen

take off (phr v) to increase or succeed quickly

figure out (phr v) to solve; to understand

budding (adj) (someone who is) embarking on an activity and (will) probably (be) successful at it in the future

overdraft (n) the amount of money owed to a bank when one has spent more money than one had in one's account

unadulterated (adj) not containing unwanted substances; pure

dash (n) a small amount of a quality that is added to something else

quirky (adj) unusual, especially in an interesting way

preservative (n) a chemical that keeps food from going bad

pint (n) a unit for measuring liquid; 0.568 litres

lager (n) a light-coloured beer

falling-out (n) a quarrel

soundbite (n) a short, quotable statement

asset (n) something or someone that is useful because they help one succeed

status quo (n) the way things are now

fiendishly (adv) extremely

preach (v) to give someone advice in a way that they think is boring or annoying

munch (v) to chew strongly on something

communal (adj) shared by a group of people

complementary (adj) complementary things go well together, although they are usually different

bust-up (n) a serious quarrel, especially one that ends a friendship

down (v) to drink or eat something quickly and finish it off

premium (adj) of very high quality

▶▶ PART 3

etching (n) a picture formed by cutting lines on a metal plate, piece of glass, stone etc.

depict (v) to paint; to draw

on a variety of counts (phr) in several ways

sheer (adj) used to emphasise that something is very large, good etc.

staggering (adj) extremely great or surprising

hold one's own (phr) to perform satisfactorily

epoch (n) a period of history

albeit (conjunction) even though; despite

inadvertently (adv) not on purpose; unintentionally

cordon off (phr v) to enclose an area

intimidating (adj) frightening

show up (phr v) to become visible

convey (v) to communicate or make known

preliminary (n) a preparation for an event

rigid (adj) very unwilling to change ideas or behaviour

tentatively (adv) provisionally

vulnerable (adj) exposed; unprotected

envisage (v) to imagine

▶▶ PART 4

devise (v) to invent (something clever); to dream up

convention (n) a method or style often used in literature, the theatre etc. to achieve a particular effect

prompt (v) to cause someone to do something

distressingly (adv) in a way that causes emotional pain

confined (adj) limited; restricted

ingenuity (n) skill at inventing things and thinking of new ideas

mount (v) to plan, organise and begin an event or a course of action

impose (v) to force someone to do something

upright (piano) (n) a piano with strings that are in a vertical position

pronounce (v) to officially state that something is true

medley (n) melodies from different tunes that are played one after the other

entrance (v) to hold someone's attention and give delight; to enchant

detract (v) to take something good from; to lower the value of someone or something

practitioner (n) a person who does skilled work

pier (n) a structure built over and into the water so that boats can stop next to it or people can walk along it

repertoire (n) the group of musical pieces, roles etc. that an artist can play, sing or speak

venue (n) the location of an event

prop (n) a small object such as a book, weapon etc., used by actors in a play or film

demise (n) death

rave (v) to praise greatly

ensemble (n) a small group of musicians, actors or dancers who perform together regularly

churlish (adj) rude; unpleasant

engage (v) to employ someone to do a particular job

scrupulously (adv) in a way that shows you are attentive to detail and correctness

percussionist (n) a musician who plays percussion instruments

acquit oneself well (phr) to perform or behave well

connoisseur (n) a person with knowledge of fine things

tribute (n) expression of praise, honour or admiration

initiate (v) to tell someone about something, or show them how to do something

piercing (adj) sharp and painful

ooze (v) if a thick liquid oozes from something, that liquid flows from it very slowly

sleuth (n) a person who tries to solve mysteries; a detective

condense (v) to shorten

PAPER 3   English in Use

▶▶ PART 2

pursuit (n) an activity such as a sport or hobby

boom (v) to flourish; to thrive

sow the seeds of (phr) to do something that will cause a bad situation in the future

disperse (v) to break up and send or go away; to scatter

reinforce (v) to make part of a structure stronger

far-fetched (adj) not likely to happen; improbable

notion (n) an idea, belief or opinion

spell (disaster) (v) if a situation or action spells trouble etc., it makes one expect trouble

▶▶ PART 4

ample (adj) more than enough; plenty

resolve to do something (phr) to make a definite decision to do something

implausible (adj) not believable; unlikely to be true

▶▶ PART 5

lukewarm (adj) mildly warm; tepid

▶▶ PART 6

opt (v) to choose

edge (n) a small advantage

TEST 2

PAPER 1   Reading

▶▶ PART 1

blur (v) to make someone unable to see clearly

compile (v) to put something together item by item

monitor (v) to observe the actions of others

patronise (v) to act in a superior manner toward someone; to be condescending

adverse (adj) difficult; unfavourable

notorious (adj) well-known, especially for something bad

blockbuster (n) a film or book that is very successful commercially

integrate (v) to incorporate into a larger unit

supplement (v) to make an addition or additions to

impetus (n) the encouragement needed to do something

evade (v) to escape; to elude

incentive (n) something that makes someone work harder; motivation

legislation (n) a proposed law or laws

rigorous (adj) having strict or high standards for behaviour or action

stipulate (v) to require by a legal paper; to specify

bestow (v) to give something formally

cite (v) to mention or quote as an example or authority

gullible (adj) easily tricked; naive

ploy (n) a trick; a manoeuvre to gain advantage or to disguise one's true intent

ammunition (n) material for use in attacking or defending a position

copy-cat (adj) closely imitating or following another

posture (v) to hold oneself or to behave in a certain, often artificial way, especially to impress others

cascade (n) something falling or rushing forth in quantity

discerning (adj) intelligent; perceptive

voice-over (n) the voice of an unseen narrator speaking (as in a film or television commercial)

incidence (n) the frequency of something happening

disembodied (adj) not having a material body

sought-after (adj) desired; wanted

strenuous (adj) needing great effort

niche (n) a specialised market

turn one's back on (phr) to reject; to repudiate

mainstream (n) a prevailing current or direction of activity or influence

prime-time (adj) during the evening hours, generally between seven and eleven pm, when the largest television audience is available

apace (adv) at a quick pace; quickly

▶▶ **PART 2**

linguist (n) a person who knows several languages and their structure

forge ahead (phr) to proceed with strength and speed despite problems or difficulties

consummate (adj) perfect

wary (adj) concerned about danger; cautious

corpus (n) a body of written work

competent (adj) having the ability to do something well

mouthpiece (n) a spokesperson; a representative

blunt (adj) frank

trek (v) to travel with difficulty

expectant (adj) pregnant

score (n) twenty

tonic (n) a medicinal liquid that gives energy

rub (n) a medicinal lotion or cream that is rubbed on the skin

potion (n) a strong liquid medicine

▶▶ **PART 3**

bewitch (v) to charm; to captivate

smitten (adj) very attracted or in love

amid (preposition) in or into the middle of; surrounded by

stock (adj) commonly used

spirit (n) a mental disposition characterised by firmness or assertiveness

enduring (adj) lasting; surviving

shortcoming (n) a fault; a deficiency

sibling (n) a person with the same parents as someone else; a brother or sister

enlightened (adj) freed from ignorance and misinformation

villain (n) a bad person, especially a criminal

empathise (v) to understand another's feelings, attitudes, reasons etc.

▶▶ **PART 4**

enhance (v) to improve; to add to

engage (v) to take part

venture (n) an undertaking involving chance, risk or danger; a speculative business enterprise

break (n) a piece of good luck

dabble (v) to work superficially or intermittently, especially in a secondary activity or interest

downside (n) a disadvantageous aspect

burnt out (phr) unable to work any more, usually from exhaustion

down the line (phr) at a point in the future

lucrative (adj) producing a lot of money; profitable

from scratch (phr) from the beginning

avid (adj) enthusiastic; eager

the ropes (phr) knowledge about a job or situation

dogsbody (n) a person who does hard, menial or monotonous work for someone else

PAPER 2 Writing

▶▶ **PART 1**

surly (adj) rude and hostile in manner or attitude

vocational (adj) related to work

PAPER 3 English in Use

▶▶ **PART 1**

feat (n) a notable act or deed

lock (n) an enclosure in a canal with gates at each end, used in raising or lowering boats as they pass from level to level

freight (n) goods to be shipped

cramped (adj) small and uncomfortable

weed (n) a wild plant that is not wanted in a yard or garden

▶▶ **PART 2**

all told (phr) in total

duplicate (v) to repeat an action or words

▶▶ **PART 3**

delicacy (n) special food that tastes great and is hard to get

surge (n) to rise suddenly to an excessive or abnormal value

▶▶ **PART 4**

consolidate (v) to strengthen; to make firm or secure

fringe benefit (n) a service or privilege provided to an employee by an employer in addition to salary, such as medical, dental and life insurance

virtual (adj) created, simulated or carried on by means of a computer or computer network

TEST 3

PAPER 1 Reading

▶▶ **PART 1**

inconsistent (adj) not compatible with another fact or claim

fallibility (n) the capacity to make errors or be imperfect

misplace (v) to set on a wrong object or eventuality

vested interests (phr) groups that seek to maintain or control an existing system or activity from which they derive private benefit

implication (n) a possible consequence

pesticide (n) a chemical used to kill pests

hindsight (n) an opinion about something after it has happened

tackle (v) to begin a job with a lot of energy

succumb (v) to show weakness or give up to a greater strength or desire

concerted (adj) mutually contrived or agreed on

clout (n) power and influence

lobby (n) a group of people who promote or secure the passage of legislation by influencing public officials

spew (v) to come out or push out with force

guzzle (v) to consume large quantities, often quickly

deed (n) a usually praiseworthy act

get worked up (phr) to become tense or upset

doom and gloom (phr) a deeply pessimistic outlook or feeling

doomsday (n) a time when an important bad event occurs

scenario (n) a sequence of events, especially when imagined

viable (adj) workable; capable of succeeding

painstaking (adj) careful to do things exactly right

moor (n) a boggy area, especially one dominated by grasses and sedges

heathland (n) an extensive area of open uncultivated land, usually with poor soil, bad drainage, and a surface rich in peat or peaty humus

▶▶ PART 2

surmise (v) to make a reasonable guess

perch (n) a resting place or vantage point

slog (v) to walk with difficulty, for example, in deep snow or mud

loot (v) to rob, especially on a large scale and usually by violence or corruption

aqueduct (n) a waterway made of stone blocks

carbon dating (n) chemical analysis used to determine the age of materials

fire (v) to fill with passion or enthusiasm

tantalise (v) to offer but not satisfy; to tempt

wry (adj) humorous, ironic or dry in manner

blue-collar (adj) blue-collar workers work with their hands in jobs that require some training

intricate (adj) having many complexly interrelating parts or elements

toil (v) to work hard with little reward or relief

pore over (phr v) to study carefully; to examine long and carefully

blunder (v) to move unsteadily or confusedly

annals (n) a written record or collection of historical events, discoveries etc., on a certain subject

proponent (n) a person who argues in favour of something

vigorous (adj) energetic; strong

undeterred (adj) refusing to be prevented from acting

hail (v) to greet, especially with enthusiasm

swashbuckling (adj) flamboyantly adventurous

rugged (adj) hilly, referring to land that is difficult to travel over

▶▶ PART 3

emblematic (adj) symbolic; representative

terrain (n) land; landscape

squat (adj) disproportionately short, low or thick

ungainly (adj) hard to handle; having an awkward appearance

hare (v) to go quickly

indulgence (n) something one enjoys, even though it may be bad or wrong

would-be (adj) desiring; professing; having the potential to be

goggles (n) plastic glasses that protect the eyes

usurp (v) to take the place of someone or something

▶▶ PART 4

transgression (n) a crime; a violation

fusion (n) a merging of diverse, distinct or separate elements into a unified whole

credible (adj) believable

evocation (n) imaginative re-creation

foster parent (n) an adult who is paid by the government to take care of a child that is not their own

inherent (adj) naturally belonging to or part of something

hard-hitting (adj) very effective; forceful

out of the blue (phr) suddenly; unexpectedly

enchant (v) to charm; to delight

floppy (adj) loose and usually oversized, like a soft toy

dilapidated (adj) falling apart; in disrepair

genre (n) a category of artistic, musical or literary composition characterised by a particular style, form or content

undertone (n) an implied meaning; an undercurrent

cuddle (n) a close embrace

premise (n) a basis for a line of reasoning; an assumption

chunky (adj) short and thick or broad

sparse (adj) with much space between; of few and scattered elements

interweave (v) to mix or blend together

overtly (adv) obviously

didactic (adj) intended to instruct

indulge (v) to allow someone to do something, even if it is not good or wise

drab (adj) dull in colour; uninteresting

hint (v) to make reference to something in an indirect way

mismatch (n) something unequal in ability, personality, strength etc.

address (v) to deal with

unreserved (adj) given without reservation; unqualified

articulate (v) to put into words

portal (n) a door or entrance

plausible (adj) appearing worthy of belief

thorny (adj) difficult; complex

nullify (v) to make invalid; to cancel

quaint (adj) unusual or different in character or appearance

backdrop (n) the general events during which something else, such as a person's life, happens

dawn on (phr v) to begin to be perceived or understood

figurative (adj) related to a word or phrase that expresses meaning in a colourful way, usually through comparison; metaphorical

medieval (adj) of, relating to, or characteristic of the Middle Ages

depict (v) to describe

alike (adv) equally; to the same degree, form or manner

PAPER 3 English in Use

▶▶ PART 1

newsworthy (adj) of sufficient interest or importance to the public to warrant reporting in the media

fad (n) a fashion that lasts a short time

▶▶ PART 4

flee (v) to run away; to escape

absorb (v) to soak up; to take in

ramble (v) to walk slowly for pleasure

stout (adj) sturdily constructed

▶▶ PART 5

culinary (adj) related to the kitchen and cooking

gourmet (n) a person who knows a lot about and enjoys fine food and drink

▶▶ PART 6

wired (adj) determined by physiological or neurological mechanisms

co-educational (adj) relating to the system of education in which both girls and boys attend the same school

TEST 4

PAPER 1 Reading

▶▶ PART 1

relish (v) to have a happy feeling about something

gratify (v) to give pleasure and satisfaction

reassure (v) to make someone believe that something will be all right

privileged (adj) having special rights or benefits

overcome (v) to fight against someone or something successfully

over the moon (phr) delighted; very pleased

two-edged sword (phr) something that can bring harm as well as benefits

trace back (phr v) to follow something to its origin

craft (n) a skilled trade

collaborative (adj) involving working with other people

intrusion (n) the act of breaking into the conversation or activity of a person

rarified (adj) belonging to or reserved for a small select group

acclaim (n) public congratulations; praise

line (n) a field of activity or interest

reap (v) to obtain as a result of effort

tangible (adj) touchable; real

forthcoming (adj) arriving in the future; due to be delivered

see the light of day (phr) to appear; to happen

overwhelm (v) to overpower in thought or feeling

▶▶ PART 2

policy (n) a rule or group of rules for doing business by industry and government

incorporate (v) to unite in or as one body

national grid (n) a network of conductors for distribution of electric power

consideration (n) a matter taken into account when formulating an opinion or plan

embrace (v) to accept an idea

electorate (n) a body of people entitled to vote

eyesore (n) an unpleasant sight

offshore (adj) away from the shoreline in the water

phase out (phr v) to remove something in gradual steps

decommission (v) to withdraw from active service

impact (n) an effect; an impression

migrate (v) to move from one place to another, as animals, birds and fish do

exploitation (n) productive use of something

▶▶ PART 3

uproar (n) clamour; people complaining or shouting

constitute (v) to make up; to compose

infringement (n) a violation of a law, regulation, agreement etc.

instructive (adj) with useful information; educational

turn a blind eye (phr) to avoid seeing something wrong; to overlook

prosecute (v) to bring legal action against someone because one considers that they have broken the law

a laughing stock (phr) an object of jokes or ridicule

sue (v) to seek justice or right from someone in a court of law

consensus (n) general agreement

wrath (n) anger

innocuous (adj) harmless; unobjectionable

distort (v) to cause to be perceived unnaturally

whine (v) to complain; to act irritably

resentment (n) a feeling of anger at something one regards as a wrong, insult or injury

steep (adj) expensive

evanescent (adj) of short duration; passing away quickly

▶▶ PART 4

paramount (adj) supreme; foremost

rural (adj) of or relating to the country, country people or life, or agriculture

commute (v) to travel back and forth regularly

enervate (v) to drain of energy; to weaken

write-off (n) something that is ruined

robust (adj) strongly formed or constructed; sturdy

on its last legs (phr) worn out; close to failure or death

woefully (adv) lamentably bad or serious; deplorably

unequivocal (adj) definite; clear; unambiguous

dismissive (adj) considering something unimportant or worthless

▶▶ **PART 1**

profound (adj) all-encompassing

heavenly body (n) an object in the sky

auspicious (adj) favourable; good

resort (v) to have recourse to something or someone

exempt (adj) free or released from some liability or requirement to which others are subject

▶▶ **PART 4**

off the beaten track (phr) an unusual route or destination

imply (v) to express indirectly

awe (v) to create a feeling of respect or admiration

boar (n) a wild male pig

underlying (adj) fundamental; basic

vein (n) any of many blood vessels that bring blood to the heart and lungs

constrict (v) to make narrow; to draw together

▶▶ **PART 5**

tenant (n) someone who rents or leases a house, flat etc. from a landlord

vacate (v) to move out of; to leave

utility (n) any basic necessity or service, such as running water, electricity or gas

remit (v) to send money

refrain (v) to keep oneself from doing, feeling or indulging in something

inventory (n) an itemised list of objects

expire (v) to cease to be valid; to lapse

▶▶ **PART 6**

grasp (v) to succeed in understanding something

detractor (n) someone who speaks against someone or something; a critic

dismiss (v) to reject serious consideration of

bond (n) a relationship of trust, cooperation, friendship, love etc.; a connection

posture (n) the way the body is held

coordination (n) the ability to move one's body well

gait (n) the way a person or animal walks, runs, gallops etc.

TEST 5

PAPER 1 Reading

▶▶ **PART 1**

corporate (adj) related to a business

fruitful (adj) productive; profitable

collaboration (n) the act of working with others, especially in an intellectual endeavour

hypothesis (n) a working theory

adherent (n) a believer; a member

root (n) the basis of something; source; origin

avidity (n) keenness; enthusiasm

scan (v) to look at something to see as much information as possible in a short time

hard-headed (adj) tough-minded; sober; realistic

portfolio (n) a set of different investments by a person

insight (n) the ability to see or know the truth; perception

riddle (n) a puzzle; a question that requires cleverness to answer

observance (n) behaviour according to laws, rules, holidays and customs

mechanistic (adj) capable of complete explanation by the laws of physics and chemistry

fervour (n) the state of being emotionally aroused and worked up

hoax (n) a deception; a trick

bamboozle (v) to cheat; to swindle

base rate (n) the standard or normal amount of something

spawn (v) to cause; to give life to

discredit (v) to show that something is of little or no truth or value

debunk (v) to show the falseness of something

pour scorn (phr) to express a feeling of disrespect in a strong or angry way

undetectable (adj) impossible to notice or observe

miniscule (adj) very small

eminent (adj) standing above others in some quality or position; famous

credibility (n) the quality or power of inspiring belief

marital (adj) related to marriage

▶▶ **PART 2**

plight (n) an unfortunate, difficult or dangerous situation

shed light (phr) to make clear; to explain

range (v) to live or occur in or be native to a region

come by (phr v) to get; to acquire

reclusive (adj) living alone and avoiding contact with others

inhospitable (adj) difficult to live in because of bad weather or geography

poacher (n) a hunter or trapper who takes game animals illegally

logger (n) someone involved in cutting down trees

bush (n) land far from towns and cities; wilderness

range (n) the region throughout which an animal naturally lives or occurs

canopy (n) the uppermost spreading branchy layer of a forest

replenish (v) to replace something that was used

fare (v) to get along; to succeed

convention (n) an assembly of people who meet for a common purpose

dwindle (v) to become steadily less or fewer

ominous (adj) being a sign of something evil, bad or threatening

slash (v) to cut with or as if with rough sweeping strokes

eden (n) a delightful place; a paradise

take a toll (phr) to cause damage

allocate (v) to plan to use an amount of money for a specific purpose; to allot

stark (adj) not cheerful; brutal

▶▶ PART 3

draw to a close (phr) to come to an end

roam (v) to go freely over a large area; to wander

glacier (n) a large mass of ice which moves slowly down a mountain valley

submerge (v) to cover something with water

deluge (n) a flood

lush (adj) having thick, healthy growth

verdant (adj) green with vegetation; covered with green growth

tusk (n) a long, thick front tooth, such as of elephants, warthogs etc.

ledge (n) a narrow flat piece of rock that sticks out on the side of a mountain or cliff

pinpoint (v) to locate exactly

scathing (adj) harsh; severe

maritime (adj) related to the sea

aggregate (n) mineral materials, such as sand or stone, used in making concrete

quarry (v) to dig stone or sand from a quarry

dredge (v) to dig up sand, mud and debris from a harbour, river etc.

artefact (n) an object produced or shaped by human craft, especially a tool, weapon or ornament

topography (n) the physical landscape

outraged (adj) feeling great anger

perception (n) the way a person sees something; a point of view

▶▶ PART 4

prospective (adj) likely to do something or achieve a position in the future

apprehensive (adj) worried or nervous about something that one is going to do

transaction (n) the act of doing business; a deal; a negotiation

interpersonal (adj) between people

babble (v) to talk without making sense

get carried away (phr) to do too much of something and lose control of oneself

go off at a tangent (phr) to leave the main point; to digress

evasive (adj) not direct, clear or frank

pedantic (adj) paying too much attention to rules and details

come across (phr v) to seem to have particular qualities

promotional (adj) related to advertising

penetrating (adj) showing an ability to understand things quickly and completely

size up (phr v) to form an opinion of someone

blurt out (phr v) to speak suddenly

component (n) one of several parts that make up a machine, system etc.

swollen-headed (adj) arrogant

complacent (adj) pleased with a situation, especially something one has achieved, so that one stops trying to improve or change things

at fault (phr) responsible

diffident (adj) shy and not wanting to make people notice or talk about one

---

PAPER 3   English in Use

▶▶ PART 1

foolhardy (adj) reckless; rash

▶▶ PART 2

ubiquitous (adj) seeming to be everywhere

▶▶ PART 4

upheaval (n) disorder; a change that disturbs daily life

▶▶ PART 5

ballroom (n) a large hall for dances

forthcoming (adj) given or offered when needed

 TEST 6

PAPER 1   Reading

▶▶ PART 1

disreputable (adj) having a bad reputation

empathy (n) the ability to share or understand another person's feelings

barrister (n) a lawyer who speaks in the higher courts of law

ingénue (n) a naive, innocent girl or young woman

induce (v) to persuade; to influence

stage struck (adj) enthralled by the theatre; eager for a career in acting

sneak off (phr v) to go quietly; to try not to be seen

matinée (n) an afternoon film or theatre performance

shed (v) to get rid of something unwanted

persona (n) the role or character someone adopts in public or for a performance

lure (n) the power of something that attracts

footlights (n) the stage as a profession; a row of lights at the front of a stage floor

incredulous (adj) not believing; very surprised

land (v) to secure or win

prior to (preposition) before; in advance of

smitten (adj) very attracted; in love

rush (n) the immediate pleasurable feeling produced by a drug

troupe (n) a group of theatrical performers

slick (adj) superficially plausible or appealing; based on stereotype

impersonate (v) to imitate; to act like someone else

concur (v) to express agreement

glaze (v) to cover or fit with glass

ventilation (n) a system of providing fresh air

conservatory (n) a greenhouse for growing or displaying plants

modish (adj) stylish

trim (v) to free of excess or extraneous matter by or as if by cutting

momentum (n) strength or force gained by motion or through the development of events

accord (n) agreement

break (n) a deduction that is granted in order to encourage a particular type of commercial activity

dim (v) to lower the force of, especially a light

synergy (n) the extra energy, power or capability produced by combining two or more agents, operations or processes

outlook (n) a prediction for the future

duct (n) a tube or passage in buildings, especially for air

come to grips with (phr) to confront squarely and attempt to deal decisively with something

compost (v) to convert (plant debris) to compost, usually for use as fertiliser

biomass (n) plant materials and animal waste used especially as a source of fuel

forefront (n) the most advanced part

juice (n) gas, electricity etc.

tumble (v) to decline suddenly and sharply

▶▶ PART 3

hitherto (adv) up to this time

instrumental (adj) helpful; causing something to happen

by-product (n) something that happens as a result of something else

outperform (v) to do better than others

ligament (n) a strong, flexible band of tissue holding bones or other body parts in place

tendon (n) tough fibrous tissue connecting muscles to bones or to other muscles

calf (n) the back part of the lower leg

confer (v) to give

scavenger (n) an animal that feeds on dead or decaying matter

carcass (n) a dead body

vulture (n) a type of bird that eats dead animals

locomotion (n) the ability to move from place to place

contentious (adj) controversial

▶▶ PART 4

prejudicial (adj) related to or causing harm by holding a biased opinion not based on fact

payroll (n) a list of employees to be paid and the amounts due to each

mortgage (n) a long-term loan from a bank for buying property, which is used as security

hefty (adj) of considerable size or amount

infuriate (v) to make very angry

outlay (n) money spent for something

dearth (n) little or none of something

concrete (adj) about real, specific things and situations, not general ideas

go bust (phr) to become bankrupt

landscape gardening (n) the art or profession of improving the ground around a building with trees, plants etc.

cut-throat (adj) relentless or merciless in competition

unsung (adj) unpraised; not seen as important; overlooked

PAPER 3 English in Use

▶▶ PART 1

misconception (n) a mistaken idea about something

span (n) a period (of time)

plague (n) an epidemic disease causing a high rate of mortality

grim (adj) ghastly; repellent; sinister

appalling (adj) shocking; deeply offensive

feudal (adj) relating to a political and social system in which a king and the people of the upper classes owned the land and people of the lower classes worked it

clergy (n) the official leaders of religious activities in organised religions

▶▶ PART 4

garish (adj) showy; ostentatious

homage (n) special honour or respect shown or expressed publicly

▶▶ PART 6

rickshaw (n) a small two-wheeled cart pulled by a person

diminutive (adj) exceptionally small; tiny

TEST 7

PAPER 1 Reading

▶▶ PART 1

festive (adj) joyful; with feasting and good spirits

precaution (n) a step taken in advance to prevent harm

affinity (n) a liking for; an attraction to

irrational (adj) not governed by or according to reason; insane

gear (n) equipment, usually connected with sports

gruelling (adj) very difficult and tiring

host (v) to receive or entertain guests

free-form (adj) done without restrictions; loose and informal

rate (n) the cost of something

aimlessly (adv) without purpose or direction

surf (n) ocean waves as they approach and break on a shore creating rolling banks of water topped by white foam and spray

gradient (n) the degree of change in a slope

stick around (phr v) to stay; to wait

mishap (n) an accident; misfortune

distraction (n) something that draws or directs one's attention to a different object or in different directions at the same time

dubious (adj) having doubts; suspicious

spurt (n) a sudden burst

▶▶ PART 2

amenity (n) something that adds to people's comfort, convenience and pleasure

boast (v) to be proud of something

following (n) a group of admirers or followers

gig (n) a performance by musicians or comedians

precarious (adj) dependent on chance, unknown conditions or uncertain developments

to boot (phr) in addition; also

hone (v) to improve

prodigy (n) a highly talented child

flautist (n) someone who plays the flute

abrasive (adj) rough; making people feel bad

thin-skinned (adj) touchy; sensitive to criticism

yearn (v) to have a strong desire for something; to long for something

demanding (adj) requiring high performance

clientele (n) a group of customers

kid (v) to make jokes

snort (n) the act of forcing air violently through the nose with a rough harsh sound

daunt (v) to make afraid; to discourage

whim (n) a sudden desire, especially an unreasonable one

bunch (n) a group

▶▶ PART 3

blunt (adj) not sharp

talon (n) a bird's claw, especially of predators

wingspan (n) the distance from the tip of one of a pair of wings to that of the other

soar (v) to fly high through the air with no difficulty

diversity (n) variety

incubate (v) to sit on an egg so as to hatch by the warmth of the body

bicker (v) to argue about little things

rear (v) to help children or young animals to grow

saunter (v) to walk without hurrying

antifreeze (n) a liquid used in engine radiators to lower their freezing point

coyote (n) a kind of wolf similar to a medium-sized dog found mainly in western North and Central America

shard (n) a piece of a brittle substance such as glass or metal

perforate (v) to make a hole through something

carrion (n) the flesh and bones of a dead animal that is unfit for human food

juvenile (n) a youth or child

pen (n) a small area of land surrounded by a fence and used to keep animals in

mentor (n) a teacher and friend

glide (v) to fly through the air without power

plumage (n) the covering of feathers on a bird

▶▶ PART 4

compatibility (n) the ability of machines to be used together

fragile (adj) easily broken; delicate

unawares (adv) without warning; by surprise

viewfinder (n) a device on a camera that indicates, either optically or electronically, what will appear in the field of view of the lens

texture (n) the way a surface or material feels when you touch it, especially how smooth or rough it is

gloss (n) a photograph that has been made shiny

come to grief (phr) to be harmed or destroyed in an accident

PAPER 3 English in Use

▶▶ PART 1

pollinate (v) to transfer pollen to the stigma of a plant so that it can reproduce

cure (v) to preserve food, tobacco etc. by drying it, hanging it in smoke or covering it with salt

tickle (v) to stimulate pleasantly

▶▶ PART 4

melancholy (adj) very sad

evaporate (v) to disappear; to vanish

in hand (phr) if something is in hand, it is being done or dealt with

▶▶ PART 5

outlet (n) a shop or store

adjacent (adj) a room, piece of land etc. that is adjacent to something is next to it

elapse (v) to go by; to pass

▶▶ PART 6

taut (adj) stretched tight

vocal (adj) loud; complaining

galling (adj) making one feel upset and angry because of something that is unfair

yield (n) the amount of profits, crops etc. that something produces

TEST 8

PAPER 1 Reading

▶▶ PART 1

décor (n) the style of a room, house etc.

wisteria (n) a climbing woody vine with fragrant purple or white flowers

clad (adj) covered with something

shimmering (adj) giving off gently moving light

Victorian (adj) of, relating to, or characteristic of the reign of Queen Victoria of England

tremendous (adj) wonderful; excellent

vinyl (n) a tough plastic used to make records

nondescript (adj) common; ordinary; with no outstanding features

sconce (n) a bracket candlestick or group of candlesticks

plush (adj) soft, luxurious and expensive

let-down (n) a disappointment

gamut (n) a range of things

obscure (adj) not well known

reflection (n) deep thought

Edwardian (adj) of, relating to, or characteristic of the reign of Edward VII of England

cavernous (adj) like a large cave

intimidating (adj) making people frightened by showing power or making threats

a touch (phr) somewhat; rather

austere (adj) with no human warmth or comfort

scone (n) a rich bread cut into triangular or round shapes and cooked on a griddle or baked on a sheet

kedgeree (n) a dish consisting of flaked fish, boiled rice and eggs

haddock (n) an edible whitefish

poach (v) to cook in simmering liquid

renowned (adj) famous; well-known

ale (n) a type of beer

fiddler (n) someone who plays the violin, especially if they play folk music

oasthouse (n) a building containing an oast (= a kiln for drying hops

give prominence to something (phr) to treat something as specially important

proprietor (n) an owner

courteous (adj) having good manners; polite

exude (v) to show in one's face and behaviour

bland (adj) having little taste

lashings of something (phr) a large amount of something

vibrant (adj) full of activity; lively

▶▶ PART 2

Velcro (n) a material used to fasten clothes, consisting of two pieces of material which stick to each other when you press them together

plunder (v) to steal; to take others' property by force and in large quantity

random (adj) happening at any time; unplanned

spur (v) to encourage someone to do something

hands-off (adj) left alone; not to be touched

on tap (phr) available on demand

win-win (adj) a win-win situation is one that will end well for everyone involved in it

intervention (n) the act of becoming involved in a difficult situation in order to change what happens

alleviate (v) to make less difficult

the real McCoy (phr) something real or authentic

concerted (adj) strong; intense

indigenous (adj) born in a place; native to a place

▶▶ PART 3

slump (v) to lose an upright position by bending or falling

vague (adj) not clearly defined, grasped or understood

hunched (adj) formed into a hump

slouch (v) to walk, stand or sit with an ungainly stooping of the head and shoulders or excessive relaxation of body muscles

pilates (n) a system of exercise that increases flexibility

tilt (v) to move upwards or to the side

daft (adj) silly

orator (n) someone who is good at making speeches and persuading people

▶▶ PART 4

phase out (phr v) to gradually stop using or providing something

lag (v) to not keep up; to delay

stumbling block (phr) an obstacle

bulky (adj) big and heavy; bigger than other things of the same type and difficult to carry or store

stationary (adj) standing still; not moving

benign (adj) harmless

lubricate (v) to put a substance like oil on something in order to make it move more smoothly

cumbersome (adj) slow and difficult

PAPER 3 English in Use

▶▶ PART 1

instigate (v) to make something happen

ingrained (adj) firmly established and therefore difficult to change

gimmick (n) a clever or unusual method or object used to attract attention

▶▶ PART 4

sparse (adj) existing only in small amounts

strive (v) to work hard for something

garment (n) an article of clothing

▶▶ PART 6

magma (n) hot liquid rock below the Earth's surface

suppress (v) to prevent something from growing or developing

crust (n) the outer layer of the Earth

trigger (v) to start a reaction

TEST 1

PAPER 1 Reading

▶▶ PART 1

1 C: 'But not long ago, a technique was developed that could ascertain reliably whether stars have planets orbiting them.'

2 A: 'There are billions of galaxies in the universe … , so to many people it seems unlikely that our own planet is unique in having the physical conditions that permitted sentient beings to evolve.'

3 E: 'We simply do not know how life originated here on Earth … we can only make educated guesses.'

4/5 A: 'This, in turn, would mean that the planet would be both too hot and too cold for life'

4/5 B: 'Venus … is too hot for life as we know it'

6 D: 'However, astronomers … now believe they have pinpointed a planetary system which resembles our own.'

7 B: 'Moreover, unlike the Earth, it lacks a magnetic field, which is crucial in shielding life from cosmic rays.'

8 F: 'There are often voices raised in opposition to the vast sums invested in space research'

9 A: 'the constituent elements of life, including carbon, … and oxygen'

10 C: 'Basically, this technique relies upon our ability to detect … how much light a star is giving off. If this changes … , it is probably because a large object – a planet – is passing in front of it.'

11 B: 'It shows signs of erosion caused in the past'

12 F: 'Matherson also hopes that by the third decade of this century, spaceships will be sent into outer space with the sole purpose of studying likely planets.''

13 B: 'From observing the planets closest to us, … only a small window of opportunity for life to have a chance.'

14 C: 'Until recently, we have confined ourselves to our own solar system … we have not had evidence for the existence of other solar systems.'

15 F: 'There is even a possibility that valuable mineral resources could be discovered on these planets and exploited commercially, which would further justify funding exploratory missions.'

▶▶ PART 2

16 E: Link between 'asked their customers for a verdict' in the previous paragraph and 'We originally wrote this massive long questionnaire'.

17 G: Link between 'Britain's leading brand of smoothie, selling about 40% of the 50 million downed annually by British drinkers' and 'The appeal of Innocent's products' in the following paragraph.

18 D: Link between 'so-called "natural fruit drinks" ' and 'Most are made from concentrated juice with water – and perhaps sweeteners, colours and preservatives – added' in the following paragraph.

19 A: Link between 'the company has always been very careful not to preach' and 'Everyone knows what they're supposed to do' in the following paragraph.

20 C: Link between 'extending their range of products into desserts' and 'Innocent plans to simply freeze some of its smoothies' in the following paragraph.

21 H: Link between 'is there a temptation to sell up and go and live on a desert island' and Richard's answer in the following paragraph.

22 F: Contrastive link between 'They also seem to have managed to stay friends' and 'We have got annoyed with each other' in the following paragraph. Also, link between 'each member of the team … complementary set of skills' and 'the areas we have had fallings-out over are things where we each think we have reasons to be right' in the following paragraph.

▶▶ PART 3

23 A: Incorrect. They are 'extremely rare', not 'unique'.

23 B: Incorrect. They are etchings, not paintings.

23 C: Incorrect. The images are not compared to other cave art in Britain.

23 D: Correct. 'But more importantly, the Church Hole etchings are an incredible artistic achievement.'

24 A: Incorrect. This is not stated or implied in the text.

24 B: Incorrect. This is not stated in the text. The point made is that ancient Britons *were part of a culture* that spread across the continent.

24 C: Correct. 'Britons were part of a culture that had spread right across the continent'

24 D: Incorrect. Britons were 'at least as sophisticated as' people in Europe.

25 A: Incorrect. The discovery of the images was made public, but the writer does not suggest this should have been avoided. She implies the images should have been protected.

25 B: Correct. 'As a result, some etchings may already have been damaged, albeit inadvertently, by eager visitors.'

25 C: Incorrect. The text states that many people *knew* about the etchings within hours of their discovery, but it does not say that many people *visited* the cave within hours of the discovery.

25 D: Incorrect. Measures were taken too late to prevent damage that had already been done, but the text does not say that the measures themselves are ineffective.

26 A: Correct. 'However, the Church Hole images are modifications of the rock itself, and show up best when seen from a certain angle in the natural light of early morning.'

26 B: Incorrect. 'They had been looking for the usual type of cave drawing or painting'

26 C: Incorrect. The images 'show up *best*' in natural light.

26 D: Incorrect. The text does not suggest that the power of the light was a problem.

27 A: Incorrect. This statement does not express the conclusion Dr Samson draws about the function of the etchings.

27 B: Incorrect. They intended the images to be visible in the early morning.

27 C: Correct. 'I think the artists knew very well that the etchings would hardly be visible except early in the morning.'

27 D: Incorrect. The text mentions 'rituals involving animal worship', but this does not mean that ice-age hunters worshipped animals in the cave.

28 A: Incorrect. It is implied that we can make inferences, but we cannot 'insist on any rigid interpretation'.

28 B: Incorrect. Dr Caruthers does not think their function 'can be determined with any certainty', but she does not imply they serve no particular function.

28 C: Incorrect. Saying someone knows 'so little' is not the same as saying they know nothing.

28 D: Correct. 'We should, in my view, begin by tentatively assuming … while of course being prepared to modify this verdict at a later date'

29 A: Incorrect. This is not stated or implied in the text.
29 B: Correct. 'To which I can only add that I felt deeply privileged to have been able to view Church Hole.'
29 C: Incorrect. This is not stated or implied in the text.
29 D: Incorrect. This is not stated or implied in the text.

▶▶ PART 4

30 B: 'Besides, who can afford to work only during the summer months?'
31 A: 'The other art form that I adore – ballet – could hardly be performed in the confined space of a normal house'
32 D: '*Death Calls* ... had me fondly recalling a production of *2001, A Space Odyssey* at the Edinburgh Fringe Festival'
33 A: 'We had made it clear that no particular requirements would be imposed upon the performers'
34 C: 'a colleague of my wife's started raving about a particular jazz ensemble. It seemed churlish to do otherwise than engage them'
35 C: 'The Hot Jazz Quintet ... appeared to make a point of being scrupulously polite and tidy. It was as though the stereotype image of the egocentric musician were being overturned in front of my very eyes'
36 D: 'In fact, one could claim that it doesn't really come under the category of theatre at all, and it is not normally presented on a stage, either.'
37 B: 'There was once a time when no seaside resort in the country was complete without a Punch and Judy show on the pier'
38 A: 'my daughter – who had previously been of the view that opera was unspeakably idiotic – was entranced'
39 B: 'They arrived with a surprising number of boxes and cases. Naively, I had expected a miniature theatre to require a minimal amount of equipment.'
40 D: 'There we stumbled – literally – over a body oozing fake blood that was so convincing it almost caused my wife to faint.'
41 B: 'William Daniels ... was suffering from a terrible cold ... . Like a true pro, though, he struggled through the performance bravely.'
42 A: 'so they gave us a medley of familiar pieces from popular operas'
43 C: 'As luck would have it, Mike is a percussionist with his school orchestra, and he was able to acquit himself creditably, to the delight of the professionals performing for us.'
44 D: 'my wife proved to be a brilliant sleuth, solving the mystery in record time'

PAPER 2 Writing

▶▶ PART 1

Question 1
Style: Semi-formal or formal article. Formal letter.
Content: Article:
    1 Describe the planning department's intentions.
    2 Say that there is a lot of opposition to the plan.
    3 Describe the results of the questionnaire.
    4 Explain that there will be a meeting.
    Letter:
    1 Explain what you are writing about.
    2 Say that there is a lot of opposition to the plan.
    3 Explain how the land is being used now.

    4 Ask why building work will be started so soon.
    5 Ask whether the houses will be for local people.
    6 Ask for some response to your letter.

▶▶ PART 2

Question 2
Style: Neutral or semi-formal
Content: 1 Suggest that travel is good for young people.
    2 Give a number of reasons, e.g. learning to be independent, learning to make decisions, seeing interesting places.
    3 Say how you would benefit from a trip, what you would like to see etc.

Question 3
Style: Semi-formal or formal
Content: 1 Introduction: explain what you will write about.
    2 Give an example of a useful machine.
    3 Give a second example of a useful machine.
    4 Give an example of an unnecessary machine.
    5 Give a second example of an unnecessary machine.
    6 Conclusion: express your opinion whether on balance technology makes our lives easier.

Question 4
Style: Semi-formal or formal
Content: 1 Introduction: give some relevant information about your region.
    2 Describe young people's attitude to your region's culture, giving examples.
    3 Describe young people's attitude to your region's history, giving examples.
    4 Conclusion: express your view on how the situation may change in the future.

Question 5
Style: Semi-formal or formal
Content: 1 Introduction: state the name of the company, what it does, where it operates.
    2 Describe the structure of the company.
    3 Describe its aims and principles.
    4 Describe its main activities.
    5 Describe its plans for the future.
    6 Conclusion: give any interesting/relevant additional information, e.g. describe the company's leisure facilities.

PAPER 3 English in Use

▶▶ PART 1

1 C **2** D **3** B **4** A **5** C **6** D **7** B **8** C **9** A **10** C **11** B **12** A **13** D **14** C **15** A

▶▶ PART 2

16 Some **17** while/whereas/but **18** in **19** However **20** be
21 the **22** how **23** Another **24** not
25 will/may/might/can/could **26** take **27** with **28** by
29 time **30** off

▶▶ PART 3

31 fortnight **32** afford **33** ✓ **34** UK **35** leisure
36 though, **37** companies **38** ✓ **39** entertainment
40 on board **41** rinks **42** modified **43** ✓ **44** their
45 services **46** break

PART 4

47 unsuccessful **48** Desperate **49** exceptionally
50 impersonate **51** unbelievable **52** brilliance **53** easily
54 replacement **55** ensure **56** destruction **57** unauthorised
58 expiry **59** essential **60** consequently
61 memorise/memorize

PART 5

62 accommodate **63** the past **64** reserved
65 politeness/courtesy **66** shortage of **67** volume
68 alternative to **69** promised **70** chilled **71** decorated
72 unhelpful **73** compensation **74** discount on

PART 6

75 G **76** F **77** I **78** D **79** A **80** B

PAPER 4 Listening

PART 1

1 ancient Egypt **2** willow tree extract **3** 1829
4 stomach **5** German company **6** research **7** fifty/50
8 vegetables

PART 2

9 frequency **10** powerful/strong **11** Deforestation/Cutting down
trees **12** (many) thousands **13** cattle disease **14** coral reefs
15 heat up/melt **16** global warming

PART 3

17 B **18** A **19** D **20** D **21** C **22** A

PART 4

Task One
23 B **24** H **25** A **26** D **27** F

Task Two
28 G **29** F **30** H **31** D **32** B

 2

PAPER 1 Reading

PART 1

1 B: 'This argument draws ammunition from the tendency among some viewers of soap operas to believe ... that events and characters on the screen are real.'
2 A: 'Though figures are notoriously hard to come by'
3 C: 'it is particularly applicable to the young, those much sought-after purchasers in the 16 to 24 age group'
4 A: 'The introduction of video recorders that can automatically skip commercials and only record the programmes'
5 D: 'But now tracking has begun; major TV networks will be scanned for placement, and it will be possible to calculate how many seconds a certain product has been visible on prime-time television.'
6 A: 'But perhaps the most powerful incentive to use product placement was the fear that legislation would be introduced to regulate conventional forms of advertising more strictly.'
7 B: 'Thus commercials for alcohol are banned entirely in the UK ... . And yet, it may be more effective than the type of commercial that is banned.'

8 C: 'One is the tendency ... of consumers ... to become more discerning in their response to advertising as they are exposed to more of it over a period of time.'
9 C: 'consumers are tired of being talked down to'
10 A: 'it seems clear that many major companies are paying high fees to see their products feature in blockbusters or even TV soaps'
11 C: 'It has even been claimed that standard advertising for certain products aimed at niche youth markets would damage sales rather than improve them'
12 D: 'This is not to say that the effectiveness of placement can be deduced from such a simple statistic alone.'
13 B: 'Moreover, placement may expose children to unsuitable products ... exposure to certain modes of behaviour can encourage copy-cat posturing among the young or the immature.'
14 D: 'However, if it is ever going to be possible to calculate the precise effects of this, or indeed, any marketing device, such figures will be necessary.'

PART 2

15 F: Link between 'As many as 1,000 languages have died in the past 400 years. Conversely, the handful of major international languages are forging ahead' in the previous paragraph, the description of the status of the world's major languages today, and the description of what is happening to many languages in the following paragraph.
16 A: Frederik Kortlandt is mentioned for the first time in paragraph A. Also, link between 'Frederik Kortlandt ... has a mission to document as many of the remaining endangered languages as he can' and 'Documenting a threatened language can be difficult' in the following paragraph.
17 C: This paragraph continues the theme of languages threatened with extinction developed in preceding paragraphs.
18 E: Link between 'Kortlandt knows a language is disappearing' and the main theme of preceding paragraphs. Also, link between 'turned up at a conference in Tallinn' and 'like-minds met in Kathmandu for a conference' in paragraph C. Link between 'Every now and then language researchers get lucky. Kamassian ... was supposed to have died out, until two old women ... turned up at a conference in Tallinn' and 'To non-linguists it must seem an odd issue to get worked up about' in the following paragraph.
19 D: Link between 'Language is the defining characteristic of the human species. These people say things to each other which are very different from the things we say, and think very different thoughts, which are often incomprehensible to us' in the previous paragraph and 'If you want to understand the human species, you have to take the full range of human thought into consideration'.
20 B: Link between 'For centuries forest tribes have known about the healing properties of certain plants ... . All this knowledge could be lost if the tribes and their languages die out' in the previous paragraph and 'There are hundreds of known remedies in Fiji's forests. ... If the languages die, so too will the medicinal knowledge of naturally occurring tonics, rubs and potions'.

PART 3

21 A: Incorrect. It is implied that this is Ellen MacIntosh's view, but it is not the writer's view.
21 B: Incorrect. 'simplicity' refers to the 'stock, two-dimensional characters', not the stories themselves.

21 C: Correct. 'Indeed, although her comment does make one wonder why simplicity of this sort should be out of place in a story for children.'

21 D: Incorrect. This is not stated or implied in the text.

22 A: Incorrect. This is a true statement in itself but it is not what Ellen objects to.

22 B: Correct. 'Instead of standing up to her cruel stepmother ... Cinderella just waits for a fairy godmother to appear and solve her problems. But wouldn't you want a daughter of yours to show more spirit?'

22 C: Incorrect. The two sisters are 'absurd', which is not the same as saying they are figures of ridicule. Also, this is not what Ellen objects to.

22 D: Incorrect. This is implied in the text, but it is not what Ellen objects to.

23 A: Incorrect. 'The character of the rich and handsome stranger, however, is retained, *and in some cases really is a prince*.'

23 B: Correct. 'the Cinderella character no longer has to clean the house and *has no siblings to make her life a misery*'

23 C: Incorrect. 'The role of the fairy godmother is often replaced by coincidence or sheer luck'. This is not the same as saying that luck plays a greater role.

23 D: Incorrect. 'the Cinderella character no longer has to *clean the house*' and 'In the majority of film versions, the heroine has a profession'

24 A: Incorrect. 'In the majority of film versions, the heroine has a profession', but the text does not indicate whether she is successful in her profession.

24 B: Incorrect. 'marrying her prince' is used metaphorically, to imply that Cinderella will 'live happily ever after', not that she will become a real princess.

24 C: Incorrect. This is not stated or implied in the text.

24 D: Correct. 'In the majority of film versions, the heroine has a profession and is even permitted to continue working after marrying her prince – *this is the twenty-first century, after all*.'

25 A: Correct. 'Most children experience a sense of inner loneliness as they are growing up and empathise with the protagonist who faces some sort of test or challenge.'

25 B: Incorrect. The text does not state or imply that little girls like to be challenged themselves.

25 C: Incorrect. This is not stated or implied in the text.

25 D: Incorrect. This is not stated or implied in the text.

26 A: Incorrect. This is not stated or implied in the text.

26 B: Correct. 'This can be seen in the original story of Cinderella ... . She has to grow spiritually, and by maturing, she becomes attractive to the prince ... In the later versions, this element is missing'

26 C: Incorrect. This is not stated or implied in the text.

26 D: Incorrect. This is not stated or implied in the text.

▸▸ PART 4

27 B: 'I enjoyed putting on plays at the local youth centre, especially coaching budding actors'

28 D: 'I also offered to help my uncle out in his studio. ... I'd go along at the weekends and act as general unpaid dogsbody.'

29 A: 'now I can really understand why someone's using a certain technique or piece of equipment'

30 E: 'I was hardly a model employee. I loathed my job, and instead of selling insurance, I used to wander around the city's numerous art galleries'

31 C: 'I'm thinking either of expanding – more shops, managers and so on – or diversifying, perhaps producing my own surf boards'

32 B: 'The classes themselves aren't terribly lucrative, but I supplement my income ... organising trips to see shows in London.'

33 F: 'and the next thing I knew, my wife was urging me to set up my own company'

34 B: 'Then someone at an organisation called Business Link ... suggested advertising on the Internet!'

35 D: 'I've had to find another way to switch off. In fact, I've taken up fishing.'

36 A: 'If I hadn't realised early on that I'd never make it as a performer, I probably would have carried on dreaming that my big break would come.'

37 B: 'I couldn't work out how to find customers who would pay for their children to attend the kind of courses I wanted to run'

38 C: 'He said he wanted to sell up and I jumped at the chance to buy the business from him!'

39 E: 'To my surprise, I've turned out to be quite a good saleswoman.'

40 F: 'I had to take a very deep breath before I finally took the plunge.'

41 B: 'I studied medicine, but when I finished medical school I had a sort of crisis. I suddenly knew I couldn't go on with it!'

PAPER 2 Writing

▸▸ PART 1

Question 1

Style: Formal

Content: 1 Suggest that the writer of the article is mistaken in some ways.

2 Explain that the new sports centre has replaced the old sports pavilion.

3 Mention increased student numbers, more students from abroad and the need for accommodation.

4 Indicate that academic standards are actually better now, not worse. Also, mention the greater range of courses now offered.

5 Describe the college's involvement in community activities.

6 Explain that the college is holding a reunion for former students (with a few details from the memo).

▸▸ PART 2

Question 2

Style: Formal

Content: 1 Introduction: explain the basic idea.

2 Describe the benefits of the radio station, e.g. a service for students, its usefulness for communicating information etc.

3 Describe possible programme types.

4 Describe the support you would need, e.g. rooms, funding, equipment.

5 Conclusion: end with a summary of your arguments.

Question 3

Style: Semi-formal or formal

Content: 1 Introduction: describe the situation you are going to discuss (people moving to cities).

2 Describe the attractions of city life.

3 Describe the problems of country life.
4 Describe the disadvantages of city life.
5 Discuss what cities may be like in the future.
6 Conclusion: end with a summary of your views.

Question 4
Style: Semi-formal or formal
Content: 1 Introduction: give some basic information about the geography of your region.
2 Describe the most popular public transport facilities, and say why they are popular.
3 Describe what is being done to improve and promote the use of public transport.
4 Discuss what more could be done.
5 Conclusion: end with a summary of your views.

Question 5
Style: Formal
Content: 1 Say how long and in what capacity you have known the applicant.
2 Describe his business skills and abilities.
3 Describe how his personal characteristics make him a good choice for the position.
4 Offer to supply more information about the applicant if necessary.

PAPER 3 English in Use

▶▶ PART 1

1 A **2** D **3** C **4** B **5** B **6** C **7** A **8** D **9** C **10** A **11** B **12** D
13 C **14** A **15** D

▶▶ PART 2

16 may **17** but **18** apart **19** their/the **20** far **21** any
22 they **23** into **24** better **25** When **26** to **27** every
28 as **29** do **30** so

▶▶ PART 3

31 eel's/eels' **32** unappetising **33** There **34** ✓
35 quite **36** European **37** different **38** salmon
39 desirable **40** ✓ **41** its **42** ✓ **43** trend,' **44** ✓
45 whether **46** long term

▶▶ PART 4

47 unprecedented **48** division **49** energetic **50** successful
51 creativity **52** aggressively **53** competitive **54** option
55 unlikely **56** operators **57** efficiently **58** confirmation
59 notification **60** dissatisfied **61** refundable

▶▶ PART 5

62 majority of **63** survey **64** opposed **65** (medical) staff
66 universal/unanimous **67** reduction in **68** number of
69 admitted **70** alternative **71** condition/state of
72 made redundant **73** permission **74** reconsider

▶▶ PART 6

75 D **76** G **77** C **78** I **79** E **80** B

PAPER 4 Listening

▶▶ PART 1

1 an amateur historian **2** farmer **3** a doctor **4** articles and essays **5** personal correspondence **6** wife's brother **7** Roman history **8** Italy

▶▶ PART 2

9 forty-eight/48 **10** (a) vacuum pack **11** oxygen
12 three/3 days **13** renting (an) **14** (a free) gift/promotional device **15** conservationists **16** (dangerous) waste

▶▶ PART 3

17 A **18** B **19** C **20** D **21** A **22** A

▶▶ PART 4

23 C **24** A **25** B **26** A **27** A **28** B **29** A **30** C **31** A **32** B

TEST 3

PAPER 1 Reading

▶▶ PART 1

1 B: 'I've read somewhere that it would be a relatively easy matter to mass-produce cars that run on non-polluting fuels ... but the oil companies are so strong they block any real progress in that direction.'

2/3 B: 'I know many people are under the impression that they are helping in their own little way'

2/3 D: 'I also feel that if everyone were responsible and organised ... it would make a huge difference in the end.'

4 A: 'I think that's the real danger facing us today – that we'll succumb to a feeling of helplessness instead of making a concerted effort to make our planet a safer and cleaner place for future generations.'

5 D: 'I think this applies in particular to places like moors, forests and heathland ... where wildlife is under threat.'

6 C: 'In the next few decades scientists are bound to find viable alternative sources of energy to fossil fuels.'

7 C: 'And I suspect the scientists who keep preaching doom and gloom are probably exaggerating.'

8 A: 'And since it's a global issue, individual countries can't tackle it by themselves. Reducing damage to the environment really must be an international effort.'

9 B: 'They don't seem to realise that you can recycle waste paper for years to save trees being cut down, but your good deeds can be cancelled out by a single plane flight!'

10 C: 'They were wrong about that, so why should we assume they are right about global warming and the rest of the doomsday scenarios?'

11 A: 'With hindsight, I think we were naive.'

12 D: 'No matter how right your ideas are, there's no justification for becoming rude or violent.'

13 B: 'So much of the waste is produced by big industry, ... put pressure on governments to pass laws in its favour.'

14 A: 'I remember being pleased when laws restricting the use of certain pesticides came in.'

15 C: 'People have to be allowed to make choices of their own – responsible choices, of course – on such matters.'

▶▶ PART 2

16 G: Link between 'remnants of the Inca civilisation' in the previous paragraph and 'the greatest Inca discovery of them all'. Also, link between 'But this region of southern Peru is still full of ruins' and 'an advanced civilisation existed here' in the following paragraph.

17 D: Link between 'firing the ambitions of those hoping to make similar spectacular finds' in the previous paragraph, 'That amounts to an awful lot of culture buried under the ground'

and 'It is the mountains of the Vilcabamba range that perhaps hold the most tantalising, spectacular ruins' in the following paragraph.

18 A: Link between 'foundations of buildings, foundations of roads, water channels' and 'The finds' in the following paragraph.

19 E: Contrastive link between 'About ninety percent has not been investigated' in the previous paragraph and 'vigorous exploration combined with serious scientific research'. Also, Johan Reinhard's name is mentioned for the first time in paragraph E.

20 C: Contrastive link between 'It's the Indiana Jones fantasy' in the previous paragraph and 'But exploring is not all about adventure'.

21 B: Link between 'In two lengthy expeditions to Qoriwayrachina in 2001 and 2002' and 'future expeditions to Qoriwayrachina' in the following paragraph.

▶▶ PART 3

22 A: Correct. 'Later came the beach buggy, a briefly fashionable, wildly impractical, single-terrain vehicle' and 'there is no doubt which pointless recreational vehicle ... it's the quad bike'

22 B: Incorrect. A snowmobile or motorcycle can be, 'in certain contexts, quite useful', but the quad bike is a 'pointless recreational vehicle', according to the writer.

22 C: Incorrect. The text implies that its only purpose is for recreation, not that it is useless *for* recreation.

22 D: Incorrect. This is not stated or implied in the text. The phrase 'briefly fashionable' is used to describe the beach buggy, not the quad bike.

23 A: Incorrect. This is not stated or implied in the text.

23 B: Incorrect. This is not stated or implied in the text.

23 C: Correct. 'There's nothing cool about a quad' and 'Spoilt children get them for Christmas.'

23 D: Incorrect. He mentions rich people, but does not imply they have 'too much money'.

24 A: Incorrect. This is not stated or implied in the text.

24 B: Correct. 'Originally, the ATV ... was developed in Japan as a three-wheeled farm vehicle, an inexpensive mini-tractor that could go just about anywhere.'

24 C: Incorrect: 'Originally, the ATV ... was developed in Japan as a *three-wheeled* farm vehicle'

24 D: Incorrect. 'Originally, the ATV ... was developed in Japan as a three-wheeled *farm vehicle*'

25 A: Incorrect. Turning a corner is not mentioned as a danger in itself.

25 B: Incorrect. 'they're much easier to ride than a two-wheeled motorcycle'. It does not follow, however, that someone who can ride a quad bike can ride a motorcycle.

25 C: Incorrect. 'With quad racing it's very rare that we see anybody having an accident'

25 D: Correct. 'the quad's recreational appeal lies in its potential to deliver a safe thrill' and 'The quad bike, in short, provides middle-aged excitement for men who think a Harley might be a bit dangerous.'

26 A: Incorrect. Wearing these is not an *obligation* – it is a *recommendation* made by retailers.

26 B: Incorrect. Basic safety instructions are offered by retailers, but quad bike riders do not *have to* follow them.

26 C: Correct. 'Employers are required to provide training to workers who use quad bikes'

26 D: Incorrect. 'there is no licence required to drive a quad bike'

27 A: Incorrect. Although he says 'police constables ride them while patrolling the Merseyside coastline', he does not imply this is the reason why the quad bike will remain popular.

27 B: Correct. 'they have all but replaced the tractor as the all-purpose agricultural workhorse'

27 C: Incorrect. It has replaced the tractor, not horses.

27 D: Incorrect. The quad bike can be used on ice, but not as a working vehicle.

▶▶ PART 4

28 E: 'Books and films for older children (and adults) that deal with time travel indicate just how, well, timeless, that interest is.'

29 B: 'The haunting pictures of the dilapidated farm buildings and scruffy animals are just one of the outstanding features in this first novel'

30 H: 'nobody must look at the old oak. Everyone in the village knows this ... except Arthur ... We learn what happens to Arthur when he looks at the tree'

31 C: 'The sparse text is cleverly interwoven with the line drawings in such a way as to encourage reading without being too overtly didactic.'

32 F: 'But a new teacher at nursery school brings out the artist in Viji'

33 E: 'As Heather ventures backwards and forwards in time, she learns fascinating details about life in different epochs, each of which is entirely plausible and very real.'

34 H: 'as in her first novel, Carson depicts brilliantly the isolation of childhood'

35 D: 'Problems begin to emerge when he discovers he is slipping in and out of his imaginary world without realising it – and then he finds he can't control which world he is living in.'

36 C: 'Even toddlers who show no interest in the usual baby bathtime books will be entranced by the delightful narrative.'

37 F: 'A useful message for every child who is unwilling to try something new because of doubts about his or her ability.'

38 D: 'the younger members of the target market for this work may find the material too unsettling' and 'If this marketing mismatch could be addressed'

39 G: 'Wilmot captures brilliantly the drabness and grey uniformity, but also the quaint quality of life in that decade.'

40 A: 'the breathtaking finale comes right out of the blue'

41 B: 'This enables young readers to understand fully the awkward issues facing the grown-ups in this world'

42 G: 'Wilmot's ability to demonstrate what is going on in the minds of the adults in the story without talking down to his young readers, as so many writers do'

PAPER 2 Writing

▶▶ PART 1

Question 1

Style: Formal

Content: 1 Introduction: briefly describe the trip (dates, number of people, places visited).

2 Say what criticisms have been expressed:
- didn't see much scenery
- the coach was slow
- a train with sleeping cars would save time
- practice with Scottish accents needed
- the language classes were hard for some people

- the lectures were boring for some people
- some people wanted an organised event on the first evening

3 Describe the positive feedback:
- people enjoyed the guided tour of the city
- country dancing was popular
- people enjoyed the museums and art galleries, though this was too much for one day

4 Conclusion: end with your suggestions for future trips.

▶▶ PART 2

Question 2
Style: Semi-formal or formal
Content: 1 Introduction: give some basic information about the region.
2 Describe the sports played in the region and the facilities.
3 Describe what other recreation possibilities there are.
4 Give some basic information about cinemas and theatres (how to get there, the kinds of films, plays one can see etc.)
5 Give some basic information about cafés and restaurants (how to get there, prices, type of food etc.)
6 Conclusion: perhaps suggest where students can get more detailed or additional information.

Question 3
Style: Semi-formal or formal
Content: 1 Introduction: describe a situation when you did manual work.
2 Describe exactly what you had to do.
3 Say how the work proved to be satisfying.
4 Conclusion: perhaps end with a reflection on the value of doing manual work.

Question 4
Style: Informal
Content: 1 Introduction: explain what you are going to write about.
2 Describe the events leading up to the accident.
3 Describe the accident itself in some detail.
4 Describe the reactions of the drivers and other people.
5 Describe your experience with the police.
6 Explain what was interesting about the whole experience for you.

Question 5
Style: Formal
Content: 1 Introduction: explain what you are proposing the company should do.
2 Describe the kind of information that would be included in the magazine.
3 Say who would read the magazine.
4 Discuss how it would be publicised.
5 Discuss how it would benefit the company.
6 Conclusion: end with a summary of your arguments.

PAPER 3 English in Use

▶▶ PART 1

1 C **2** B **3** D **4** B **5** D **6** C **7** D **8** A **9** A **10** C **11** D **12** B **13** B **14** C **15** A

▶▶ PART 2

16 than **17** number **18** them **19** in **20** as **21** what **22** why **23** worth **24** less **25** though/if **26** the **27** such **28** will/can/could/may/might **29** mind **30** in

▶▶ PART 3

31 the **32** actually **33** ✓ **34** been **35** out **36** to **37** ✓ **38** such **39** who **40** all **41** ✓ **42** it **43** although **44** ✓ **45** up **46** a

▶▶ PART 4

47 unbearably **48** electricity **49** temporarily **50** heatwave **51** penetration **52** insulation **53** disobeying **54** commonly **55** waterproof **56** simplicity **57** attractions **58** actually **59** indispensable **60** recreation **61** unbelievably

▶▶ PART 5

62 takes off/leaves **63** driver **64** come/get out **65** taken/driven **66** address **67** on foot **68** the sights **69** fluent **70** to eat/drink **71** popular/successful **72** restaurant **73** appeal **74** (boat) trip

▶▶ PART 6

75 B **76** C **77** I **78** A **79** F **80** D

PAPER 4 Listening

▶▶ PART 1

1 a (new) motorway **2** skeleton **3** ceremonial **4** cattle **5** leader **6** France **7** west **8** the British Museum

▶▶ PART 2

9 purple **10** a/one tenth/1/10 **11** (rare) birds **12** deer **13** tourist attractions **14** landowners **15** trees **16** decline/deterioration

▶▶ PART 3

17 C **18** C **19** D **20** B **21** A **22** A

▶▶ PART 4

Task One
23 A **24** H **25** G **26** E **27** B

Task Two
28 F **29** D **30** B **31** H **32** C

TEST 4

PAPER 1 Reading

▶▶ PART 1

1 C: 'If you go to art school, you get feedback from tutors and your peers, but I never had the opportunity'
2 E: 'This success has come overnight ... I enjoy being invited to parties.'
3 B: 'classical ballet is a collaborative art, which is one aspect of it I particularly appreciate'
4 D: 'my teacher at art school, who advised me to give up any idea of being a graphic designer and think about some other line of work'
5 B: 'I'd like to work in a company that mounts productions for children and tries to attract people who wouldn't normally dream of going to the ballet, just to give them a taste of it.'

6 A: 'And I have to say, writing is more demanding and less glamorous than I had ever imagined.'

7 C: 'However, what matters most to me is not public acclaim but the praise of other artists and those critics I respect, especially because I sometimes doubt my own talent.'

8 D: 'I've started taking pottery classes there just for fun'

9 A: 'I wrote *Strange Tales* the summer after I graduated from university, and the words just poured out; it didn't seem to require any struggle at all.'

10 B: 'Ballet can be such a rarified world, and you feel you are performing for a small, rich elite.'

11 D: 'I've been reaping some more tangible benefits as well. Funding for future projects is more readily forthcoming'

12 E: 'I never would have imagined I'd get back pain from standing on stage for so long, for instance.'

13/14 B: 'I'm uncomfortable about the whole concept of being a star because the publicity can be an intrusion into your private life'

13/14 C: 'What's more, public attention can be exhausting, and I feel awkward about being interviewed.'

15 C: 'This was hard, especially since I had to rebel against the wishes of my family; my father was determined I should become a lawyer like him.'

▶▶ PART 2

16 D: Link between 'almost eight percent of the electricity that the country needs will be generated in this way' in the previous paragraph and 'This is in line with the target ... of producing ten percent of Britain's electricity from renewables'.

17 A: Link between 'the principle ... has only very recently been used successfully' and 'the delay' in the following paragraph.

18 G: Contrastive link between the risks described in the previous paragraph and 'In fact, there is very little risk involved'. Also, contrastive link between 'Britain may well become a world leader in offshore wind exploitation' and 'The way ahead is not without problems, however' in the following paragraph.

19 F: Link between the problems and complaints described in the previous paragraph and 'Another cause for concern'.

20 C: Link between 'solar energy is hardly going to be a great success here' in the previous paragraph and 'Some form of water power would seem a far more likely candidate for development'.

21 E: Link between 'Existing nuclear power stations are to be phased out' in the previous paragraph and 'this is only a small step in the right direction'. Also, link between 'when the existing power stations are shut down' and 'In the meantime' in the following paragraph.

▶▶ PART 3

22 B: ' "The industry is completely overreacting; it'll be a laughing stock," says Mayes.'

23 D: 'The scratchy, distorted cassette copy is a poor version of the original recording, whereas an MP3 file is of high quality and can be stored'

24 C: 'The companies are simply hoping that one of these new bands or singers will be a hit'

25 B: 'the recording industry can't be held responsible for the evanescent nature of fame, given the teenage appetite for anything novel'

26 C: 'The problem isn't going to vanish if the industry carries on trying to make a quick profit.'

▶▶ PART 4

27 A: 'Consequently, she uses a car mainly to commute to her office'

28/29 B: 'when the weather is bad she has to drive the children to their school nearby'

28/29 C: 'she mostly uses the car to stock up with groceries from the local supermarket on Friday evenings'

30 D: 'she only passed her driving test three and a half years ago'

31 C: 'She is rather dismissive of SUVs ... they are a danger to cyclists because SUV drivers tend not to notice them.'

32 B: 'When asked about what influenced her choice of vehicle, she is unequivocal: safety was the crucial point'

33 A: 'They wanted a car that would be fuel-efficient and that would produce as few harmful emissions as possible.'

34 D: 'Heather herself then reluctantly took charge of the car'

35 A: 'Megan left the choice of car to her husband; she claims she is ignorant of the technical issues involved'

36 C: 'The new charges for drivers ... she would far rather take the train to the city'

37 B: 'Vera is one of the growing number of people who have purchased an SUV.'

38 B: 'her SUV seats eight people ... she needs this room'

39 D: 'She says she never expected to get such enormous pleasure from sitting behind the wheel ... a sense of independence and confidence that she lacked when she was younger.'

40 A: 'She stresses she would rather be able to manage without a car at all. However, ... a viable option'

41 C: 'Some good neighbours ... were thinking of buying a new one ... use hers whenever they wanted to.'

PAPER 2 Writing

▶▶ PART 1

Question 1

Style: Formal

Content: 1 Suggest that the writer of the article is mistaken in some ways.

2 Answer the writer's criticisms:
- most people were satisfied
- refreshments were served from twelve to two
- other entertainment was available, apart from rides
- students paid for the party, not the college

3 Admit that the layout was bad and apologise.

4 Refer to the survey results.

5 Conclusion: perhaps end with a summary.

▶▶ PART 2

Question 2

Style: Neutral or semi-formal

Content: 1 Introduction: Describe how the situation came about.

2 Say who was involved.

3 Describe what you felt.

4 Say whether you succeeded in concealing your feelings.

5 Conclusion: perhaps discuss any lessons you learnt from this experience.

Question 3

Style: Semi-formal or formal

Content: 1 Introduction: give some basic information about the area.

2 Describe one or two places of historical interest.

3 Describe one or two areas of natural beauty.

4 Describe one or two theme parks/amusement parks.

5 Conclusion: perhaps tell readers where to find additional or more detailed information.

Question 4

Style: Semi-formal or formal

Content: 1 Introduction: describe where and when you had this teacher.

2 Describe the teacher's appearance and personality and how he/she taught.

3 Describe the response of the pupils.

4 Discuss what made him/her a good teacher.

5 Discuss what you learnt from this teacher.

6 Conclusion: perhaps summarise briefly what makes a good teacher.

Question 5

Style: Formal

Content: 1 Introduction: briefly re-state why this experiment was introduced.

2 Describe the benefits arising from the experiment in practice.

3 Describe the problems arising from the experiment in practice.

4 Conclusion: summarise the situation and make suggestions for the future.

PAPER 3 English in Use

▶▶ PART 1

1 B 2 A 3 A 4 D 5 B 6 C 7 B 8 D 9 A 10 C 11 D 12 B
13 A 14 C 15 D

▶▶ PART 2

16 due 17 how/where 18 keep 19 which/that 20 despite
21 its 22 can/could 23 everyone/everybody/anyone/anybody
24 or 25 back 26 on/to 27 against 28 In 29 whether/if
30 no

▶▶ PART 3

31 of 32 convinced 33 days,' 34 physical 35 lives
36 out 37 ✓ 38 years 39 ✓ 40 believes 41 ✓
42 peak 43 until 44 claims, 45 your 46 ✓

▶▶ PART 4

47 exploration 48 architectural 49 impressive 50 attractions
51 comprehensive 52 picturesque 53 cautiously
54 knowledge 55 extremities 56 indication 57 pressure
58 acceptable 59 malfunctioning 60 elasticity 61 disregard

▶▶ PART 5

62 share 63 downstairs 64 to keep 65 too/as well 66 go up
67 the most 68 to pay 69 allowed to 70 look after 71 list
72 turn down 73 writing 74 end of

▶▶ PART 6

75 C 76 F 77 A 78 H 79 B 80 E

PAPER 4 Listening

▶▶ PART 1

1 winter 2 two/2 3 direct 4 not descended
5 became extinct 6 tools 7 groups 8 a mystery

▶▶ PART 2

9 two hundred/200 metres 10 overhead cables/power lines
11 children 12 (model aircraft) fuel 13 connect (the) battery
14 (the) starter spring 15 step backwards
16 climbs and dives

▶▶ PART 3

17 B 18 A 19 C 20 A 21 D 22 C

▶▶ PART 4

23 B 24 A 25 C 26 A 27 C 28 A 29 C 30 B 31 B 32 A

TEST 5

PAPER 1 Reading

▶▶ PART 1

1 D: 'Its author is Percy Seymour, a former astronomy lecturer'

2 A: 'a few years ago it emerged that one large bank was using astrology to help manage its £5 billion investment portfolio'

3 B: 'Is there, after all, anything to astrology, or is the whole "science" an elaborate hoax to bamboozle the gullible?'

4 E: 'Working with psychologist Ivan Kelly, Dean studied 2,000 people'

5 A: 'Even former British Prime Minister Margaret Thatcher once told MPs: "I was born under the sign of Libra, it follows that I am well-balanced".'

6 B: 'Can an expert astrologer armed with the details of your exact time and place of birth produce an accurate reading of your character?'

7 D: 'Most scientists and astronomers have poured scorn on Seymour's suggestions ... so small as to be virtually undetectable.'

8 A: 'The roots of astrology are probably almost as old as humanity's first attempts to map the heavens. ... most cultures throughout history have believed that the stars influence our lives'

9 E: 'They found no evidence of the similarities that astrologers would have predicted'

10 A: 'and to judge by the avidity with which modern-day Britons scan the pages of newspapers for their daily horoscope, astrology is as popular today as ever it was'

11 C: 'Mars is found in certain positions in the sky more often at the birth of sports champions than at the birth of other people'

12 A: 'Nor is it a secret that several politicians have relied on astrologers to provide insight on matters of state'

13 E: 'But ironically, it is research done by an ex-astrologer, Geoffrey Dean, that has done the greatest damage to the credibility of astrology.'

14 B: 'Paradoxically, however, the resultant mechanistic view of life has caused many to feel that their life has no purpose ... Is this, perhaps, why growing numbers of people are turning to astrology with such fervour?'

PART 2

15 C: Link between 'Gorillas, chimpanzees, bonobos and orangutans ... could vanish from the wild within fifty years' in the previous paragraph and 'The clock is standing at one minute to midnight for the great apes'. Also, link between 'They have appealed for £15 million to save the world's great apes' in the previous paragraph and 'the sum required'.

16 B: Link between 'the decline in ape numbers has not only continued but accelerated' in the previous paragraph and 'the rapidly dwindling numbers'.

17 G: Link between 'In one population studied, researchers knew of 140 gorillas. After an outbreak of the Ebola virus, they could only find seven alive' and 'The future looks equally bleak for the other African apes' in the following paragraph.

18 D: Link between 'To survive and breed, the great apes need undisturbed forest. But such earthly edens are becoming increasingly scarce' and the destruction of natural habitats discussed in the following paragraph.

19 E: Link between 'Unesco officials are working to improve law enforcement in African national parks' and 'We cannot just put up fences to try and separate the apes from people' in the following paragraph.

20 A: Link between 'one official' in the previous paragraph and 'Another official'.

PART 3

21 C: 'all that remains to tell us that it was once lush and verdant – and inhabited – is the occasional tool stone, harpoon or mammoth tusk brought up from the sea bed by fishing boats'

22 D: 'While previous devices have only been able to produce two-dimensional images, bathymetry ... accurate and remarkably detailed maps. ... an ancient river bed leaps out of the three-dimensional image ... . The sites of pre-historic settlements can now be pinpointed, ... to see in stunning detail the sunken shipwrecks'

23 A: 'She is however, scathing about the scale of government funding' and 'it's an absolute scandal that we know so little about the area just off our shores'

24 B: 'The idea of Britain as a natural island kingdom will be challenged ... . It remains to be seen how far this new awareness is taken on board among our "island" people.'

25 D: 'In addition, commercial applications are a real possibility.'

PART 4

26 E: 'Preparation is of extreme importance; things like finding out what form the interview will have ... will you be talking to one person or a panel?'

27 A: 'But I got carried away and went off at a tangent, which made a bad impression.'

28/29 B: 'I wondered if perhaps I had been too direct, but I later discovered ... they were impressed by my enthusiasm and ambition.'

28/29 F: 'Show that your ambition is the force that drives you'

30 E: 'Actually, it's not so much what people say ... as the way they sit, how they hold their heads, whether they meet the interviewer's eye'

31 C: 'find out as much as you can about the company you have applied to from its website and promotional material'

32 D: 'I turned up in a smart business suit and tie, only to find that my prospective employers were in jeans!'

33 E: 'Another question interviewers sometimes ask ... is about mistakes you have made. ... admit that you were at fault'

34 B: 'Firstly, a candidate should not learn a speech off by heart; you will come across as insincere, as if you have practised everything in front of a mirror.'

35 D: 'A candidate should decide in advance on at least ten things to ask the interviewer'

36 F: 'Being nervous can make you forget things ... this will help you feel less nervous.'

37 D: 'I was so relieved that the interview was over that I just smiled and blurted out: "No thanks!"'

38 C: 'Make it clear that the interview is a two-way process'

39 D: 'They believed in being casual ... people all used first names with each other etc.'

PAPER 2 Writing

PART 1

Question 1

Style: Formal

Content: 1 Introduction: briefly describe what you are going to propose.
2 Describe the schedule you propose.
   • Saturday morning: a talk on regulations
   • Saturday early afternoon: use of the library
   • Saturday late afternoon: visit the sports hall
   • Saturday evening: a talk about social life, followed by a disco
   • Sunday morning: use of the computer room
   • Sunday afternoon: an introduction to student societies
3 Conclusion: make any other relevant comments and suggestions.

PART 2

Question 2

Style: Semi-formal or formal

Content: 1 Introduction: perhaps explain how history can be boring.
2 Summarise the relevant part of history.
3 Describe the situation you were in.
4 Explain why it made history come alive.
5 Conclusion: write an appropriate ending to round off.

Question 3

Style: Formal

Content: 1 Describe briefly how you met the applicant.
2 Describe his/her skills and abilities.
3 Describe the personal characteristics that make him/her a good candidate for the position.
4 Offer to supply more information if necessary.

Question 4

Style: Semi-formal or formal

Content: 1 Introduction: describe the situation (i.e. many young people leave school early).
2 Discuss the benefits of further education.
3 Discuss why many young people do not appreciate these benefits.
4 Discuss what could be done to encourage young people to go to college.
5 Conclusion: perhaps end with a brief summary of your points.

Question 5

Style: Formal

Content: 1 Introduction: describe briefly the proposed changes.
2 Describe the advantages.
3 Describe the disadvantages.
4 Discuss the possible short-term and long-term effects.
5 Conclusion: end with a brief summary of your views.

PAPER 3 English in Use

▶▶ PART 1

1 B **2** C **3** D **4** A **5** B **6** C **7** A **8** D **9** C **10** B **11** D **12** C
13 A **14** B **15** A

▶▶ PART 2

16 any **17** on **18** which **19** for **20** do **21** have/need
22 like **23** why **24** In **25** not **26** If/When **27** without
28 account/consideration **29** As **30** their

▶▶ PART 3

31 Gulf **32** agree **33** occurrence **34** ✓ **35** soon.
36 raging **37** convinced **38** ✓ **39** tides **40** considerable
41 sea **42** ✓ **43** of **44** whatever **45** criticism **46** ✓

▶▶ PART 4

47 characterised/characterized **48** versatility **49** costly
50 execution **51** inadvisable **52** essentially **53** indestructible
54 maintenance **55** transformations **56** predominantly
57 recognisably/recognizably **58** Agricultural **59** irreversible
60 increasingly **61** perception

▶▶ PART 5

62 fortnight **63** accommodation **64** co-operation/cooperation
65 an expert/authority **66** a number **67** unwilling/reluctant to
68 appearance **69** no longer **70** available **71** vehicles
72 access/connection **73** on time **74** was delayed

▶▶ PART 6

75 I **76** D **77** A **78** C **79** H **80** F

PAPER 4 Listening

▶▶ PART 1

1 subject **2** on Earth/earth **3** extraterrestrial life **4** history
5 (geological) period **6** five million/5,000,000
7 (very) different from **8** (the) dinosaurs

▶▶ PART 2

9 hard work **10** passive exercise **11** vibrates
12 fit **13** aerobic **14** resistance **15** (basic) equipment **16** push

▶▶ PART 3

17 A **18** D **19** C **20** B **21** A **22** C

▶▶ PART 4

Task One
23 B **24** C **25** G **26** A **27** D

Task Two
28 E **29** A **30** F **31** G **32** H

TEST 6

PAPER 1 Reading

▶▶ PART 1

1 C: 'she suddenly lost interest – whereas I was smitten. I certainly wasn't prepared for the adrenalin rush I experienced'

2 B: 'She simply couldn't conceive of anybody choosing to become an actor after making a living in a *proper* profession.'

3 A: ' "I enrolled in a drama school when I was eighteen." Duncan made her first professional stage appearance shortly afterwards … enjoy a considerable measure of success.'

4 B: 'acting was not a career that I dared to suggest for myself'

5 A: 'I had worked as an actor, and I knew what it was like to struggle, to be unemployed.'

6 D: 'I used to resent it if anybody said that lawyers lived in the real world, whereas actors were just acting.'

7/8 A: 'Then one day she was asked for advice in a case involving Equity, the actors' union.'

7/8 B: 'I went to an agent and told her I was a lawyer but I wanted to become an actor.'

9 C: 'she is also keen to get to grips with the art of directing'

10 A: 'No longer young enough to play ingénue roles … play the relatively unglamorous parts available to older women?'

11 B: 'Fortunately, I have a private income and I don't have to depend on acting to earn a living'

12 D: 'Now I spend a lot more time applying my lawyerly skills to uncover the real nature of the character I am impersonating.'

13 B: 'I come from a long line of hard-headed Yorkshire businessmen, and my family would have thought that a stage career would be a waste of time and energy, not to mention money!'

14 C: 'One thing that continually surprises me is the fact that I do it at all, because deep down I'm a very shy and private person.'

15 A: 'she also felt she was not being stretched intellectually'

16 C: 'Alicia Bolton had no interest in the theatre, either at school or as a law student.'

▶▶ PART 2

17 F: Link between the description of the 'community for the deeply green' in the previous paragraph and 'This might sound like a high-tech oasis'.

18 G: Link between 'a matter of intelligent design' in the previous paragraph and 'The key is finding ways to maximise efficiency in the simplest ways possible'.

19 A: Link between 'more zero-energy communities are under construction' in the previous paragraph and 'Much of the technology involved'.

20 C: Link between the 'European Union directive' described in the previous paragraph and 'The US government, too, has been doing its part'.

21 E: Link between the innovations described in the previous paragraph and 'Even more exciting developments are creeping onto the market'.

22 B: Contrastive link between 'Who cares … costs a relatively small amount?' in the previous paragraph and 'Still, as governments, scientists and builders continue to provide the "market push" towards energy efficiency, the "consumer pull" will be stimulated'. Also, link between 'a combination of increasingly efficient appliances and building techniques' and 'The technologies will be able to support each other' in the following paragraph.

▶▶ PART 3

23 C: 'the ability to run was a crucial factor in the development of our species'
24 C: 'However, this is only true if we consider fast running, or sprinting, over short distances. Even an Olympic athlete can ... only keep up a top speed for fifteen seconds or so.'
25 B: 'When we run, it is this ligament that prevents our head from pitching back and forth or from side to side. Therefore, we are able to run with steady heads, held high.'
26 D: 'Then there are our Achilles tendons ... which have nothing to do with walking. When we run, these tendons behave like springs, helping to propel us forward.'
27 C: 'running evolved in order for our direct ancestors to compete with other carnivores for access to the protein needed to grow the big brains that we enjoy today'

▶▶ PART 4

28 D: 'One thing that did surprise me at the start was how much official paperwork I have to deal with.'
29/30 C: 'It seems to me that people who start up businesses at my age ... are less inclined to take unnecessary risks.'
29/30 E: 'I figured I'd be better off sticking to what I know'
31 B: 'I know a lot of people in the industry. They have been great, offering advice as well as concrete help.'
32 A: 'I was infuriated by the arrogance of the company, which appeared to believe I was too old to be useful any longer'
33 F: 'I do almost all my work from home, using my PC for e-mails and video conferencing'
34 D: 'It was something I'd longed to do for years.'
35/36 A: 'The initial outlay for office equipment was pretty low, all things considered.'
35/36 D: 'When I left the company ... I had a reasonable amount of cash to invest in my own company.'
37 E: 'I'm sure I wouldn't have had the nerve to do it when I was younger, but I'm very glad I did.'
38 C: 'we're about to expand into glassware as well'
39 E: 'software showing people exactly how to go about it'
40 B: 'There seemed to be a dearth of companies catering for the over sixties'
41 C: 'Most of the people who work for me are more or less my generation. I find they tend to be more loyal'
42 F: 'I was in advertising for almost thirty years, but it's a very cut-throat business'
43 E: 'I've deliberately not tried to expand the business'

PAPER 2 Writing

▶▶ PART 1

Question 1
Style: Informal
Content: 1 Introduction: advise your friend to ask for further information.
2 Your friend should ask about:
● the exact location and how he/she can get to London
● the kind of accommodation available; can he/she stay with a family to improve his/her conversational English?
● the number of students in each class

● classes for students who already have a good level of English
● the number of class hours per week
● facilities for sports and other activities
3 Conclusion: perhaps end by wishing your friend a pleasant stay if he/she eventually decides to attend the school and offer to help further if necessary.

▶▶ PART 2

Question 2
Style: Semi-formal or formal
Content: 1 Introduction: describe the situation (some young people have to specialise at an early age).
2 Discuss the benefits of specialisation.
3 Discuss the benefits of getting a more general education.
4 Discuss what employers might want.
5 Conclusion: perhaps end with some general conclusions and/or suggestions.

Question 3
Style: Semi-formal or formal
Content: 1 Introduction: describe the situation (there are many sources of information).
2 Discuss the benefits of access to so much information.
3 Discuss the possible problems, e.g. getting bored or becoming unable to absorb it all.
4 Conclusion: perhaps end with your views of what will happen in the future.

Question 4
Style: Semi-formal or formal
Content: 1 Introduction: give some basic information about the region.
2 Describe some sights that might be of interest to young people.
3 Describe some places of cultural interest.
4 Describe some places of historical interest.
5 Describe some places of entertainment.
6 Describe some places where young people can socialise.
7 Conclusion: perhaps end by telling readers where to find additional or more detailed information.

Question 5
Style: Formal
Content: 1 Introduction: describe what you intend to propose (sponsoring a cultural event).
2 Describe the event, giving some background information and explaining what the event involves.
3 Discuss why it would be a suitable event for your company to sponsor.
4 Describe how the event could be publicised.
5 Conclusion: perhaps end with a brief summary of your points.

▶▶ PART 1

1 A **2** C **3** B **4** D **5** B **6** C **7** D **8** A **9** B **10** C **11** A **12** D
13 D **14** C **15** B

▶▶ PART 2

16 forward **17** While/When/If **18** how **19** It **20** such
21 to **22** each/every **23** Then **24** far **25** could/would
26 of **27** as **28** They **29** which **30** down

▶▶ PART 3

31 down **32** same **33** to **34** ✓ **35** in **36** an **37** ✓
38 been **39** are **40** all **41** is **42** ✓ **43** had **44** of
45 together **46** ✓

▶▶ PART 4

47 faithfully **48** revolting **49** width **50** overlooked
51 wholesome **52** setting **53** ageing/aging **54** importance
55 relationship **56** adolescents **57** unimaginable
58 negotiations **59** masterpiece **60** accessible
61 fragmentation

▶▶ PART 5

62 access **63** restricted **64** forbidden to **65** inform/tell
66 ask/consult **67** attempt **68** borrow **69** obtained
70 number of **71** fee/charge **72** at least **73** entitled
74 requirements/needs

▶▶ PART 6

75 D **76** I **77** B **78** G **79** E **80** H

▶▶ PART 1

1 map (out) **2** conserve the site **3** humid
4 coach park **5** an underground stream **6** (loose) stones **7** leg
8 tour guide

▶▶ PART 2

9 (our) civilisation/civilization **10** gold **11** processed food
12 the food industry **13** blood pressure **14** heart attacks
15 third/1/3 **16** roads

▶▶ PART 3

17 D **18** D **19** B **20** A **21** C **22** B

▶▶ PART 4

Task One
23 F **24** E **25** C **26** H **27** A

Task Two
28 A **29** G **30** H **31** C **32** E

TEST 7

▶▶ PART 1

1 B: 'It all started when I became interested in running the marathon in London, our home town, after a back injury.'
2 D: 'The second half of the route also takes you past Notre Dame and the Eiffel Tower, along the banks of the Seine'
3 C: 'London has a real carnival atmosphere for the marathon'
4 B: 'You turn up in a fascinating city, relieved you are not there to wander aimlessly and get bored'
5 A: 'One tip: it makes sense to plan a trip like this well in advance since important marathons frequently have arrangements with airlines and hotels for special rates.'
6 D: 'Three-quarters of the way through the marathon, I started to get tired and I was rather dubious about completing it.'
7 C: 'I often manage to arrange business trips so that my stay in a city coincides with a marathon'
8 B: 'There are some steep gradients'
9 A: 'I can finally compensate my nearest and dearest for all those Sundays I went missing for the better part of the day'
10 D: 'That eliminates race-day nerves about getting there on time.'
11 B: 'My physiotherapist suggested some regular exercise, so I took up jogging and soon became very keen on running.'
12 C: 'I'd also suggest that you check your insurance before each event to make sure you're covered in case of mishaps.'
13 A: 'My wife loves jazz'
14 D: 'I've decided that the appealing thing about running a marathon is that it's basically an illogical thing to do'

▶▶ PART 2

15 A: Contrastive link between 'An enviable position to be in' in the previous paragraph and 'Yet she is clutching her saxophone like a petrified child'.
16 E: Link between 'an extraordinary combination' in the previous paragraph and 'As if this weren't unusual enough'. Also, link between 'she's a vet by training' in the previous paragraph and 'she suddenly decided to sell her thriving veterinary practice'.
17 G: Link between 'I was satisfied with my life' and 'contentment of this sort' in the following paragraph.
18 D: Link between 'it was as if she was hearing music for the first time' in the previous paragraph and 'I thought I'd gone to heaven'.
19 F: Link between 'Oddly enough' in the previous paragraph and 'the other curious factor'.
20 B: Link between 'little opportunity to feed her brain', 'reading books only goes a small way towards intellectual fulfilment' and 'her latest project will provide what's missing' in the following paragraph.

▶▶ PART 3

21 B: 'Their appeal begins to become evident when they take flight.'
22 D: 'From studying wild condors, they already knew that if a pair lost an egg, the birds would often produce another. So the first and sometimes second eggs laid by each female in captivity were removed'

23 A: 'As a result, the scientists, zookeepers and conservationists who are concerned about condors have bickered among themselves over the best ways to rear and release the birds.'

24 D: 'Most recently, some of the first chicks hatched in the wild died after their parents fed them bottle caps ... and other man-made objects that fatally perforated or blocked their intestines.'

25 C: 'The real key to successful condor reintroduction, he believes, lies in properly socialising young condors as members of a group that follow and learn from older, preferably adult birds.'

▶▶ PART 4

26 D: 'And though manufacturers stress the saving on film, they may fail to mention that you need expensive memory cards. What's more, some digital cameras use up batteries at an alarming rate.'

27 B: 'you can put your own information on each picture you take, such as the time, day and place where it was taken'

28 A: 'On the other hand, the flash will probably be of poor quality, with an effective range of only about four metres.'

29 C: 'you will learn how to make all the adjustments yourself, for different types of light etc.'

30 C: 'With SLRs you must make sure the lens and body will fit together since they come in different sizes.'

31 D: 'You will have to store your photos on your computer ... what happens if it breaks down'

32 C: 'Get a camera with a metal body ... delicate lenses are less likely to come to grief.'

33 B: 'The Advanced Photo System (APS) was launched in 1996 by several manufacturers who established a common standard.'

34 A: 'the image will not be clear if you blow up the picture bigger than 15cm x 21cm'

35 B: 'these famous names ... These often offer comparable features, build qualities and guarantees for a lower price.'

36 H: 'It's tiny, so you can ... get those special shots without anyone realising they're being captured on film.'

37 F: 'You learn better without the modern electronic gadgetry, which will probably break down in a couple of years anyway.'

38 F: 'Nobody will take you seriously as a photographer with anything other than an SLR.'

39 E: 'You develop as a photographer by taking lots of shots, studying them ... this is how you learn what makes a good picture.'

40 G: 'you can use any 35mm film with a compact – a definite advantage when you're in some tiny village where shops only have normal films'

PAPER 2 Writing

▶▶ PART 1

Question 1

Style: Semi-formal or formal article. Formal letter.
Content: Article:
1 Explain what is being proposed:
- to merge the Whitewall College library with the Technical College library
- to house the libraries in the Technical College library building
- to introduce charges for borrowing
- to open the library to members of the public

2 Encourage opposition to this plan by explaining the disadvantages:
- the Technical College has no humanities books in its library
- the charge for borrowing will affect poor students unfairly
- the library will be overcrowded

3 Describe opposition to the plan from students and staff.
Letter:
Reply to the principal's points. Point out that:
- students were not informed of the plan until now; ask why there was no discussion
- the humanities are not taught at the Technical College, so the libraries do not overlap
- the new library will be overcrowded; when will it be enlarged?
- the charge for borrowing is unfair to poorer students

▶▶ PART 2

Question 2

Style: Semi-formal or formal
Content: 1 Introduction: describe the situation (it is getting easier all the time to download books)
2 Discuss the benefits of downloading.
3 Discuss the benefits of conventional books.
4 Discuss why conventional books have the ultimate advantage.
5 Conclusion: perhaps end with a brief summary of your points.

Question 3

Style: Neutral or formal
Content: 1 Introduction: describe the situation (the increasing number of fast food outlets).
2 Discuss the convenience of fast food, especially for young people.
3 Describe the attitude of young people to healthy foods.
4 Describe how an appreciation of good food and the art of cooking could be promoted in schools and colleges.
5 Conclusion: perhaps end with a brief summary of your points.

Question 4

Style: Semi-formal or formal
Content: 1 Introduction: state briefly what you are going to describe.
2 Discuss the role played by the family in the past, mentioning both the nuclear and the extended family.
3 Describe a typical family in your country today and the relationship between family members.
4 Say whether the situation today is different from what it used to be.
5 Discuss how the family might change in the future and the factors that may contribute to this change.

Question 5

Style: Semi-formal or formal
Content: 1 Introduction: describe briefly the region in which your company operates.
2 Describe the history of the company in this region.
3 Describe the structure and character of the company.
4 Describe the company's role in the region with reference to the workforce, sales etc.

5 Describe the company's social contacts with the people and other organisations in the region with reference to sporting events, cultural events etc.

6 Conclusion: perhaps end by discussing how the company's status could be further enhanced.

PAPER 3 English in Use

▶▶ **PART 1**

1 C **2** D **3** B **4** A **5** C **6** B **7** D **8** D **9** C **10** A **11** B **12** D **13** A **14** C **15** B

▶▶ **PART 2**

16 in **17** which **18** What **19** only **20** no/little **21** were **22** the **23** had **24** case **25** more **26** While/Whereas/Although/Though **27** too **28** as **29** They **30** with

▶▶ **PART 3**

31 where **32** says **33** role **34** ✓ **35** 'The **36** ✓ **37** University **38** monitor **39** ✓ **40** won't **41** ✓ **42** separate **43** outside **44** making **45** anything **46** person's

▶▶ **PART 4**

47 modifications **48** entitled/titled **49** publication **50** admission **51** complimentary **52** unfulfilled **53** forthcoming **54** architectural **55** deterrent **56** confidently **57** saying **58** credibility **59** disbelief **60** knowledge **61** apparent

▶▶ **PART 5**

62 shops **63** put **64** stamps/prints **65** make use **66** an inspector **67** a look **68** a timetable **69** due **70** takes **71** next **72** about/approximately **73** frequently **74** how long

▶▶ **PART 6**

75 E **76** C **77** H **78** I **79** A **80** F

PAPER 4 Listening

▶▶ **PART 1**

1 chains **2** ninety-eight percent/98% **3** a few/several hours **4** flour **5** (rather) tasteless **6** stale **7** allergies **8** lose money

▶▶ **PART 2**

9 complex **10** right angle **11** small and unimportant **12** in (the) rear **13** sixty-seven/67 (long) **14** corridors **15** (a) god **16** official functions

▶▶ **PART 3**

17 A **18** C **19** D **20** B **21** C **22** A

▶▶ **PART 4**

23 C **24** B **25** A **26** C **27** A **28** B **29** B **30** A **31** B **32** A

TEST 8

PAPER 1 Reading

▶▶ **PART 1**

1 D: 'No evening meals, but ten minutes' drive away is Oban's Eeusk, a fabulous restaurant specialising in seafood, for which the region is renowned.'

2 F: 'It emerges that he is the proprietor, Walter, and he remains courteous and helpful throughout our stay, exuding a genuine pleasure in having guests.'

3 D: 'The Ferryman in Connel village … prides itself on its ales, malts, fiddlers and the warm welcome so typical of the entire area.'

4/5 B: 'You can leave the windows open at night and listen to the sounds of the harbour.'

4/5 D: 'Splendidly isolated, this fine Edwardian hotel is in beautiful grounds with tremendous views across Ardmucknish Bay to the Isle of Mull.'

6 A: 'Even if you get up late, you'll find it easy to get breakfast, which is the kind of service found only rarely these days.'

7 E: 'There are low-slung pine beds with fresh-coloured linen and tasteful cushions, which nicely set off the austere but interesting contemporary prints on the walls.'

8 C: 'a leisurely stroll brings you to Westbourne Grove, which has a whole gamut of restaurants specialising in ethnic cuisines'

9 B: 'the blend of modern and traditional design in this townhouse hotel is far more stylish'

10 A: 'Adventurous gourmet dinner menus, changing nightly'

11 C: 'A nondescript front door opens to reveal a magnificent staircase, which is lit by candles in sconces in the evenings.'

12 B: 'drinks are available in the lounge, which gives you a chance to enjoy the hotel's excellent collection of 70s and 80s rock on the original vinyl'

13 F: 'Decorated with a genuine sense of enjoyment in colour, which may be overpowering for some tastes.'

14 D: 'The cavernous main hall is rather intimidating and encourages conversation in hushed whispers.'

15 F: 'a delicious breakfast is provided, featuring delicacies of the region, such as goat's cheese and smoked salmon'

16 E: 'Sefton Peaks Theme Park is just minutes away, with attractions for all ages, though especially good for teenagers.'

▶▶ **PART 2**

17 B: Link between 'There are definitely more and more people seeking wildlife experiences now' and 'an increased demand for wildlife tours or the addition of a wildlife-watching component to traditional holidays' in the following paragraph.

18 D: Link between 'It seems people want to discover nature for themselves' in the previous paragraph and 'There's no way to compare seeing an animal in the wild with watching one on TV'.

19 G: Link between 'They use the services of local communities, train local guides and have close ties to conservation projects' in the previous paragraph and 'Thus tour operator Rekero has established its own school – the Koyiaki Guide School and Wilderness Camp'.

20 E: Link between 'Some offer the opportunity to participate in research and conservation' in the previous paragraph, 'Earthwatch … does just that' and 'offer members of the public the opportunity to be on the front line, not the sidelines, of conservation'.

21 A: Link between 'Volunteers ... take part in various activities including snow leopard, wolf and bear surveys and whale and dolphin research' in the previous paragraph and 'People have a unique experience while contributing to conservation directly'.

22 F: Link between 'it's worth remembering that you don't have to go to the ends of the Earth to catch rewarding glimpses of animals' and 'some of the best wildlife-watching opportunities on offer are on our doorstep' in the following paragraph.

▶▶ PART 3

23 A: 'I consulted an osteopath ... Go off and learn the Alexander technique.'
24 C: 'It trains you to use your body less harshly and to perform familiar movements and actions with less effort.'
25 B: 'The key is learning to break the bad habits ... a habit the body has formed which can be hard to break.'
26 D: 'This may sound daft, but it is an important element in the process of learning how to hold yourself upright.'
27 D: 'Frederick Matthias Alexander, an Australian theatrical orator ... with dramatic results.'
28 C: The text as a whole.

▶▶ PART 4

29 B: 'The alternative technologies we have at present are lagging far behind the petrol-guzzling internal combustion engine in terms of speed and the distance that can be travelled before refuelling.'
30 E: 'However, a new generation of turbines – microturbines – has been developed ... . They are small, high-speed engine systems ... all the other vital components and control electronics.'
31 A: 'The motor industry is finally showing some serious interest ... as can be seen by the amount of money they are spending on research and development.'
32 C: 'But these vehicles are virtually confined to urban settings'
33 D: 'First developed for use in missions to the moon, fuel cells appear to be the most serious challenger to the internal combustion engine'
34 F: 'For example, most diesel cars can now be converted to run on biodiesel fuel, which is made from used vegetable oils and animal fats.'
35 C: 'electric cars have a toy-like appearance which is definitely not appealing'
36 A: 'Governments throughout the world are demanding restrictions ... replaced by vehicles that run on alternative power sources.'
37 D: 'the reformer ... takes up so much space that the vehicle can only seat the driver and one passenger'
38 E: 'These large turbines shine when in steady-state applications but are not as efficient when speed and load are continually changing.'
39 B: 'This vehicle ... can go from 0 to about 100 kph in around 10 seconds'
40 F: 'Some experts even believe that the future may lie with steam cars ... it could be that the wheel is coming full circle.'
41 A: 'nowadays a significant number of people would prefer to buy a vehicle that did not emit greenhouse gases into the atmosphere or pollute the environment in other ways'
42 B: 'When you start the hybrid car and when you are driving normally ... the petrol engine provides that power.'

PAPER 2 Writing

▶▶ PART 1
Question 1
Style: Formal
Content: 1 Describe the purpose of a career day.
2 Suggest a day and date for it.
3 Describe what space and facilities might be needed and describe the layout of the lecture hall.
4 Discuss how many companies should be invited.
5 Discuss what kind of publicity is needed.
6 Suggest a suitable person to give a talk on planning a career.
7 Suggest that information on how to write a CV should be made available.
8 Conclusion: end by stating what the next steps should be.

▶▶ PART 2
Question 2
Style: Neutral, semi-formal or formal
Content: 1 Introduction: say a few introductory words about the activity.
2 Describe how you became interested in this activity.
3 Describe what equipment is needed.
4 Describe the attractions this activity has for you.
5 Conclusion: perhaps end by describing what you plan to do in the future in connection with the activity.

Question 3
Style: Neutral or formal
Content: 1 Introduction: perhaps begin by stating that more and more people change employers or even careers these days.
2 Describe the attitude of young people to the traditional idea of working at one job for life.
3 Describe the attitude of young people to developing a range of skills.
4 Describe the attitude of young people to job security.
5 Conclusion: perhaps end by describing how you think most young people think about employment these days.

Question 4
Style: Neutral or formal
Content: 1 Introduction: explain that you are going to talk about two films that are supposed to be good: one that you liked and one that you didn't.
2 Discuss the first film:
• give a brief summary of the plot
• describe the characters briefly
• describe some interesting or appealing aspects of the film, e.g. the acting, the soundtrack, the dialogue etc.
• summarise why you liked the film
3 Discuss the second film:
• give a brief summary of the plot
• describe the characters briefly
• describe any aspects of the film that you think are worth mentioning, e.g. the acting, the soundtrack, the cinematography etc.
• summarise why you didn't like the film

Question 5

Style: Formal

Content: 1 Introduction: explain that a recruitment programme has been tried out by your company.
2 Describe what activities this has involved.
3 Discuss any direct benefits the programme has had for your company, e.g. hiring of good staff.
4 Discuss any indirect benefits the programme has had for your company, e.g. improving the image of the company.
5 Conclusion: end by giving your view on how effective the programme has been.

PAPER 3 English in Use

▶▶ PART 1

1 C **2** A **3** B **4** C **5** C **6** A **7** D **8** B **9** C **10** A **11** B **12** A
13 D **14** C **15** B

▶▶ PART 2

16 which **17** as **18** A **19** they **20** from **21** there
22 less **23** in **24** on **25** at **26** to **27** what **28** when
29 yourself **30** long

▶▶ PART 3

31 attempt **32** step **33** ✓ **34** rhythm **35** quite **36** hadn't
37 phenomenon **38** ✓ **39** performed **40** similarities.
41 surprising **42** they're **43** ✓ **44** pronounced
45 Further **46** nineteenth

▶▶ PART 4

47 astonishingly **48** numerous **49** departure **50** phenomenally
51 admirable **52** authenticity **53** compassionate **54** leading
55 steadily **56** preferably **57** responsive **58** adaptability
59 opportunities **60** assurance **61** irrespective

▶▶ PART 5

62 are residents **63** eligible/considered **64** submit
65 In addition **66** expressing/stating
67 the importance/significance **68** selection
69 informed/notified by **70** awarded **71** intervals **72** free
73 participate **74** held

▶▶ PART 6

75 B **76** G **77** E **78** A **79** F **80** I

PAPER 4 Listening

▶▶ PART 1

1 (long-distance) running **2** long jump **3** nephew **4** build
5 shooting **6** proper diet **7** equipment **8** attitude

▶▶ PART 2

9 a (poor) tailor **10** original **11** the eighteenth century/18th century
12 social mobility **13** the details **14** Arabic cultures **15** exotic
16 budget

▶▶ PART 3

17 D **18** D **19** A **20** C **21** B **22** C

▶▶ PART 4

Task One
23 F **24** D **25** G **26** A **27** C

Task Two
28 C **29** H **30** D **31** F **32** B

TEST 1

▶▶ PART 1

You will hear a writer talking about a book she has written on the subject of aspirin. For questions 1–8, complete the sentences. You will hear the recording twice.

Writer: We are all familiar with aspirin, that common household remedy which provides relief from pain. But few people are aware of just how fascinating the subject of aspirin actually is.

The key ingredient of this wonderful drug is found in several plants, and five thousand years ago physicians in ancient Egypt were using an extract from the bark of the willow as a cure for a variety of complaints. But it was to be many centuries before the scientific basis of this medication was understood.

Then, in the eighteenth century, an Englishman, Edward Stone, accidentally rediscovered the medicinal properties of willow tree extract, although he mistakenly attributed its efficacy to its bitter taste and its supposed resemblance to another drug, quinine. Later on, in 1829, a pharmacist isolated the active ingredient, salicylic acid. Unfortunately, the chemical has several undesirable side effects, the most serious of which is that it can upset the stomach.

However, at the end of the nineteenth century, a chemist working for Friedrich Bayer, a German company, found a way of combining salicylic acid with an acetyl group. A few years later, Bayer marketed the first aspirins, and for the next seventy years it was regarded as a miraculous painkiller. Curiously, during all that time, hardly any research was done into the way aspirin works.

Then, in 1971, groundbreaking findings were published that showed how aspirin slows down swelling and the coagulation of the blood. This means it also dramatically reduces the risk of heart disease. As you can imagine, this was exciting news. Further research showed that a third of all people at risk from a heart attack will not have one if they take aspirin regularly. Although that sounds too good to be true, most doctors now accept that aspirin really does possess these miraculous qualities. More controversially, some scientists believe that nearly everyone over the age of fifty would benefit from taking aspirin regularly as a preventative measure.

Now it seems that the active ingredients of aspirin can also be found in many organically grown vegetables – and regular consumption of such foods might be an alternative to an aspirin a day …

TEST 1

▶▶ PART 2

You will hear a talk on the subject of desert dust storms. For questions 9–16, complete the sentences. Listen very carefully as you will hear the recording once only.

Man: Few of us realise how dust storms in the Sahara Desert can affect us directly in this country, but in fact, the consequences of such storms can be felt many miles away. This has become more apparent in recent years as the frequency with which dust storms occur has risen sharply. To understand how this situation has come about, you need to know something about the desert landscape. Under normal circumstances, there is a thin crust of small stones and lichen lying on top of the soft sand. The winds that sweep across the desert, although they may be powerful, don't blow away the sand because the crust keeps it in place. But this protective covering, which has been in place for thousands of years, has been disturbed, especially over the last decade or so. One reason for this is that people who travel across the desert nowadays prefer jeeps to camels, and these vehicles are destroying the crust. Of course, there are other contributing factors as well, the main two being overgrazing of the grassland areas and deforestation on a large scale.

But how is it that these dust storms have such far-reaching effects? Well, storms in the Sahara send dust high into the atmosphere, and it can descend many thousands of miles away. If you fly over the Alps, you can sometimes see red desert dust on the snow below! And this dust can bring with it quite unexpected dangers. It can, for example, carry cattle disease to distant places. In addition, a layer of dust can fall on the sea, preventing the rays of the sun from penetrating into the water over large areas. Experts believe that the destruction of coral reefs in the Caribbean, 3,000 miles from the Sahara, can be traced back to this effect. Perhaps more worryingly, the dust can even land on the ice in Greenland. The ice, which is now dark in colour, no longer reflects the sun's rays, so it heats up more readily and melts. So it appears that the increase in dust storms is yet one more of the many factors contributing to global warming.

TEST 1

▶▶ PART 3

You will hear part of an interview with Stan Levin, a dance critic, about a modern ballet production involving animals. For questions 17–22, choose the correct answer A, B, C or D. You will hear the recording twice.

Interviewer: Stan, you are known as being something of a conservative as far as dance is concerned, so I was intrigued when you told me you wanted to discuss Alain Platel's ballet *Wolf* on tonight's programme. *Wolf* generated a furore in certain circles when it was first performed, didn't it?

Stan: Yes, it's attracted its fair share of criticism, but it's also been welcomed as one of the most fascinating modern dance productions in recent years.

Interviewer: Some of our viewers may not have seen the ballet and they may be wondering why all the fuss, so could I ask you to describe briefly what *Wolf* is about.

Stan: Well, basically, it's about homeless people living in a disused shopping mall and returning to some sort of pre-civilised life. And it features some startling innovations, including the use of dogs as characters.

Interviewer: How do the dogs come into it?

Stan: Well, as I understand it, the pack of dogs represents this return to a primitive state. At least, that's the idea Platel is trying to convey.

Interviewer: What do you think of the idea of using animals on stage in this way? Can it be justified?

Stan: Well, more and more choreographers these days are moving beyond the traditional limits of dance, and I don't disapprove of this in principle. Many are turning to technology, for instance, using computers to plan the actual choreography.

Interviewer: Sometimes even using projections of dancers alongside the real ones ...

Stan: Exactly. I find all this very interesting – take the work of Annette Sanderson in New York, for instance – but I think it's now going beyond the genre of dance and turning into something else. Whereas I think Platel is coming from the other direction, if you like, working more with improvisation and basic ensemble techniques.

Interviewer: How do audiences respond to *Wolf*?

Stan: By and large, quite enthusiastically. I think some people are surprised at how well it all works. The dogs generally keep very close to one of the characters. Apparently, the dancer works intensively with them during rehearsal, and the dogs have learned to imitate his movements. That fascinates audiences. Of course, sometimes the dogs distract attention from an important piece of dancing, but I don't feel this is a real problem.

Interviewer: Do the dogs do anything special during the performance?

Stan: No. Their main function is to add atmosphere. It's not like a circus, with the dogs performing tricks! At the same time, you realise they have been trained and are, in a sense, putting on a show simply by remaining on stage with the human performers. During the performance I saw, a member of the audience in the front row tried to call the dogs over to him, which made them look away from the dancers towards the audience. It spoiled the mood – though of course, this wasn't the dogs' fault.

Interviewer: So the dogs fulfil a kind of symbolic function in the story?

Stan: Yes and no. They are attached to one of the characters, a tramp, and we are meant to understand that they have become a pack. I must say this works rather well: you really *do* get the impression that the dogs and the tramp have bonded to form a sort of community. But for me, the most striking aspect of the production was the lurking possibility of aggression, largely as a consequence of the presence of the animals.

Interviewer: Well, Stan, I must say it all sounds fascinating. Thank you for coming along tonight and sharing your insights with us.

Stan: My pleasure.

TEST 1

▶▶ **PART 4**

You will hear five short extracts in which different people talk about fitness and health. For questions 23–27, match the

extracts with what each speaker says about his or her reasons for attending a gym regularly, listed A–H. For questions 28–32, match the extracts with the opinion each speaker expresses about fitness and health generally, listed A–H. You will hear the recording twice. While you listen you must complete both tasks.

Speaker 1: I think getting fit is like many things in life: it's much easier if you arrange a regular routine for yourself. Then after a while it becomes a source of pride to continue the way you've started – as if you'd be breaking a promise to yourself if you stopped. And of course, having a definite goal helps, too. That's why I've entered for the London Marathon next year, despite being over forty! I want to be ready for it, and every time I go to the gym that's what I focus on while I work out.

Speaker 2: I'm not what you'd call a fitness fanatic but about three years ago I was knocked off my bike by a car, and I had to stay in hospital for a month. It took me a long time to regain the full use of my legs. And the physiotherapist made me promise to exercise in a gym at least three times a week. She also said I needed to stop smoking and lose weight, which makes sense. I mean, you can't expect to be fit if you have such unhealthy habits, can you?

Speaker 3: I suppose if I'm honest, one of the reasons I work out in the gym is that I've got to know a lot of people here, and I enjoy seeing them. Now and then we meet up outside the gym for a drink, or to go to the cinema. Of course, I do think keeping fit is important as well. Although I think it's harder for some people to keep slim and healthy. It's as though it's in the blood. I have a friend who doesn't eat much and takes regular exercise, but he's still overweight. It's as if his body doesn't *want* to be thin.

Speaker 4: It's getting harder and harder to stay fit. I used to go for a walk every morning to the local shops; plenty of healthy exercise. But now they've all closed, there's one of those massive supermarkets on the edge of town, and I have to take a bus there. I've decided I have to be serious about exercising, which is why I joined a gym, and I generally manage to get there three times a week. I have high blood pressure, you see, and I don't want to end up having a heart attack like my father and grandmother.

Speaker 5: As a professional golfer I don't really have any choice: I simply must do my three hours in the gym every morning to make sure I can play the game properly. Fortunately, I love golf and I like the lifestyle, so all the exercise doesn't bother me too much. In fact, it's become so much part of my life that I think it would be hard to stop. The people I admire are those who start doing serious exercise late in life; it must be so hard to do that when you aren't accustomed to it.

TEST 2

▶▶ **PART 1**

You will hear part of a talk by a writer who has written a biography. For questions 1–8, complete the sentences. You will hear the recording twice.

Writer: I've just finished writing the biography of Robert Tewbridge, an amateur historian who achieved a certain notoriety in his day. It probably comes as no surprise that I find him a fascinating character, and I hope I've managed to convey this in my book.

One of Tewbridge's most endearing personal qualities was his fierce independence of spirit. Throughout his life, he stubbornly followed his own instincts rather than sticking to the accepted norms. He was born in Scotland, the son of a farmer. Robert's parents had ambitions for their only son, a quick-witted lad, and hoped he would study medicine at Edinburgh University, the idea being that he would return to the highlands as a doctor and set up his own practice. But Robert was determined to see the world and so, at the age of nineteen, he left home for London with only a few shillings in his pocket.

In the great metropolis, Robert had to find some way to keep body and soul together, and being of a literary turn of mind, he started writing for newspapers and journals. Indeed, during his lifetime Tewbridge was known primarily for his articles and essays on some of the more controversial social and political issues of the day. I was able to study most of his published work while I was doing research for the biography, but I would hardly have had an insight into the private man without access to his personal correspondence. Tewbridge wrote literally thousands of letters during his lifetime, including an astonishing number to his wife's brother, a learned chap by all accounts. The two men became very intimate, and in these letters Tewbridge felt able to be frank and honest. It was while I was reading one of these letters that I discovered how Tewbridge first became interested in history. Apparently, it was after seeing a performance of Shakespeare's *Julius Caesar*. This prompted him to begin a lifelong study of Roman history, and the fascination never left him. In fact, when Tewbridge was in his fifties, he and his wife moved to Italy, where they lived for the next thirty years, until his death, in fact. Tewbridge did not live to publish his monumental work on Rome and died without seeing his native Scotland again, but it was ...

▶▶ PART 2

You will hear a talk on the subject of disposable DVDs. For questions 9–16, complete the notes. Listen very carefully as you will hear the recording once only.

Woman: This morning I'm going to be describing a product that was launched at an unsuspecting public a couple of years ago, but has since faded from view.

As we all know, DVDs, or digital video discs, replaced video cassettes as the preferred means of storing films some time ago. Then someone came up with the idea of a *disposable* DVD, which works just like an ordinary one – except that it self-destructs after 48 hours. It simply won't work after that; you have to throw it away. How does it work? Simple. The DVD is stored in a vacuum pack until you decide you want to watch the film. Only then do you break the seal and play the DVD, which has the picture and sound quality we have come to expect. But from that moment on, a chemical compound on the disc combines with oxygen in the air, making the DVD

opaque and unreadable after a couple of days. In fact, the technology exists to make a DVD that is playable for as long as three days before it self-destructs.

I imagine you're wondering exactly who would want to buy or use a disposable DVD. Well, when the product was launched, a number of possibilities were discussed. It was suggested, for example, that the customers of film rental businesses would benefit because they would no longer have to worry about being fined for returning DVDs late. Instead, they could just buy a disposable DVD and throw it away when it became unusable. This idea assumed, of course, that the cost of buying a disposable DVD would be less than the cost of renting one. Then there was a whole range of other ideas: the disposable DVD could be a free gift in magazines, showing extracts from new films, for example – as a promotion device to encourage people to buy the regular DVD of the film!

However, the disposable DVD almost immediately fell foul of conservationists, and there was a storm of protest. Once discarded, disposable DVDs merely add to the huge amount of dangerous waste being generated by new technologies. In the end, the disposable DVD seems to be one of those products that we don't really need. And so, another idea ...

▶▶ PART 3

You will hear part of an interview with Betsy Boom, owner of a chain of fashion shops. For questions 17–22, choose the correct answer A, B, C or D. You will hear the recording twice.

Interviewer: Betsy, it's only five years since you opened your first shop, but today your chain is one of the success stories of the retail market in the UK. Perhaps one way to gain an understanding of how you managed such a phenomenal feat would be to find out a little about your personal tastes. Shopping is your business, but is it one of your pleasures? Are you an avid shopper?

Betsy: Not really, which I think helps explain the philosophy behind my stores. I mean, I like finding a bargain as much as the next person, but what I adore is trying things on – seeing how I look in outfits I wouldn't normally buy. Then there's the other aspect of shopping: going from one shop to another, being ignored in the cheaper shops or treated with disdain by aloof staff in the expensive ones – and feeling you are obliged to buy something if you've been in a shop longer than ten minutes. I can't stand that.

Interviewer: Did your personal attitudes shape the concept of your first store?

Betsy: Absolutely. I thought: wouldn't it be wonderful to go into a shop that was fun! And for me, that means friendly staff who come up to you and suggest all sorts of ideas, some of them wild, about how you might like to look. So you're persuaded to try on loads of things – but nobody minds if you don't buy them! It's more like romping around a huge fancy-dress emporium than going shopping!

Interviewer: Did the idea for your shop take off right away?

Betsy: More or less. I mean, when we opened the first place, most people who came in felt a little stunned, not sure how to respond, I suppose. But once they got used to the idea they loved it! And it was the same with the staff. I asked the assistants to be far more outgoing and upfront than usual. They were a bit shy at first, partly because they weren't sure whether customers would take it the right way or get offended and storm out. But they get quite a kick out of it now.

Interviewer: Now that success is assured, can you pick out the most satisfying aspect of the work for you personally?

Betsy: Well, it's lovely being able to turn round to all the people who said it would never work and say: 'Look! I did it!' But what never fails to thrill me is the sight of someone who isn't at all sure at first about wearing something new, and then she thinks she might as well because the atmosphere's so friendly, and in the end she's delighted by a completely different, daring outfit she'd never have tried on otherwise. It's like seeing a person discover a new self.

Interviewer: So what comes next? Where do you go from here?

Betsy: Good question. To be honest, I haven't a clue! Or at least, I do have a few ideas, but I'm being careful. The shops have worked for me, but that doesn't make me a top business brain by any means! Having said that, I'm deeply aware that I tend to be lazy. I'm quite capable of just sitting back and letting the cash roll in.

Interviewer: That doesn't sound too bad!

Betsy: No, but after a while I'd become frustrated. I know I have to take a risk and try something else, even if it fails. Otherwise my self-respect will be in tatters within a couple of years.

Interviewer: Whatever you do try next, good luck. And thanks for being with us today, Betsy Boom.

Betsy: I've enjoyed talking to you.

TEST 2

▶▶ PART 4

You will hear five short extracts in which different people talk about environmental initiatives in the workplace. Each extract has two questions. For questions 23–32, choose the best answer A, B or C. You will hear the recording twice.

Speaker 1: I don't think offices are environmentally friendly places at all. All the stuff that gets thrown away! People just can't be bothered to recycle paper, equipment is left on all the time, wasting electricity. The average worker thinks it's up to the bosses to do something. Hardly anyone realises they could make a significant difference, just by turning off monitors and electrical equipment at the end of the day.

Speaker 2: These days more people are conscious of a company's environmental image when buying products and services, which is a big change when you remember the situation ten or fifteen years ago. I think it's the hard economics of the marketplace that's making companies do something for the environment. And you've got a new generation of university graduates who want to work for an employer whose environmental concerns are similar to their own. So recruitment is harder for companies without a good attitude towards the environment.

Speaker 3: I think we should feel more encouraged about the environment these days. After all, there are some positive signs. For instance, one big insurance company no longer uses energy derived from the burning of fossil fuels. It uses clean, 'green' sources instead: solar energy and wind energy. Its staff now drive company cars that run on gas fuel, so they don't burden the atmosphere with so many dangerous emissions. And considering the number of reps that travel all over the country every day, this does make a difference.

Speaker 4: One thing about environmental awareness: everyone agrees it's a good idea to encourage it. So companies benefit from a kind of association of ideas. We somehow assume, for example, that a company that cares about recycling waste will also care about delivering goods on time. But a business has to put real effort into making environmental initiatives work. It's no good simply introducing new regulations in the workplace. You have to motivate employees to follow them by showing how much energy can be saved by adopting particular practices.

Speaker 5: Communication is definitely the key, because staff can easily think that environmental schemes are there simply to save money for the company – reducing electricity bills and so on. There's also the danger of cynicism. A big car manufacturer recently started a scheme to plant trees, which is fine – except that people are just going to see it as a public relations exercise. It would be more useful if people knew just how much harm they were doing by, say, driving to work and back each day. Then planting trees could be some sort of compensation for the damage done by the manufacturer's cars.

▶▶ PART 1

You will hear an archaeologist talking about a recent find. For questions 1–8, complete the sentences. You will hear the recording twice.

Archaeologist: This find was really the most astonishing stroke of luck! You see, while we know quite a lot about Roman Britain, comparatively little is known about the era before that, when various tribes inhabited different parts of the country. And then, quite by chance, builders excavating the foundations for a new motorway in Yorkshire unearthed a limestone chamber with the remains of a chariot from that period! The chariot is 2,500 years old and from it we can deduce quite a lot about the history of this region.

First of all, we know the chariot was rather special. It contained the skeleton of a man aged between thirty and forty years old, and this suggests that the chariot served a ceremonial, not a utilitarian purpose. The hypothesis was borne out when it was discovered that it did not have matching wheels, so it could not have been used for transport. The chamber also contained the bones of over 250 cattle, and slaughter on this scale can only be explained if the person interred in the chariot was very important – a tribal leader, in fact.

Secondly, burials like this indicate a belief that in the afterlife a person would have need of his worldly possessions. Such beliefs were by no means confined to ancient Britain, of course – one immediately thinks of the ancient Egyptians. So in view of the similarities, we wonder if there had been any contact between Egypt and pre-Roman Britain.

Thirdly, we know from other sites that chariot burial was practised by a tribe known as the Parisii. These people had arrived on these shores from France, and it is not inconceivable that they were in communication with lands further south.

Finally, the finding is significant because it shows us that the Parisii inhabited regions of the country farther west than has previously been thought.

Unfortunately, the authorities have decided that work on the motorway has to continue, which means we are working non-stop in an effort to excavate as much of the surrounding area as we can in the time available. We're hoping that a place for the chariot will be found at the British Museum, if we can succeed in the very tricky task of lifting the remains out of the ground …

TEST 3

▶▶ PART 2

You will hear a talk about the heather moors of Scotland. For questions 9–16, complete the sentences. Listen very carefully as you will hear the recording once only.

Man: It's a sight that is a symbol of Scotland itself: the heather blooming on the moors in all its purple glory. But it is one that is becoming far less common. Rather alarmingly, the moors have shrunk drastically, and nowadays only about a tenth of the land is covered with heather, whereas in the not too distant past, this area was much greater: in the 1940s there was twenty-five percent more heather than there is today.

Why should any of this matter? Aside from the fact that it looks picturesque, does heather have any other value? The answer must be an emphatic yes. First of all, quite a number of rare birds would be very hard pressed to survive without it. In fact, twenty-one species are associated solely with heather. Secondly, the heather moors provide the backdrop for certain sports such as deer stalking, which constitute an important source of income for the rural economy. Thirdly, this small bushy plant features prominently among the country's tourist attractions, and as is the case in many countries today, tourism is an important source of revenue for Scotland's economy.

So, if the heather moors are of such great value to Scotland, why have they been allowed to shrink so drastically? To a certain extent, the damage is due to mismanagement and a short-sighted attitude on the part of landowners: overgrazing by sheep is one of the major factors that have contributed to the deterioration of the heather moors. On top of that, large tracts have been cleared so that trees could be planted.

It is becoming increasingly obvious that something should be done to halt this decline as soon as possible. Now, there is no disputing the fact that abuse of the land over a long period has been one of the main causes of the problem, so there is no reason why large-scale projects to manage the heather moors properly shouldn't likewise bring positive results. Such programmes have recently got under way in certain areas, although it could be several years before the results become apparent.

TEST 3

▶▶ PART 3

You will hear part of a radio discussion with Ellen Harrington of the Meadow Lane Residents Group, and Tim Barlow from them Carton Town Planning Department. For questions 17–22, choose the correct answer A, B, C or D. You will hear the recording twice.

Interviewer: Good morning, and welcome to *City Life*, our weekly look at some aspect of life in towns and cities. Today my guests are Ellen Harrington of the Meadow Lane Residents Group in the town of Carton, and Tim Barlow from the Carton Town Planning Department. Ellen, perhaps I can start by asking why you formed a residents' group?

Ellen: Because our lives have been a misery recently, that's why! You see, three months ago the town council decided to turn the centre of Carton into a pedestrian precinct – no cars at all. Which seemed like a terrific idea at first. I was over the moon. Until I realised that all the traffic diverted from the centre of town was going to come through Meadow Lane. And I suspect the planners knew all along this would happen.

Interviewer: And Meadow Lane is – or was – a quiet suburban street.

Ellen: Exactly! With two schools and lots of children playing in the street. Now it must be one of the most dangerous roads in the county! And we're not going to stand for it. We're livid, we really are, and we're going to do whatever it takes to get satisfaction, starting with our protest at the town hall tomorrow!

Interviewer: If I could turn to you now, Tim. What's your reaction to what Ellen has been saying?

Tim: Well, naturally, I have every sympathy with her situation. But I really don't think the Carton Town Planning Department is entirely to blame for this. Closing the town centre to traffic was the right thing to do, and I think it's to the credit of the town council that a measure like this was put into practice, despite considerable opposition. Changing the status quo is never an easy course of action – somebody's always going to be unhappy with the new situation. But in this case, if cars drive too fast along quiet streets, that's a matter for the police. Irresponsible drivers are to blame for the problem, which is why the protesters have chosen the wrong target. I'm not even sure exactly what Mrs Harrington's Meadow Lane Residents Group is trying to accomplish.

Interviewer: Do you accept that point, Ellen?

Ellen: I certainly do not! Drivers will take the shortest possible route to get where they're going – that's just human nature – and it's the Town Planning Department who decide what that route is. I think Mr Barlow is trying to dodge the responsibility for the problem – probably because the planners hadn't realised quite how bad the situation in our street would be.

And I don't believe they can wash their hands of the whole matter. And even if they weren't entirely to blame for it, they could still do something now to solve it.

Interviewer: What would you like to see happen now?

Ellen: First of all, a new traffic system should be installed in the area of Meadow Lane to stop motorists using the street the way they do. Then we'd like a review of the whole road system in and around the town. Obviously, that will take some time to set up – in fact, we don't want any rush jobs here – but we want a firm commitment from the town council that they'll listen to our demands.

Interviewer: And this protest you're planning: do you feel it will be a success?

Ellen: I certainly do! You see, we plan to have a big demonstration outside the Town Hall, which will attract a lot of media interest – and that's what really makes people sit up and take notice these days. I'm sure we'll get some reaction. After all, the people in charge here are our representatives, councillors who should listen to the views of the people who elected them …

 3

▶▶ PART 4

You will hear five short extracts in which different people talk about children's free time activities. For questions 23–27, match the extracts with each person's explanation of how his or her child became interested in this activity, listed A–H. For questions 28–32, match the extracts with the opinion each speaker expresses about these activities, listed A–H. You will hear the recording twice. While you listen you must complete both tasks.

Speaker 1: Michael's been a member of a rugby club for two years now. He'd never played until he went to the local comprehensive, but he was hooked immediately! We were nervous at first about him getting hurt, but he's never been injured, not really. I'm glad he's got a hobby, although it *is* quite expensive. We take him to away games, which could be anywhere in the country, so petrol costs mount up. But he's learning to be one of a team, which is a good skill to have in general.

Speaker 2: Our daughter Jane's wild about skiing! Obviously, she can only actually go skiing when we're on holiday or during skiing excursions. She got the idea from a novel about some girls at finishing school in Switzerland, and kept pleading with us to let her try it. Now she's got all the equipment, which cost quite a lot – but she enjoys it so much it's worth the money. She gets anxious about the exams they have at the ski club, which is not altogether a good thing. I mean, the whole point of a hobby is that it should be fun.

Speaker 3: Dan was spending the summer with some horsy friends in Cornwall, and so of course it was inevitable that they should take him riding one day. Their enthusiasm must have rubbed off, because when Dan came home, he asked us to arrange riding lessons for him. Luckily, there's a good stables nearby, and he goes twice a week – more in the summer holidays. I'm glad he has an outdoor hobby; before

he started riding, he used to get colds all the time and was rather pale, but now he's full of beans and he's got a healthy glow.

Speaker 4: I enrolled Wendy in a ballet class when she was five because our doctor told me it would help strengthen her spine, and she took to it straight away. My mother had been a professional dancer, but I don't think that influenced Wendy in any way. She goes to classes three times a week, and although she'll never be good enough to be a professional, she still enjoys it. She's become friends with some of the girls in her class, and we have a fair bit of contact outside ballet, which is nice, especially since Wendy is an only child.

Speaker 5: One Sunday night, Jim suddenly announced he was going to be a painter! My brother had been taking him to various art galleries all summer, but it seems that an exhibition of Impressionists was what really began it all. At first, my wife and I thought it was just a passing craze, and we tried to dissuade him. We thought he should have a healthy outdoor hobby. But Jim's been attending art classes for a number of years now, and I must say, some of the things he's done are very nice. He's quite dedicated to his art!

 4

▶▶ PART 1

You will hear an anthropologist talking about a recent find. For questions 1–8, complete the sentences. You will hear the recording twice.

Anthropologist: A most exciting discovery has been made in a remote region of Ethiopia, and I don't think it's too much of an exaggeration to say this may change the way we think of evolutionary history! Last winter an international team of anthropologists unearthed some fossil hominid skulls that have been reliably dated as being 160,000 years old. Three of the skulls – two belonging to adults and one to a child – were in quite good condition, but fragments of other skulls were also found. Now, this in itself isn't the exciting part because skulls of hominids – we use the word to mean species similar to our own – have been found that are considerably older than this. But it seems that these people were our direct ancestors, whereas the older hominid skulls are from species which died out. To put it simply, the fossils were the skulls of *Homo sapiens*, the species to which modern humans belong.

Another reason why this discovery is causing great excitement in the world of anthropology is because it ties in with other research indicating that we are not descended from Neanderthals at all. You see, the Neanderthals only vanished from the the fossil record about 30,000 years ago. So if the hypothesis is correct, it paints a fascinating picture. For an incredibly long time, tens of thousands of years in fact, at least two different species of humans co-existed on the planet, and then – for reasons we don't understand – the Neanderthals became extinct.

It is also interesting that a number of tools were found near the fossil skulls in Ethiopia, and it may well be that these people's superior technological skills allowed them to drive the Neanderthals away. Moreover, there are suggestions that they lived in groups, and there is a close correlation between advances in human development and social interaction. This may explain why *Homo sapiens* prevailed as the dominant human species! On the other hand, I must remind my listeners that the distant origins of mankind, those early days lost in the mists of prehistoric time, continue to be a mystery. Nobody really knows what happened – which naturally makes my work even more fascinating.

 TEST 4

▶▶ PART 2

You will hear instructions for the use of a model aircraft. For questions 9–16, complete the notes. Listen very carefully as you will hear the recording once only.

Man: Now, let me run through the basic instructions for use of your Burnley Flier. I must stress how important it is *not* to try and fly the model before you're prepared. You'd be surprised how many people are careless about obvious things like choosing a site carefully. A large park is ideal, or a field out in the country. You must be at least 200 metres away from the nearest houses, and you have to ensure there aren't any overhead cables nearby; it's dangerous to fly model aircraft near power lines. Also, remember that this model has a real, working petrol engine and could seriously injure someone if it hit them. Adults are usually sensible enough to keep out of the way when they see you flying your plane, but you must keep a lookout to make sure children don't get too close. They may think your model is just a harmless toy, and that sort of attitude can have terrible consequences.

Once you've chosen a place and set out your model with the control wires and control handle, make sure the wires aren't tangled. Remember, your plane will fly in a circle around you, and you'll be turning slowly, using the control handle to operate the controls in the plane. Check the tank is full – and use only the approved brand of model aircraft fuel. When you're ready to start the engine, connect the battery to the top; as you know, the aircraft's engine is a glowplug, with a tiny sparking plug heated up by a battery when you start up. Once the engine is running, you can disconnect the battery. So if you're ready to start the engine, use the starter spring to kick-start the propeller, and the engine should fire first time.

When you've adjusted the throttle to get full power from your engine, get into the centre of the circle, grab the control handle and signal your assistant to release the plane, which will then take off. A few tips about your first flight: don't step backwards to pull the plane into the air. Stand still, pull the control wires gently, and the plane will respond perfectly well. The power of the engine keeps the wires taut, so you don't need to move. And on this first flight, don't try any fancy aerobatics like loops! Practise simple climbs and dives, and wait until you are proficient before you try anything more ambitious.

 TEST 4

▶▶ PART 3

You will hear part of a radio discussion about iris recognition systems. For questions 17–22, choose the correct answer A, B, C or D. You will hear the recording twice.

Interviewer: My guest on *Technology Matters* this week is Jim Davies, a leading expert in the field of IRS or iris recognition systems. Jim, perhaps I could start by asking you to explain exactly what IRS is?

Jim: In fact, it's a simple system in theory, one that was first suggested back in the 1930s. Basically, it's a way of recognising a person by analysing the pattern of his or her iris. This pattern is different for every individual on the planet; even identical twins have different iris patterns. The way it works is, you have a camera linked to computer software that can compare the iris pattern it sees with iris patterns on a database; the computer makes a match and then reports on the identification.

Interviewer: It just provides a report?

Jim: No. That's simply the first step. An iris recognition machine can be connected to any number of devices. For instance, at airports it will be possible for barriers to be opened by a machine, and this will, in turn, speed the flow of passengers through checkpoints. I must say, though, I don't think it's speed that is the biggest appeal of iris recognition machines – the fact that they are reliable will guarantee their popularity in the future.

Interviewer: Are iris recognition machines actually being used at the moment?

Jim: Oh, yes. As a matter of fact, we've just completed a pilot scheme in northern England. We installed machines at a school there to identify pupils as they came into the canteen. That way they could be given their correct meals automatically, which meant they didn't have to wait around to be served. It was a great success! And the kids loved it. I think they regarded it as something out of a science fiction film.

Interviewer: What about adults? Do you think they will be as impressed?

Jim: That's a good question. I admit there are many people who feel that the use of iris recognition machines is a civil liberties issue and infringes on their privacy, but I think people said the same thing about the use of X-ray machines at airports, and now everyone accepts them. So I'm confident that the vast majority of people will come to see the sense behind using these machines, especially when they realise how efficient they are. When they're properly set up, they take a mere twelve seconds to scan someone's iris, and of course the customs people themselves are very attracted to the idea because of the time it saves.

Interviewer: So is it simply a matter of time before we find iris recognition machines everywhere?

Jim: Nobody knows as yet just how widespread they'll be. A lot depends on how quickly the public comes to accept them, and I think the government wants to monitor public reaction before committing itself to the technology.

Interviewer: What about the costs involved?

Jim: The computerised cameras themselves don't cost a great deal, but the really huge cost will be when we have to register the whole population. I can quite understand that the government might be nervous about this sort of expense, although of course you wouldn't ever have to repeat it on such a huge scale once you'd done it.

Interviewer: So you believe the future lies with IRS?

Jim: I do, yes, primarily because every government wants to be able to confirm identity at places like airports, and iris recognition machines are simply the most effective way of doing this as yet available to us ...

▶▶ PART 4

You will hear five short extracts in which different people talk about holidays that went wrong. Each extract has two questions. For questions 23–32, choose the best answer A, B or C. You will hear the recording twice.

Speaker 1: We went to Tunisia last year, and the whole thing was a fiasco from start to finish. The flight was delayed for three hours, so we were in a foul mood before we even left! Then we were diverted to a different airport in Tunisia, so we spent an extra hour on the bus to get to our hotel – which turned out to be well below standard. That's what really spoilt it for us. And when we got back and complained to the tour company, the girl there said a refund was out of the question; we should have read the small print, she said. Absolutely useless.

Speaker 2: We had been so looking forward to our walking tour of the Lake District! We decided to make use of a tour company: they transport you to the starting point and pick you up at the end of your walk. It sounded appealing – but they could hardly have foreseen that such a bad storm would hit, leaving us stranded until a rescue team came out. We did get back safe and sound, but we vowed to be more modest in our plans for walking tours in future.

Speaker 3: It was my fault, really. I'd hired a car while we were in France, and I was involved in a minor accident with another car. The other driver was terribly decent and spoke excellent English, but when the police came they said I'd have to go to the police station because I wasn't a resident! I lost my head and started yelling at them, which was a mistake. I ended up spending the night in jail, and that's no fun, I can tell you. In the end, I got away with just a small fine. But the whole experience shook me a bit.

Speaker 4: Last year I booked an all-inclusive trip to Russia. And everything was very interesting, until the last day, when I woke up with awful abdominal pain. I couldn't keep anything down, not even water. It was clear I was running a fever. At the hospital they told me I had a ruptured appendix and an operation was unavoidable! Well, in a way, it was an interesting experience. Once I realised the doctor was first-rate I was so relieved; I even felt fortunate to have been in Russia when my appendix burst!

Speaker 5: We were on holiday in Spain and someone suggested going to a nearby island. Bad idea! Because the trip was by hydrofoil and the astonishing thing is the way those things move when they encounter waves: they jerk up and down violently. Which left me sick as a dog. I felt downright miserable, and I was left with the absolute conviction that I'd react in precisely the same way if I ever got on one of those things again. And since the only way back

from the island was on another hydrofoil, I soon had the chance to find out.

▶▶ PART 1

You will hear an astrobiologist talking about her work. For questions 1–8, complete the sentences. You will hear the recording twice.

Astrobiologist: When I tell people what my particular branch of science is, I often get funny looks. In a way, I understand because astrobiology is the study of life on other planets. Well, obviously, life has *not* been discovered on other planets, which would appear to make astrobiology a science without a subject! However, everything we know about life on our *own* planet suggests we have to try to understand if there are any universal requirements for life to evolve, as well as the processes involved in evolution. Consequently, astrobiologists are deeply interested in the beginnings of life on Earth. Once we know more about what happened on home ground, as it were, we will be in a better position to understand any life forms we may one day find on other planets.

When most people think of extraterrestrial life, they conjure up images of so-called 'higher' life forms: they imagine humanoid creatures or bizarre and probably dangerous animals of some kind. But if we consider the whole history of life on Earth, a very different picture emerges. For billions of years the only forms of life on the planet were organisms consisting of single cells. It was only about 550 million years ago, during the geological period we call the Cambrian, that the seas suddenly became filled with a whole array of multi-cellular life.

So how do humans fit into this time frame? Well, human-like creatures first appear in the fossil record about five or so million years ago: in geological terms, this is just a blink of an eye compared to the long history of life on Earth. And *Homo sapiens*, our own species, has only been around for about 130,000 years. The point is if we *do* find life on other planets, it will almost certainly be relatively simple – of the sort that populated the Earth for most of its existence so far.

And of course, we must be prepared for these life forms to look very different from life on Earth. We must not forget that many modern life forms came about as a result of chance, their fate shaped by floods, continental drift and comet or meteor strikes. It is interesting to reflect that if a giant asteroid had not hit the Earth and wiped out the dinosaurs, they might still be ruling the planet and we might never have evolved ...

▶▶ PART 2

You will hear a fitness expert talking about different methods of keeping fit. For questions 9–16, complete the notes. Listen very carefully as you will hear the recording once only.

Woman: The thing about getting fit, if you're like most people – don't do enough exercise, spend too much time sitting down at work and then slumped on the sofa at home – is that there's no easy solution. That's the first thing I tell people who come to see me: there's no substitute for hard work. You hear an awful lot about new methods of exercising that are supposed to give results without any pain – you see adverts for these 'passive exercise' machines on television all the time. But the point is that none of them are any good by themselves. It's not that the adverts are telling lies – they're just not telling you the whole truth. Take the latest one I've heard about. This machine sounds very appealing. Apparently, you just stand on it and it vibrates, so you shake all the time. This is supposed to strengthen your muscles, and it *does* work, but it's virtually no good at all unless you're fit already! People like football players will benefit from it because they are already in good shape. But if you're overweight and flabby, it won't do much good on its own!

So what do I recommend to people who want to get into shape? Well, when someone comes to see me, first of all I put them on an exercise regime that will make them breathe good and hard and increase their heart rate at least four times a week! Naturally, the type of exercise depends on the individual, but it will usually include some activity like jogging, cycling or swimming – one that has aerobic benefits. Now, that in itself won't make anyone really fit; you also need to target the muscles directly. We call this resistance training: something like weight-lifting or push-ups. No way around it, I'm afraid, if you want to be really fit.

So there you are; that's a summary of my experience in over fifteen years at this job. Basically, if you want to be fit, I don't think it's necessary to enrol in an expensive fitness centre. You can do all this at home with some very basic equipment. On the other hand, you'll never get fit if you don't push yourself! And even joining the best and most expensive gym in the world is no substitute for that.

 TEST 5

▶▶ **PART 3**

You will hear part of a radio interview with Pete Birtwhistle, a playwright. For questions 17–22, choose the correct answer A, B, C or D. You will hear the recording twice.

Interviewer: This evening on *Arts Alive* I'm talking to Pete Birtwhistle, whose new play, *Time Talking*, has just opened at the Court Theatre in London. Pete, thank you for joining us.

Pete: Glad to be here.

Interviewer: Before we talk about your new play, I'd like to ask you how you started writing for the theatre in the first place. I think I'm right in saying that your background isn't exactly typical for a playwright?

Pete: I suppose you could put it like that! You see, I was a miner until my mid-thirties, but then my health got bad and I had to leave the pit. But the theatre was the last thing on my mind! I don't think I'd ever been to a play – apart from taking the kids to pantomimes at Christmas – and I wasn't even curious about it: I didn't feel it had any bearing on me and my life at all.

Interviewer: So what prompted you to write your first play?

Pete: Doctor's orders. Being out of work was terrible – it really got me down when I realised I had to stop working down the mine, and in the end I was in such a bad way that my local GP sent me to a psychiatrist. She suggested I write a story about

what had happened to me, how I felt about working in the mine and then having to leave. All therapy, really. Well, of course, it was pretty hard at first, writing a play from scratch.

Interviewer: Getting the dialogue and story right, I imagine?

Pete: Funny you should say that. I started off thinking I could invent a group of characters and have them put forward different views. But when I sat down to write, I couldn't get them to do what I wanted, no matter how hard I tried. In the end, I discovered I had to let them do and say what *they* wanted.

Interviewer: What do you mean, exactly?

Pete: They took on a life of their own. So I had to sit back and let them go whichever way they wanted. And once I let myself give them that freedom, the play wrote itself. The odd thing is I feel all the characters I create are part of me, so I'm revealing different aspects of myself.

Interviewer: Is that the most profound effect writing has had on you?

Pete: I think so, yes. Practical things have changed as well, of course – we've just bought a new house – but material benefits are fairly peripheral in the end.

Interviewer: Turning to your new play about time travel – isn't that an unusual theme for the theatre?

Pete: Definitely! But it's not deliberate. I mean, I don't go round looking for novel subjects just to be different. It's more a case of finding an issue that doesn't have easy answers, a topic that stretches you when you start thinking about it.

Interviewer: I hear you're going to start work on a screenplay for a film in the next few months. Is that an exciting prospect?

Pete: Yes, but there are so many stories of films that never get made, writers and directors who throw themselves into the task of making a film and then get terribly disappointed when it all falls apart. So I have to watch out that I don't take the whole thing too seriously ...

TEST 5

▶▶ **PART 4**

You will hear five short extracts in which different people talk about tracing their ancestors. For questions 23–27, match the extracts with what each person says about the discoveries he or she made, listed A–H. For questions 28–32, match the extracts with the emotions aroused in each speaker by these discoveries, listed A–H. You will hear the recording twice. While you listen you must complete both tasks.

Speaker 1: The first bit of new information was quite exciting. It turned out my grandfather's only brother had slipped out of the house one day when he was about sixteen and disappeared! At first, the family thought he'd gone off to Australia, but it turned out that he'd joined a circus and become a clown. Romantic, isn't it? I managed to track down his descendants, and I found out they were all circus performers, too. It's fantastic to know that the two branches of our family are in touch again.

Speaker 2: I wanted to know something about my roots, and with a name like O'Dwyer, I knew I probably had some Irish ancestors. Eventually, I did find out a bit about them, though this is going back to the end of the nineteenth century. It was my great-grandparents who came over to the States because life was so hard back home. People were starving in Ireland – literally. And apparently, my great-grandmother's family were worse off than most. I get furious at the idea of ancestors of mine having to leave their homes because they were so hungry.

Speaker 3: After a lot of work I established that one branch of the family exists to this day in Australia, though regrettably, the background to the story is a family row. Apparently, my great-grandmother's brother wanted to marry a girl his family didn't approve of, so he just walked out and never came back. He ended up in Australia with his wife, and his parents never saw their grandchildren. A family tradition has it that his mother died of a broken heart. Imagine a family being torn apart by something like that!

Speaker 4: My great-grandfather was a doctor, which has been a sort of family tradition ever since. He seems to have been a man of strong religious feeling, and he worked for years in a hospital in Africa. Apparently, he paid his own way over and volunteered his services to a missionary hospital. By all accounts, he never boasted about what he'd done; he seems to have thought everyone should help their fellow human beings if they can. It makes me glad to think there was someone so genuinely *good* in my family.

Speaker 5: There was a story passed down in the family that we're distantly related to an aristocratic family from Scotland, complete with an estate, manor house and so on. Well, it turns out that my great-great-grandmother really *did* live in a posh house, but only because she was a servant to the family who owned it! It wasn't exactly what I had been expecting, and it took me a while to get over it, but now I can see the funny side of the whole business.

▶▶ **PART 1**

You will hear an archaeologist talking about an experience he had in South America. For questions 1–8, complete the sentences. You will hear the recording twice.

Archaeologist: A couple of years ago I was working in an ancient Aztec city in South America. This city is becoming more and more popular with visitors, and I was part of a team employed to map out the city and its environs. We were half-way through our contract when we were approached and asked if we could come up with some ideas about how best to conserve the site, because it was feared that the increasing numbers of visitors could be damaging it. The worst damage is caused by the mere presence of people. Their breathing makes the air very humid, which causes the plaster on the walls to crumble. At the time I'm talking about, this was one of my special interests, so I was only too pleased to undertake the job.

Anyway, one day I had to go into one of the minor tombs – we were making a survey of it because the authorities were going to build a coach park nearby, and we had to ensure the tomb wouldn't be damaged any further by the construction work. To my horror, the tomb was in a worse state than we thought it would be. There were signs of recent erosion, apparently caused when an underground stream flooded. But it was when I was climbing into the tomb itself that disaster struck. The stones underfoot were loose, you see, and I twisted my ankle. I fell awkwardly and rolled down a slope. I heard a terrible cracking noise, rather like a pistol shot, and I knew I had fractured my leg. The pain was excruciating, but once I got over the initial shock I became far more worried about the fact that it was now dark outside, which would lessen my chance of being discovered. As the hours went by, I began to feel very cold and pretty scared, but in the end I was incredibly lucky. A tour guide was out for an evening stroll and just happened to come close enough to hear me shouting from the hole in the ground, so he alerted the rest of the team. The break wasn't too bad, fortunately, but the whole thing was quite a frightening experience ...

▶▶ **PART 2**

You will hear a talk on the subject of salt. For questions 9–16, complete the sentences. Listen very carefully as you will hear the recording once only.

Woman: We tend to take salt for granted, but from a historical perspective, it is hard to imagine how our civilisation could have developed without it. The use of salt to preserve food allowed people to settle down – they no longer needed to go hunting for food every day. Soon salt came to be worth literally its weight in gold, which seems curious when the salt we put on our table is so cheap.

Actually, most of the salt in the modern western diet doesn't come from a salt cellar: it is added to a very wide range of processed food in the factory, as can be seen from looking at the list of ingredients on the packaging, though we're seldom told just how much has been added. Interestingly enough, the function of salt in the manufacture of food is not related purely to taste or preservation: the food industry likes adding salt to food because of its water retention properties, which means that a fair proportion of the weight of processed food is quite simply water.

This may sound like a relatively harmless trick to increase profits, but in fact, the presence of all this salt is potentially harmful. In many people, high salt intake is linked to high blood pressure, or hypertension, which in turn can cause heart attacks and strokes. Therefore, anyone suffering from hypertension should keep their salt intake low, and doctors estimate that cutting down on salt would benefit about a third of the population.

So should governments be doing more to limit salt consumption, for example by forcing food manufacturers to cut down on the salt used in processed foods? Predictably, the food companies are opposed to the idea. The salt manufacturers also object, although the amount of salt used in foods accounts for less of their output than the salt used for application to roads during icy spells, at least in this country.

Industry representatives point out that only those suffering from medical abnormalities would be harmed by consuming too much salt. However, that description applies to more and more of us these days – and salt may be part of the reason why.

TEST 6

▶▶ PART 3

You will hear part of an interview with Professor Hector Williams, a linguist. For questions 17–22, choose the correct answer A, B, C or D. You will hear the recording twice.

Interviewer: Professor Williams, I know you've made a special study of artificial languages. I suppose most people think of Esperanto when this subject comes up, but is Esperanto the most widespread of the various artificial languages in existence?

Williams: I think that's the case today, yes, but you must remember that the idea of an artificial language isn't new. Esperanto dates back to the 1880s, but even in medieval times people were fascinated by the idea of a language created by man. Of course, their aims would have been quite different back then.

Interviewer: What do you mean?

Williams: Well, in the Middle Ages there was a theory that the universe was constructed on logical principles and that everything in it could be classified and named according to a regular and logical system. Ultimately, the nature of the universe itself could be understood through a language created in this way.

Interviewer: That all sounds rather complicated. Would such a language be easy to learn?

Williams: That one wouldn't have been, no, but there were other artificial languages that did have this goal. One man, for instance, struck by the fact that the notes of the musical scale were known by the same syllabic value all over the western world, felt this could be of use in the creation of a universal language, so he invented words based on the syllables *do, re, mi, fa* etc.

Interviewer: Was there the same kind of logic behind Esperanto?

Williams: In a way, and if I may digress for a moment, I must confess that the first time I heard it, Esperanto did seem musical to my ears. I think it was because the syllables of Latin origin aroused in me vague memories of the operas my father used to play on the gramophone when I was a child. Anyway, the man who came up with Esperanto, Dr Zamenhof, wanted his artificial language to be easy to learn, so he chose word stems and roots from major European languages, hoping they would sound familiar to most Europeans. And most experts believe he did a remarkably good job in that sense. A person with average linguistic skills can gain a working knowledge of Esperanto in a matter of months.

Interviewer: So do you feel it could have a future as a universal language?

Williams: To be perfectly honest, I don't. And there are a number of reasons for this. I have some sympathy with those who claim that the words of an artificial language seem one-dimensional, as it were, because they don't have any flavour derived from past usage; no word could have connotations in such a language. And this is not just a theoretical problem; it really does make the language seem rather mechanical.

Interviewer: You'd describe advocates of Esperanto as idealists then, would you?

Williams: Possibly – though that isn't such a bad quality! In my experience, people who have taken the trouble to learn Esperanto are marked by a refreshing enthusiasm for the task; I imagine many language teachers would be delighted to have students with such single-minded determination to master the details of a language. The difficulties with imagining Esperanto as the language of the United Nations, say, or the European Union, are not based on any deficiencies among the speakers.

Interviewer: Well, you've mentioned one problem with artificial languages; what others are there?

Williams: The fundamental difficulty is psychological. For the vast majority of the world's population, the sense of self is inextricably bound up not just with location but also with what is aptly referred to as their mother tongue. So any attempt to replace that native language meets with very strong resistance – and that is why I am convinced that the applications of an artificial language are very limited.

Interviewer: Professor Williams, thank you for being with us.

Williams: My pleasure.

TEST 6

▶▶ PART 4

You will hear five short extracts in which different people talk about the Internet. For questions 23–27, match the extracts with what each person says about starting to use the Internet, listed A–H. For questions 28–32, match the extracts with the views each speaker has about the influence of the Internet, listed A–H. You will hear the recording twice. While you listen you must complete both tasks.

Speaker 1: The problem was that my neighbour, who showed me how to use the Internet in the first place, didn't really know what he was doing – and of course, I didn't know that at the time! So it was pretty discouraging. Back then, everything was so slow, and you were always losing your connection. But now I wouldn't want to be without it. I even read my daily paper online, and I expect that's the way it is for lots of people, especially those of us who live in remote areas.

Speaker 2: A work colleague of mine was really into virtual reality games, you know, the sort you play with other users in real time online. Well, I watched him playing one day, and I got hooked! I still play games like that today, despite the fact that I'm now a grandmother. But I must admit, I wouldn't like my two-year-old granddaughter to grow up doing everything online and never interacting with real people! And that's the way I can see things going.

Speaker 3: While I was writing my thesis for my master's degree, I realised the best way to compile a list of the reading I had to do was to use the Internet, so I took a deep breath and started to learn. These days I use it at work, like most people, but the best aspect of the Internet for me personally is online shopping. I love ordering books and having them delivered to my door a couple of days later. The only problem is that it's so easy you sometimes forget how much money you're spending!

Speaker 4: Growing up with the Internet the way I did – we've had it at home since I was eleven – it never seemed a big thing. I mean, I'm used to having it around, the way I'm used to television. But I realise that there are parts of the world where people don't have Internet access, so if you're growing up there, you're missing out on a terrific resource. That should be changed so every kid has the same opportunities to learn.

Speaker 5: A couple of years ago I decided I wanted to know more about my family tree, and a friend told me there was a website listing the births, marriages and deaths during the last 150 years in many parts of the UK. I thought I'd give it a try, and it was fascinating! As for the future, I think the Internet's going to have a huge impact in lots of ways. For instance, libraries as we know them won't exist in a decade or so because we will all be able to access the book we want online and even print it out if we choose.

▶▶ PART 1

You will hear part of a talk by a writer who has written a book about bread. For questions 1–8, complete the sentences. You will hear the recording twice.

Announcer: Here in the studio with me today on *Food Matters* is Algernon Lacey, who's just written a book called *Half a Loaf* about that most basic of foods: bread. Algernon, what first aroused your interest in the subject?

Algernon: My grandmother, actually. One day she was describing to us how she used to make bread in the old days, and I was interested enough to start doing some research. I found out that all the big manufacturers use the same process to make bread these days. Even the supermarket chains, who think it makes them look good if customers see bread baking in their stores, use the same ingredients as everyone else. 98% of bread is made in this way – that's all the bread on sale in this country except for the products of small independent bakeries. And this process is a basic departure from the traditional techniques. You see, bread used to be made by allowing the yeast to ferment in water, which takes a few hours. But the modern method uses rapid mixing to shorten the time necessary for fermentation. This method is preferred because it saves money: less flour is needed to make bread. Unfortunately, there is a downside: you need a lot more water and fat, which makes the bread less wholesome. And since it's the fermentation process that gives bread its natural flavour, the modern method would produce rather tasteless bread if a great deal of salt weren't added. Some modern bread is also given a coating of calcium propionate to make sure it doesn't go stale. The loaf will last for a couple of weeks that way. But of course, there's a problem here, too – an increasing number of people are developing allergies to bread and wheat

products, and I think there's a connection. The modern method doesn't ferment the ingredients properly, and it's hard for consumers to do anything about this because bread-making methods are dictated by the large supermarkets, who don't make a profit on bread. They don't even sell it at cost price. They're prepared to lose money to bring customers into their stores. So they dictate the methods used in the big bakeries.

▶▶ PART 2

You will hear an archaeologist talking about an important discovery. For questions 9–16, complete the notes. Listen very carefully as you will hear the recording once only.

Archaeologist: One of the most fascinating archaeological discoveries of recent times was made quite by chance, in the Valley of the Kings, where the pharaohs of ancient Egypt were buried. It happened like this. Some years ago, the archaeologist Kenneth Weeks was making a detailed map of the area. This was a huge job, far bigger than he and his team originally expected it to be, because once they started looking closely at the tombs, it turned out they were more complex than they'd imagined. What made these tombs so interesting was the fact that their construction was rather odd – for instance, the corner angle of a tomb might be 85 degrees instead of a right angle of 90 degrees, as one would expect.

Now, one of the tombs Weeks was surveying, KX5, had been discovered years before, but nobody had paid much attention to it because it was basically just a hole in the ground, full of rubble, small and unimportant – or so everyone thought.

Anyway, while Weeks and his colleagues were inside this tomb, measuring away, they glimpsed some inscriptions in the rear of the chamber. It's doubtful if anyone had noticed them before, but it turned out they were the names of the sons of Rameses II, one of Egypt's greatest pharaohs, and king for sixty-seven long years. Naturally, after this discovery, excavations were speeded up. But it was a slow job, nevertheless, and it was a long time before they emptied out enough rubble to see a large number of corridors leading off from the back of the chamber. It turned out that the tomb is massive, with at least 130 chambers hidden away inside!

Why was it built so large? The answer is that Rameses had himself declared a god while he was still alive. Very nice for him, but it meant he couldn't perform official functions like other pharaohs – acting as a judge in legal cases, for example. So his sons had to stand in for him. And when they died, their funeral and burial had to be suitably grand. After all, their father was no mere mortal. And that is why this huge tomb was built!

▶▶ PART 3

You will hear part of a discussion between Velma Andrews, a lawyer, and Sergeant William Bailey, a police officer. For questions 17–22, choose the correct answer A, B, C or D. You will hear the recording twice.

Interviewer: Today on *Legal Issues* we have Velma Andrews, a lawyer, and Sergeant William Bailey, a police officer who helps to run a scheme which trains police officers in the art of giving evidence in court. William, perhaps I can start by asking you why this training scheme is necessary?

William: Well, you must remember that in a criminal case the police have gathered evidence to show that someone – the defendant – is guilty of a crime. And the defendant's lawyer is trying to show that this evidence is wrong or unreliable. Now, the way the defence lawyer goes about doing this can be very tricky. For instance, the first time I gave evidence in court twenty-five years ago, the lawyer for the defence made me look like a right fool. He annoyed me by interrupting me all the time, and when I tried to argue with him I got confused, and the people in court laughed at me. That made my evidence look bad. I simply had no idea what I was up against.

Interviewer: Velma, you are a defence lawyer; do you agree with William?

Velma: Absolutely. A police officer has to learn how the system works. You must get used to the idea that the lawyers are just doing a job, and even if it seems they are attacking your honesty in a rude or brutal manner, they have nothing against you as an individual.

Interviewer: It must be hard to think like that when you're giving evidence and some lawyer is trying to trip you up.

Velma: It is, but a police officer has to develop the right attitude. You need to think of your evidence as one piece in a jigsaw puzzle, the picture being the whole case against the defendant. If you start giving opinions about other pieces, other parts of the case that aren't your responsibility, it weakens the case as a whole. Your piece of the puzzle is the only thing you should think about!

Interviewer: Do you find Velma's advice helpful for police officers on your training scheme, William?

William: Definitely. For a young officer, appearing in court is an intimidating experience. It's hard to get used to the system. I mean, there are two lawyers, one acting for the defendant and one for the crown, and in the courtroom they are adversaries but they probably know each other professionally. They may even go off together after the trial and have dinner. As if it were all a game!

Interviewer: Would you advise William's trainees to treat a court case as a game, Velma?

Velma: would tell them to remember that the defence lawyer is trying to discredit them and their evidence. One tip to help you develop the right attitude so you don't get drawn into an argument with the lawyer is to stand so you're facing the judge, and direct all your answers to the bench. That should make it easier to avoid any sort of personal exchange with the lawyer.

Interviewer: William, is your training scheme having results?

William: Yes. I think police officers are more confident in court. And this is not just about making people less nervous! I've seen some pretty terrible things happen in court. You get an inexperienced officer who starts arguing with the lawyer and ends up making the judge and jury think there's something wrong with the police case – there's a risk that dangerous criminals might be found not guilty and set free. That's the main reason why officers need this training.

Interviewer: Velma Andrews and William Bailey, thank you.

 TEST 7

▶▶ **PART 4**

You will hear five short extracts in which different people talk about wind power. Each extract has two questions. For questions 23–32, choose the best answer A, B or C. You will hear the recording twice.

Speaker 1: I've just been reading about some sheep farmers in Wales who were losing money and looked into a different way of earning a living. So they took the plunge and decided to set up a wind farm. But apparently, some neighbours resented the fact that they'd had a brilliant idea and managed to capitalise on it. As a result, there was a good deal of opposition to the farm in the area. However, I did think it was an encouraging story.

Speaker 2: The whole issue is an emotional one, but it's the *look* of these wind farms that's causing the greatest outcry, it seems to me. I know quite a few people in rural areas are getting together and starting wind farms to serve their local community, and though I think they have the best of intentions, it does seem that they're going about it the wrong way. Everyone knows wind turbines are not a reliable source of energy and need some kind of backup.

Speaker 3: I find it odd that people object to having wind turbines miles offshore, where nobody except a passing ship would ever see them. What's wrong with that? After all, it's a question of using fossil fuels, other renewable energy sources or nuclear power. Obviously, there's no real future in fossil fuels, but I can't see any feasible way of generating enough electricity from wave power or hydroelectric stations either, at least not in this country. Which leaves the third option, though we have to make sure sufficient safeguards are in place.

Speaker 4: I get quite angry about the whole question, actually, because everyone goes on and on about how wonderful wind power is, but there's only enough wind to generate electricity about thirty percent of the time. I think the whole method is fundamentally impractical. And the irony is that we could save much more energy than wind can ever generate if we just had a better energy conservation policy with full government backing and industry participation. Improved insulation in the roofs of houses, for instance, would save an incredible amount of electricity.

Speaker 5: There's been a lot of talk about birds flying into turbines, and that has turned a lot of people against wind energy. But if you look at the figures, you'll see that the number of birds killed in this way is insignificant. On the other hand, I think we have to see wind power in perspective as just part of a move towards energy from renewables. We can't rely on wind power to cover all our needs, but that doesn't mean we should abandon it; it simply needs to be supplemented by other sources.

TEST 8

▶▶ **PART 1**

You will hear part of a talk by the director of a sports academy. For questions 1–8, complete the sentences. You will hear the recording twice.

Helen: I'm Helen Waterman, director of the Waterman Sports Academy, a school that helps promising young athletes fulfil their dreams. We coach youngsters who want to swim faster than anyone else in the world and children who dream of running the marathon at the Olympic Games one day.

I've coached many athletes in my life, going back to the day when the daughter of a friend announced she had entered for the long jump in an amateur athletics event. I enjoyed coaching her, and that was the start of my career. I also became interested in sports medicine at about that time, when my nephew fell off his bike and hurt his back. He'd been a keen athlete before his accident, but unfortunately, he never really got over his injury sufficiently to get back into serious training. That's when I realised the importance of sports medicine, and the staff of the academy includes two doctors.

Perhaps at this point I should answer a question often asked by young people when they enrol at the academy: how important is an athlete's build? Well, nobody can deny that build *does* matter, and one cannot hope to be a world-class long-distance runner, say, if one is built like a weightlifter. But other factors also play a vital role. For a start, good general health and fitness. These are important, even in sports where you might not think they are a priority. In shooting, for instance, athletes have to be fit to lower their heart rate. This enables them to fire between heart beats and so achieve maximum accuracy. At the academy, we encourage healthy eating habits. Without a proper diet, young athletes cannot achieve their optimum physique. Nor will they have the energy for training. Then there's the role of technology in sports. These days, athletes cannot compete successfully at the highest level without access to state-of-the-art equipment. I've already mentioned sports medicine, and it goes without saying that young athletes need to be able to consult specialists in case of an injury. But above all, at the academy we stress the importance of *attitude*. Without the will to succeed, you may as well not bother to take up any sport seriously. In my opinion, it is this that …

TEST 8

▶▶ **PART 2**

You will hear a talk about the popular fictional character, Aladdin. For questions 9–16, complete the sentences. Listen very carefully as you will hear the recording once only.

Man: The basic elements of this hugely popular story are as follows. Aladdin, the son of a poor tailor, finds a lamp with a magic spirit inside – a genie – who grants him every wish and enables him finally to marry the king's daughter. The story of Aladdin is associated with the collection most of us know as *The Thousand and One Nights*, though like other well-known tales in that volume – that of Sinbad the Sailor springs to mind – it was probably not part of the original canon. It seems to have been made up in the eighteenth century by a Frenchman who translated a manuscript of these tales and simply inserted the Aladdin story into the collection.

So why is the story of Aladdin so popular? Well, it suggests that a person's life can change radically for the better, and that is a very attractive idea, even though magic may be required for the transformation. That's why it's been particularly popular in ages when social mobility has been difficult, or in cultures with rigid class systems.

Over the years there have been many different versions of the story. The details have changed, but they're of no real consequence, and the basic elements remain in place – whether in films, theatrical performances or illustrated children's books. The first film version was released in 1924, and though there has never been much realism in Hollywood portrayals of Arabic cultures, that hasn't damaged the success of movies featuring Aladdin. Audiences love stories with exotic settings, especially when they can identify with the characters. There is also a purely practical reason why stage performances of Aladdin are popular: only a few elements are crucial to the story, and the rest can be improvised if necessary. For instance, if a company is strapped for cash and wants to perform Aladdin on a shoestring budget, some roles can easily be cut out altogether. Similarly, topical references can be inserted so the story becomes a comment on contemporary life, and the very adaptability of Aladdin is a further reason for its appeal.

TEST 8

▶▶ **PART 3**

You will hear part of an interview with Harold Mackenzie, who has written a book about early adolescence. For questions 17–22, choose the correct answer A, B, C or D. You will hear the recording twice.

Interviewer: Harold Mackenzie, your book *Talking to Pre-Teens* is coming out later this month, and I'm sure that parents who read your best-selling *Talking to Teens* will be queuing up to buy it. But let's begin by asking you exactly what a pre-teen is.

Harold: A pre-teen – or 'tweenie' as some people prefer – is a child aged between eight and twelve, in other words, a child hovering on the brink of adolescence. Oddly enough, this age group didn't attract much attention in the past, but in recent years there has been quite a dramatic growth of interest. There are several reasons for this. Psychologists are beginning to understand how important this period is in an individual's development, and much more research is being done. However, that's not the main reason pre-teens are featuring in the news more and more. It seems that businesses have woken up to the fact that these youngsters are a force to be reckoned with. They have considerable spending power, so marketing managers who previously focused on teenagers are now also targeting these younger consumers. The trouble is that pre-teens are so impressionable.

Interviewer: Mm. In your book you suggest that marketing campaigns aimed at pre-teens should be carefully vetted. Can you expand on this?

Harold: We are all susceptible to advertising, but pre-teens are especially vulnerable. Advertisements can suggest that everything the child does – the food he eats, the clothes he wears, the toys he chooses to play with – are regarded as a statement by his or her contemporaries. He feels he has to 'keep up', so it's bewildering for a child when he tries to follow a fashion that is succeeded after a brief time by a different, equally arbitrary one.

Interviewer: Can you tell us something about the kinds of changes a child experiences during the pre-teen years?

Harold: Well, this is the age when children start to measure themselves against people outside their families for the first time, and one way in which they develop their sense of self is by forming friendships with other children. The way your peers react to you plays an enormous role in how you see yourself in later life.

Interviewer: It sounds as though the pre-teen years are quite eventful emotionally.

Harold: Yes, and they can be a trying time as well. It's unfortunate that for many children this period is full of stressful situations. For example, at this age children have to face real examinations at school for the first time – examinations that may determine what sort of education they will have in future. If a child's ability could be evaluated in different, less stressful ways, we might reduce the tensions that pre-teens are subjected to. I outline several possibilities in my book.

Interviewer: Harold, what can concerned parents do in concrete terms to help their pre-teen children?

Harold: Helping them gain self-confidence is crucial. Parents should respect their children's views about how their lives are conducted, but they should not make the mistake of indulging all their offspring's wishes and allowing them complete control of their lives. Children still need guidance! Buying them everything they want is not the best response; it can even be dangerous because it suggests that the things you have matter more than the kind of person you are. Find a way to discuss important issues with your children and listen – really listen – to what they tell you about their fears and desires.

Interviewer: Harold Mackenzie, thanks for being with us.

Harold: My pleasure.

TEST 8

▶▶ **PART 4**

You will hear five short extracts in which different people talk about their experiences at the theatre. For questions 23–27, match the extracts with what each person says about the show he or she enjoyed most, listed A–H. For questions 28–32, match the extracts with the views each speaker has about why theatre is an interesting medium, listed A–H. You will hear the recording twice. While you listen you must complete both tasks.

Speaker 1: The first time I went to the theatre, I was twelve, and my mother had to drag me along. But it was a fantastic play – a murder mystery – and I was entranced. Ever since then I've enjoyed the theatre, and I go whenever I can. I love the atmosphere you get at a good play, as if you are all in an enchanted circle for those two hours the play is on. I don't think you get that feeling in the cinema.

Speaker 2: When I was at university, I saw a production of a comedy by Tom Stoppard called *After Magritte*. It was absolutely hilarious! I liked it so much that I went back the next night with two friends! There were some very simple jokes, there was slapstick humour, and there were some very witty lines. I don't think you'd get that in a film these days – the cinema has become so formulaic. For me, it's the theatre's ability to jolt you out of your complacency that makes it so special.

Speaker 3: As a child I saw a performance of the musical *My Fair Lady* with my Aunt Emily. My family weren't sure I'd enjoy it, but the actor playing the lead was marvellous! He could sing, his acting was great – he dominated the whole performance. I do some acting myself – I'm in an amateur dramatics society – and I love watching the way different actors go about interpreting a role. It definitely helps me when I have to take on a big part.

Speaker 4: My most memorable theatrical experience was a performance of Shakespeare's *Romeo and Juliet*. I went because we were studying it at school. I didn't expect to be affected, but to my intense surprise I was in tears at the end! That's when I finally understood how magical the theatre is. Seeing a play on stage is special; all the emotions come across to the audience if it's a good production. While you are watching there's a suspension of disbelief, and what's happening on the stage becomes real, at least for a while.

Speaker 5: I'd read a review of a production of *Antigone* by Sophocles in a very small theatre, so I went along. The acting was excellent, and because you were so close to the actors you felt very involved in the play – it became a sort of personal experience, as if you were in the play yourself! I suppose what I've come to love about the theatre is that no two performances are ever exactly the same: the actors do not always deliver their lines in the same way and there are subtle differences of timing and interpretation.